The Muslim Brotherhood

The Muslim Brotherhood

Ideology, History, Descendants

Joas Wagemakers

Amsterdam University Press

This publication has been made possible by financial support from Dokumentationsstelle Politischer Islam.

 Dokumentationsstelle
Politischer Islam

Originally published as: Wagemakers, Joas, *De Moslimbroederschap. Ideologie, geschiedenis, nakomelingen*. Amsterdam university Press, 2021

Cover illustration: Getty Images. © László Mihály

Cover design: Mijke Wondergem
Lay-out: Crius Group, Hulshout

ISBN	978 94 6372 768 6
e-ISBN	978 90 4855 670 0
DOI	10.5117/9789463727686
NUR	717

Table of Contents

Part III   Descendants

Preface

It happens every so often: accusing politicians or other prominent public figures of 'supporting' or 'having ties to' the Muslim Brotherhood. In America, perhaps the best-known example of this is Huma Abedin, who held several senior positions on Hillary Clinton's staff, including as vice-chair of the latter's 2016 presidential campaign. In 2012, several Republican politicians questioned Abedin's loyalty and reliability because of her alleged ties – through family members and in other ways – to the Muslim Brotherhood and wondered whether she should receive security clearance. These claims were later debunked as conspiracy theories, however, and widely rejected by both Democrats and Republicans.

Such accusations are certainly not limited to America and can also be found in European countries. In the Netherlands, for instance, Kauthar Bouchallikht, a member of the GroenLinks ('GreenLeft') party elected to parliament in March 2021, was accused of having ties with the Muslim Brotherhood through her former position as vice-chair of the Forum of European Muslim Youth and Student Organizations (FEMYSO). Ihsan Ha-ouach, a Belgian politician, found herself in a similar situation in July 2021 when it became known that she had given a talk, in 2019, to the European Forum of Muslim Women (EFOMW), another group supposedly tied to the Muslim Brotherhood. Both denied having connections to the organization.

Quite apart from the question of whether or not these politicians sympathized, or still sympathize, with this organization, these incidents made abundantly clear that many apparently see the Muslim Brotherhood as somehow undesirable. Politicians, journalists, commentators and people writing on social media frequently claimed that the Muslim Brotherhood is in favour of jihad and would like to (violently) impose the Sharia, sometimes with reference to the early ideologues of the Egyptian Muslim Brotherhood. Even some of the people who defended those accused of having ties to the organization and who dismissed these charges as Islamophobic or conspiratorial thinking apparently took it for granted that the Muslim Brotherhood was, indeed, a group one would not want to be associated with.

What is the Muslim Brotherhood and what is so frightening about it? Does this organization actually incite violence through military jihad? Does it really want to impose its will on both Muslims and non-Muslims in the form of the Sharia? How does the organization relate to groups like Al-Qaida? Is there a difference between the Muslim Brotherhood in Egypt, where the organization was founded almost a century ago, and the situation in European countries? This book answers these and other questions. It does not seek to defend the Muslim Brotherhood, but instead to explain and contextualize it, as well as to provide nuance to a discussion in which this is often sorely lacking.

This is not an academic publication and, as such, it contains little new information that cannot also be found in other, scholarly works. This book, by contrast, is intended for a broader audience, particularly for people who are professionally interested in the Muslim Brotherhood, such as policymakers and students taking courses on history, the Middle East, religion and political science. I have therefore refrained from using Arabic sources as much as possible. Instead, this book seeks to address an apparent need for reliable information on the transnational Muslim Brotherhood. As such, it is intended as an introduction to those who know little about the organization, but – through the numerous references – it can also serve as a good starting point for research.

Acknowledgements

Although this book was written and translated in 2021–2022, it is based on research that goes back several years. It is rooted in a Veni research grant that I was awarded by the Dutch Research Council (NWO) in 2011 for a project that I started working on in 2012 and formally finished in 2016. The project focussed on Islamic activism in Jordan, which resulted in – among other publications – the book *The Muslim Brotherhood in Jordan* (Cambridge University Press, 2020) and which stimulated me to think about writing a book on the Muslim Brotherhood for a broader audience. I published the latter in Dutch as *De Moslimbroederschap: Ideologie, geschiedenis, nakomelingen* (Amsterdam University Press, 2021), of which the present book is the updated, slightly revised and translated version. I would like to thank NWO for the financial support it provided for a project of which this book is the latest – albeit indirect – product.

Under normal circumstances, this would be the place to thank my colleagues in the Department of Philosophy and Religious Studies at Utrecht University for the collegial and friendly atmosphere they provided while writing this book. The truth is, however, that this book was not written under normal circumstances, but during the corona pandemic that has swept the world since 2020. This meant that I hardly saw my colleagues during the period in which I conducted research for and wrote this book, except via Teams or Zoom. Although I have recently been able to actually meet my colleagues and teach offline again, I can only hope that the world will be in better shape once this book is published than when it was written.

There are several people that I would like to thank personally. First, I thank Saskia Gieling at Amsterdam University Press for her faith in the Dutch version of this book. I would also like to thank her successor, Annelies van der Meij, for continuing Saskia's work and supporting the translation of this book. Chantal Nicolaes guided the production process and Anna Yeadell-Moore was a great copy editor, for which I thank them both. The translation of this book was made possible by no-strings-attached financial support from the Dokumentationsstelle Politischer Islam in Vienna, for which I would like to thank Ferdinand Haberl and Lisa Fellhofer. Moreover, Mehdi Sajid, Brynjar Lia, Kiki Santing, Thomas Pierret, Stéphane Lacroix, Nina ter Laan, Sami Zemni, Roel Meijer, Pieter Nanninga, Martijn de Koning and Ellen van de Bovenkamp were kind enough to dedicate some of their precious time to commenting on parts of this manuscript or the original Dutch version of this book. Precisely because I know how busy they are, I greatly appreciate their contribution and would like to thank them here. Although the book has improved because of their insights, it goes without saying that all remaining errors are my responsibility.

Finally, while this book might have seen the light of day without the wonderful jazz that I surround myself with every day by listening to, for example, accujazz.com, it would certainly have been a much less pleasant experience. This is even more true, of course, regarding the support I received from my family during this project. Writing a book often means working long hours, at least if one wants to keep it going, and the months in which this book was written have been no exception. Fortunately, my wife was always patient and understanding whenever I was up late at night working on this project. She has also made an invaluable contribution to the manuscript by lending me her wireless keyboard when the letter 'd' on my laptop suddenly gave up. It is because of her patience – and because of the fact that, thanks to her, this book is not about 'the Muslim Brotherhoo' but about 'the Muslim Brotherhood' – that I dedicate this work to her. I hope she is as happy as I am that the long working days will be over for a while.

List of Abbreviations

The abbreviations below are given in the language of the abbreviation itself and, in the case of a non-English-language organization, in English translation.

AEIF   Association des Étudiants Islamiques de France ('Association of Islamic Students of France'), French

AIVD   Algemene Inlichtingen- en Veiligheidsdienst ('General Intelligence and Security Service'), Dutch

BMI   British Muslim Initiative, British

CBSP   Comité de Bienfaisance et de Secours aux Palestiniens ('Charity and Relief Committee for Palestinians'), French

CDLR   Committee for the Defence of Legitimate Rights, Saudi

CFCM   Conseil Français du Culte Musulman ('French Council of the Muslim Religion'), French

CGI   Contact Groep Islam ('Contact Group Islam'), Dutch

CPR   Congrès pour la République ('Congress for the Republic'), Tunisian

DMG   Deutsche Muslimische Gemeinschaft ('German Muslim Community'), German

ECFR   European Council for Fatwa and Research, European

EIHS   European Institute of Human Sciences, European

EFOMW   European Forum of Muslim Women, European

EMF   Étudiants Musulmans de France ('Muslim Students of France'), French

Fatah   Harakat al-Tahrir al-Watani al-Filastini ('Palestinian National Liberation Movement'), Palestinian

FEMYSO   Forum of European Muslim Youth and Student Organizations, European

FIO   Federatie Islamitische Organisaties ('Federation of Islamic Organizations'), Dutch

FIOE   Federation of Islamic Organizations in Europe, European

FJP   Freedom and Justice Party, Egyptian

FOSIS   Federation of Student Islamic Societies, British

GIF   Groupement Islamique en France ('Islamic Group in France'), French

Hadas   Al-Haraka al-Dusturiyya al-Islamiyya ('Islamic Constitutional Movement'), Kuwaiti

Hamas	Harakat al-Muqawama al-Islamiyya ('Islamic Resistance Movement'), Palestinian
IAF	Islamic Action Front, Jordanian
ICE	Islamic Council of Europe, European
ICF	Islamic Charter Front, Sudanese
IFC	Islamic Front for the Constitution, Sudanese
IGD	Islamische Gemeinschaft in Deutschland ('Islamic Community in Germany'), German
IGSD	Islamische Gemeinschaft in Süddeutschland ('Islamic Community in Southern Germany'), German
IS	Islamic State, Iraqi/Syrian/international
ISB	Islamic Society of Britain, British
ISI	Islamic State of Iraq, Iraqi
ISIS	Islamic State in Iraq and Syria, Iraqi/Syrian
JMF	Jeunes Musulmans de France ('Muslim Youth of France'), French
LFFM	Ligue Française de la Femme Musulmane ('French League of the Muslim Woman'), French
LIIB	Ligue Islamique Interculturelle de Belgique ('Intercultural Islamic League of Belgium'), Belgian
MAB	Muslim Association of Britain, British
MCB	Muslim Council of Britain, British
MIRA	Movement for Islamic Reform in Arabia, Saudi
MPDC	Mouvement Populaire Démocratique et Constitutionnel ('Popular Democratic and Constitutional Movement'), Moroccan
MSS	Muslim Students Society, British
MSV	Muslim Studenten Vereinigung in Deutschland ('Muslim Students Association in Germany'), German
MTI	Mouvement de la Tendance Islamique ('Movement of the Islamic Tendency'), Tunisian
MUR	Mouvement de l'Unicité et de la Réforme ('Movement of Unity and Reform'), Moroccan
MWH	Muslim Welfare House, British
NIF	National Islamic Front, Sudanese
PAIC	Popular Arab and Islamic Congress, Sudanese
PJD	Parti de la Justice et du Développement ('Justice and Development Party'), Moroccan
PLO	Palestine Liberation Organization, Palestinian
PNA	Palestinian National Authority, Palestinian

SCAF	Supreme Council of the Armed Forces, Egyptian
UOIE	Union des Organizations Islamiques en Europe ('Union of Islamic Organizations in Europe'), European
UOIF	Union des Organizations Islamiques de France ('Union of Islamic Organizations of France'), French
YMUK	Young Muslims United Kingdom, British
ZMD	Zentralrat der Muslime in Deutschland ('Central Council of Muslims in Germany'), German

Glossary

Several terms that have been explained below have multiple meanings. I have chosen to focus only on the meanings used in this book. Less important terms, or those only used once in the book, are not mentioned here, but are explained in the text.

al-amr bi-l-ma'ruf wa-l-nahy 'an al-munkar – commanding right and forbidding wrong. This Koranic duty can take many forms, but to the Muslim Brotherhood it includes holding the ruler to account.

dar al-da'wa – the abode of preaching. This term is used to signify non-Muslim countries where Muslims can profess their faith to emphasize the need for preaching in those countries and to legitimize Muslims' settlement there. See also *dar al-harb* and *dar al-Islam*.

dar al-harb – the abode of war. This refers to the area with which the *dar al-Islam* (q.v.) is theoretically at war. To the present-day Muslim Brotherhood, this classical Islamic term is increasingly irrelevant. See also *dar al-da'wa*.

dar al-Islam – the abode of Islam. This term signifies the area where Muslims are in the majority, where Islamic law is applied or where Muslims can profess their faith, depending on the interpretation used. Some in the Muslim Brotherhood claim that the entire world has become *dar al-Islam*. See also *dar al-da'wa* and *dar al-harb*.

darurat – necessities. This term denotes matters that, despite perhaps being at odds with the Sharia, are necessary and therefore allowed. See also *hajat, maslaha, taysir*.

da'wa – call (to Islam), preaching. This has long been an important activity of the Muslim Brotherhood.

dhimmi – a member of a protected minority. This term has long been applied to Jews and Christians who could live under Muslim rule as a protected minority under certain conditions (including payment of a poll tax (*jizya*, q.v.)). The Muslim Brotherhood has largely dropped this concept in its approach to non-Muslim minorities throughout the years.

fiqh – jurisprudence, the study and development of the Sharia. See also *fiqh al-aqalliyyat*.

fiqh al-aqalliyyat – jurisprudence of minorities. This was specifically developed for Muslim minorities in non-Muslim countries. See also *fiqh*.

hajat – needs. This term refers to matters that, despite perhaps being at odds with the Sharia, represent an important need among Muslims and are therefore allowed sometimes. See also *darurat, maslaha, taysir*.

hakimiyya – sovereignty. In the work of Mawdudi, Qutb and others, this term refers specifically to Gods sovereignty in all aspects of life, particularly legislation.

hisba – control, the application of *al-amr bi-l-ma'ruf wa-l-nahy 'an al-munkar* (q.v.), which can take multiple forms.

'ibadat – matters pertaining to the worship of God. See also *mu'amalat*.

ijtihad – independent reasoning on the basis of the Koran and the Sunna without necessarily remaining within the boundaries of a school of Islamic law. This has been an important instrument for the reform (*islah*, q.v.) of the Sharia.

infitah – opening. This refers specifically to the economic open-door policy of Egyptian President Anwar al-Sadat (r. 1970–1981).

islah – reform. This term has a positive connotation for Islamists, who see Islam as the source of reform.

jahiliyya – pre-Islamic period of ignorance. Qutb and others also use this term to describe the situation of Muslim societies today.

jama'at (sing. *jama'a*) – groups.

jam'iyyat (sing. *jam'iyya*) – associations.

jizya – poll tax. Only a *dhimmi* (q.v.) needed to pay this tax.

maqasid al-Shari'a – purposes of the Sharia. This refers to the underlying purposes of Islamic law, not its specific judgements.

maslaha – interest. This concept can be used within *fiqh* (q.v.) to create exceptions in which matters that are forbidden may be allowed after all to serve the interest of the Muslim community. See also *darurat, hajat, taysir*.

mu'amalat – matters related to relations between people amongst themselves. See also *'ibadat*.

sahwa – revival. This refers specifically to a movement that combines Wahhabism with the activism of the Muslim Brotherhood in Saudi Arabia.

salafi – 'like the forefathers'. This word originally had a theological meaning and was used by modernists from the nineteenth and twentieth centuries who also influenced the Muslim Brotherhood. This should not be confused with modern-day Salafis, who have the same theological ideas as *salafi* modernists, but are not modernists themselves.

shura – consultation. Many members of the Muslim Brotherhood see this as the Islamic alternative to or the equivalent of democracy.

tajdid – renewal. This is an important term for Muslim reformers who have also influenced the Muslim Brotherhood.

takfir – excommunication, accusation of unbelief. Muslim Brothers sometimes use this, but are generally very hesitant in its application.

tariqa – order, referring to a Sufi order.

taysir – facilitation. This is part of *fiqh al-aqalliyyat* (q.v.) and intended to impose the least difficult rules on Muslims in difficult situations. See also *darurat, hajat, maslaha.*

ulama – scholars.

umma – Muslim community, nation.

usra – family. This refers to the smallest cell within the hierarchical structure of the Muslim Brotherhood.

wasatiyya – centrism. In the context of Islamism, this refers to the supposed golden mean that some scholars apply in *fiqh* (q.v.) between too much emphasis on texts, on the one hand, and too little attention for them, on the other.

Note on Transliteration

Arabic words used in this book are transliterated according to a simplified version of the system applied by the *International Journal of Middle East Studies*. This means that I do not use dots and macrons to indicate emphatic letters or long vowels, but that I do use an English transliteration, including for Arabic names and words that are often rendered into Latin script with, for example, a French transliteration. Concretely, this entails the transliteration of, for example, the name 'Rachid al-Ghannouchi' as 'Rashid al-Ghannushi'. The apostrophe with the opening to the right (') and with the opening to the left (') represent the Arabic letters *'ayn* and *hamza*, respectively. Arabic words that one can find in a good English dictionary (e.g. 'Koran', 'Sharia' and 'jihad') or well-known names ('Saddam Hussein', 'Yasser Arafat') are left unchanged. Slightly less well-known names ('Burqiba/Bourguiba', 'Ibn 'Ali/ Bin Ali') are first given in the correct transliteration and then in the more popular form. Names presumed unknown and without a popular spelling are rendered in the correct transliteration. The spelling of originally Arabic names of European Muslim Brothers depends on how they themselves spell them in Latin script.

Introduction

The Koran refers to Muslims as 'brothers' several times. Sura 3:103, for instance, states: '[...] remember God's blessing upon you when you were enemies, and He brought your hearts together, so that by His blessing you became brothers (*ikhwanan*) [...]'.[1] This seems to be a reference to the pre-Islamic situation in the seventh century CE, in which inhabitants of the Arabian Peninsula often fought each other because of their tribal conflicts, but were unified through the arrival of Islam. This verse may suggest that the message of the Prophet Muhammad (570–632) brought about a period of harmony and peace in which his followers conducted themselves as 'Muslim Brothers', but this was often not the case in practice. Not only did internal conflict quickly rear its head after the death of the Prophet, but the various Islamic empires that succeeded each other throughout history were often also each other's competitors.

Verses like the one mentioned above nevertheless seem to show that unity was the goal Muslims should strive for. The organization that is the focus of this book – the Muslim Brotherhood – may have wanted to hint at this ideal with its name.[2] Ironically, however, the Muslim Brotherhood has turned out to be an important source of division: both among Muslims and non-Muslims, there is much resistance against its use of Islam as a politically and socially relevant ideology, its activism and its specific ideas, while the organization simultaneously has millions of supporters around the world. In addition, the Muslim Brotherhood itself – as we will see in the chapters to come – is also strongly internally divided on several issues. Finally, academics are not united in their analysis of the organization: some see the Muslim Brotherhood as a dangerous group that differs only marginally from terrorist organizations such as Al-Qaida, while others see it as a flexible, pragmatic and democratic club that can make a constructive contribution to the politics of the countries in which it operates.

To clarify these different academic positions on the Muslim Brotherhood, this introduction will first deal with the scholarly debate about Islamism, the trend that the organization is part of and that is known under various names. We will subsequently look at the different points of view that academics have with regard to the Muslim Brotherhood. Finally, I will give an overview of what the reader can expect in the chapters to come. The goal of this book is not just to give an overview of the various expressions of the Muslim Brotherhood in different Arab and European countries, but also to show that stereotypes about the organization do not do justice to the gradual, organic and ideological developments that it has gone through over the past decades.

Islamism as a Concept and as a Phenomenon

The term 'Islamism' refers to the idea that Islam, apart from being a religion of rituals, beliefs and texts, is also a politically and societally relevant ideology that forms the basis for activism. In practice, this is expressed in the idea that Islam should not just be applied in the religious sphere, but also in the political and societal spheres, mostly by implementing the Sharia. So, whereas Islam can be limited to the private sphere, Islamism is something that is, by definition, also related to the public sphere. For this reason, Islamism – much more than Islam itself – touches upon the lives of others.

The effects of Islamism on the public sphere and the possible tensions that emanate from them are probably also the reason that several labels for Islamism underline politics and society. One of these is 'political Islam', a term that emphasizes the politically relevant aspect of Islamism.[3] Other terms more or less embody the activist aspect of Islamism: 'Islamic extremism',[4] which is usually tied to violence (and is regularly used in the media), the more neutral 'Islamic revival',[5] the less common 'Islamic reformism/modernism'[6] (because Islamism is a modern reformist movement), 'militant Islam'[7] or the often-heard 'radical Islam'.[8]

Although none of these terms is perhaps entirely incorrect, each one of them is lacking in some respect: political Islam suggests that Islam itself is a-political, which is doubtful; extremism is rather a subjective term; revival is somewhat vague and may refer to a much broader phenomenon and is therefore less applicable; reformism/modernism is easily confused with more progressive trends within Islam; militant Islam seems to imply violence; and radical Islam does not take into account that Islamists often take a gradual approach and, in some contexts, have left the opposition and have attained power (and are therefore not so radical), as we will see in later chapters.

Academics are perhaps even more divided about the use of the term 'fundamentalism' in Islam as an alternative to Islamism. Apart from the fact that this term has a reputation for being associated with things like fanaticism,[9] some researchers reject the term because it has roots in Protestantism and is not indigenous to Islam[10] or because it seems to accept as true the claim that Islamists are the ones who go back to the 'foundations' or 'fundamentals' of

the faith.[11] Other academics do use the term fundamentalism with regard
to Islam. They state that fundamentalism, with its rejection of 'passive'
and 'tainted' conservatism in favour of an activist return to the 'pure' faith
(perhaps linked to a specific historical period) and the political and societal
application thereof, are typical of Islamism.[12]

Just like the latter group of scholars, I believe that the term fundamentalism – separated from its negative image and coupled with a specific
approach to a religious tradition – can be applied to Islam, particularly if
that also includes groups other than the Muslim Brotherhood.[13] Still, the
description of fundamentalism as given above does not entirely fit the
Muslim Brotherhood's gradual and flexible approach that we will see in the
chapters to come.[14] That approach is characterized much more by the image
described before, of an ideological form of Islam that is applicable in politics
and society; in other words: Islamism.[15] Moreover, this book is not about
Islamic fundamentalism in general, but only about the Muslim Brotherhood,
an organization whose members label themselves *Islamiyyun* ('Islamists')
in Arabic, to distinguish themselves from *Muslimun* ('Muslims').[16] In this
book, the term Islamism will therefore be used to indicate the broader
ideological trend of which the Muslim Brotherhood is also part.

Yet Islamism is more than a concept. The word also represents a phenomenon about which academics wonder how exactly it should be interpreted.
This, too, has led to division. Various approaches of reading Islamism can
be distinguished, which we can roughly divide into three categories. A
first approach is one that sees Islamism primarily as anti-modern and
describes it as a phenomenon stemming from resistance to modern (Western)
developments in the cultural, technological, political and societal spheres.
Particularly when this is tied to secularization, Islamism is said to be a
response to encroaching modernization in Muslim countries. Although
scholars use (elements of) this approach, it has also been criticized because
of its somewhat essentialist character and its apparent lack of attention for
context.[17]

A second academic approach to Islamism is its treatment as a protest
movement, such as those that also exist in non-Muslim countries. In this
approach, Islamism may have its own, contextualized form, but it is simultaneously part of broader trends that are not limited to the Muslim world.
As such, Islamism has been compared to communism and fascism,[18] but it is
sometimes also seen as the anticolonial movement that resisted British and
French rule in the Muslim world in the twentieth century or that employs
today's reality in developing countries to turn against the West.[19] A different
perspective within this approach is to consider Islamism as an alternative

to the economic, political and social crises that people find themselves in. Wherever (relative) poverty, repression and exclusion are prominently present, Islamism is said to be an alternative to the systems from which these emanated.[20] Although this approach, unlike the first one, pays great attention to the contexts in which Islamism develops, it has been criticized for its lack of attention for the role of Islam.[21]

A third way academic scholars approach Islamism – based on the idea that it is a diverse phenomenon – tries to look at it from all the perspectives mentioned above. As such, Islamism is seen as a dynamic and heterogeneous movement that tries to offer solutions to both internal and external challenges[22] and for whom both cultural resistance against (Western) modernity and socio-economic considerations can be important.[23] In this approach, both contextual factors – for example, the extent to which people are able to mobilize or the political structure of a country – and ideological influences are taken into account by treating Islamic movements as social[24] movements.[25] Because of its complete and nuanced treatment, this book also follows this third approach.

The Muslim Brotherhood as an Object of Study

Just like Islamism in general, the Muslim Brotherhood as a specific organization has also been the subject of academic study for decades. Partly related to the positions on Islamism given above, we can also see different trends here. We can roughly distinguish four different approaches. The first of these clearly draws a connection between the Muslim Brotherhood, on the one hand, and terrorist organizations like Al-Qaida, on the other. The attempts by American and European politicians to criminalize the Muslim Brotherhood or to have it listed as a terrorist organization by their governments have gone on for years,[26] but a similar tendency can also be discerned in academia. As such, some researchers portray the Muslim Brotherhood as an organization that is bent on grabbing power and merely refrains from using violence out of tactical considerations.[27] Others point to the alleged ideological similarities between the Muslim Brotherhood and Egyptian terrorist groups[28] and Al-Qaida,[29] paint the organization as a terrorist wolf in sheep's clothing,[30] as a group that cooperates with terrorist organizations[31] or even as a group that 'has operated as a terrorist entity for almost a century'.[32]

The second approach in the academic analysis of the Muslim Brotherhood, which can somewhat overlap with the first, sees the organization mostly as an unchangeable group for which a strict reading of the Koran and the Sunna and a severe application of the Sharia are and will remain decisive.[33] One element that is often discussed in this approach is the allegedly fundamentally undemocratic character of the Muslim Brotherhood.[34] Another theme we encounter among adherents to this view is that the organization wants to establish an Islamic theocracy on the basis of the Sharia in individual countries or even the entire world.[35]

The third trend does not actually represent an academic point of view, but is nevertheless important to mention because it can frequently be seen in media sources about the Muslim Brotherhood and sometimes even in books professing to be serious. This concerns the idea that the Muslim Brotherhood is an international conspiracy against the West and that the organization has a secret agenda, which it has cunningly concealed. These types of accusation against the Muslim Brotherhood in popular and media sources have been analysed in various academic publications[36] and still occur, for example in a Dutch newspaper article about the alleged influence of Islamists in local politics in Rotterdam. This article labels one of the persons involved 'a spider in the Islamic web' and refers to the 'tentacles' of the Muslim Brotherhood that 'reach into the town hall',[37] suggesting that we are dealing with a central and controlling power. The organization is described in similar fashion in a recent book, which explicitly calls the Muslim Brotherhood a 'conspiracy'.[38] Thus, some groups 'have taken on different names in order to conceal their links to the leading organisation in Egypt'.[39] Moreover, the author views the Muslim Brotherhood as a dangerous organization that – through guidance from Qatar and Turkey – extends its 'tentacles' and whose presence in the West is labelled a 'beachhead' and a 'Trojan horse'.[40]

The fourth and by far the most common approach among academics who have done research on the Muslim Brotherhood is one that starts from the idea that the organization has a pragmatic, dynamic and flexible character. This expresses itself in, among other things, its ability to adjust to the systems of the countries in which it is active, its acceptance of the rules of the political game, its urging of regimes to adopt democratic and constitutional reforms and its susceptibility to the wishes of the peoples from which it sprang. Within this academic trend, this conclusion has been drawn with regard to the Muslim Brotherhood in Egypt,[41] Jordan,[42] Morocco,[43] the Palestinian territories,[44] Syria[45] and Tunisia,[46] to name just a few countries that will be dealt with in this book. This is not to say that adherents to this trend believe the Muslim Brotherhood has become a liberal-democratic organization, but that they acknowledge the actual, organic, intensely discussed and ideologically underpinned changes within the Muslim Brotherhood. This book has also been written on the basis of this approach.

Overview

As indicated before, this book is intended for professionally interested readers, not for academic specialists of the Muslim Brotherhood, and provides a detailed overview, be it as an introduction or as the basis for further research. For that reason, this book is overwhelmingly based on secondary literature and the number of Arabic sources has consciously been kept to a minimum. As a result, the book enables the broadest possible audience to actually look up the works cited in the notes and use them for further study. At the same time, this book is structured in a way that facilitates readers looking up specific information on, for instance, the Muslim Brotherhood in Syria or learning something of the relationship between the organization and Al-Qaida, but that also sketches the development of the Muslim Brotherhood in general and deals with related debates.

The book is divided into three parts. Part I deals with the theme of 'Ideology' and delves into the earliest ideas of the Muslim Brotherhood in two chapters. Chapter 1 has the general ideology of the organization as its subject and it analyses where the Muslim Brotherhood's ideas come from and how they are rooted in nineteenth-century reformist thought. It subsequently deals with the organization's ideas on Egypt and the view of the West among the earliest ideologues of the Muslim Brotherhood. Chapter 2 deals with the ideology of the organization regarding three themes that will recur throughout this book, namely, the state, political participation and societal rights and freedoms; or, to be more specific about the latter, the position of religious minorities, women's rights and civil liberties.

Part II (History) deals with the historical development of various Muslim Brotherhoods in a series of nine Arab countries, divided into three themes, each of which has a dedicated chapter. Chapter 3 has 'Repression' as its theme and deals with three countries in which this was an important part of the Muslim Brotherhood's history: Egypt, Syria and Saudi Arabia. The theme of Chapter 4 is 'Participation' and it deals with the Muslim Brotherhoods in Kuwait, Jordan and the Palestinian territories, precisely because those have been given the space to participate in the political system. Finally, in this part, Chapter 5 examines the theme of 'Power', and features analysis of the Islamist organizations that have actually attained power in, respectively, Sudan, Morocco and Tunisia.

Part III of this book delves into what I refer to as 'Descendants' of the Muslim Brotherhood: groups and trends that, strictly speaking, are no longer part of the Muslim Brotherhood, but that somehow – directly or indirectly – stem from or are connected with the organization. Chapter 6 zooms in on the 'radicals', who strive for drastic political and societal changes: the transnational Hizb al-Tahrir; the Palestinian Islamic Jihad; Tanzim al-Jihad and Al-Jama'a al-Islamiyya from Egypt; as well as Al-Qaida and the Islamic State. Chapter 7, by contrast, deals with the 'Liberals': those who have shown a greater ideological flexibility than the Muslim Brotherhood itself has often done. In this chapter, I deal with, respectively, the *wasatiyya*-trend, post-Islamism and an example of the latter – the so-called ZamZam-initiative. Finally, the focus of Chapter 8 is the Muslim Brothers as 'Europeans' and analyses the migration of the Muslim Brotherhood from the Middle East to Europe, the expressions of the organization in five European countries (Great Britain, France, Belgium, Germany and the Netherlands) and how these developments have been ideologically justified.

In the conclusions of each of the chapters in Part II and III, I will deal with one of the alternative approaches to the Muslim Brotherhood as they have been distinguished above. Concretely, this means that I will examine the view of the Muslim Brotherhood as a (potential) terrorist organization in Chapters 3 and 6, analyse the image of the group as theocratic and anti-democratic in Chapters 4 and 7 and I return to the idea of the Muslim Brotherhood as an international conspiracy in Chapters 5 and 8. That way – and in the conclusion of the book as a whole – it not only becomes clear why I have chosen the fourth approach to the Muslim Brotherhood myself, but also why this is the only one that does justice to the ideological, historical and geographical development that the organization has undergone over the past century.

Part I

Ideology

1. The General Ideology of the Early Muslim Brotherhood

The ideology of the Muslim Brotherhood is rooted in Islam or, more precisely, in the ideas of an Islamic reform movement that arose in the nineteenth century and which itself was rooted in earlier reforms. The desire to reform was a response to the established order of that time. This was an order that took shape after the death of the Prophet Muhammad in 632 around the so-called caliphate, a political system whose leader was seen as the successor (*khalifa*; 'caliph') of the Prophet. This succession did not pertain to the prophetic gifts of Muhammad – who is, after all, seen by Muslims as *khatim al-anbiya'* ('the seal of the prophets') – but to his duties as a ruler of Muslims, which was underlined by the title the caliph bore in the following centuries: *amir al-mu'minin* ('the commander of the faithful'). The latter showed the politico-religious character of the caliph's leadership. In practice, this was mostly expressed through the application of the Sharia and the organization of the Friday prayers. The process of developing and shaping the Sharia is called *fiqh* ('jurisprudence'), which was led by the ulama ('scholars') and particularly the *fuqaha'* ('legal scholars'), who had specialized in this subject through their studies, in the centuries after Muhammad's death.[1]

Various Islamic empires came into existence after the death of the Prophet Muhammad, partly on the basis of the idea of the caliphate. With respect to this book, the most important of these was the Ottoman Empire (1299–1923), which provided the context for the nineteenth-century reform movement that the Muslim Brotherhood grew out of ideologically. In this chapter, I will deal with the attempts at religious renewal that arose after the Middle Ages and how a reform movement that – ideologically speaking – can be seen as the cradle of what later became the Muslim Brotherhood grew out of this in the nineteenth century. I subsequently analyse the ideological development of the early Egyptian Muslim Brotherhood (1920s–1970s) by focussing on the ideological background of Hasan al-Banna, the organization's founder, its ideas about what was wrong in Egypt and why and how Islam could provide an answer to this. Finally, this chapter deals with the early Muslim Brotherhood's views on the West, particularly in the context of the British colonial rule under which Egyptians lived in the early twentieth century.

Status Quo and Reforms in Islam After the Middle Ages

The Ottoman Empire, which had Istanbul as its capital and which (at its territorial peak) stretched from Europe to Iraq, was still a powerful and largely centrally led entity in the sixteenth and seventeenth centuries. As was the case in other Islamic empires, the ulama also played an important role in the Ottoman Empire. These scholars legitimized the authority of the sultans in Istanbul, as it were, and, in return, were given room to fulfil their Islamic-legal duties in relative freedom. In the Ottoman Empire, scholars worked under the supervision of the state, but this also allowed them to assign a greater role to the Sharia in politics.[2]

Although Islamic scholars had an important position in the Ottoman Empire, a considerable part of religious life within this context was constituted by Sufism, which existed partly – but certainly not entirely – separate from the ulama's sphere of influence. This mystical trend within Islam was organized through *tariqa*s ('orders') that were concentrated around a master (*pir*, *shaykh*), who sometimes had a large number of followers. Due to their major spiritual and religious authority – partly based on their experiences with earlier masters that formed a *silsila* ('chain'), which sometimes reached all the way back to the Prophet Muhammad himself – popular rituals would often develop around these masters, particularly after their deaths. They were seen as being able to ensure blessing, fertility or healing and, consequently, their graves sometimes became sites of pilgrimage.[3]

The spread of Sufism was partly facilitated by the claim that the mysticism of the Sufi masters did not clash with the Sharia of the legal scholars, but rather complemented and perfected it.[4] Thus, partly because of the previously mentioned claims of indirect connection with the Prophet, Sufism became acceptable to the ulama. This acceptance of Sufi orders did not create a greater legitimacy for the practices around the graves of Sufi masters described above, however, which the scholars often viewed as contrary to the Sharia.[5] Because of the popularity of Sufism, the connecting structure that the Sufi orders offered and the widespread piety that they brought with them, such great support for these practices developed that scholars often did not speak out against them.[6]

Although there had also been opponents of certain forms of Sufism in the Middle Ages who saw them as incongruous with the Sharia (as well as the theological and legal trends that often accompanied them), this remained limited. This was because Sufi orders were sometimes tied to scholars, who, in turn, enjoyed state support in the Ottoman Empire. As such, this situation was partly maintained by means of the authorities. This changed somewhat in the seventeenth century, when some scholars from the Middle East, but also from India, expressed fierce criticism of what they saw as unacceptable Sufi ideas or rituals that involved dancing and music. They also sometimes did their best to push these allegedly bad practices back into a Sharia-compliant form.[7]

Reforms in the Eighteenth Century

The ability to express criticism of the religious and political establishments was strengthened by political developments that occurred in the Ottoman Empire in the eighteenth century. The first of these was a clear decentraliza-tion, at the expense of Istanbul's authority. This decentralization was tied to increasing competition from European economies, which sometimes offered favourable prices for the goods of local traders in the Middle East. As a result, the export – over which the central authority had little control – increased. This coincided with a rise in power and autonomy among local rulers who were unwilling to cede these to the sultan again.[8] Therefore, centrally led reforms to re-establish Istanbul's grip on the situation were often not structural in nature because they were opposed by local rulers, bureaucrats, army officers and even religious scholars who refused to give up their own autonomy.[9] Thus, some ulama or local politicians, like those in Egypt or in the holy cities of Mecca and Medina, gained more and more power at the expense of the sultan.[10]

A second eighteenth-century development that strengthened opposition against the religious and political authorities was the weakening of the Ottoman Empire by Russian and Western European influences. This was tied, on the one hand, to the military losses that the Ottoman Empire suffered at the edges of its territory, for example because of Russian military invasions in the Caucasus and the Balkans in the second half of the eighteenth century and the French occupation of Egypt in 1798. On the other hand, this was related to the increasing economic wealth that particularly Christians amassed as a result of the foreign protection they enjoyed. In the sixteenth century, France had already arranged that it would manage the interests of Roman Catholics in the Ottoman Empire. The agreements about this arrangement, the so-called capitulations, allowed France to privilege Roman Catholic Christians, which Russia also did later with Orthodox Christians.[11]

The Ottoman Empire thus weakened both from the inside and from the outside in the eighteenth century. More or less simultaneously, a reformist trend could be discerned in various places in the empire, one which strove for a return to the Koran, the Sunna, the Sharia and the practices of the earliest

Muslim community, albeit expressed differently in different areas.[12] This built on the seventeenth-century criticism of certain 'problematic' aspects of Sufism mentioned earlier and this trend therefore influenced some tariqas. Because Sufi orders functioned partly outside of official Ottoman circles of scholars, they could serve as the basis of opposition movements against the existing religious and/or political establishment.[13] As a result of this return to the textual basis of Islam, which was not limited to the Ottoman Empire, reformist movements came into existence that challenged the authorities in various places.[14]

The Islamic reform movements that emerged in the eighteenth-century Muslim world varied from Wahhabism on the Arabian Peninsula to revivalist developments in Africa, India and Southeast Asia.[15] This geographical span shows that this was a diverse phenomenon that occurred beyond the boundaries of the Ottoman Empire. It is therefore important to emphasize that the roots of these reformist movements differed.[16] Within the Ottoman Empire, these movements continued into the nineteenth century and gave impetus to a new generation of reformers.

Reforms in the Nineteenth Century

The Ottoman Empire of the nineteenth century was partly characterized by the same challenges as those of the eighteenth century. Among others, the European threat caused the empire to adopt military, political and administrative reforms once again, this time with greater success. This was partly expressed in the increase of modern education. Whereas traditional education used to be based on the authority of the teacher (and his own teachers) and was often limited to religious subjects, new education was less traditional and placed greater emphasis on profane subjects. This different type of education resulted in the ulama and the Sufi orders that were tied to them being partly side-lined. Moreover, these educational developments led to the rise of a new elite, who had enjoyed a modern education, which, in turn, catalysed a new reformist movement. This movement started forming what may be described as an intellectual alternative to the ulama and did not object to opposing the religious authorities.[17]

The new elite of modern-educated reformers emerged at a time when European involvement in the Middle East did not limit itself to economic influence or control of parts of the Ottoman Empire, but also expressed itself in the colonial occupation of various areas. Algeria became a French colony in 1830, for example, and Egypt came under British colonial control in 1882. Apart from the ensuing military and political consequences, the European cultural influence that emanated from this was interpreted differently by nineteenth-century reformers: whereas secular reformers embraced it, believing that true reform could only happen by adopting European cultural norms, modernists took a different view. While they strove for religious reform, they also wanted to accept modernity through the prism of Islam. In other words, they wanted to modernize Islam rather than abolish it as a politically and societally relevant religion, as many secularists wanted.[18]

This partial acceptance of European cultural insights expressed itself among modernists in the continuation of the above-mentioned eighteenth-century reforms aimed at a return to the Koran and the Sunna (and undermining the power of the religious authorities), although this was done in different ways. Some reformers strove for renewal that was tied to specific theological ideas about how the Koran should be read, which they referred to as *salafi* ('like the forefathers'). Examples of this included the Syrian Jamal al-Din al-Qasimi (1866–1914) and the Iraqi Mahmud Shukri al-Alusi (1856–1924); other thinkers shared these scholars' broad, modernist, reformist agenda but did so outside of the framework of *salafi* ideas. Examples of the latter included the Iranian Jamal al-Din al-Afghani (1838–1897)[19] and the Egyptian Muhammad 'Abduh (1848–1905).[20] The word '*salafi*', however, was also used in the twentieth century to denote the broad, modernist, reformist movement as a whole (even though this was, strictly speaking, incorrect).[21] Hence, '*salafi*' came to be seen by many as simply meaning 'reformist' and in a limited way it has also entered the discourse of the early Muslim Brotherhood as such, as we will see later on.[22]

Salafi or not, these modernist thinkers partly had the same reformist ideas. On the one hand, they shared a critical attitude towards the ruling religious authorities and certain 'problematic' Sufi practices with those espousing renewal in the previous century and they also pursued a Sharia-compliant form of Sufism.[23] On the other hand, within a more generally anti-colonialist framework, they also had a broader agenda of religious *tajdid* ('renewal') and *islah* ('reform'), terms that Islamic reformers have used throughout the centuries.[24] Concretely, this meant that, unlike what they saw as the rigid ulama elite or those they viewed as superstitious 'extreme' Sufis, the modernists accorded rationalism a major role in their way of thinking and preferred direct interpretation of the sources (*ijtihad*) to following legal precedents (*taqlid*) drawn up by the schools of Islamic law (*madhahib*, sing. *madhhab*).[25] They also reinterpreted old Islamic concepts such as *shura* ('consultation') and *ijma'* ('consensus') in such a way that they could be used to embed ideas like popular representation in Islam.[26]

Apart from the above-mentioned representatives of this modernist Islamic reform movement from the nineteenth century, the most important exponent of these ideas is possibly the Lebanese scholar Muhammad Rashid Rida (1865–1935), who had *salafi* sympathies but was also closely associated with people like 'Abduh.[27] Rida was not just a modernist reformer who developed ideas in various spheres of life and published them in his magazine *Al-Manar* ('The Lighthouse'), but he was also a staunch proponent of Islamic unity. Possibly bitter about the West – as were other reformers sometimes[28] – which became increasingly present as a colonial power in the Middle East after World War I, Rida became closely connected to the (not at all modernist) Wahhabi movement on the Arabian Peninsula. He believed its leader – the later king of Saudi Arabia, 'Abd al-'Aziz Ibn Sa'ud (1876–1953) – to be capable of bringing about Islamic unity.[29]

Apart from this tendency to emphasize Islamic unity, Rida also had a strongly politicized discourse, which dealt with politics in the region and, at the time of the abolition of the caliphate in 1924, he openly pondered about how a new form of the caliphate could take shape in these changed circumstances.[30] Given this emphasis on unity and on political issues, it was perhaps not surprising that Rida's publications drew the attention of and had a major impact on Hasan al-Banna (1906–1949) and on the Muslim Brotherhood as a whole.[31] Al-Banna and his organization, for instance, published the magazine *Al-Manar* after Rida's death.[32] Although the relationship between Rida and al-Banna should not be exaggerated, and it has been correctly pointed out that the latter was also influenced by others, Rida does constitute one of the links between the Muslim Brotherhood and the broader reform movement of the nineteenth century.[33] The concrete ideas that this generated form the subject of the next two sections.

The Early Muslim Brotherhood's Views on Egypt

The Muslim Brotherhood was founded by Hasan al-Banna in Egypt in 1928, based on the same idea that had driven so many reformers in the years before, namely, that the Muslim world was threatened from the inside as well as from the outside. Although existing traditions can change and, therefore, can also be the source of renewal,[34] many nineteenth-century reformers argued against the traditional Islam of the Ottoman Empire, whose structures and ideas they considered rigid, impure or backward. In a sense, the Muslim Brotherhood started as the activist and populist expression of this reformist thought.

Whereas traditional Islam – embodied by the Ottoman state scholars with their time-honoured beliefs that have been handed down through the generations – was expressed within existing frameworks, made use of existing institutions and changed its positions only slowly, reformers had an entirely different approach. They – and particularly the Islamists that were partly inspired by them – stepped outside the existing frames of reference, had less structural ties with existing institutions and wanted direct change. While traditional Islam is characterized by what we may call institutionalized conservatism and is, as such, perhaps less interested in (and less susceptible to) threats, Islamism – including the Muslim Brotherhood – does not refrain from confronting challenges.[35]

Hasan al-Banna's Ideological Background

An important difference between the nineteenth-century reform movement and the Muslim Brotherhood was that the former was an ideological trend directed by intellectuals. The Muslim Brotherhood, on the other hand, directed its attention towards ordinary people and was much more geared towards activism. This can be seen in the early activities of Hasan al-Banna himself, who had been educated as a teacher.[36] In the 1920s and 1930s, the founder of the Muslim Brotherhood visited coffee houses to preach his simple message of a return to Islam.[37] He used to educate people about, for example, the way to ritually cleanse themselves and how to perform prayers,[38] based on a vision that he would later describe as 'a pure (*naqiyan*), clear (*safiyan*), simple (*sahlan*), total (*shamilan*), complete (*kafiyan*), perfect (*wafiyan*) understanding' of Islam.[39]

Al-Banna's simple message was embedded in a broader religious background. As we have seen already, he had been influenced by Rida and he was also interested in other modernists with a *salafi* bent.[40] Al-Banna also shared theological ideas typical of *salafi*s,[41] although he paid relatively little attention to theology in his writings[42] and '*salafi*' possibly meant 'reformist' to him. At the same time, al-Banna had been raised with Sufi rituals[43] and he had already been involved in social activism in a Sufi context prior to founding the Muslim Brotherhood.[44] This diverse religious background also partly explains why he would later call the Muslim Brotherhood 'a *salafi* call (*da'wa salafiyya*) [...], a Sunni path (*tariqa sunniyya*) [...] and a Sufi truth (*haqiqa sufiyya*)'.[45]

Al-Banna's ideological background was as broad as it was diverse, which meant that his message appealed to Muslims with wide-ranging ideas. Instead of emphasizing sectarian differences, al-Banna – like Rida before him – was known for his desire for unity and brotherhood, as well as his willingness to cooperate with other Muslims on the basis of what they had in common and to compromise where they differed.[46] For the same reason – and because he was not a trained scholar – al-Banna avoided discussions about theological details.[47] Although this may sound tolerant and perhaps even ecumenical, in al-Banna's case this resulted in a message that was not always very clear and sometimes seemed contradictory, perhaps in an attempt to keep the members of the organization together. The discourse of the Muslim Brotherhood's later leaders is sometimes characterized by a similar ambiguity.[48]

Criticism of Egypt

The challenge that nineteenth-century reformers had constituted to the religious and political authorities of their time was expressed in al-Banna's and the early Muslim Brothers' work through their criticism of the political system in Egypt. The Muslim Brotherhood fiercely opposed the British colonial occupation of Egypt – to which we will return in the next section – but believed that beside this *al-isti'mar al-khariji* ('foreign imperialism') there was also *al-isti'mar al-dakhili* ('internal imperialism') in the country. The latter consisted of internal Egyptian forces that – consciously or not – aided the British occupation or kept it in power, thereby supposedly contributing to the corruption of Islam in Egypt and the country in general. This was particularly problematic because the early Muslim Brotherhood saw Egypt as a country that, as one of the oldest civilizations in the world and with its long history as a Muslim country, had a unique relationship with Islam and should also be a pioneer in restoring that connection with the religion.[49]

The early Muslim Brotherhood expressed relatively little criticism of the Egyptian royal family, which descended from a ruling family that had been in power in Egypt since the early nineteenth century and governed the nominally independent country under British colonial rule until the military coup in 1952. Perhaps the Muslim Brotherhood adopted this attitude because al-Banna remained loyal to the monarchy or perhaps it was because the organization feared being banned.[50] In any case, much more criticism was directed at the political rulers below the level of the king: ministers, members of parliament and party leaders. These people were not only said to be corrupt and in politics to serve their own interests, but their lack of concrete plans and non-representative character led to accusations that they were primarily an instrument in the hands of the colonial powers.[51]

The early Muslim Brotherhood also viewed economic relations through the lens of colonialism. It tied British rule to the presence of foreigners, who were said to exploit the country as tools of imperialism. According to the Muslim Brotherhood, this happened in cooperation with major landowners in a capitalist system in which supporters were more interested in money than in the country's interests. Moreover, they supposedly failed to pay their taxes, while they had the government represent their interests. Apart from the economic consequences that this would have for the people, this system weakened the country, robbed the population of its dignity, corrupted the character of the country, deprived people of their security, made communism more attractive and was also contrary to Islam.[52]

Finally, the Muslim Brotherhood expressed fierce criticism of the societal developments that took place in Egypt as a consequence of Western influence. It lamented British control, not just as a military occupation, but also as a source of cultural influence, with all that this entailed. It believed, for instance, that family life was undermined by the supposedly evil message that emanated from cinematic films (seen as filthy) or by some types of popular music. It also criticized the presence of 'naked' women in the streets and connected this with the moral problems Egyptian youngsters were suffering from. Lastly, the Muslim Brotherhood stated that people were starting to lead split lives – Islamic and Western – in which some Egyptians turned out to be even more Western than Westerners themselves. This was supported by a dual educational system, in which one track turned pupils into religious scholars while another was completely detached from this and concentrated only on profane subjects.[53]

From the above, it becomes clear that the Muslim Brotherhood did not believe that politicians in Egypt would change this situation. The organization was equally pessimistic about the extent to which other forces in society would be capable of doing this. Although al-Banna himself, for example, was influenced by Sufism, he was also critical of this trend and the parts within it that he considered extreme.[54] In his view, these were not just inherently detrimental to society, but the large number of Sufi orders also created division within the Muslim community. In addition, al-Banna was ultimately also sceptical about the extent to which Sufi orders could shape the general political reforms that he strove for.[55]

Al-Azhar University, a renowned institute that had produced Muslim scholars for centuries, was also unable to turn the tide of decline in Egypt, according to the Muslim Brotherhood. Although al-Banna personally respected the ulama, was friendly towards them, and some Al-Azhar students also joined the Muslim Brotherhood,[56] he and the organization were highly critical of Al-Azhar University as an institute. On the one hand, they blamed the scholars for their alleged lack of passion for Islam, which had supposedly become a dead religion in their hands, instead of a living faith. It was claimed that the ulama emphasized only the memorization of texts and paid no heed to rationalism or modern methods. As a result, al-Banna believed Al-Azhar only produced people who were religiously literate, but who could not function as spiritual leaders.[57] On the other hand, the Muslim Brotherhood saw Al-Azhar scholars as people who collaborated with corrupt rulers and major landowners, instead of rebelling against them or resisting British colonial rule.[58]

Thus, the criticism of the Muslim Brotherhood directed at the Egyptian state and society in the first half of the twentieth century strongly resembled that of the earlier reformers from the nineteenth century, but applied to a local situation. Just like the earlier reformers, it was critical of the rulers, the interpretation of Islam used by – among others – certain Sufis and the way in which traditional scholars dealt with this, but then applied specifically to Egypt. The Muslim Brotherhood presented itself not just as a contemporary and activist alternative for all of these, but also had a message that was very different from what Egyptians had been used to.

'Islam is the Solution'

The Muslim Brotherhood offered an alternative to the malaise that it experienced in the Egyptian state and society, beginning with the idea that Islam encompasses all spheres of life. According to al-Banna, Islam had:

> [A] broad meaning (*ma'na wasi'*), unlike the narrow meaning that most people understand it to have. We believe that Islam has an all-encompassing meaning (*ma'na shamil*) that organizes all of life's affairs. It gives a legal judgement on every matter and provides it with a precise, solid system (*nizaman muhkaman daqiqan*).[59]

This does not just apply to the religious aspects of life. Al-Banna explicitly states that:

> [T]hose who think that these teachings only deal with the worship-related or spiritual side [of Islam], without [dealing] with others, are wrong in thinking this. Islam is creed and worship (*'aqida wa-'ibada*), homeland and nationality (*watan wa-jinsiyya*), religion and state (*din wa-dawla*), spirituality and work (*ruhaniyya wa-'amal*), Koran and sword (*mushaf wa-sayf*).[60]

This *shumuliyya* ('universality', 'comprehensiveness') also explains why '*al-Islam huwa l-hall*' ('Islam is the solution') became the Muslim Brotherhood's most important slogan: in the organization's view, Islam offers tools to deal with problems in all aspects of life and, as such, the slogan epitomizes the activist (and populist) character of the Muslim Brotherhood. Later ideologues of the organization, such as the Egyptian Sayyid Qutb (1906–1966),[61] confirmed this in their own writings[62] and the Muslim Brotherhood as a whole has continued to use the slogan until today.[63]

The words 'Islam is the solution' not only indicate that all answers can be found in religion, but also imply that Islam has a positive effect on and forms the basis of life. According to Qutb, perhaps the Egyptian Muslim Brotherhood's most important ideologue during the 1950s and 1960s, Islam functioned as a dynamic force that, on the one hand, had a constant and unchanging core, but, on the other, could also be adapted to different situations and manifest itself in various ways. Although the latter meant that Islam was broadly applicable, the constant core ensured that people would not drift away from the truth too much and also gave life direction. Thus, Islam does not just act as a barrier against unwanted influences, but also functions as a criterium on the basis of which all things in life can and must be judged.[64]

That Islam should be used as a criterium was obvious to the early Muslim Brotherhood, which saw this religion as better than all other systems, partly because it was believed to encompass the best of all of them. Moreover, Islam was claimed to conform to the principles of the Egyptian people – the overwhelming majority of whom were Muslims – and a return to that religion would confirm people's identity and thereby provide hope, perseverance and national self-respect.[65] The early Muslim Brotherhood also believed that the necessity of confirming Islam was clear from their reading of history, i.e. that the problems in the Muslim world – both in the distant past and in the twentieth century – stemmed from a deviation from 'true' Islam. To rise from the crisis in which Egypt found itself, it was therefore necessary to return to the Koran and the Sunna, so that the religion, as well as the Muslim world, could be restored.[66] According to the Muslim Brotherhood, this version of Islam to which one should return was not represented by Al-Azhar or a different actor in Egyptian society, but by the organization itself.[67]

In the hands of Qutb, al-Banna's message, which seemed to be especially directed at Egypt, became a universal declaration of Islam as a liberating force. Qutb believed that by returning to Islam, people could throw off the yoke of their oppressors and replace it with a better alternative. As such, submission to the rule and laws of God was not a new yoke, but actually a liberation for humankind,[68] which – as Qutb explicitly indicates – not only applies to Arabs, but to everyone.[69] It is in this context that we should see the Muslim Brotherhood's views on the application of the Sharia, which we will encounter regularly in the pages to come: whereas among many people in the liberal-democratic West, Islamic law conjures up images of cutting off hands and stoning adulterous women and, as such, embodies a lack of freedom, Muslim Brothers see the Sharia entirely differently. To understand this, it has to be borne in mind that the Muslim Brotherhood was founded and developed in a period of foreign repression through colonialism and – later – internal repression through dictatorship, the latter of which remains prevalent in Egypt and the Arab world. In such a context, where people's rights are often partly dependent on the whims of what many see as unjust rulers, the Sharia is seen as an alternative to repression and a sign of freedom, precisely because it is viewed as deriving from a fundamentally just God. As such, it is no coincidence that ideas such as Qutb's are sometimes compared with Latin American Christian liberation theology.[70]

Although the Muslim Brotherhood's specific political philosophy will be dealt with in Chapter 2, it is important to note here that the view of Islam as an ideology of liberation was given concrete form in Egypt. The organization strove for the Islamization of Egyptian legislation under the slogan 'the Koran is our constitution', which was intended to affect various aspects of political and societal life, such as parliament, corruption, the civil service and the army. It is not surprising that the Muslim Brotherhood, precisely because it viewed Islam as an all-encompassing ideology, resolutely rejected criticism from others in Egypt and elsewhere of its interference in these wide-ranging issues.[71]

The subject of the economy was also not left untouched by the Muslim Brotherhood, although this was initially not a priority for al-Banna. The organization's economic vision was characterized by the idea of economic independence, which it saw as the basis of true, political independence, and the improvement of the plight of the many poor people in Egypt. In this context, the Muslim Brotherhood called for industrialization, the nationalization of the National Bank of Egypt, land reforms and social security, among others. As such, the Muslim Brotherhood's economic vision was an extension of its political views on independence and standing up for the people's interests.[72]

With regard to social changes, the Muslim Brotherhood primarily spoke about educational reforms. Starting from the idea that children are the future, it neither strove for purely religious education – such as that provided at traditional institutes like Al-Azhar –nor did the Muslim Brotherhood only want to see profane subjects taught in schools. Instead, the organization believed that Egyptians should become proficient in secularism in order to overcome it. Partly for this reason, al-Banna argued in favour of modern, academic education in which religious schooling was harmoniously integrated.[73] The Muslim Brotherhood could play a part in this through its emphasis on *da'wa* ('call [to Islam]', 'preaching'), an important means for the organization to direct the Egyptian people towards the alleged need to embrace Islam.[74] Moreover, the organization viewed *da'wa* as a duty for all Muslims (also in later years), so that Egyptians themselves could contribute to reforming the country.[75]

The Early Muslim Brotherhood's Views on the West

According to the Muslim Brotherhood, every Muslim should engage in the task of preaching. The message of this preaching was strongly influenced by the British colonial occupation as well as the Arab-Israeli conflict, which took shape in the first half of the twentieth century and has remained an important topic for the Muslim Brotherhood until today. This, in turn, influenced how members of the organization viewed the West in general and how they placed it in a religious framework. That way, the Muslim Brotherhood's *da'wa* carried a message that was relevant with regard to both domestic and foreign affairs and contributed to the general worldview of those who were influenced by it.

The West as a Political Problem

To the early Muslim Brotherhood – and to Hasan al-Banna in particular – 'the West' was first and foremost a concrete political problem that manifested itself in the form of the British colonial occupation of Egypt. After the rise of the nationalist Wafd Party in 1918 and a popular uprising against British rule in 1919, Egypt became officially independent in 1922. The conditions on which this took place, however, were such that the colonial rule partially remained intact, Egypt did not become truly independent and the British army remained present in the country. The agreement underpinning independence was renegotiated by an elected Egyptian government in 1936, but retained certain privileges for the British – troops in the Suez Canal Zone and partial responsibility for Egypt's foreign policy – which ensured that there was still no real independence.[76]

Although al-Banna was still a teenager when the uprising against British rule took place in 1919, this event and its aftermath seem to have had a great impact on him. Later, he claimed that he and his classmates had been involved in protests and that he had vivid memories of the demonstrations against British control that had taken place during his childhood. This not only left a lasting influence on the young al-Banna, but it was also the beginning of his growing political consciousness.[77] This was underlined in 1927, when he left for Isma'iliyya, a city in the Suez Canal Zone, where he went to work as a teacher and where he was directly confronted with the major differences in wealth and lifestyle between the colonial rulers, on the one hand, and the local population, on the other. To al-Banna, his stay in Isma'iliyya confirmed how wrong the British military dominance in Egypt was.[78] In his later writings, he blames the British for repressing Egypt and states that the agreement that the country had with Great Britain is 'a chain (*ghull*) around Egypt's neck and a shackle (*qayd*) around its hand'.[79]

Considering this background, it is not surprising that British colonialism has had a great impact on the early Muslim Brotherhood's thought and its views on the West. In fact, decades after the British had left Egypt, Muslim Brothers still portrayed Western influence as 'colonialism' sometimes.[80] This does not mean, however, that nothing has changed in the Muslim Brotherhood's attitude towards the West: not only has anti-Western rhetoric become less fierce over the past few decades, but the organization has also justified this revised stance more recently by pointing to Western violence or policy in the Middle East,[81] although themes such as Western 'moral decay'[82] and Western materialism[83] remain present in its discourse. This response is partly inspired by secularization in the Arab world, which the Muslim Brotherhood had to accept and for which it was easier to blame the West than the local population, particularly given the fact that anti-Western views are shared much more broadly in the Arab world than just among the Muslim Brothers.[84]

A specific problem not directly related to Egypt but equally connected to British colonialism and the West was the situation in Palestine, which became increasingly violent during al-Banna's life. The British, who were given a mandate over Palestine by the League of Nations (the United Nations' predecessor) in 1922, had already made (seemingly) contradictory promises to Arab and Zionist leaders, who both claimed the territory for themselves, in the years before. Although many Egyptian politicians and religious scholars did not seem to worry much about Palestine in the first three decades of the twentieth century,[85] this was different for the Muslim Brotherhood. It had been concerned with developments in Palestine since its founding and called for the defence of the holy places in Jerusalem, rejected the sale of land to Zionists and wanted to bring a halt to Jewish immigration to the area. Moreover, it paid much attention to Palestine in its early publications, called for the collection of money for the Arab inhabitants of the mandate area and visited the contested land with a small delegation in 1935.[86]

All of this increased when, in 1936, an uprising against the British broke out among the Arab population of Palestine, which was to last until 1939. Apart from the local meaning the uprising had, it was also of great importance to the Egyptian Muslim Brotherhood since it made many Egyptians aware of the possible influence a future Jewish state could have on the cultural, economic and security position of their own country. This caused a shift in Egyptian public opinion in the direction of Islamism (and thus in the direction of the Muslim Brotherhood).[87] In 1936, the organization set up a committee that became the central organ for the activities it organized around Palestine. During the uprising, the Muslim Brotherhood sent telegrams to the authorities to call attention to the issue, published articles on the subject, handed out leaflets, organized demonstrations and took part in conferences on the topic.[88]

Apart from the role that Great Britain had played in the creation of the Arab-Israeli conflict in Palestine, the Muslim Brotherhood also believed America was partly responsible and it blamed the country for allowing Jewish survivors of the Holocaust to go to Palestine rather than allowing them into the United States after World War II.[89] The organization also accused the United States of supporting Israel because of 'Jewish gold and Zionist influence'. Moreover, the Muslim Brotherhood claimed that Zionists dominated the media in America to such an extent that they were said to incite people there against Muslims in order to gain support for a pro-Zionist policy in Palestine.[90]

Such statements show that the early Muslim Brotherhood's criticism sometimes went further than anti-Zionism and turned against Jews or included age-old anti-Semitic stereotypes about Jews and money, power and secret control, with 'Zionists' as the guilty party rather than Jews. This manifested itself first and foremost in the context of Egypt itself. The Muslim Brotherhood spoke out firmly against Jews and Jewish organizations in Egypt that supported the Zionist cause in Palestine, but also went so far as to call communism a Jewish ideology and to label Freemasonry a Jewish sect.[91] The Muslim Brotherhood also launched a boycott of Jewish businesses in Egypt, in which it openly published the names and addresses of the owners, arguing that the money spent at these businesses would go to Jews in Palestine.[92]

Although these statements were made in the context of the Arab-Israeli conflict (and particularly during the uprising of 1936–1939), about which the Muslim Brotherhood and at least some Jews strongly disagreed,[93] part of the criticism seemed to derive from anti-Semitic ideas of European origin. The organization also pointed to the supposedly long history of Jewish enmity towards Islam and seemingly related verses from the Koran, such as sura 5:82 ('Thou wilt surely find the most hostile of men to the believers are the Jews and the idolaters [...]').[94] This hostility not only led to incidents of (sometimes deadly) violence directed at Jewish Egyptians,[95] but in the context of the continuing Arab-Israeli conflict, which kept feeding into this sentiment, it also set the tone for some of the Muslim Brotherhood's later rhetoric about Israel and Jews.[96]

The West as a Religious Problem

From what we have seen above, it is clear that the early Muslim Brotherhood saw certain connections between Europe, America, Israel and Jews based on the political circumstances in which it found itself. Yet, the early Muslim Brotherhood also tried to interpret the challenge that the West represented in religious terms. We have already seen that the organization ascribed certain 'immoral' elements in Egyptian society to Western influence and to the willingness of some Egyptians to go along with that, but these were more than just incidents in the eyes of the early Muslim Brothers. Firstly, the organization pointed to concrete initiatives such as the so-called British Councils that – under the guise of education in English and British culture – spread values about freedom and gender relations that the Muslim Brotherhood did not like.[97] This was also said to apply to academic researchers and missionaries, who supposedly misrepresented Islam in their work or allegedly attacked it based on their Christian beliefs.[98] In the 1970s and 1980s, the Muslim Brotherhood still portrayed this as part of a global conspiracy against Islam and in favour of Christianity.[99]

The early Muslim Brotherhood also put colonialism and related factors in historical perspective by connecting them with the Crusaders, whose confrontation with Muslims in the Middle East was claimed to have led to hatred of Islam in Europe.[100] Qutb consequently wrote about '*al-isti'mar al-Urubbi wa-l-Amriki al-salibi*' ('European and American Crusader imperialism')[101] and stated that 'the spirit of Crusaderism (*ruh al-salibiyya*)' was 'in the blood of the Westerners'.[102] This was framed further by viewing the struggle with colonialism in the context of a battle between the 'materialist' Western civilization and the 'spiritual' Eastern civilization, with Islam as its centre.

According to al-Banna – in line with statements from Qutb[103] – the West was fundamentally anti-Islamic. Secularism that entered the Muslim world should therefore not be seen as an organic process or a natural development, but as a conscious attack from the West[104] that was allowed by Muslims because they had deviated from Islam.[105]

Yet, the West, in general, and Europe, in particular, were not always associated with Christianity. In fact (and perhaps in contradiction with the above), early Muslim Brothers painted the West as a source of moral decline, atheism and individualism.[106] This was not always based on ignorance. Through colonialism in Egypt, the organization learned about Western 'immoral' influence, as demonstrated above. Moreover, in the 1950s, Qutb also spent a few years in the United States, where he visited several places and actually got to know life in America without it causing him to abandon the idea of the West as immoral.[107] Qutb even went so far as to deny that Europe was ever Christian because 'the tolerant principles of Christianity (*mabadi' al-masihiyya al-samha*)' had supposedly never been accepted on the continent and had therefore never occupied anything more than a marginal position.[108] 'The real intellectual bases (*al-usus al-fikriyya al-haqiqiyya*) in the West', Qutb writes, 'must be sought in the understanding of life by the ancient Romans', who limited their actions to material and intellectual endeavours that they could control and for whom absolute moral considerations played no role.[109]

All of this does not mean that the early Muslim Brotherhood viewed anything remotely Western as evil. Not only did the organization show an openness to, for example, education in which Western knowledge was dealt with, but leaders like al-Banna also cited Western thinkers and scholars to buttress their message. Furthermore, the Muslim Brotherhood admired the freedom and democracy in Western countries and stated that Great Britain made some Muslim countries look bad with regard to justice and equality.[110] This shows the ambivalent attitude that the early Muslim Brotherhood had regarding the West. Some members of the organization tried to explain this by claiming that Western successes had actually been adopted from Islam. Thus, Qutb states that 'the current European industrial culture (*al-hadara al-sina'iyya al-Urubiyya al-hadira*) did not originally emerge in Europe, but emerged in Islamic communities in Andalusia and the East (*al-Mashriq*)'.[111] The Renaissance also supposedly sprang from European contacts with Islam[112] and the same was allegedly true for concepts often associated with the West, such as democracy.[113] As Lia shows, this attitude of the early Muslim Brotherhood should be explained as a desire to emphasize and promote what is authentic about Egypt and

Islam – which al-Banna viewed as being constantly under fire from the West – at the expense of an (alleged) enemy, rather than as a fundamental antipathy towards the West.[114]

The solution that the Muslim Brotherhood proposed to counter the challenges emanating from the West lay in the intra-Islamic unity and the aforementioned *da'wa*, but also in jihad. To al-Banna, jihad was the fifth step in a series of seven: 1) the building of the individual personality; 2) the establishment of the Islamic family; 3) the rise of the Islamic nation; 4) the creation of an Islamic government; 5) the use of jihad to retake all Islamic countries that were conquered by Western powers; 6) the foundation of an Islamic empire consisting of all Muslim countries; and 7) to reach the whole world with the message of Islam. As such, al-Banna called upon his followers to wage jihad, using this term to refer to a broad struggle that was not necessarily military in nature, but certainly did include that dimension.[115]

'Abd al-Qadir 'Awda (1906–1954), one of the most important ideologues of the Egyptian Muslim Brotherhood in the 1940s and 1950s, made clear in his work that jihad was a duty for every Muslim 'when the unbelievers enter an Islamic country [...], because fighting for the defence of the religion (*qital difa' 'an al-din*) is not an offensive fight (*qital ghazw*)'.[116] This even applied to the elderly, women and children, who usually do not have to fight under different circumstances, but should do so now because it is a defensive fight.[117] It is clear that this call for jihad was made in the context of a colonial occupation, not as a general call for some sort of eternal struggle. Al-Banna made his call for jihad in the framework of the liberation, independence and sovereignty of Egypt[118] and 'Awda, too, called on his readers to fight imperialism.[119]

When the Egyptian Muslim Brothers used the word 'imperialism', they possibly referred to the British occupation of their own country first, but certainly also to the British and Zionist presence in Palestine. The early Muslim Brotherhood believed that only jihad could bring a solution to the conflict in Palestine and the organization therefore used the years immediately after World War II to prepare itself for this by gathering political support for their military efforts in this conflict.[120] In the war that broke out between the newly founded state of Israel and the Arab countries in 1948, the Egyptian Muslim Brotherhood actually participated in the fighting with three battalions of fighters. Although the eventual military contribution that the Muslim Brotherhood made in this conflict appears to have been small, for those involved it was nevertheless a source of pride.[121]

***

The Muslim Brotherhood is thus an ideological outgrowth of the nineteenth-century modernist reform movement that resisted traditional Islam by criticizing certain Sufi rituals and the established religious and political order and that was opposed to Western colonialism, but without rejecting European ideas outright. The Muslim Brotherhood was essentially the Egyptian, activist and populist version of this intellectual trend of reformers. In the belief that Islam, as they expressed it, offered a solution to all problems, the Muslim Brothers therefore strove for reforms in Egypt itself, as well as for a removal of the British colonial influence. Although the Muslim Brotherhood principally favoured a pragmatic and gradual approach, it argued for jihad against foreign occupation – be it in their own country or in Palestine, an issue that remains important to the organization to this day. The later history of the Muslim Brotherhood is essentially a negotiation between the heritage of this important early period and the demands of new times and contexts in which the organization finds itself. Before we deal with those, however, we must first take a closer look at the Muslim Brotherhood's specific political ideology.

2. The Political Ideology of the Early Muslim Brotherhood

In the previous chapter, we saw that the early Muslim Brotherhood was a broad, diverse organization with an ideological message to match. This does not mean, however, that it did (or does) not have specific Islamist ideas on how the state, politics and society should take shape. Building on the nineteenth-century reformers that we saw in Chapter 1, ideologues affiliated with the Muslim Brotherhood have thought about what should happen in Egypt and beyond. The results of this thinking form the subject of this chapter. In the first section, I will delve into the subject of the state, where I will deal with how the early Muslim Brotherhood viewed the idea of an Islamic state. The second section subsequently shows how the organization viewed political participation. Finally, I deal with the early Muslim Brotherhood's ideas on societal rights and freedoms, where I will concentrate on the rights of non-Muslims, women's rights and civil liberties.

The State

In Chapter 1 we learned that, for centuries, the most important form of government in Islam has been the caliphate. It is not surprising, therefore, that discussions on the state within the Muslim Brotherhood implicitly or explicitly start there. Whether Muslims wanted to re-establish the caliphate after it had been abolished in 1924 was not a clear-cut matter. Several scholars – including, for example, the Egyptian Sharia judge 'Ali 'Abd al-Raziq (1888–1966) – stated that it was not necessary or even desirable to do so, because they believed that the caliphate actually had little (if any) basis in the Koran and the Sunna.[1] The early Muslim Brotherhood did not agree with this. Influenced by Rida[2] – which, in this case, meant that they lamented the fall of the caliphate, but realized that it should not be directly resurrected in its old form – early Muslim Brothers stated that the caliphate was a duty that rested on the Muslim community as a whole.[3]

At the same time, al-Banna was realistic enough to see that any future caliphate would require a lot of preparation, including 'complete cultural, social and economic cooperation between all of the Islamic peoples' and various treaties between the countries concerned.[4] Moreover, the early Muslim Brotherhood's support for the re-establishment of a caliphate was somewhat half-hearted. It did not seem convinced, for example, of the necessity of returning to one Islamic empire. As such, al-Banna spoke of a 'league (*'asabat*) of Islamic peoples' as a goal,[5] suggesting he took the reality of the various nation states in the region into account. 'Awda wrote similar things. Although he uses his work to sum up the (somewhat exclusive) conditions that a caliph traditionally had to meet,[6] he simultaneously seems to suggest that Muslims in general are the heirs to the caliphate,[7] apparently arguing for an inclusive approach to Islamic leadership. Moreover, 'Awda minimizes the importance of the term 'caliphate' and states that this is just a word for leadership that can be compared with equivalent modern terms.[8]

Islamic State

So, the early Muslim Brotherhood expressed its support for a caliphate (if it did so) mostly in theory, but was much more pragmatic in practice by directing its attention to existing Muslim countries and by making an effort to set up an Islamic *state* instead of an empire or a caliphate. According to the early Muslim Brotherhood, the belief that not only the lives of individual Muslims, but also the state, should be Islamic was rooted in the idea that God the Creator rules over everything and has appointed human beings as rulers on earth.[9] This had several consequences. On the one hand, it meant that earth was ultimately God's possession and that human beings therefore had absolutely no right to claim ownership of it and to do with it whatever they wanted;[10] on the other hand, it entailed that God – as the ultimate owner of earth – must also take possession of legislation and government. The human ruler, to quote 'Awda, 'does not have the right to rise up against the order of the one who has made him a caliph (*amr man istakhlafahu*)'.[11]

Viewed this way, an Islamic state is actually a natural product of Islam. In fact, according to 'Awda, it was Islam that 'created the Islamic state'.[12] Building on al-Banna's ideas, 'Awda states: 'Islam is not just a religion. On the contrary, it is a religion and a state (*din wa-dawla*) and it is in the nature of Islam (*tabi'at al-Islam*) that it has a state (*an takuna lahu dawla*)'.[13] According to 'Awda, these two things could therefore not be separated.[14] Precisely because the Islamic state was such an important part of the religion as a whole, prominent Muslim Brothers, such as al-Banna and Qutb, claimed that it was necessary for the revival and the recovery of Islam.[15] Given all of this, it is not surprising that the re-establishment of an Islamic state has become a central goal for the Muslim Brotherhood,[16] although the exact way this takes shape in practice has not always been the same throughout the years, as we will see later on.

The Muslim Brotherhood claimed the Islamic state should have a constitution[17] that was based on the rules derived from the Koran and the Sunna.[18] Al-Banna writes that if the first article of the constitution stipulates that Islam is the official religion, this should also be apparent from the rest of the constitution.[19] 'Awda adds that the ideal state, as he envisions it, should have multiple parts, including an executive, a legislative and a judicial power.[20] In this context, he pays special attention to the role of the leader as a feature of executive power,[21] who is responsible for various tasks, such as preserving and applying Islam, protecting the country and punishing criminals.[22] 'Awda also acknowledges a 'financial authority' (al-sulta al-maliyya), by which he refers to the financial independence the state should have, and 'the authority of holding to account and improvement' (sultat al-muraqaba wa-l-taqwim'), which he places in the people's hands and to which we will return later.[23]

The emphasis on the religious influence on the constitution and the Islamic constitution as the basis of an Islamic state show the importance that the early Muslim Brotherhood attached to the application of the Sharia.[24] 'Awda, a legal scholar himself, states that the Sharia is superior to other laws because Islamic legislation is based on Islam and, therefore, according to him, is derived from God.[25] He adds, however, that Islamic legislation also has an advantage over other rules because the Sharia emanates from the religion of the Egyptian people, which is primarily Muslim. Because of this, the rules of the Sharia closely match the sense of justice felt by the Egyptian people, which gives Islamic legislation an authority that other systems lack – 'Awda calls this the 'spiritual component' of a law.[26]

Considering the allegedly divine origin of the Sharia and its ties to the Egyptian people's everyday life, 'Awda states that Muslims may not obey non-Islamic laws, even if that means going against the will of a ruler.[27] 'Awda did not consider legislation in Egypt as Islamic, however. The Egyptian constitution may have stated that Islam was the official state religion, but, to 'Awda, this implied that individual laws should also stem from Islam, which he believed was not the case. This way, 'Awda claimed, Egyptian legislation not only violated the Sharia, but also the constitution itself.[28] Instead of implementing the Sharia, the state was said to apply laws that had been transported from Europe.[29]

According to 'Awda, these European laws were used in the service of the imperialist powers that had introduced them to Egypt.[30] They had also led to all kinds of forbidden things, like earning interest, wine, pork, gambling and adultery.[31] Although 'Awda blames the rulers of Egypt (and the Muslim world) for this in his work,[32] his verdict on them is, in a sense, also mild, because he states that they are not aware of the seriousness of non-Islamic legislation and its consequences,[33] and he believes that they are afraid of the colonial powers.[34] The latter happens in a context of loyalty and obedience to Western rulers that has not yielded anything good for Muslim leaders to date, 'Awda states,[35] quite apart from the Islamic prohibition of subjection to non-Islamic powers (especially if they are ill-disposed towards Muslims).[36] Although the colonialist argument was used less frequently in later years, the application of the Sharia and the alleged lack of this in Egypt remained important themes in the Muslim Brotherhood's discourse.[37]

The Sovereignty of God

The above may suggest that there was agreement among early Muslim Brothers on the application of the Sharia and, to a certain extent, this was, indeed, the case. Yet the organization nevertheless became increasingly divided regarding the subject of the Islamic state and the application of the Sharia, which was closely connected with the term *hakimiyya* ('sovereignty'). This concept neither originated in Muslim Brotherhood discourse nor can it be found literally in the Koran. Instead, it had been coined by the Indian-Pakistani Islamic scholar Abu l-A'la Mawdudi (1903–1979), who founded the Islamist Jama'at-I Islami party in 1941.[38] Although he was not organizationally tied to the Muslim Brotherhood and was rooted in a different ethnic and geographical context, Mawdudi did share the organization's Islamist ideology, including its view of Islam as an all-encompassing system and the need for an Islamic state.[39] Moreover, he had also had his own (yet similar) experiences with British colonialism.[40]

In his work, Mawdudi derived the term *'hakimiyya'* from the Arabic verb *hakama* ('to judge'),[41] which occurs in various forms in the Koran, such as in sura 5:44: '[...] Whoso judges not (*wa-man lam yahkum*) according to what God has sent down (*bi-ma anzala llah*) – they are the unbelievers'. According to Mawdudi, verses like these suggest that believers should obey God. He also states that other passages from the Koran – such as sura 3:154: '[...] "The affair belongs to God entirely (*al-amr kullahu li-llah*)" [...]' – show that people owe this obedience in all aspects of life, including in politics.[42] Yet, the problem, according to Mawdudi, is that people have turned themselves or others into a *rabb* ('lord') or *ilah* ('god') by appropriating the sovereignty that belongs to God alone. The human dominance over others for their own interests that is said to have been the result of this has been responsible for much misery in the world, Mawdudi claims. An Islamic state should therefore unconditionally submit itself to the sovereignty of God.[43] The role of human beings in such a state would not be one of *uluhiyya* ('divinity'), then, but of *'ibada* ('worship').[44] In Mawdudi's thought, *hakimiyya* therefore boils down to the sole sovereignty of God and, in that sense, can be called theocratic,[45] although he himself refers to this system as a 'theo-democracy' because it does – within its own framework – give people some influence.[46]

The reason Mawdudi's views on *hakimiyya* are so important to the Muslim Brotherhood is that they were an important source of influence to Sayyid Qutb, who read Mawdudi's work when he was in prison in 1954.[47] Although adherents to Mawdudi's thought have accused Qutb of pushing his ideas on *hakimiyya* too far, and, moreover, of taking them out of their original context of a non-Muslim country (India) and applying them to a Muslim country (Egypt), Mawdudi has been a great influence on certain Muslim Brothers.[48] Starting from the same pre-suppositions with regard to the broad (and thus also political) applicability of Islam as Mawdudi's,[49] the influence of the latter on Qutb is evident. Qutb writes:

> Complete worship (*al-'ubudiyya al-mutlaqa*) of God alone is represented in taking God alone as a god, with regard to creed (*'aqidatan*), worship (*'ibadatan*) and law (*Shari'atan*). So, a Muslim does not believe that 'the divinity' (*al-uluhiyya*) is for any other than God – may He be praised – and he does not believe that 'worship' (*al-'ibada*) is for any other from his creation and he [also] does not believe that 'sovereignty' (*al-hakimiyya*) is for any of his servants.[50]

According to Qutb, this meant that the Sharia (as a total system that encompasses all spheres of life) should be fully applied in Muslim countries.[51]

Qutb's conclusion about sovereignty seems to come down to what we saw earlier, namely, the application of the Sharia. Qutb's ideas about *hakimiyya* go further than that, however. As becomes clear from the above, Qutb – like Mawdudi – establishes a clear connection between the sovereignty of God in legislation, on the one hand, and the worship of God, on the other, in which recognition and acceptance of the former is a necessary expression of the latter.[52] Moreover, according to Qutb, because the worship of God is tied to Muslims' relationship with Him, this cannot be changed from place to place and from period to period, but rather must remain a constant, unchanging factor.[53] As such, *hakimiyya* becomes an essential part of God's divinity. Qutb connects God's sovereignty directly to the Islamic confession of faith ('There is no god but God and Muhammad is the messenger of God'), which forms the basis of Islam.[54] Thus, faith in and support for the sovereignty of God becomes a litmus test for someone's faith, as it were. According to Qutb, the alternative to this was *kufr* ('unbelief').[55]

The far-reaching importance that Qutb ascribes to the acceptance of the sovereignty of God (and particularly to the accusation of unbelief that he connects with the refusal thereof) is further underlined when we see what Koranic verses he uses to legitimize this point of view. In the context of this subject, Qutb emphasizes the relationship between following non-Islamic legislation and worship of idols by pointing to sura 9:31, which says of Jews and Christians that: 'They have taken their rabbis and their monks as lords (*arbaban*) apart from God [...] and they were commanded to serve but One God (*ilahan wahidan*) [...]'.[56] With regard to *hakimiyya*, Qutb,[57] like Mawdudi, cites sura 5:44,[58] which he – in the political contexts in which he reads this – interprets as an accusation of unbelief (*takfir*) against rulers who do not apply the Sharia in full. Qutb believes that no compromises are possible in this regard. In his exegetical work *Fi Zilal al-Qur'an* ('In the Shade of the Koran'), he writes about this part of sura 5:

> God – may He be praised – says that the question – in this entirely – is a question of faith and unbelief (*iman aw kufr*) [...] and that there is neither a middle way in this matter (*la wasat fi hadha l-amr*) nor a truce or reconciliation! For the believers are the ones who judge according to what God has sent down (*bi-ma anzala llah*) – they do not forbid a letter of it (*la yuharrimuna minhu harfan*) and they do not exchange anything of it (*la yubaddiluna minhu shay'an*) – and the ungodly, evildoing unbelievers (*al-kafirun al-zalimun al-fasiqun*)[59] are the ones who do not judge according to what God has sent down.[60]

With this point of view, Qutb not only criticized secularism in Egypt or the policies of a certain government, but he also undermined the basis of the state as such.[61]

Although Qutb deals with many more subjects than *hakimiyya* in his numerous books and even though his ideas on this notion are partly the result of a process of radicalization that we will deal with in more detail later on, it is clear that he went further than other ideologues of the Muslim Brotherhood.[62] This resulted in him being criticized for his ideas within the Egyptian organization. The key person in this respect was Hasan al-Hudaybi (1891–1973), the second leader of the Muslim Brotherhood.[63] The title of his book about this, *Du'at La Qudat* ('Preachers, Not Judges'), epitomizes al-Hudaybi's criticism of Qutb, namely, that it is the Muslim Brotherhood's job to call people to lead Islamic lifestyles, not to condemn them for not doing so.[64]

Al-Hudaybi's criticism of Qutb's ideas on God's sovereignty points out that *hakimiyya*, as we have already seen above, is neither mentioned in the Koran, as such, nor in the traditions of the Prophet that he considers authentic.[65] This is crucial to al-Hudaybi, since 'the verses and the traditions are the ones that determine the Sharia verdict (*al-hukm al-Shar'i*), the conditions of its realization (*shurut tahqiqhi*) and the limits of its use (*hudud isti'malihi*)'. He states that there is no need for 'technical terms (*mustalahat*) that fallible people (*bashar ghayr ma'sum*) have invented'.[66] Although al-Hudaybi equally states that following the Sharia is a duty for Muslims,[67] that Muslims should not go against the rules of God,[68] and that all of this should also happen on a political level,[69] he writes that those who fall short in this respect should not immediately be accused of unbelief. Such people may be ignorant about the Sharia or may have wrong ideas about it, al-Hudaybi states, but – implicitly criticizing Qutb's reading of sura 5:44 – that does not make them unbelievers.[70]

Al-Hudaybi also criticizes Qutb's interpretation of sura 9:31, in which the latter equates following non-Islamic laws with the worship of idols. Al-Hudaybi points out that it is important to look at a person's intentions.[71] If one does not know those, he states, then Muslims should follow the Prophet's order and judge people on the basis of what is outwardly visible and what they say.[72] This means, on the one hand, that one cannot apply *takfir* against entire groups of people, simply because one first has to investigate someone's individual faith or unbelief;[73] on the other hand, it means that, as long as people say the Islamic confession of faith, one should accept them as Muslims, even if they are guilty of sinful behaviour.[74] It is this 'live-and-let-live' view on the state that ultimately became dominant within the Muslim Brotherhood, as we will see in greater detail later.

Political Participation

The different ideas on an Islamic state found within the early Muslim Brotherhood were divided between the opponents of Qutb, who argued in favour of *takfir* of the regime, and al-Hudaybi, who was much more willing to obey the rulers. The points of view held by other prominent ideologues, such as al-Banna and 'Awda, were in between these two. All of this was, of course, related to how such an Islamic state should be reached. This, too, was a point about which division existed among early Muslim Brothers, namely, between those who were willing to work peacefully within the boundaries of the system and those who were prepared to confront them and did not shy away from using violence in the process.

Peaceful Means of Political Participation

The dominant trend within the early Muslim Brotherhood regarding political participation was characterized by a peaceful and gradual approach, within which the above-mentioned *da'wa* played an important role in terms of convincing society of the organization's message from the bottom up.[75] Apart from preaching, the Muslim Brotherhood also developed ideas about parliamentary participation and about what the role of the people should be in any future Islamic state. In this context, it is clear that al-Banna was not a supporter of party politics. About this subject, he writes that 'we are not like that and we will not be'. Muslim Brothers, according to him, are different:

> We are politicians in the sense that we are interested in the affairs of our community (*shu'un ummatina*). We believe that the executive power (*al-quwwa al-tanfidhiyya*) is part of the teachings of Islam that fall within its sphere (*tadkhulu fi nitaqihi*) and is included under its rulings (*tandariju tahta ahkamihi*) and that political freedom and nationalist might (*al-'izza al-qawmiyya*) is one of its pillars and one of its duties. We work diligently for the perfection of the freedom (*li-stikmal al-hurriyya*) and the reform of the executive means (*li-islah al-adat al-tanfidhiyya*). That is what we are.[76]

Al-Banna also states that the attitude of the Muslim Brotherhood vis-à-vis Egyptian governments is one of 'brotherly advisor (*al-nasih al-shaqiq*)',[77] not of a party that challenges the powers. In fact, he sees (oppositional) political parties as organizations that create divisions in the Muslim community and possibly bring about chaos. He therefore distinguishes between freedom of expression and:

> [T]ribalism of opinions (*al-ta'assub li-l-ra'y*), rising up against the community (*al-khuruj 'ala l-jama'a*), untiring work to widen the chasm of division (*tawsi' huwat al-inqisam*) in the community and overthrowing the authority of the rulers (*za'za'at sultan al-hukkam*). This is what party politics requires and what Islam refuses and strongly forbids (*yuharrimuhu ashadd al-tahrim*).[78]

Al-Banna also claims that many political parties in Egypt act mostly out of self-interest or have come into existence through specific circumstances and, as such, perhaps have little future in the long term.[79] It is for these reasons that al-Banna calls on political parties in Egypt to continue in one coalition[80] or prefers that they are abolished altogether.[81] Considering al-Banna's view that Egyptian politics was characterized by elites and corruption, it is highly probable that his opposition to political parties should also be interpreted in this context.[82]

The Muslim Brotherhood's views on electoral participation – not parties – was strongly connected with several Islamic concepts that had sometimes also been used for this purpose by nineteenth-century reformers. The first concept that plays a role in this is *al-amr bi-l-ma'ruf wa-l-nahy 'an al-munkar* ('commanding right and forbidding wrong'), a duty that is mentioned multiple times in the Koran and that boils down to the idea that Muslims should do good things and prevent or stop bad things.[83] Whereas this term was perhaps mostly an ethical concept in earlier contexts, al-Banna saw it as an Islamic basis for the legal and political right of Muslims to hold the government to account. The ruler, in his eyes, was not just answerable to God, but also to the Muslim community (*umma*).[84] Hence 'Awda states that rulers come from the *umma* itself and represent it, not to dominate the Muslims, but to lead them.[85] The Muslim community, in turn, has a duty – based on the concept of *al-amr bi-l-ma'ruf wa-l-nahy 'an al-munkar* – to hold them to account,[86] particularly if the rulers go against the rules of Islam.[87]

Part of holding rulers to account is the aforementioned concept of *shura*.[88] Al-Banna states that rulers have the duty to consult the *umma* and to respect its opinion and – with reference to two Koranic verses[89] – that God has also commanded rulers to do so.[90] 'Awda also points to the religious duty of consultation[91] and, like al-Banna, he pairs this with the relationship between the ruler and the people.[92] Precisely because *shura* means 'consultation' and people like al-Banna and 'Awda tie this explicitly to the political involvement of the people, it is not surprising that this concept is frequently connected to democracy. Seen as such, *shura* could be a form of popular government derived from Islam.[93] 'Awda strenuously denies this, however. According to him, democratic countries partly fail because politicians there are influenced by personal and party interests that come at the expense of the general interest.[94] He believes this is not the case with *shura* since both the ruler and the ruled have to adhere to Islamic norms in that system. These flow from things like justice and equality, which are derived from Islam in a system of consultation, while, in democracies, the contents of these are left to the people themselves.[95]

According to prominent members of the early Egyptian Muslim Brotherhood, there did not have to be any consultation with the people if there was definitive proof for a certain point of view from the Koran or the Sunna. In such a case, the matter was clear to them and they believed that point of view should be followed. At most, there could be consultation about how to execute it.[96] If there was no textual evidence for a specific point of view, then consultation with the people should take place, so the ruler could – according to al-Banna – subsequently choose from among the collected viewpoints what he deemed best.[97] 'Awda, moreover, writes that the ruler also needs to be elected via consultation with the people,[98] a custom that also took place in early Islam, when a select group of prominent Muslims was consulted to choose the new caliph.[99]

Just like at the beginning of Islam, the ideologues of the early Muslim Brotherhood did not consider it practical or even possible to consult all Muslims about who should be the ruler. According to al-Banna, the group of people consulted should therefore be limited to the *ahl al-hall wa-l-'aqd* ('the people of loosening and binding'; more freely translated: 'the people of decision-making'), a term also applied to religious scholars who were responsible for appointing a new caliph in the past.[100] These representatives of the people could, according to al-Banna, be religious scholars, 'experts (*ahl al-khibra*) in general matters', or people with a societal leadership position.[101] 'Awda adds to this that the Sharia does not prescribe a specific number or way of electing these 'people of decision-making', but does state that they need to be righteous, have knowledge of the matters at hand and possess a measured opinion and wisdom.[102] As the final stage of this selection process, according to 'Awda, 'the people of decision-making' should pledge an oath of fealty (*bay'a*) to the ruler[103] – again an old Islamic custom[104] – after which the believers own the leader their obedience (*ta'a*), except when this goes against the rules of Islam.[105]

Violent Means of Political Participation

Thus, the early Muslim Brotherhood strove for an Islamic state through peaceful means that clearly ascribed a role to the people, but within the boundaries of the Sharia. Not everybody agreed with this, however. Again, it was Qutb who formulated an alternative to al-Banna's ideas – which he essentially considered naïve – in the years after his death. Unlike the founder of the Muslim Brotherhood, Qutb did not believe that a mass movement's preaching could bring about an Islamic state and he therefore increasingly emphasizes the use of violence by a small group of people to reach the same goal.[106]

The starting point of Qutb's radical views was the conviction that, because it did not accord full sovereignty to God, Egyptian society lived in *jahiliyya*.

In Islam, this term usually refers to the pre-Islamic period of 'ignorance', when the Prophet Muhammad had not yet received his alleged revelations.[107] According to Qutb, however, *jahiliyya* was:

> [N]ot a historical period (*fatra tarikhiyya*), but a situation that you will find anywhere where its components are present in a situation (*wad'*) or a system (*nizam*). It is, at its core (*fi samimiha*), the returning of ruling (*al-hukm*) and legislation (*al-tashri'*) to the desires of humankind (*ahwa al-bashar*), not to the method of God (*manhaj Allah*) and his Sharia of life (*Shari'atihi li-l-hayat*).[108]

In his work, Qutb distinguishes between two kinds of societies: the Islamic society, 'in which Islam is applied with regard to creed (*'aqidatan*), worship (*'ibadatan*), the Sharia (*Shari'atan*), the system (*nizaman*), morality (*khulqan*) and behaviour (*sulukan*)', and the ignorant society, in which none of this can be found.[109]

As was the case with *hakimiyya*, Qutb did not coin the term '*jahiliyya*' himself, but had borrowed it from the work of the Indian scholar Abu l-Hasan Ali Hasani Nadwi (1913–1999),[110] whom he had met in Saudi Arabia[111] and who, in turn, had adopted it from Mawdudi.[112] Qutb's use of this term has received much attention in academic literature,[113] but its scope in his work is not entirely clear. Some scholars claim that Qutb only applies the term to the regime,[114] others suggest that it applies to all of society,[115] while still others point out that the use of the term *jahiliyya* is not the same as *takfir*.[116] Whatever the case, Qutb's use of this terminology – together with his use of *hakimiyya* – lay the foundations for a radical road towards an Islamic state.[117]

Qutb's ideas on *jahiliyya* do not mean that he remains entirely silent about the concepts that people like al-Banna and 'Awda used. Like them, Qutb states that *shura* only offers people the possibility to make decisions about matters within the boundaries of the Sharia, not about whatever falls outside of those.[118] As a result of this attitude, Qutb also rejects democracy, precisely because sovereignty in that system lies with the people and not with God.[119] He also warns against the tendency to transform *shura* into a system that moves in the direction of European democracies.[120] That would result in a shift in sovereignty from God and the eternal values of Islam to people and their fickle *jahili* ideas.[121]

Qutb's radical views – whether his positions on *hakimiyya* and *jahiliyya* or his fierce denunciation of democracy – should be seen in the context of the increasingly heavy repression by the Egyptian regime of the Muslim Brotherhood's opposition, in general, and his, in particular, in the 1950s and 1960s.[122]

The periods he spent in Egyptian prisons and the torture he endured there because of his ideas and his membership of the organization made him bitter, encouraged him to read the Koran as a revolutionary book and partly pushed him in the direction of considering violence as an option against the regime.[123]

His ideological development in the direction of using violence against the state expressed itself in the re-appreciation of jihad. Although this word literally means 'effort' and can therefore stand for a broad range of activities among Muslims, in an Islamic-legal sense, the word is mostly used to denote a religiously legitimized struggle against non-Muslims in defence of or to expand Islamic territory.[124] Qutb denies, however, that jihad is a defensive war that can be compared with other wars.[125] Even if jihad were a defensive struggle, it would be a '"defence of man" himself against all factors that limit his freedom (*tuqayyidu hurriyyatahu*) and hinder his liberation (*ta'uqu taharrurahu*)'. According to Qutb, these factors can be found in:

> [P]olitical regimes based on economic, class and racist blockades (*al-hawajiz al-iqtisadiyya wa-l-tabaqiyya wa-l-'unsuriyya*) that prevailed on the entire earth (*kanat sa'ida fi l-ard kulliha*) on the day Islam came and forms of which still prevail in the current *jahiliyya* (*al-jahiliyya al-hadira*) at this time![126]

Because Qutb sees Islam and the Sharia as means to liberate people, it is not surprising that he treats jihad in this context and states that all of this amounts to a 'total revolution (*al-thawra al-kamila*) against the sovereignty of humankind in all its forms (*suwariha*), shapes (*ashkaliha*), systems (*an-zimatiha*) and situations (*awda'iha*)'.[127]

To Qutb, jihad was thus a means to overthrow existing political regimes and to replace them with Islamic systems and, as such, liberate people from the yoke that they had burdened themselves with and apply the Sharia instead.[128] In this context, he wonders how 'the process of the revival of Islam' begins and answers his own question by pointing to the necessity of having a *tali'a* ('vanguard').[129] This elite of pious Muslims should take the lead in all of this by seceding from the *jahiliyya*, preparing themselves for the struggle and guiding the rest of the Muslim community.[130] Should all of this succeed, then Muslims would owe their obedience to the eventual leader of the Islamic state, who rules according to the Sharia.[131]

It was not just the revolutionary, violent aspect of Qutb's ideas that clashed with al-Banna's earlier thought, but the isolationist and elitist character of Qutb's vanguard also contrasted starkly with the popular organization of lay people that the Muslim Brotherhood tried to be. It was no coincidence, therefore, that al-Hudaybi – the leader of the organization when Qutb wrote his most important books – resists his ideas in his own work and hews much more closely to al-Banna's line. He recognizes that jihad is still a legitimate defensive struggle, but rejects it as a means to found an Islamic state because of his opposition to *takfir* of the regime. That, he claims, could lead to *fitna* ('chaos'), a term that goes back to the internal struggle that the earliest Muslims waged after the death of the Prophet Muhammad and that has a very negative connotation.[132] Instead, al-Hudaybi – like other Muslim Brothers – argued in favour of commanding right and forbidding wrong as an Islamic form of opposition that moves the regime in the direction of an Islamic character, on the one hand, but also accepts the authority of the state (even if it does not apply the Sharia), on the other.[133]

In al-Hudaybi's ideal Islamic state, we can see the same aspects that we saw with other prominent members of the early Muslim Brotherhood. For him, too, 'the people of decision making' were responsible for the selection of a leader[134] – although al-Hudaybi was less inclined than al-Banna and 'Awda to involve a broad group of Muslims in this[135] – who would eventually pledge an oath of fealty to the person chosen.[136] If such a ruler applies the Sharia, then obedience is compulsory. This duty expires, however, if the leader demands disobedience to the Sharia from the people.[137] Still, even in such a situation al-Hudaybi does not call for revolution against the regime, but rather for preaching Islam.[138] Al-Hudaybi's gradual and non-violent approach (through *da'wa* and political participation) has become the strategic choice of the Muslim Brotherhood since the 1960s, at the expense of Qutb's.[139] Moreover, the organization has also increasingly embraced democracy,[140] as we will also see in the chapters to come.

Societal Rights and Freedoms

The extent to which the early Muslim Brotherhood offered space to societal rights and freedoms[141] for various groups was, just like with earlier subjects, dependent on the context in which the organization found itself and the extent to which it was prepared to adopt the reformist ideas from the nineteenth century. To the Muslim Brotherhood, the application of the Sharia was not just a political issue, but also a societal necessity; after all, Muslims' lives played out in society and it was therefore important that the rules in the societal sphere were Islamic.[142]

None of this takes away the fact that the Muslim Brotherhood's idea of the exact contents of the Sharia was rather vague, although it did seem to agree that the 'true' rules of God should not be confused with Islamic jurisprudence. In other words, one should distinguish between rules truly derived from the Koran and the Sunna and the many rules that Muslim scholars had added to these throughout the centuries. By viewing this last group of rules as contextually and temporally bound, and therefore not as sacred, space was created to set them aside and formulate solutions to contemporary problems through direct interpretation of the sources rather than exclusively relying on the rulings of, for example, mediaeval scholars. This way, the Muslim Brotherhood not only continued the reformist agenda from the nineteenth century, but it also laid the foundation for a flexible approach to the Sharia that took the demands of the time and context in which one lived into account.[143]

Reforms of the Sharia pursued by the Muslim Brotherhood did not just happen randomly or without limits, however. Firstly, the Koran and the Sunna offered the textual framework that one could not simply ignore. Moreover, scholars affiliated with the organization – like Islamic legal scholars in the centuries before – distinguished between *'ibadat* and *mu'amalat*. The first term applies to matters pertaining to the worship of God, while the second one refers to relations between human beings amongst themselves.[144] Because *'ibadat* are connected with rituals of worship detached from context and time (and thus hardly change, if at all), but *mu'amalat* do depend on changing contexts and times, the Muslim Brotherhood believed that reforms of the Sharia were only possible within the latter category of rules.[145]

This way, even clear Koranic texts could be skirted, for example by interpreting the commandment to amputate the hand of a thief,[146] as only valid in an Islamic state in which people are provided with all material means. Since such a situation did not exist, one could effectively invalidate this commandment without actually challenging its correctness.[147] Since Qutb, as we have seen, connected legislation and God's sovereignty with worship, he often viewed *mu'amalat* as falling into the sphere of *'ibadat*, which is why he was sceptical about the extent to which these were allowed to be reformed.[148] Partly in response to Qutb,[149] al-Hudaybi disagreed with this, however, which illustrates that the opening up of the Sharia to reforms created space that even members of a single organization did not fill in the same way.

Rights of Religious Minorities

As we have already seen in the context of the Arab-Israeli conflict and the attitude of the Muslim Brotherhood towards Jews, the early Muslim

Brotherhood's discourse on the societal issue of religious minorities' rights should be viewed in the colonial context in which it came about. This could suggest that the Muslim Brotherhood's views on Christianity – which is essentially what this section is about – are also characterized by hostility, given that the British colonial occupier of Egypt in the first half of the twentieth century was also Christian. The reality was slightly more complicated, however.

Firstly, the Muslim Brotherhood was apparently capable of making a distinction between Western (Protestant) missionaries and the local (Coptic) Christians, in which the organization also viewed the latter as victims of the alleged distortion of the faith by the former.[150] Secondly, the organization also based its views on the Islamic tradition regarding non-Muslims in Muslim countries,[151] according to which these groups ought to live as *dhimmi*s (members of a protected minority): contractually protected by Muslims in return for payment of a poll tax (*jizya*) while living under discriminatory measures that varied from place to place and from period to period. The traditional relationship between Muslims and *dhimmi*s therefore was certainly not one of hostility, although it was equally clear that the two groups did not enjoy the same rights.[152]

Building on this tradition, the basic attitude of the early Muslim Brotherhood towards Christians appears to have been one of religious, societal tolerance: in this context, al-Banna cites sura 60:8 ('God forbids you not, as regards those who have not fought you in religion's cause, nor expelled you from your habitations, that you should be kindly to them, and act justly towards them; surely God loves the just') to legitimize that Muslims not only protect non-Muslims who do not engage in hostilities, but also treat them well.[153] These were not just empty words: relations between the Muslim Brotherhood (and particularly al-Banna) and Coptic Christians in Egypt appear to have actually been good.[154] The same attitude could be seen among other early Islamists,[155] including the first leader of the Syrian branch of the Muslim Brotherhood, Mustafa al-Siba'i (1915–1964).[156]

Still, these good personal relationships were not necessarily translated into a clear position of equality between Muslims and Christians in all respects. 'Awda may state in his work that 'Islam establishes equality (*al-musawat*) between all people'[157] and that no distinction is made in Islam between people of, for example, different skin colours or origins,[158] but he, too, continues to speak of *dhimmi*s (although he says that they have the same rights as Muslims).[159] This is not surprising, because the nationality (*jinsiyya*) of all inhabitants of the *dar al-Islam* ('the abode of Islam') is the Islamic one, 'whether they are Muslims or *dhimmi*s', Egyptian, Syrian,

Iraqi or Moroccan.[160] This essentially means that the deciding identity of the country is a religious one that Christians – precisely because they are Christians – will not subscribe to, which means that they do not really fit in after all.

The above-mentioned question of identity and the unequal rights that flowed from it were expressed in people's political inequality in an Islamic state as the early Muslim Brotherhood envisioned it. As such, Qutb states that non-Muslim men of the age of conscription should, in such a scenario, pay the *jizya*, which would serve as compensation for the fact that they are not willing to fight in the Islamic army of an Islamic state.[161] Qutb also assumes that Christians are hostile towards Islam,[162] seems to take the *dhimmi* status of non-Muslims – rather than equality – as his starting point[163] and views the poll tax as a sign of their submission.[164]

In the previous sections, we saw that Qutb is often more radical than other thinkers in the early Muslim Brotherhood. With regard to this subject, he also expresses more negative views on Christians than al-Banna and 'Awda. Still, they had in common that all of them strove for an Islamic state with an Islamic identity, which seemed to imply inequality that, though perhaps small, was nevertheless fundamental, because everything should be subordinate to the political order of an Islamic state. In such a context, non-Muslims can presumably not hold the same positions as Muslims, such as in the army or in politics. This attitude among Muslim Brothers did not truly change until later, when they began to adjust the ideal of an Islamic state or even dropped it from their agenda altogether.

Women's Rights

Although Muslim women – unlike Christians – do belong to the Muslim community and are therefore not directly tied to a non-Muslim country such as Great Britain, the issue of women's rights cannot be seen as completely detached from British colonialism because of the latter's alleged evil moral influence. The Muslim Brotherhood, for example, lamented that Muslim women were said to have lost their virtuousness by participating in parties and dances, because they wanted to look like Europeans.[165] The organization also condemned this tendency in the 1970s and 1980s. It pointed out that Muslimas who modelled themselves after Western women attached greater value to the outside (appearances and good looks) than the inside (piety and dignity). While 'Western' things like feminism suggest to women that they need to be liberated and encourage them to reject Islam, the Muslim Brotherhood believed that Islam and womanhood were a natural fit.[166]

Apart from the supposedly evil Western influence on Muslim women, the early Muslim Brotherhood also believed that an 'Eastern' view of this matter – which wrongly described women as inferior and reduced them to objects of procreation, chastity and sexual pleasure for men – should be rejected.[167] Building on this, the aforementioned Mustafa al-Siba'i made an important contribution to the subject of the position of women within the early Muslim Brotherhood.[168] This author states that earlier civilizations – such as the Greeks, the Romans and the inhabitants of ancient India – treated women badly, gave them hardly any rights and made them almost completely subservient to their husbands.[169] Jews, Christians and pre-Islamic Arabs also used to treat their wives badly by viewing them merely as, for example, servants, objects of lust in the hands of Satan or marriage partners without any rights.[170] According to al-Siba'i, Islam changed this by viewing women as equals to men with regard to their humanity and their piety and by providing them with social and legal rights.[171]

This golden mean that Islam supposedly represented did not mean that the Muslim Brotherhood believed men and women should have completely equal rights: according to their way of thinking, women were not inferior to men, but they were different in nature.[172] On the one hand, this was due to the idea that women were not just physically but also mentally less strong than men,[173] which results in the idea that men should supervise women (in line with sura 4:34: 'Men are the managers of the affairs of women for that God has preferred in bounty one of them over another [...]');[174] on the other hand, this idea was connected to the fact that women had a less important social status, for example because they had usually received less education or had fewer social responsibilities. This, according to the Muslim Brotherhood, explains why the Koran states[175] that the testimony of a women is worth only half of that of a man[176] and also[177] that men inherit twice as much as women.[178]

In this framework, the early Muslim Brotherhood believed that women's most important task was within the family, which was very important to the organization.[179] As such, women could function in their natural state as wives and – especially – as mothers and educators of a new generation,[180] which remained an important theme in the Muslim Brotherhood's publications for years afterwards.[181] With regard to the family, the early ideologues of the organisation were not fiercely against polygyny, but they were certainly not supporters of it either because this would be detrimental to family life. To be sure, they acknowledged that the Koran allows a man to marry up to four women,[182] but they also pointed out that this was a limitation of earlier, non-Islamic forms of polygyny and that the Koran sets the condition that the man treats his different wives equally, which they considered virtually impossible.[183] Moreover, al-Siba'i emphasizes that women should have a say prior to and during – and, in case of a divorce, also after – their marriages and that this should be respected.[184]

The emphasis on the family and marriage does not mean that the early Muslim Brotherhood denied women the chance to play a role outside the house. They should be dressed modestly – which, in any case, entailed the wearing of a headscarf and a body that was largely covered[185] – and interaction with unrelated men should be kept to a minimum to prevent seduction and possible adultery.[186] Education for women was encouraged and, in principle, all studies were open to them, although careers in medicine and education were encouraged because these were said to fit women's nature best and to help them with their family duties later.[187] This was slightly more complicated with regard to a job because this was often seen as the duty of a man. The Muslim Brotherhood therefore did allow women to work outside the house, but naturally only if the rules of Islam were respected and provided there was enough room for a job on top of family life, which remained a women's primary task.[188]

One type of job that needs to be mentioned specifically is political positions. To the early Muslim Brotherhood, this was a controversial subject because it was related to working outside the house in general (with all the possible sinful behaviour that this entailed), but also because it could lead to the leadership of women over men, which the organization rejected because of texts such as the aforementioned sura 4:34.[189] Still, the Muslim Brotherhood did not reject the presence of women in politics. Although al-Siba'i states that politics is not something that the first Muslim women were actively involved in, he does not deny that they were involved in, for example, preaching.[190] He also writes that there is no specific objection based on Islam against women voting during elections or standing for parliament, provided the Islamic rules regarding behaviour and clothing are observed, although he continues to stress that women should primarily care for their families.[191] Leadership positions are also not definitively closed off to women, except that of head of state, which al-Siba'i believes is exclusively reserved for men.[192]

Civil Liberties

Freedom was a subject that the early Muslim Brotherhood paid less attention to than to other subjects. Yet, it is clear – particularly in Qutb's writings – what freedom should be based on. To Qutb, the most important obstacles to true freedom are the tyrannical characteristics of human sovereignty, which bound people to rules and laws that they impose on each other as a yoke that keeps everyone enslaved. His alternative – God's sovereignty – is the source of true freedom that will enable all people to be free to live their lives.[193] By extension, 'Awda states that 'Islam founds society on the basis of freedom in its widest [possible] meaning (*fi awsa' ma'aniha*)'.[194] According to him, this encompasses the freedom of conviction, the freedom of thought and the freedom to speak,[195] as well as the freedom of education and the freedom to own property.[196]

The way Qutb and 'Awda speak about freedom again provides us with another glimpse of the context in which they made these statements: they mostly formulate freedom as a situation in which there is no dictatorial government to stifle people's thinking and limit their actions. This does not mean, however, that they advocated total freedom of choice themselves. In fact, things that were allowed in Egypt at that time – such as adultery, asking for and receiving interest, alcohol and gambling – were believed by them to be in conflict with the Sharia and, as such, should be forbidden. They do not so much argue in favour of this to curb people's freedom, but rather because a prohibition of these things came from God and was, therefore, by definition infallible.[197] The same applies to freedom of expression. On the basis of 'Awda's ideas mentioned above, this appears to be quite extensive in the Muslim Brotherhood's thought, but in practice it is also formulated in opposition to a tyrannical government, not at the expense of Islam, which sets divine limits to what is and what is not allowed. According to 'Awda, freedom in an Islamic state must therefore not only happen within certain practical boundaries, but it should also be 'limited so that what is written or said does not go against the texts or the spirit of the Sharia'.[198]

***

The Muslim Brotherhood thus rather quickly let go of the caliphate and accepted the idea of a nation state, which they clearly wanted to have an Islamic character. The early Muslim Brotherhood's activist approach to the Egyptian state was expressed in two different ways: Qutb's concept of *hakimiyya* and al-Hudaybi's opposition against it. This was also apparent in the early Muslim Brotherhood's views on political participation, about which two opposing views could be discerned: the ultimately dominant strategy of peaceful and gradual participation (but not democracy), as al-Hudaybi advocated, and Qutb's minority position that was expressed through jihad and revolution.

On societal rights and freedoms, the early Muslim Brotherhood seems to have been more united and to have advocated a flexible approach to the Sharia if there was no definitive textual basis for a rule concerning relations between people (rather than the worship of God). With regard to non-Muslims, this was expressed in religious and societal tolerance, but not true equality; regarding women's rights, this resulted in the idea that women had different capacities and responsibilities than men and therefore also had different rights, but were equal and similar in their humanity; the Muslim Brotherhood formulated civil liberties on the basis of Islam and in opposition to a tyrannical state, which meant that true freedom implied that there were only 'divine' limits. In the chapters that follow, we will see that the Muslim Brotherhood reformed itself and developed further from these ideas, but in different ways and not to the same extent in each of the three subjects mentioned.

Part II

History

3. Repression

The Muslim Brotherhood has encountered repression many times throughout its history in different contexts. Although repression of the Muslim Brotherhood has taken many forms – such as limiting its ability to act, closing media, prohibiting activities and imprisoning, expelling and torturing activists – this chapter will focus on the countries where the latter forms of repression took place the most: Egypt, Syria and Saudi Arabia, respectively. Moreover, the conclusion of this chapter deals with the extent to which this extensive repression has led to the radicalization of the Muslim Brotherhood and to what degree the organization can be seen as (potentially) terrorist, as some researchers claim.

Egypt: The Cradle

Chapters 1 and 2 make clear that Egypt is the cradle of the Muslim Brotherhood. It is here that the organization was born and where it initially developed, in a country that had been Islamic for centuries, was part of the Ottoman Empire, lived under the influence of British colonial rule and had a monarchy that cooperated to a certain extent with this imperialist regime. In addition to the famous Al-Azhar University and other traditional forms of Islam, there was a flourishing discussion going on in society about what direction the religion should go in. This discussion included a secular camp, but also a modernist trend, from which the Muslim Brotherhood sprang.

Origins and Early Developments (1928–1952)

The beginning of the Muslim Brotherhood and the year of its founding is somewhat shrouded in mystery, but 1928 is generally taken as the organization's starting point.[1] What is clear is that it originated in Isma'iliyya, a city in the north of Egypt, where Hasan al-Banna worked as a teacher. According to several sources, six men who had been influenced by al-Banna's earlier teaching are said to have come to him to express their worries about Islam and the Arab world and to ask him to lead them to a better future. Al-Banna agreed and became the leader of an organization named the Muslim Brotherhood.[2] Under his direction, mostly elementary educational activities were organized in Isma'iliyya, such as Koran study, lessons in Islamic history and reading prophetic biographies. This way, the organization strove for the practical upbringing and education of a new, consciously Islamic generation of Muslims,[3] which largely comprised people from the educated middle class, but which at that time also included working-class Egyptians and agricultural workers.[4]

The organization grew spectacularly and ten years after its foundation there were 300 local branches throughout Egypt[5] with a total membership that probably ran into the tens of thousands.[6] Although education and preaching – complemented with charitable, social and sports activities – continued in the 1930s and 1940s[7] and led to new branches of the organization being established in neighbouring countries,[8] the Muslim Brotherhood increasingly steered its activism in a political direction. This manifested itself in conferences and publications,[9] but also in involvement in national politics by means of electoral participation[10] and an increasingly fierce rhetoric against British colonial rule.[11]

Meanwhile, the Muslim Brotherhood became an increasingly formalized organization. At the top of the organizational hierarchy was the Murshid 'Amm ('General Guide'), the leadership position held by al-Banna. Below that were the Maktab al-Irshad ('Guidance Bureau'), the organization's Executive Council, the Majlis al-Shura ('Consultation Council'), its legislative body, and the Maktab Idari ('Administrative Bureau'). Below this level, the organization was divided into cells that varied from big (*mintaqa*; 'district') via intermediate (*shu'ba*; 'division') to small (*usra*; 'family'). Within this structure, there were also committees and sub-groups that focussed on specific tasks, such as preaching or student activities.[12] New members joined an *usra* and subsequently worked their way up through the internal education[13] and the different stages to the various bodies,[14] pledging fealty to the organization.[15]

In the early 1940s Al-Nizam al-Khass ('The Special System'), also known under the name Al-Jihaz al-Sirri ('The Secret Apparatus'), was founded as a separate entity within the Muslim Brotherhood. It emerged in a context in which the relationship with the Egyptian regime was growing worse and the opposition against the British was gaining strength.[16] As the Muslim Brotherhood became more critical towards the Egyptian government for its cooperation with the colonial rulers, so the regime increasingly began to distrust the organization. In 1942, the Muslim Brotherhood was excluded from participating in parliament and, in 1945, the regime rigged the elections in such a way that the organization did not win a single seat.[17] In the late 1940s, the enmity between the Egyptian government and the Muslim Brotherhood resulted in a confrontation between the two, in which members of Al-Nizam al-Khass were responsible for several assassinations of senior officials[18] and a student member of the organization shot and killed Egyptian Prime Minister Mahmud Fahmi al-Nuqrashi in December 1948.[19] Although it is not exactly clear to what extent these attacks were centrally controlled, the Muslim Brotherhood as a whole was banned in December 1948 and al-Banna was assassinated by the regime a few months later, in February 1949.[20]

Although the repression of the Muslim Brotherhood continued after the death of al-Banna, in 1951 a new government was installed that allowed the organization to be active again, albeit under restrictive conditions. Part of the Muslim Brotherhood agreed to this, but there was also resistance against it among some less compromising members.[21] One of them, Salih 'Ashmawi (1910–1983), had been the organization's de facto leader after al-Banna's death, but because it was clear that a confrontation with the state was undesirable, the Muslim Brotherhood chose the aforementioned Hasan al-Hudaybi as its new General Guide in 1951, partly because of his close contacts with the regime. The internal tensions between 'Ashmawi's radical tendency and al-Hudaybi's careful approach remained, however.[22]

Crushed Hope (1952–1970)

The frustration and anger over the Egyptian regime and the influence of the British was certainly not limited to the Muslim Brotherhood. In 1952, a group calling itself 'the Free Officers' staged a military coup that brought an end to the Egyptian monarchy. Consequently, an authoritarian regime under the guidance of General Muhammad Najib (Naguib, 1901–1984) came to power, which governed independently of the British, had a strongly socialist character and put much emphasis on the Arab identity of Egypt.[23] The first two years after the coup, however, were characterized by an internal power struggle between Naguib and his rival and fellow-Free Officer Jamal 'Abd al-Nasir (Nasser, 1918–1970), which the latter won in 1954. Under his direction, the last vestiges of the old regime were dismantled.[24]

In the context of its confrontation with the previous regime, the Muslim Brotherhood had established close ties with some Free Officers, including Nasser. The organization had put its hope in these soldiers, through whom it saw a possibility to gain true independence and achieve its own goals, while the Free Officers wanted to get the Muslim Brotherhood behind them because of its large popular base.[25] Just like many other Egyptians, the organization therefore agreed with the coup and initially supported it enthusiastically.[26] Yet, the tide quickly turned: al-Hudaybi had envisioned a greater role for himself in Egyptian politics than Nasser was willing to grant him. Moreover, al-Hudaybi and other Muslim Brothers had chosen Naguib's side in his power struggle with Nasser. The latter, who had become president in the meantime and was no longer as dependent on the Muslim Brotherhood's support as he used to be, therefore turned against the organization.[27]

The year 1954 was the beginning of a period of new and fiercer repression of the Muslim Brotherhood. While the organization increased its criticism of the regime, Nasser launched a propaganda campaign against al-Hudaybi. In this context, members of Al-Nizam al-Khass decided to try to assassinate the president. Although their attack failed, it did give Nasser a direct reason to ban the Muslim Brotherhood again and to have many of its members – including al-Hudaybi – arrested, tortured and (in six cases) executed.[28] It was in this context that many Muslim Brothers not only decided to flee abroad (a topic we will deal with later), but some also expressed the idea of re-forming Al-Nizam al-Khass and of setting up a truly revolutionary organization. This came into existence outside of prison under the name Al-Tanzim al-Sirri ('The Secret Organisation'), but it was strongly connected with the ideas of the imprisoned Sayyid Qutb, who would eventually also become its leader.[29]

The ideological discussions between Qutb and al-Hudaybi that we dealt with in Chapter 2 built on differences between radical and gradual ways of thinking within the Muslim Brotherhood that had existed before this time, but which crystallized in the period of repression in the 1950s and 1960s that became known among Muslim Brothers as the *mihna* ('inquisition'). These discussions, however, went further than ideology and were, in fact, also an internal struggle for power.[30] Despite the internal differences, this struggle was, in a way, ultimately decided by the regime. Although Qutb was released again in 1964, in 1965 the regime accidentally discovered the existence of Al-Tanzim al-Sirri – which had not been engaged in a single attack – after which seven of its members gave testimonies that had been acquired through torture. They were sentenced to death. While some of these were commuted into life sentences and al-Hudaybi's life was spared as well, Qutb was executed in 1966.[31]

'The Believing President' (1970–1981)

After Nasser's death in 1970, a new era began in Egyptian history. The socialist president was succeeded by Anwar al-Sadat (1918–1981), who reversed the policies of his predecessor in some ways and wanted to liberalize the economy.[32] This policy, which was referred to as *infitah* ('opening'), was half-hearted, however, and did not lead to truly drastic reforms.[33] The Muslim Brotherhood initially welcomed the policy, but ultimately rejected it.[34] The new president also 'cleansed' politics of elements related to the old regime by imprisoning Nasser's supporters.[35] In order to achieve this, al-Sadat had to search for a new ideology that he could use as a guidance for his regime. He found this in Islam. He became known as 'al-ra'is al-mu'min' ('the believing president'), applied Islamic terms in his use of language and offered more space for public expressions of religion.[36] This emphasis on Islam also entailed giving more room to Islamists (who had long opposed Nasser), including the Muslim Brotherhood: prisoners were released, publications were allowed to appear again and more space became available in politics for calls to apply the Sharia.[37]

The Muslim Brotherhood welcomed this new policy and used it to rebuild the organization, recruiting new members and, for example, organizing new educational activities. Under the leadership of its new General Guide – 'Umar al-Tilmisani (1904–1986), who had succeeded al-Hudaybi in 1973 – the organization also restored its relationship with the regime,[38] through which al-Tilmisani confirmed the gradual and peaceful method of his predecessors.[39] Moreover, the Muslim Brotherhood used the space it received under al-Sadat to lobby members of parliament for more influence of the Sharia on Egyptian legislation.[40] The new president joined forces with Syria to start a war against Israel in 1973 and initially enjoyed several military successes. The regime repeatedly imbued these wins with religious meaning and portrayed them as a divine victory, which meant it could count on the Muslim Brotherhood's approval.[41]

The Muslim Brotherhood's positive attitude towards the regime – which, incidentally, still refused to officially legalize the organization[42] – changed when al-Sadat visited Jerusalem to address the Israeli parliament in 1977 and made peace with his former enemy the following year. The Muslim Brotherhood – which was fiercely pro-Palestinian – and other (often more radical) Islamist groups were very unhappy about this and began to criticize the government, which was increasingly under fire anyway because of the growing gap between rich and poor and the failing economic policy.[43] In response, the regime once again increased the pressure on Islamists, which led, for example, to a continued delay in the legal recognition of the Muslim Brotherhood. Yet, it also contributed to a process of such radicalization that members of a different Islamist group (which will be dealt with in more detail in Chapter 6) attacked and assassinated al-Sadat during a military parade in 1981.[44]

Slow Changes (1981–2011)

While the policies of Nasser and al-Sadat were characterized by major changes, the new president, Husni Mubarak (1928–2020), chose to go on with the policy of his immediate predecessor, albeit more carefully. Thus, he continued al-Sadat's policy regarding Israel and the better relationship with America that this had brought about, but he simultaneously tried to restore ties with the Arab world, which had been very critical of the peace agreement with Israel.[45] Mubarak also cautiously continued the infitah policy of his predecessor[46] and offered more space to political and societal actors, such as professional syndicates, to engage in their activities. Moreover, to create a counterweight to the radical Islamists who had been responsible for the assassination of al-Sadat, the new president offered more space to alternative forms of Islam, such as Al-Azhar and the Muslim Brotherhood.[47]

In this context, a debate grew within the Muslim Brotherhood about whether it wanted to participate in parliamentary elections. Members wanted to rebuild the Muslim Brotherhood and re-integrate into society, but they were afraid to rush this since the organization had already been repressed by the regime several times. Moreover, legislation from 1983 compelled all candidates to participate through a political party, a method of participation that – as we saw in Chapter 2 – was not approved of by Hasan al-Banna. Apart from this, some Muslim Brothers preferred to focus on *da'wa* rather than on parliamentary participation. In the end, al-Banna's criticism of political parties was discarded as specific to his context or as no longer relevant[48] and the organization decided to participate in the elections because political integration was important, the different activities did not have to be mutually exclusive and parliamentary participation could yield more influence.[49] Because the Muslim Brotherhood was not allowed to participate in the elections with a party of its own, the organization formed alliances with other political parties, such as the Neo-Wafd, in 1984,[50] and the socialist Labour Party and the Liberal Party in the elections of 1987.[51]

Thus, the Muslim Brotherhood integrated into Egyptian party politics. Moreover, it supported the regime in its campaign against radical Islamist groups,[52] it carefully directed its criticism at the government (not at the legitimacy of the regime) and – once it was in parliament – it even took the (internally controversial) decision to vote for a second term for Mubarak.[53] Still, the repression of the organization continued. This was due to the fact that the regime feared the Muslim Brotherhood, which was experiencing growth in the 1980s and 1990s[54] through its social activities at universities,[55] professional syndicates[56] and hospitals.[57] This popularity coincided with an increasing assertiveness within the organization, which boycotted the elections of 1990[58] and criticized government policy during the Gulf War of the same year.[59] In response to this growing influence, the regime rigged the elections,[60] excluded the Muslim Brothers from participating,[61] limited their activities at universities[62] and repressed them under the guise of anti-terrorism measures.[63]

Despite this repression, the Muslim Brotherhood did not revert to the radicalization that Qutb had expressed in the 1960s, but held on to the peaceful and gradual method previously expressed by al-Banna and al-Hudaybi.[64] The organization also started participating in elections in the 1990s and 2000s again.[65] None of this was coincidental or merely based on the ideas of earlier leaders, but also stemmed from the ideological reforms that the Muslim Brotherhood was going through, stimulated by the experience the organization had gained through contacts and negotiations with others in professional syndicates.[66] These ideological reforms included a clear acceptance of the institutions of the Egyptian state and the will to work within that framework, internal democratization (which led to new leaders being elected rather than appointed)[67] and the acceptance of a multi-party system.[68] Such ideological reforms should have prepared the Muslim Brotherhood for a long political life in the Egyptian system. For several reasons, however, this turned out not to be the case.

The 'Arab Spring' and Its Aftermath (2011–2021)

On 17 December 2010, a Tunisian fruit vendor named Muhammad al-Bu'azizi (1984–2011) set himself on fire out of frustration over the trouble the security services in his country were giving him. His act, which led to his death, set in motion an uprising that would spread throughout Tunisia and other Arab countries in what came to be popularly known as the 'Arab Spring'. Inspired by this act, building on frustration over dictatorship in their own country and precipitated by the death of Khalid Sa'id (1982–2010) – who had been murdered by Egyptian police because he had revealed corruption in their midst – Egyptians also revolted against their regime.[69] Although the Muslim Brotherhood was initially surprised by this,[70] was initially reluctant to join the protests because of its careful approach[71] and even started negotiating with the regime against which it was protesting,[72] the organization quickly became an important factor in the demonstrations taking place in the streets.[73]

When Mubarak's regime – like several other regimes in the Arab world – fell in 2011, the Supreme Council of the Armed Forces (SCAF) – headed by Field Marshall Husayn Tantawi (1935), who was succeeded by Field Marshall 'Abd al-Fattah al-Sisi (1954) in 2012 – temporarily took over power. In this post-revolutionary context, the Muslim Brotherhood was involved in plans to rewrite the constitution prior to presidential and parliamentary elections.[74]

The organization also prepared itself for the elections by setting up its own party in April 2011: the Freedom and Justice Party (FJP).[75] Like so many other Islamist groups who do not want to 'provoke' the regime by winning too big a victory,[76] the FJP initially indicated that it would participate in the elections in only 35 per cent of electoral districts,[77] but after opposition from the SCAF, the party decided to participate in every district after all.[78]

When parliamentary elections took place in a phased manner (because of the size of the electorate) in 2011 and 2012, the FJP won nearly half of the seats, after which the SCAF limited the space for the party by retaining the existing government and threatening to dissolve parliament if the FJP did not respect the power of the SCAF.[79] To counter this attempt to limit its mandate and because an ex-member of the Muslim Brotherhood, 'Abd al-Mun'im Abu l-Futuh (1951), had decided to nominate himself as an independent presidential candidate, the FJP decided to participate in the presidential elections with Khayrat al-Shatir (1950) as its candidate. By doing so, just like in the parliamentary elections, the FJP reneged on an earlier promise.[80] The SCAF responded by disqualifying al-Shatir because he had previously been imprisoned and had not yet been out of prison for the compulsory period of six years. The FJP countered by presenting its second-choice candidate, Muhammad Mursi (1951–2019).[81]

Although Mursi (just) won the presidential elections in 2012 and the Muslim Brotherhood seemed to have achieved everything it wanted, the reality of the situation had changed less than it seemed for the organization. Not only was Mursi not a charismatic leader, but the FJP had little vision and only a few vague plans for the future.[82] Moreover, the party created distrust and irritation among members of the SCAF with its decision to renege on its own promises and participate in the presidential elections and, at full strength, in the parliamentary elections, only to subsequently translate this win into power.[83] This resulted in a policy that saw Mursi trying to remain on good terms with both the revolutionaries in the streets and the Muslim Brotherhood as well as the SCAF.[84] Although this attitude stemmed from a lack of experience, to some people it confirmed the idea that the Muslim Brothers had a hidden agenda.[85] As such, the period in which the FJP was in power was characterized by, on the one hand, attempts by state institutions to sabotage the party and, on the other hand, attempts by Mursi and his supporters to prevent this by gaining control over those same institutions. In this power struggle, the people became increasingly frustrated with the lack of results and with what many considered a coup by the FJP vis-à-vis the institutions and demands for Mursi's removal were increasingly shouted during demonstrations.[86]

This tug of war between the SCAF and the FJP was reflected in numerous (and sometimes violent) demonstrations by supporters and opponents of Mursi and the Muslim Brotherhood in 2012 and 2013, during which the army presented itself as the protector of the people, thereby implicitly siding against the Muslim Brotherhood. Meanwhile, amidst the chaos in the country, the opposition chose the army's side, which left Mursi and the FJP increasingly isolated. While they did not take decisive action, in June 2013, SCAF leader and Defence Minister al-Sisi gave the government an ultimatum to come to an agreement within a week. Although Mursi made concessions, he let the ultimatum pass and refused al-Sisi's proposition to accept a referendum on his political future. Consequently, the Minister of Defence used a coup to grab power.[87] The Muslim Brotherhood protested against this en masse, part of which involved setting up a camp at the Rabi'a al-'Adawiyya square in Cairo,[88] where the regime committed a bloodbath against the Muslim Brotherhood on 14 August 2013, killing more than 800 people.[89] After 2013, the organization's central leadership maintained its peaceful approach and condemned the sporadic violence against the state instigated by individual Muslim Brothers.[90] While the incidental violence by members was exceptional, the Rabi'a massacre was part of the state's broader policy of repression. This included a complete ban on the Muslim Brotherhood (and its labelling as a 'terrorist organization'), whose members were killed, imprisoned (Mursi died in prison in 2019) or had to flee to Qatar and Turkey.[91] The organization's current acting General Guide, Ibrahim Munir (b. 1937), resides even further away, namely, in London.[92] It is in places such as these that the Egyptian organization – fragmented and in exile – continues to exist today.[93]

Syria: The Trauma

Like Egypt, Syria has a long history within Islam: Damascus was the capital of the Islamic Umayyad Empire and the area as a whole was part of the Ottoman Empire for hundreds of years, including in the nineteenth and twentieth centuries. After World War I, however, Syria, in contrast to Egypt, came under the colonial rule of France, which had local interests in the country, but also strove for a balance of power with British imperialism. To retain control in the country and to prevent the population from developing a common national identity, France divided Syria into several parts and generally pursued a divide-and-conquer policy (that met with stiff resistance in several areas of the country).[94]

In a sense, French policy was facilitated by the ethnic and religious divisions in the country. For decades, Syria has had a population whose overwhelming majority consisted of Sunni Muslims, but it has long had various religious minorities as well, such as Christians and Shiites who are also minorities within Shiism, including Alawites, Isma'ilis and Druzes.[95] In addition, the country is ethnically diverse, because although its population is largely Arab, there is also a significant Kurdish minority.[96] It was in this diverse context that the Syrian branch of the Muslim Brotherhood came into existence in the 1930s and 1940s.

Origins and Early Developments (1946–1963)

Mirroring the Muslim Brotherhood in Egypt, the Syrian branch of the organization also had a diverse ideological background. On the one hand, it was rooted in a reform-minded and Sharia-oriented trend within Sufism,[97] just as al-Banna had also had Sufi sympathies. On the other hand, the organization, like its Egyptian counterpart, descended from the reform movement that had been associated with *salafi* ideas at the beginning of the twentieth century.[98] In the late nineteenth and early twentieth century, these two ideological trends partly manifested themselves organizationally in Syria through politically engaged *jam'iyyat* ('associations'), which mobilized around themes such as the French influence on education, charity and the role of women in the public sphere.[99] One of these associations, Shabab Muhammad ('Muhammad's Youth'), was led by Mustafa al-Siba'i, who had studied at Al-Azhar University in Egypt where he had taken part in Muslim Brotherhood activities.[100] In 1945–1946, several Syrian *jam'iyyat* merged to become the national Muslim Brotherhood, with al-Siba'i as its Muraqib 'Amm ('General Controller').[101]

Unlike the Egyptian Muslim Brotherhood, the Syrian branch was less broad based and less of a populist movement of lay people; it was, rather, rooted – through the *jam'iyyat* – in the families of religious scholars and traders in the various cities of Syria. As a consequence, the members of the Syrian Muslim Brotherhood were often relatively highly educated and the organization had a more elitist character than its Egyptian counterpart.[102] In spite of the organization's character and al-Siba'i's background as a religious scholar, actual ulama in the leadership of the Syrian Muslim Brotherhood were exceptions.[103] The Syrian organization was also far smaller than in Egypt; whereas the Muslim Brotherhood in that country had many tens of thousands or perhaps even hundreds of thousands of members in the 1940s, the membership in Syria did not rise much higher than ten thousand in the same period.[104] The Syrian Muslim Brotherhood, like the one in Egypt, did have a hierarchical structure, in which the General Controller stood at the head of Al-Lajna al-Markaziyya al-'Ulya ('The Supreme Central Committee'), which directed the activities of the organization and was elected by local bureaus. The direct executive tasks were fulfilled by Al-Maktab al-'Amm ('The General Office'), which, in turn, was elected by the Supreme Central Committee. The members themselves varied – from least to most influential – from subscriber, through supporter and active, to honorary.[105]

The early years of the Muslim Brotherhood in Syria were characterized by major political instability, during which at least eight coups took place in a span of sixteen years, periods of democratic openness alternated with dictatorial repression, and the organization was banned several times.[106] Because the Syrian branch of the Muslim Brotherhood – just like the Egyptian one – subscribed to the idea of Islam as an all-encompassing ideology that was relevant to all aspects of life, the organization was engaged in a broad array of activities, such as education, sports, raising children, publishing and possibly also military training.[107] The latter was applied in the war for Palestine in 1948, in which a number of Syrian Muslim Brothers took part and in which dozens of members of the organization are said to have died.[108]

Parliamentary participation was another important activity that the Syrian Muslim Brotherhood engaged in in the 1940s–1960s. Before the elections of 1947, the organization – together with the Syrian League of Muslim Scholars – expressed its support for the electoral list of a number of independent candidates and several Muslim Brothers also stood for election themselves. In 1949, the Muslim Brotherhood itself participated under the name 'Islamic Socialist Front'. Although this combination between Islam and socialism was controversial, it also enjoyed support (including from al-Siba'i). Moreover, members of parliament from the Muslim Brotherhood were part of the government, including as prime minister, in 1949–1951.[109]

In this period, al-Siba'i also took part in a constitutional committee that would write a constitution, during which he took a pragmatic stance in his demands to give the constitution an Islamic character. Although he had wanted Islam to become the state religion, he ultimately accepted a separate declaration that Islam was the religion of the leader of Syria and that Islamic jurisprudence would be the most important source of legislation.[110] In 1952, all political parties (including the Muslim Brotherhood's) were banned under the dictatorship of Adib al-Shishakli, who had staged a coup in 1949. In response, the organization tried to keep a low profile and refrained from participating in the 1954 elections that followed al-Shishakli's fall,[111] but in 1961 the organization did participate again and even became part of the government.[112]

The First Two Decades Under Ba'th Rule (1963–1982)

In 1963, there was another coup in Syria, but this time the consequences were less short-lived than after earlier coups and brought the secular, socialist and pan-Arab Ba'th Party to power. This party, which was led mostly by religious minorities, has ruled Syria from that time until today.[113] The regime has probably been able to stay in power for such a long time because of its heightened repression, including of the Muslim Brotherhood. The organization was banned in 1964 and 'Isam al-'Attar (1927), who had succeeded al-Siba'i as General Controller of the Muslim Brotherhood in 1961, was sent into exile in the same year.[114] These measures by the government led to protests by the Muslim Brotherhood and an increasing willingness to use violence against the regime, particularly in the city of Hama, where riots broke out in 1964 that were put down by the authorities, leading to dozens of people being killed. A central role in all of this was played by Marwan Hadid (1934–1976),[115] a lay preacher who had studied in Egypt in the 1960s where he had befriended Sayyid Qutb, while the leadership of the Muslim Brotherhood clearly spoke out against the riots.[116]

Incidents like the Hama riots and the increasing repression in the 1960s led to a discussion within the Syrian Muslim Brotherhood about whether or not it was allowed to use violence against the regime. Moreover, the allegedly passive attitude of al-'Attar, the General Controller in exile, also increasingly came under fire. This – in combination with regional divisions, ideological differences and other factors – led to the organization splitting in the early 1970s,[117] after which 'Abd al-Fattah Abu Ghudda (1917–1997) became the new General Controller in 1971.[118] This did not put a stop to internal conflicts, however. In fact, the organization became even more divided after the Alawite Hafiz al-Asad (1930–2000) staged an internal coup and came to power in 1970. Although the economic policy of the new president initially bore fruit, it was strongly focussed on developing the countryside and helping the poor through subsidies and cheap state products, which did not benefit the more urban and trade-oriented base of the Muslim Brotherhood,[119] Moreover, al-Asad also made an attempt to secularize the constitution further.[120]

The combination of repression, socialist economic policy and secularization drove the different trends within the Muslim Brotherhood further apart. Although this division was partly the result of the differences between the distinct local branches of the Muslim Brotherhood in cities such as Damascus, Aleppo and Hama,[121] mostly younger members of the organization, like the scholar Sa'id Hawwa (1935–1989), also spoke out against what they saw as the passive attitude of the Muslim Brotherhood's leadership. As a result of this, and also because of the growing influence of Qutb's ideas and the increasing sectarian discourse that was used to talk about the Alawite president, the more radical 'Adnan Sa'd al-Din (1929–2010), from Hama, was elected General Controller in 1975. This made the organization as a whole tend towards the local branch in Hama, which was more inclined towards confrontation anyway.[122] A direct consequence of this was the founding of the militant Al-Tali'a al-Muqatila ('The Fighting Vanguard'), which more or less functioned under the leadership of Hadid and whose ties with the Muslim Brotherhood as a whole remained vague.[123]

Hadid was arrested in 1975 and died of the torture he had been subjected to the year after.[124] In response to this, the mostly young members of the Fighting Vanguard started a campaign of attacks against the regime – of which the Muslim Brotherhood's leadership may have been aware[125] – during which they assassinated several representatives of the state.[126] This regime increased its repression on religious networks, including the Muslim Brotherhood, which led to peaceful members of the organization being imprisoned or exiled, which strengthened the relative influence of the Fighting Vanguard. Partly encouraged by the increasingly painful consequences of al-Asad's economic policy, particularly in Hama, many radical youngsters joined the organization, which radicalized even further as a result.[127]

In this context, the Fighting Vanguard attacked the Aleppo Artillery Academy on 16 June 1979, killing dozens of Alawite cadets, possibly without the Muslim Brotherhood's leadership – which was in exile in its entirety by that time – having any knowledge of this.[128] From that moment on, the regime cracked down on the Muslim Brotherhood in an unprecedented fashion: membership of the organization became punishable by death, thousands were arrested and – once imprisoned – many were tortured and hundreds were killed.[129] In return, Islamists – including the Muslim Brotherhood – founded Al-Jabha al-Islamiyya ('The Islamic Front') in 1980,[130] and openly declared war on the regime,[131] which manifested itself most concretely in the uprising in Hama in 1982.[132] The regime surrounded the city, however, and crushed the revolt, killing tens of thousands.[133]

The events in Hama of 1982 were the culmination of a struggle between the Syrian regime and the Muslim Brotherhood that had gone on for decades. Although the central leadership of the organization may not have been involved in the uprising, the regime's response was a major blow to the Muslim Brotherhood as a whole. Moreover, the trauma of Hama has continued to play an important role in the historical narrative of the Syrian

Muslim Brotherhood.[134] It remains a controversial heritage, however, and the members of the organization itself continue to be unsure about exactly who was responsible for it.

After the Trauma of Hama (1982–2011)

After the regime had crushed the uprising in Hama in 1982, the Muslim Brotherhood basically ceased to exist in Syria as an organizational unit and was essentially entirely in exile. Although Syrian Muslim Brothers – like Egyptian members of the organization that were repressed in the 1960s – fled to numerous countries, some of them went to Iraq and Jordan, two countries that had difficult relations with Syria in the 1970s and 1980s. The fact that these two states' treatment of the Syrian Muslim Brotherhood partly depended on their own ties with their neighbouring country made the position of the organization untenable and subject to policy changes, however. Meanwhile, the exiled members were supported by the limited financial contributions they received from the organization.[135]

Thus, the Syrian Muslim Brotherhood existed across several countries after the trauma of Hama, but this event had also further divided the members of the organization: not only did tensions remain between the more radical Hama faction of the organization led by Sa'd al-Din and the less confrontational members from Aleppo around Abu Ghudda, but Brothers also wondered how things could have got this far and therefore sought to blame someone within their own ranks for the bloodbath at Hama. While the Fighting Vanguard continued its struggle from Iraq for some time, but ultimately petered out (or continued in Afghanistan, which we will deal with in Chapter 6), the more radical members split off under the direction of Sa'd al-Din in the mid-1980s and did not re-join the organization until 1991.[136] In the 1980s, Zuhayr Salim succeeded the more radical Hawwa as the most important ideologue within the Muslim Brotherhood and the Aleppo faction became increasingly dominant in the organization, which started a process of ideological moderation that was consolidated under the guidance of 'Ali al-Bayanuni (1938), who became General Controller in 1996. Under his leadership, the Muslim Brotherhood openly distanced itself from the violence that it had used against its own regime.[137]

Based on this changed attitude, the Muslim Brotherhood started establishing ties with the Syrian regime in the 1980s and 1990s, but although this led to several thousands of Brothers being allowed to return to their country, the organization as a whole did not receive permission to become active again in Syria.[138] This appeared to change when Bashar al-Asad

(1965) became president of Syria in 2000, after the death of his father. He released hundreds of Muslim Brothers and also closed several infamous prisons. The space that this created led to a limited blossoming of Syrian civil society, but this was quickly nipped in the bud again. The Muslim Brotherhood nevertheless responded by publishing its 'National Honour Charter' in 2001, in which it presented its peaceful method and its acceptance of honest and free elections.[139] This was confirmed in 'The Political Project for the Syria of the Future: The Vision of the Muslim Brotherhood in Syria', a document published in 2004 in which the organization recalled the democratic practices of al-Siba'i and described its use of violence in the 1970s–1980s as exceptional and deviating from the norm. Moreover, the organization confirmed its support for democracy, tolerance, pluralism and women's rights.[140]

In 2005, the Muslim Brotherhood (together with other groups) reinforced the values expressed in these documents by signing the Damascus Declaration, which called for a modern, free, democratic and independent Syria.[141] Yet, several months after this declaration, the Muslim Brotherhood joined the National Salvation Front, the opposition group led by former Vice President 'Abd al-Halim al-Khaddam (1932–2020), who had turned his back on the regime. Although the organization explained this choice by stating that al-Khaddam was a political leader (and not a military one) and that it had made this choice for the future of Syria, the Muslim Brotherhood's actions were nevertheless interpreted by others as opportunist. They had created the impression that the organization cared most about power and influence.[142] Still, one might ask whether the organization's behaviour could not be better explained by interpreting its actions as stemming from the fear of repression and the accompanying necessity to have multiple irons in the fire and desperately grab every chance to negotiate and cooperate with possible partners, as we saw in the case of the Muslim Brotherhood in Egypt. Whatever the case may be, the alliance ended in 2009, after which the organization was left without a clear agenda.[143]

The Arab Spring and Its Aftermath (2011–2021)

Just like in Tunisia and Syria, it was an incident that sparked the Arab Spring against the Syrian regime and this, too, happened against a background of decades of repression and frustration. In Syria, the precipitating factor was the arrest of a number of youngsters in Dar'a, who had spray painted slogans against the regime on a wall, after which protests broke out that spread across the country. The regime responded with cosmetic reforms and the crushing of the demonstrations, which had initially been peaceful, and did not take the opposition against its rule very seriously. Although the Muslim Brotherhood supported the revolt and spoke out in favour of it, the organization was simultaneously reluctant to get involved and remained vague about the extent to which its members – to the extent that it still had 'members' inside Syria – participated in the demonstrations. In spite of this, the regime quickly tied the uprising to the organization and tried to frighten people by suggesting that the Muslim Brotherhood was aiming for a second Hama.[144]

In reality, the organization had participated in the uprising almost from the outset, but – because of the absence of a legal Muslim Brotherhood in Syria itself – often did so indirectly, via online activism, by supporting others or through individual members.[145] The Muslim Brotherhood's participation took on more serious forms when the Syrian opposition formed the Syrian National Council, a kind of parliament-in-exile that enjoyed international recognition and which the organization was also part of.[146] Although the Muslim Brotherhood's presence on this council certainly did not constitute a majority and it also expressed its support for non-Brothers in leadership positions, opponents of the organization nevertheless claimed that it dominated the Syrian National Council or abused it for its own interests. The same accusations were levelled at the Muslim Brotherhood when the Syrian National Council was replaced by the National Coalition for Syrian Revolution and Opposition Forces in 2012.[147] Although the Muslim Brotherhood was the biggest and perhaps the only organized opposition group, and therefore did have more influence than others, its tendency to exert influence here was probably also connected with the organization's cautiousness and strong survival instincts, the result of decades of repression.[148]

The carefulness and the tendency to seize all chances to influence things ultimately yielded little for the Muslim Brotherhood, despite the fact that the organization initially did receive support from Qatar, Saudi Arabia and Turkey.[149] This was because of the internal divisions over several issues and the regime's propaganda against the Muslim Brotherhood, which was still influential among the Syrian people,[150] but especially because it was impossible for the organization to seriously establish a foothold in Syria This was not due to a lack of vision on the part of the Muslim Brotherhood, which had explicitly spoken out in favour of a peaceful revolution and a democratic system in which the application of the Sharia should be subject to the will of the people,[151] but to the increasing militarization of the uprising against the regime, especially after 2012.

The increasingly violent character of the uprising against the Syrian regime developed gradually and was initially mostly defensive in nature, a response to the military actions by the state. With the involvement of all kinds of radical Islamist groups, both Syrian and foreign, the uprising against the regime became more of an armed revolutionary struggle within a conflict that slowly changed into a civil war. Participation in this rebellion was not an option for the Muslim Brotherhood, however, as it had explicitly renounced armed struggle after the bloodbath at Hama. It was therefore primarily other militant groups that recalled Hama and people like Marwan Hadid, not the Muslim Brotherhood. Yet, the latter believed that it could not stay entirely on the side lines in this struggle and provided financial support to militias or allowed Brothers to become members of armed groups. It also tried to take the wind out of radical factions' sails by setting up its own militias, which were initially intended to serve self-defence purposes and to protect civilians.[152] Although the civil war cost hundreds of thousands of lives and we may safely conclude that the regime has won (just like in Hama in 1982), the Muslim Brotherhood (unlike in Hama at the time) did not resort to radical Islamist revolutionary discourse, let alone act upon it.

Saudi Arabia: Beyond the Safe Harbour

Throughout the years, the Muslim Brotherhood has argued in favour of an Islamic state in many contexts. This was somewhat different in Saudi Arabia, on whose territory Islam not only came into existence, but whose regime also claims to be an Islamic state and believes it actions reflect this.[153] The character of the state has its origins in a pact from 1744 between the Arab warlord Muhammad Ibn Sa'ud (1710–1765) and Muhammad Ibn 'Abd al-Wahhab (1703–1792), a religious reformer, who led conquests and thereby brought a large part of the Arabian Peninsula under their rule. This not only laid the foundation for the first Saudi-Wahhabi state (1744–1818), but through biological and ideological descendants of both men – respectively, the Al Sa'ud ('the family of Saud') and the Al al-Shaykh ('the family of the sheikh') – it did the same for the second (1824–1891) and the current (1932–) Saudi states.[154]

The Islamic character of Saudi Arabia did not originate from modernism, of which the Muslim Brotherhood is an heir, but rather from the central-Arabian variation of Salafism that is often labelled 'Wahhabism' and that has its roots in the thought of the aforementioned Ibn 'Abd al-Wahhab. Salafis (and 'Wahhabis') claim to emulate the first three generations of Muslims (the *salaf*; 'predecessors') as strictly and in as many spheres of life as possible and are therefore often much stricter than Muslim Brothers.[155]

Based on this attitude, Ibn 'Abd al-Wahhab and his followers checked Saudi policies on and provided them with religious legitimacy, but they were much more focussed on purity and specific religious reforms than the Muslim Brotherhood. Moreover, over time, Wahhabism in the current Saudi state has mostly become a ritual and societal ideology whose adherents are often loyal to the state, and less a basis for actual policies.[156] This means that there is room for Islamist activism in the country, including for that of the Muslim Brotherhood. Saudi Arabia initially seemed to be a safe harbour for the organization, but ultimately this country also ended up being a place of repression.

Origins and Early Developments (1954–1979)

Although Islamist activism existed in Saudi Arabia, it is perhaps not surprising – given the character of the state – that it had its roots abroad.[157] The same applies to the Muslim Brotherhood in Saudi Arabia, which grew out of a Saudi movement that came to be known as the *sahwa* ('renaissance'), which, in turn, was rooted in two different developments.[158] The first of these is that of foreign Muslim Brothers who emigrated or fled to Saudi Arabia because of repression in their own countries.[159] This included several waves from Egypt after 1954, when the regime increased its repression of the organization there,[160] but there were also waves of Syrian Islamist refugees who ended up in Saudi Arabia from the 1960s onwards.[161] Partly because of their high educational levels, several of these Muslim Brothers went on to hold positions in Saudi education and in international organizations, such as the Muslim World League (founded in 1962).[162] Two of them, the Egyptian Muhammad Qutb (1919–2014), who was Sayyid's brother, and the Syrian secondary school teacher Muhammad Surur (1938–2016), played an important role in laying the intellectual groundwork of the *sahwa*, namely, the coupling of the Muslim Brotherhood's activism and the ideological tradition of Wahhabism.[163]

The second development in which the *sahwa* was rooted was an organizational one. This was connected with the presence of the Muslim Brotherhood in Saudi Arabia itself,[164] although this was not an official branch of the organization. Al-Banna regularly travelled to Saudi Arabia, maintained contacts with like-minded people there, and is even said to have asked the king for permission to open a Saudi branch of the organization, although the monarch allegedly refused this.[165] The organizational backbone of the *sahwa* in Saudi Arabia (and thereby also that of the Muslim Brotherhood's thought in the country) was thus not a clearly structured organization, like in Egypt and Syria, but rather a collection of informal, clandestine *jama'at* ('groups'). These *jama'at* are said to have been started by Manna' al-Qattan (1925–1999), an Egyptian Muslim Brother who had already come to Saudi Arabia in 1953. The *jama'at* that he and others founded consisted of people who had encountered Islamist ideas in their student years through individual Muslim Brothers who worked at educational facilities and wanted to build on that experience by studying or spreading this thought. One of these *jama'at* had been started by Saudis who were originally from Zubayr, a city in the south of Iraq where a small community of Wahhabi Muslims had lived since the nineteenth century. This community was open to the activist beliefs of the Muslim Brotherhood, as were other *jama'at*, including one that was tied to Muhammad Surur. What all of them had in common, however, was that they were informally organized and were a cross between the Wahhabism dominant in Saudi Arabia and the Muslim Brotherhood's attitude of political engagement.[166]

These developments took place in a period that brought major changes to Saudi Arabia, both from a religious as well as a societal point of view. Firstly, the Wahhabi scholar Muhammad Ibn Ibrahim Al al-Shaykh (1893–1969), the mufti of Saudi Arabia and the most influential religious scholar of the country, died in 1969. Because of his great religious authority and his independent position, his death left a major void that the regime did not fill by replacing him with an equally authoritative scholar, but by expanding the Islamic institutional infrastructure of the country – which had been limited until then – in a way that was dependent on the rulers. As such, the religious influence in the country did not lessen; rather it was channelled in favour of and made subservient to the regime.[167] Moreover, Saudi Arabia also announced an oil boycott against the United States to punish the country for its support for Israel in 1973. The major rise in oil prices that this caused led to an enormous increase in wealth in Saudi Arabia and also to drastically changed lifestyles in the 1970s, during which material needs seemed to have the highest priority for many.[168] It was in this context that Islamists – and not just the *sahwa* – made themselves heard.

The Development of the Sahwa (1979–1990)

The years after 1979 were a period in which the *sahwa* rose to become an influential societal factor. Yet, this was partly due to a different group of Islamists that had no connection to the *sahwa* and the Muslim Brotherhood. In the 1970s, Juhayman al-'Utaybi (1936–1980), a Saudi ex-soldier and religious student, led a group of like-minded militants who wanted to resist the societal developments taking place as well as the Saudi regime and who, moreover, claimed to have a messianic figure in their midst who would introduce the beginning of a new era.[169] Juhayman's plan was to recover 'true' Islam (unlike that of the state), to usher in a new and messianic era and to reject everything that deviates from the religion.[170] In 1979, he put his ideas into practice by gathering a large group of his armed supporters and occupying the Grand Mosque of Mecca, which led to many people getting killed and for which almost all the culprits were executed by the Saudi regime after the uprising had been crushed.[171]

Although the uprising was ultimately overcome, it was nevertheless a huge shock to the regime because it had been challenged on religious grounds. It responded by implementing greater public religiosity and maintaining stricter Islamic rules in the public sphere.[172] This context opened society to solutions that were framed in the language of Islam and, as such, it more or less facilitated movements like the *sahwa*. The latter's adherents, however, were not satisfied with the greater public religiosity expressed by the regime. The politically activist and engaged adherents to the *sahwa* believed that the Saudi scholars loyal to the state were ignorant of the world and unfamiliar with the reality of life outside the details of religious doctrines and rituals. Based on this reasoning, they essentially ignored an important part of Islam and left it to the regime.[173] In addition, one *sahwa* scholar also accused the ulama of *irja'* ('postponement'), a reference to a historical trend in Islam that postponed judgement over someone's beliefs, with which the author seemed to want to say that the state scholars were not prepared to condemn the supposedly un-Islamic behaviour of the Saudi rulers.[174] As such, the *sahwa* showed that it was not just an engaged, politically savvy alternative to the religious scholars, but also a challenge to the rulers themselves.

The Gulf War and Its Aftermath (1990–1993)

What we have seen thus far shows that the *sahwa* was at least somewhat sceptical of the regime. The latter reciprocated this attitude. In 1989, the authorities imprisoned one of the most prominent scholars of the *sahwa*, 'A'id al-Qarni (1959), on the basis of accusations of which he was later found not guilty.[175] This incident, which incurred the wrath of many *sahwa* adherents, preceded a wave of criticism that washed over the Saudi regime in the context of the Gulf War. This conflict started when Iraq invaded its neighbour, Kuwait, in 1990. The Saudi regime – out of fear of a possible Iraqi invasion of its own territory – subsequently sought (and received) approval from the scholars loyal to the state to allow 500,000 American troops into the country to defend it.[176] To many Saudis, who had strongly anti-American feelings or saw this as non-Islamic interference in an intra-Islamic conflict, this was unacceptable and the regime's decision led to much protest and, by extension, a reform movement.[177]

The movement that came into existence as a response to the Saudi decision to let American troops in was broad in character and consisted of different elements that wanted to seize this moment to state their own demands towards the regime. Some of them had a far more liberal character than the *sahwa* and demanded that the regime pay more attention to equality, human rights (and specifically women's rights), a parliament and reform of the judiciary.[178] The *sahwa*, which was much better organized, took the lead in the protests, however, and dominated the demonstrations against the regime, also partly in opposition against the liberals, whom they dismissed as 'secularists'.[179]

The adherents to the *sahwa* were not only better organized than the liberal activists, but they were also more representative of Saudi Arabia as a whole, in the sense that they were from all parts of the country and were more diverse in their professional backgrounds.[180] Around the time of the Gulf War, the *sahwa* consisted of three groups. The biggest of these was a broad layer of Islamist intellectuals who had mostly become politicized during their studies and whose most prominent adherents[181] were Muhammad al-Mas'ari (1946)[182] and Sa'd al-Faqih (1957).[183] A second, smaller group within the *sahwa* consisted of scholars who were tied to the state, but who – unlike most of their loyal colleagues – were politically active and therefore supported the *sahwa*.[184] The final, smallest group consisted of the so-called *sahwa* scholars or *sahwa* sheikhs, of whom Salman al-'Awda (1956)[185] and Safar al-Hawali (1950)[186] were the most important.[187] These two scholars were not just the pioneers of the movement, but they were also the epitome of the influence of refugee Muslim Brothers from Egypt and Syria within Saudi Arabia: al-'Awda had been influenced by Surur and al-Hawali was a former student of Muhammad Qutb.[188]

Sahwa scholars used the shock that the Gulf War and the invitation to the American soldiers had caused in Saudi Arabia to speak out against the American military presence within the country's borders.[189] The *sahwa*'s activities went further, however, and also took on practical forms through the petitions that it offered to the regime, which – at the time – was a highly uncommon thing to do in Saudi Arabia, where the king would essentially only accept private advice. The first petition was the Khitab al-Matalib ('The Letter of Demands'), which was presented by 52 Islamists in 1991, and the second one was the Mudhakkirat al-Nasiha ('The Memorandum of Advice'), which followed in 1992 and had been signed by more than a hundred Islamists. The Letter of Demands was a document that – just like the liberals – called for political reforms, but that framed them in a much more explicitly Islamic way by emphasizing the Sharia with regard to legislation, the media, foreign policy and human rights.[190] The Memorandum of Advice went even further by, for instance, suggesting a greater role for the scholars, calling for a ban on the financing of stadiums, exhibitions and palaces and demanding censorship of foreign magazines and television programmes.[191] Through these petitions, an increasingly well-organized activist group had developed that, in 1993, was given concrete form in the Lajnat al-Difaʿ ʿan al-Huquq al-Sharʿiyya ('The Committee for the Defence of Legitimate Rights' (CDLR)),[192] an organization that acted as the official representative of the ideas that were expressed within the *sahwa*.[193]

The Repression of the Sahwa (1993–2021)

Although the *sahwa* was not violent, expressed an ideology that squared with the Islamic character of Saudi Arabia that the state wished to present and, moreover, had the support of a number of scholars, the regime was against it. While the state made some concessions towards the *sahwa*'s political demands,[194] it also exerted pressure on adherents to the movement by limiting their activities or preventing them from travelling from 1993 onwards.[195] More generally, the regime became increasingly involved in institutions that could act as a springboard for Islamist activities, such as higher education, to try to prevent *sahwa*-type activism.[196] The pressure on the *sahwa* was further increased by arresting dozens of its adherents. Among them were people like al-Masʿari,[197] who had become the spokesman for the CDLR and was imprisoned (and released again) in 1993, as well as the increasingly critical al-ʿAwda and al-Hawali, who both received five years' imprisonment in 1994,[198] which led to major protests.[199] The CDLR was also essentially outlawed by ensuring that its members lost their jobs or by arresting them.[200]

In the period 1993–1999, several prominent adherents to the *sahwa* who were not in prison chose to leave the country. Thus, al-Masʿari and al-Faqih fled to London to continue their opposition against the regime through the CDLR there.[201] The former was often seen as a human-rights activist and was frequently asked to comment in the media as such. At one point, al-Masʿari was well-known in Great Britain – where he received asylum as a political refugee – and beyond, to the annoyance of Saudi Arabia,[202] whose (foreign) policy he frequently criticized.[203] In 1996, a split occurred within the

CDLR, however, which led to Sa'd al-Faqih going his own way and founding Al-Haraka al-Islamiyya li-l-Islah fi Bilad al-Haramayn (Movement for Islamic Reform in Arabia (MIRA)).[204] Although MIRA's ideology was equally rooted in the *sahwa* movement,[205] the most important difference between the two organizations seemed to be that MIRA focussed exclusively on Saudi Arabia, while the CDLR had a broader view.[206] The latter also gradually ceased to exist after al-Faqih's departure.[207] Initially, this activism at a distance mostly took place by faxing newsletters from London to Saudi Arabia to stimulate local support for Islamist reforms,[208] but with the advent of the internet, MIRA's opposition has gone almost entirely online,[209] where it remains active.[210]

Meanwhile, those *sahwa* scholars who had been imprisoned in Saudi Arabia in 1994 were released in 1999. The scholars loyal to the state, who increasingly turned against the political opposition in the country, tried to portray adherents to the *sahwa* as members of the Muslim Brotherhood organization and as followers of Sayyid Qutb.[211] The authorities also accused them of sympathizing with the attacks committed by radical Islamist groups in Saudi Arabia in the 1990s and, more generally, of having dangerous and destructive ideas.[212] When, however, 'Abd al-'Aziz Ibn Baz (1910–1999) and Muhammad Ibn Salih al-'Uthaymin (1929–2001) – two of the most important Wahhabi scholars of the twentieth century – died in 1999 and 2001, respectively, the regime lost two loyal ulama. At a time of increasing terrorism in Saudi Arabia, the regime sought scholars with authority, who could condemn the attacks in the country. They found precisely that in those *sahwa* scholars it had repressed several years before.[213] Although the *sahwa* had never been in favour of terrorism and its adherents had no trouble condemning this,[214] all of this did simultaneously imply a quietism that the *sahwa* scholars conformed to. Some of them – including al-'Awda and al-Hawali – therefore kept quiet, ceased their criticism of internal Saudi politics or only talked about it in muffled voices and limited their comments to societal affairs, just like the scholars loyal to the state.[215] This way, the ulama who had once led the opposition were now co-opted by the regime.

The *sahwa* scholars did speak out on foreign policy sometimes, such as about the situation in Afghanistan or Iraq,[216] but they also had to be cautious in this regard. During the Arab Spring – which was of little consequence in Saudi Arabia – the country developed a strong antipathy towards Qatar, which had shown itself to be a proponent of the uprisings in the Arab world and, as such, supported the Muslim Brotherhood. Several *sahwa* scholars, however, including al-'Awda, have spoken out in favour of the uprisings abroad and of reform in Saudi Arabia. This led to them being imprisoned in 2017, on the pretext that they refused to conform to Saudi policy vis-à-vis

Qatar. In 2018, al-'Awda was charged – in a court session that was closed to the public – with 37 counts, including membership of the Muslim Brotherhood, for which he may receive the death penalty.[217]

***

The Muslim Brotherhood made use of violent methods against the state in Egypt and Syria in its early history. Although this was partly due to the radical ideology that was mostly rooted in the ideas of Sayyid Qutb, both this thinking and the violence came about in a context of state repression in the form of arrests, torture and executions. The use of violence against the state has never been the policy of the Muslim Brotherhood, however. Moreover, it was sworn off in the 1960s (Egypt) and 1980s (Syria) and has never been used or propagated at all by the *sahwa* in Saudi Arabia. Furthermore, the Muslim Brothers in Egypt and Syria have accepted the state as their framework of political activism and in Saudi Arabia *sahwa* scholars have been integrated into the system. Finally, the international terrorism that is used by Al-Qaida in the form of attacks in multiple countries is completely alien to the Muslim Brotherhood. We can therefore conclude that the assertion that the Muslim Brotherhood is a (potential) terrorist organization is problematic, because it seems to be based on a selective and obsolete reading of history that pays little attention to the context in which the aforementioned events took place.

4. Participation

In Chapter 3, we saw that the Muslim Brotherhood has turned its back on violence and has never had terrorism as a policy. That said, there is one Muslim Brotherhood organization that has engaged in terrorism until the twenty-first century, namely, Hamas. This organization does so, however, in the specific context of the Israeli occupation, not in other situations. This makes Hamas a violent exception to a peaceful rule, but it simultaneously constitutes a continuation of the anti-Zionist struggle that the Muslim Brotherhood has propagated as jihad against colonialism from the outset. This struggle is not a stepping stone towards more terrorism, but rather an isolated and violent expression of an ideal that is broadly supported within the Muslim Brotherhood, although Hamas, in particular, has also developed its views on this point, as we will see in this chapter.

Over the years, Hamas – like many other branches of the Muslim Brotherhood – has also engaged in political participation and this will be the focus of this chapter. This topic will be treated against the background of a second approach to the academic analysis of the Muslim Brotherhood, namely, one that sees the organization as an unchanging, theocratic and undemocratic group to whom the strict application of the Sharia remains all-important. In this context, this chapter deals, respectively, with the Muslim Brotherhood in Kuwait, its version in Jordan and the Palestinian branch of the organization.

Kuwait: Political Participation in Relative Freedom

As a part of the Arabian Peninsula, the area now called 'Kuwait' has been Islamic for centuries. Today, it is mostly Sunni, although the country also has a substantial Shiite minority. It has been ruled by the Al Sabah family since the eighteenth century. From 1899, the country was under a British protectorate, but Kuwait became independent in 1961. Meanwhile, oil was found in the country and the ruling family has reaped the financial rewards of this discovery since the 1930s. The emir of Kuwait, also from the Al Sabah, rules as an inviolable ruler who appoints the government, although the country has had an elected parliament – in which political groups (or, in the absence of a political parties law, 'proto-parties')[1] can actually form an opposition – for decades.[2] The same situation can be seen in the space that civil society in Kuwait is given and the amount of freedom of the press the country has, both of which are greater than in neighbouring countries.[3] This semi-authoritarian system offers oppositional powers, including the Muslim Brotherhood, the opportunity to truly participate in politics, although it does not allow them to actually win.[4]

Origins and Early Developments (1951–1963)

Just like the Muslim Brotherhoods in Egypt and Syria, the branch of the organization in Kuwait was also influenced by the reformist thinkers from the nineteenth and twentieth centuries that we have seen in Chapter 1. Kuwaitis inspired by these reformers concentrated especially on education and founded several schools in the country in the 1910s and 1920s.[5] Moreover, in the 1940s, they received guidance from outside, from Egyptian and Iraqi Muslim Brothers, whose representatives and writings reached Kuwait in this period.[6] In 1951 or 1952, this combination of reformist activism at home and Islamist influence from abroad led to the founding of the Jam'iyyat al-Irshad al-Islami ('The Association of Islamic Guidance'; Irshad), which formed the Kuwaiti branch of the Muslim Brotherhood, with 'Abd al-'Aziz al-Mutawwa' as its first General Controller.[7] Because the organization was not officially registered, however, it operated informally and shunned publicity.[8]

Irshad consisted mostly of young Islamists, conservative Muslims who were looking for an Islamic organization, members of prominent families and foreign Muslim Brothers. In terms of activities, Irshad primarily concentrated on education (among other things, it founded a school of its own), preaching and charity with religious and social goals, such as reforming and spreading Islam and promoting a pious lifestyle. These activities manifested themselves through the work by parts of the organization that concentrated specifically on students, labourers, traders and preaching. The organization also started publishing a monthly magazine, *Irshad*, in 1952. Its political activities mostly focussed on foreign affairs, such as the Suez Crisis in 1956. With regard to internal affairs, Irshad supported political reforms – not revolution – but it did not have a clear ideology or agenda on this topic. It was partly for this reason that considerable divisions could develop within the organization about its attitude towards the Egyptian President Nasser and his repression of the Muslim Brotherhood: whereas younger members like 'Abd al-Rahman al-'Atiqi wanted to openly speak out against him, older members – among them al-Mutawwa' – preferred to remain neutral. As a consequence of this division and the disappointing results from activities such as the school the organization had founded, Irshad fell apart in 1959.[9]

After several years, Islamists in Kuwait re-grouped and founded a new organization in 1963, the Jam'iyyat al-Islah al-Ijtima'i ('The Association of Social Reform'; Islah), led by Yusuf al-Hajji.[10] Unlike Irshad, Islah was a truly Kuwaiti organization that only allowed citizens of the country to become official members[11] and it also had a more formal structure.[12] As far as its members and networks were concerned, the organisation built on Irshad and Islah also concerned itself with preaching and education, including setting up Koran schools, which led to an influx of new members. Yet, Islah's goals were more explicitly political than those of its predecessor and it concentrated more on legislation and on the role the authorities could play in this regard.[13] Partly facilitated by the good relationship that Islah had with the regime, which saw the Muslim Brotherhood as obedient and a reliable opponent to Nasser's revolutionary Arab nationalism, this opened the door to truly parliamentary participation.[14]

Political Participation Until the Gulf War (1963–1990)

In the early 1960s, Islah was still a religious and social organization with many Muslim Brothers among its members, but not a formal representative of the Muslim Brotherhood. Partly for that reason Islah did not create a political group or organization that could participate as such in the first parliamentary elections in the country in 1963. Islah did, however, field individual candidates, who won three seats in the elections of 1963 and one seat in 1967. Moreover, its members also participated in governments in the late 1960s and early 1970s.[15] In this period, however, Islah representatives concentrated mostly on social issues, such as a ban on the sale of alcohol, and did not truly constitute a clear opposition that criticized the government's policies or held it to account.[16]

This attitude changed in 1967, when Kuwaiti Muslim Brothers cooperated with like-minded people from Egypt – who were still traumatized from the persecution they suffered in their own country and therefore did not want public activities – to found Al-Tanzim al-Sirri ('The Secret Organization'), which would function as a mass movement alongside Islah. This organization was also formally integrated into the network of Muslim Brotherhoods by pledging fealty to the General Guide in Cairo and by setting up a hierarchical internal structure similar to the one the organization in Egypt had.[17] During the 1970s, the Secret Organization increasingly took over Islah from within, which made the latter the official channel for the Muslim Brotherhood in Kuwait.[18]

In the 1970s, Islah remained heavily involved in numerous civil society activities, such as student associations, professional syndicates and trade unions,[19] but Muslim Brothers also took part in elections in 1971 and 1974 through coalitions with independent candidates, just like the Muslim Brotherhood had done in Egypt.[20] That was not the only parallel with other countries in which the organization had a presence: in 1976, the regime dissolved parliament, which led to protests from the opposition. Because the Muslim Brothers did not condemn this act by the regime and even retained their cabinet seats, they were criticized for being too closely linked with the authorities.[21] As in other contexts, the reason for the organization's behaviour was probably the fear of being repressed – as happened in Egypt and elsewhere – if it claimed the oppositional role too much.

The idea that caution – not opportunism – motivated the Muslim Brotherhood in Kuwait was confirmed by its behaviour in the 1980s, when it participated in elections for the first time through Islah. Although this was controversial within Islah itself – it allegedly diverted attention away from preaching and some members were also wary of participating in a non-Islamic system – the organization decided to take part anyway to set a good, Islamic example and to strive for Islamic legislation. Islah won three seats in the 1981 elections through its participation in the Islamic Bloc, a coalition of Islamic groups, a result it would repeat in the elections of 1985. However, the 1980s in Kuwait were chaotic, economically difficult and violent, as a result of the war that its neighbour Iraq waged with Iran from 1980 to 1988. Because the regime could not get this situation under control, the parliamentary opposition – including Islah – became increasingly critical, which the regime responded to by arresting critics, limiting freedoms and dissolving parliament again in 1986. Unlike in 1976, Islah – after its decision to openly and explicitly participate as a political bloc – actively tried to get parliament reinstated. When the state responded to this with repression, Islah backed down, but it eventually refused the regime's proposals to solve the crisis and sided with the rest of the opposition by boycotting the 1990 elections.[22]

Meanwhile, the Islamic Bloc (including Islah) continued to push for a greater role of the Sharia in societal matters in the 1980s, such as a stricter separation of the sexes in society and a ban on public Christmas celebrations.[23] Still, the controversy surrounding political participation continued: part of Islah, represented by 'Abdallah al-Nafisi, rejected parliamentary participation in an 'un-Islamic' system and considered the regime to be the enemy. Yet, Isma'il al-Shatti spoke for a different part of the organization, pleading in favour of participation and gradual reforms. In 1987, al-Nafisi left Islah out of frustration, which made the organization less oppositional, but did cause it to choose the path of participation more explicitly and – unlike during the internal division of Irshad in the 1950s – it did not collapse, but it grew.[24]

The Gulf War and the Islamic Constitutional Movement (1990–2011)

The aforementioned Gulf War was a major issue for the entire Middle East, but more so for Kuwait, which was invaded by Iraq in August 1990 and subsequently liberated by an international coalition headed by the United States in the months that followed.[25] By extension, the Kuwaiti Muslim Brotherhood also changed drastically. During the Iraqi occupation, which resulted in torture, looting and the displacement of more than half of the Kuwaiti population, the organization made an effort to provide people with food and medical care through its network of mosques.[26] It also founded Harakat al-Murabitun ('The Movement of Garrison Fighters'; Murabitun), a movement that resisted the Iraqi occupation through media and arms.[27]

Many Arabs viewed Saddam Hussein (1937–2006) as a hero rather than an occupier, partly because Iraq also fired missiles at Israel during its occupation of Kuwait. To a certain extent, this was also the case for several Muslim Brotherhoods in the Arab world. Although they were against the Iraqi occupation of Kuwait, their sympathies were often more with Iraq than with the American-led coalition. The Kuwaiti branch of the organization did not agree, however, and ultimately decided to leave the international network of Muslim Brotherhoods and to continue completely independently.[28] This was given concrete organizational form by making use of the political opening that the Gulf War offered – just like the *sahwa* in Saudi Arabia had done – and founding Al-Haraka al-Dusturiyya al-Islamiyya ('The Islamic Constitutional Movement'), better known as Hadas, in 1991.[29] The name of this organization was intended to underline its loyalty to the Kuwaiti constitution and it therefore became the arm of the Muslim Brotherhood in the country, while Islah remained its societal branch.[30]

The founding of Hadas also meant the end of Murabitun, which was, after all, tied to the Iraqi occupation, which came to an end in 1991.[31] The old group did bring in many new members for the organization who were more democratic than the older generation of members[32] and were also more inclined to focus on a broader audience.[33] Precisely because Hadas was its own, political organization, separate from Islah,[34] it became possible to formulate more political goals, to argue in favour of more participation and to strive for constitutional reform.[35] As such, Hadas participated in the parliamentary elections in 1992, 1995 and 1999, in which it won, respectively, five, five and four seats (out of a total of fifty).[36] In this period, Hadas showed its pragmatism, for example by cooperating with secular groups in favour of reforms and – lacking an Islamic system – by accepting 'un-Islamic' measures after all,[37] but simultaneously kept emphasizing the importance of the Sharia in legislation.[38] The latter was expressed, for example, in its support for more restrictive rules on women's rights[39] and gender-mixed education.[40]

In the first decade of the twenty-first century, Hadas continued to participate in the elections, in which it consistently received between one and six seats.[41] Perhaps more importantly, in this period, the organization got a younger leadership again, which started directing Hadas in a more professional way that was also more focussed on the people.[42] In this context, the issue of women's rights came to the fore again in 2005. Hadas believed that women lacked the skills to hold political office and that their primary job was taking care of the family. It also believed that being in contact with the people could compromise a woman's honour.[43] Despite a large majority of parliament sharing Hadas's point of view, the emir of Kuwait still decided to give women their political rights. Although this clashed with Hadas' stand, the fact that it was presented as a fait accompli meant that it simultaneously solved divisions about this issue within the organization. As such, this not only cleared the way for Hadas to accept women's rights but also to actively work to mobilize women for its own political activities.[44]

The Arab Spring and Its Aftermath (2011–2021)

Unlike in some other Arab countries, the Arab Spring had few consequences in Kuwait. Still, from 2010 onwards, tensions in this country rose, too. Yet, this was mostly due to the fact that the emir of Kuwait had primarily appointed his own allies as ministers that year and that allegations of corruption surfaced in 2011 as well. This led to large-scale protests in September 2011 and a victory for the opposition (including Hadas) in the parliamentary elections of February 2012. When the emir dissolved parliament again in response, the opposition (again including Hadas) boycotted the new elections in December 2012 and also those in July 2013.[45]

Despite the political problems in the country and the increasingly op-positional role that the Muslim Brotherhood has adopted in recent years, the organization has remained active in Kuwaiti politics and society. Islah continued its social activities and Hadas participated again in the elections of 2017.[46] In this process, the group has repeatedly renewed and adjusted itself. As a result, Hadas displays a high degree of internal democracy, transparency and pragmatism towards people it disagrees with today. The organization has also developed itself into a proponent of political liberalization and democratization in the country. Although this eases cooperation with liberal and secular political forces in Kuwait, this is different with regard to societal issues, such as freedom of expression and women's rights. While the organization has also made concessions on these points, it reaches its own limits far more quickly here than with political freedoms.[47] This can partly be explained by the fact that Kuwait itself is generally a socially conservative country[48] and that, as a democratic organization, the Muslim Brotherhood wants to reflect these norms and represent them in politics.[49] Something similar also happened in Jordan.

Jordan: From Favourite to Outcast

The area we know as Jordan today is essentially a creation of the colonial powers of the early twentieth century. Although the area was conquered by Muslims in the seventh century and remained part of several Islamic empires – including the Ottoman Empire – in the hundreds of years after that, it was not until the beginning of the 1920s that it became a territorial unit under the colonial rule of the British. Because the emir of Mecca, Husayn Ibn 'Ali (1853–1931), and his family chose the side of the British during the First World War, Great Britain appointed Husayn's son 'Abdallah (1882–1951) emir of Transjordan, as the country was called at the time.

Although the rulers of the country have never presented themselves as leaders of an Islamic state, the state was characterized by tribal and Islamic values from the beginning, giving it a certain conservative character. Among other things, this was expressed in the tribal elite that played an important role in the country's politics,[50] the fact that Emir 'Abdallah descended from the Prophet,[51] and the state's Islamic institutes.[52] Meanwhile, the area was essentially under control of the British, who were ultimately calling the shots both with regard to home issues as well as foreign affairs, but who gave the country its independence under the rule of King 'Abdallah in 1946.[53] This was also the year in which the local branch of the Muslim Brotherhood was officially founded.

Origins and Early Developments (1946–1989)

As was the case with the Muslim Brotherhoods in Egypt, Syria and Kuwait, the Jordanian branch of the organization was also influenced by nineteenth- and twentieth-century reformers such as Rashid Rida.[54] Yet, the trader 'Abd al-Latif Abu Qura (1906–1967), the founder of the Jordanian Muslim Brotherhood, was especially motivated by his unease about Zionist activities in Palestine in the 1930s and 1940s. After having been in touch with al-Banna,

Abu Qura set up a local branch of the Muslim Brotherhood in Jordan in 1945.[55] The organization explicitly asked for and received King 'Abdallah's blessing: the king, who perhaps wanted to underline his own reputation as a descendant of the Prophet by endorsing an Islamic organization and who also saw the Muslim Brotherhood as a safe alternative to secular opposition, gave his official approval to the organization in 1946, on the condition that it would only function as a religious group.[56] These close ties to the regime, which were unique to the Muslim Brotherhood, were continued after the assassination of King 'Abdallah in 1951 by his grandson Hussein (1935–1999), who succeeded him in 1953.[57] Moreover, the new king allowed the Muslim Brotherhood to act as a broader organization that could also engage in cultural and political activities.[58]

The Muslim Brotherhood clearly made use of the space that the regime offered: on the basis of a hierarchical structure that was similar to that of the Muslim Brotherhood in other countries – General Controller, Executive Council, Consultation Council, local branches, etc.[59] – the organization engaged in all kinds of educational, religious and societal activities. In practice, it was engaged in setting up schools and mosques and involved in various types of Islamic non-governmental organizations.[60] The most important of these were the Jam'iyyat al-Markaz al-Islami ('The Association of the Islamic Centre'), an umbrella organization for societal activities that was founded in 1963, and the Islamic Hospital, which was founded in the capital Amman in 1982.[61] At the same time, with permission from the regime and together with Palestinian militant organizations in Jordan, the Muslim Brotherhood took part in armed attacks on the Israeli army in the period 1968–1970.[62] This again showed that the struggle against Israel was of the utmost importance to the Muslim Brotherhood, but also that jihad against a foreign enemy was really something different than terrorism or revolution.

In the period until 1970, there was also a trend of greater politicization within the Muslim Brotherhood as a result of an influx of new, younger members, including Muhammad 'Abd al-Rahman Khalifa (1919–2006), who took over the position of General Controller from Abu Qura in 1952.[63] This politicization manifested itself in an increasingly strong involvement with international and regional issues, such as the influence of Great Britain and (later) America, the support for the Egyptian president Nasser and the Palestinian question. Although the regime sometimes viewed these matters differently from the Muslim Brotherhood, the organization still (implicitly) chose the state's side every time, even when Palestinian militants threatened to stage a coup in September 1970 ('Black September') and the regime banned Palestinian organizations and killed thousands of their members. While this also brought an end to the Muslim Brotherhood's anti-Israeli attacks, the organization remained on the side of the regime,[64] for which it was rewarded with governmental seats.[65] Incidentally, this was not the first time the organization was rewarded for its support to the regime: the Muslim Brotherhood had participated in parliamentary elections several times in the 1950s and when the regime banned all political parties in response to an alleged coup attempt by supporters of Nasser in 1957, the Muslim Brotherhood, which was not actually a political party, was the only one allowed to remain in existence.[66]

Thus, the Jordanian Muslim Brotherhood was, in a sense, the regime's political favourite, because of its support for the state during the first four decades of its existence. After Jordan had got rid of the direct influence of colonialism, the Nasserist threat and Palestinian militants in the 1970s, however, the Muslim Brotherhood's support was less crucial to the regime. Moreover, the organization was used by the state to mount opposition to Syria, which – as we saw in Chapter 3 – had its own problems with the Muslim Brotherhood. When the regime strove for better ties with Syria in the mid-1980s, however, it limited the organization's possibilities again.[67] By doing so, the regime embarked on a course that would only gain in strength from 1989 onwards.

Political Participation Revived and Limited (1989–1999)

The end of the 1980s was a turbulent period for Jordan: the war between Iraq and Iran (1980–1988) had just ended, the Palestinian intifada against the Israeli occupation had begun in 1987 and economic problems had piled up inside the country itself. To confront the economic crisis, the regime implemented a number of reforms that led to major protests in 1989.[68] To meet the demands of the people, the regime decided to have parliamentary elections again for the first time in over twenty years.[69] These had not taken place in the country since 1967, when Jordan lost the West Bank, which it had occupied in 1949, to Israel, which meant that many citizens now fell outside of Jordan's sovereignty. Yet, because King Hussein renounced his claim on the West Bank (apart from Jerusalem) in 1988, this issue became moot, clearing the way for new elections.[70] This offered possibilities for all kinds of actors – including the Muslim Brotherhood – to translate their political engagement into parliamentary participation, even if this seemingly democratic opening was intended as a means to channel societal unrest into something more manageable, rather than to truly end dictatorial rule.[71]

The 1989 elections were a major success for the Muslim Brotherhood, which won 22 seats (out of a total of 80), apart from twelve seats for independent Islamists.[72] Although the organization was allowed to take part in important political activities, such as a brief period in government,[73] the Muslim Brotherhood did not have a clear programme and was not successful in its attempts to apply aspects of the Sharia in the country.[74] Moreover, the undemocratic intentions of the regime (and its unease about the Islamist victory) became clear from the measures it took against the (electorally successful) Muslim Brotherhood. This manifested itself in the ban on *Al-Ribat*, the newspaper that the organization published at the beginning of the 1990s,[75] but mostly in the changes that the regime made to the electoral law and the number of seats allocated to individual constituencies, making it more difficult for the Muslim Brotherhood to achieve another electoral victory.[76]

In the meantime, the elections, the electoral success and the participation in government by the Muslim Brotherhood confronted the organization with difficult questions about participation in a system not based on the Sharia, as the Kuwaiti Islah had also discussed. Within the Jordanian Muslim Brotherhood, extensive and detailed discussions were held about this in the early 1990s, making clear that the organization – unlike the early Muslim Brotherhood in Egypt – did not consider the aforementioned concept of *shura* to be a superior Islamic alternative to democracy, but that it equated the two terms.[77] Members of the Muslim Brotherhood even wrote books about participation in 'un-Islamic' governments to lay out the different perspectives about this. Although there was no consensus on the issue, the organization as a whole chose the pro-participation point of view that was presented during the discussions about this topic.[78]

Yet, like in Kuwait, this far-reaching reform with regard to the acceptance of the state and participation in the political system did not go hand in hand with an equally far-reaching reform of the Muslim Brotherhood's ideas about the rights of religious minorities, women rights or civil liberties. Although the Jordanian Muslim Brotherhood has recognized the religious and societal rights of non-Muslims and often speaks of them as citizens (instead of *dhimmi*s, as used to happen with the early Muslim Brotherhood), the organization – just like al-Banna, 'Awda and Qutb – is somewhat reluctant to accord them full political rights.[79] This is even more the case with women's rights, on which the Jordanian Muslim Brotherhood essentially still more or less adheres to the views expressed by the early leaders of the organization. Although the number of women with an active role within the Muslim Brotherhood's bodies has increased,[80] members have long voted against measures to ban honour killings of women because they believed outlawing this practice would legitimize extra-marital sex.[81] With regard to civil liberties, the Muslim Brotherhood is a fervent proponent of press freedom and freedom of expression, except when it crosses the lines of what is admissible according to the Sharia, which has concrete consequences for criticism of Islam (or blasphemy), apostasy and atheism.[82]

Despite this lack of drastic reforms on societal matters, the organization did develop further politically. When the Muslim Brotherhood participated in the elections of 1993 by means of its political party – Jabhat al-'Amal al-Islami ('The Islamic Action Front'; IAF)[83] – which had been specifically founded for this purpose in 1992, this resulted in a loss for the organization. The IAF won sixteen seats (six fewer than the Muslim Brotherhood in 1989) and other Islamists won six seats instead of twelve in the previous elections. Although disappointment about the Muslim Brotherhood's performance also played a role,[84] this loss was probably mostly due to the changes to the electoral law and the seats allocated to constituencies.[85] The IAF's parliamentary experience suffered another blow in 1994, when the regime made peace with Israel. Although the peace agreement was not popular in Jordan[86] and the opposition (including the IAF) voted against it in parliament,[87] it was adopted anyway. Moreover, the continuing resentment against the peace agreement from, among others, the IAF and the Muslim Brotherhood led to growing unrest and a limitation of freedoms for the opposition.[88] In this context, the IAF chose to boycott the parliamentary elections in 1997.[89]

A New Reign (1999–2011)

Pressure from the regime meant that the reasoned and conscious choice for political participation by the Muslim Brotherhood and the IAF did not translate into more seats. This pressure increase further under King 'Abdallah II (1962), who succeeded his father after the latter's death in 1999. Unlike King Hussein, for whom the Muslim Brotherhood was primarily a political group, the new monarch saw the organization as a security issue. This was probably because he had lived in Great Britain and the United States for a long time and most of his time in Jordan was spent in the army, ensuring that he had little familiarity with local politics. Yet, there were also specific factors that caused King 'Abdallah II to pursue this policy. The Palestinian branch of the Muslim Brotherhood – Hamas – had been present in Jordan for years, for example, but was exiled in 1999 because of alleged attempts to infiltrate the Jordanian Muslim Brotherhood and to return Jordan to a state comparable with that of September 1970. Jordanian Islamists saw

Hamas as fellow Muslim Brothers and, as such, were not happy about this, which had negative consequences for their relationship with the state. This relationship was tested further when the police attacked dozens of Islamists during an unauthorized anti-Israel demonstration in 2001.[90]

The state's policy vis-à-vis the Muslim Brotherhood after 2001 should probably also be seen in the context of the 'War on Terror' that the United States launched after Al-Qaida's terrorist attacks on 11 September 2001. King 'Abdallah II supported the American policy,[91] while the Muslim Brotherhood rejected it.[92] Moreover, that terrorism could also strike Jordan became clear in 2005, when Al-Qaida in Iraq – the local branch of the worldwide organization – attacked several hotels in Amman, killing dozens of civilians and wounding more than a hundred. The Muslim Brotherhood had nothing to do with this and, moreover, represented a different type of Islamism than Al-Qaida; yet, many failed to see this distinction when several members of the Muslim Brotherhood expressed their condolences to the family of Abu Mus'ab al-Zarqawi (1966–2006), the Jordanian leader of Al-Qaida in Iraq, when he was killed in 2006. Although they were probably acting out of politeness to a family from their constituency – not out of sympathy for Al-Qaida – and other politicians had done the same but were left unpunished, two members of the Muslim Brotherhood were fined and imprisoned for eighteen months to two years for this.[93] In the aftermath of this affair, which led to demonstrations against the Islamists, the regime also chose to exert greater control over the Muslim Brotherhood's umbrella organization for social activities, the aforementioned Association of the Islamic Centre.[94]

The consequences of all this were also noticeable in the parliamentary arena. The regime delayed the elections of 2001 due to worries about the Palestinian Al-Aqsa Intifada, which had started in 2000, and the impending American attack on Jordan's neighbour Iraq.[95] When, in 2003, the elections took place after all, the IAF concluded that the situation for the party had mostly deteriorated. Because several Muslim Brothers ascribed this deterioration to the absence of the IAF in politics as a result of the electoral boycott of 1997, the party decided to participate again[96] and won seventeen seats (out of a total of 110).[97] Although this was a smaller number than in the earlier elections, this result was still more positive for the party than the outcome of the elections of 2007. In that year, the Muslim Brotherhood was internally divided, unpopular (because of the al-Zarqawi incident the year before) and limited by the regime's repression.[98] The IAF therefore only won six seats in 2007. Partly because of these disappointing election results, but also because of increasing repression by the regime, the internal elections within the Muslim Brotherhood itself led to the election of less accommodating people to prominent positions.[99] All of this ultimately resulted in the IAF's boycott[100] of the elections of 2010,[101] mirroring the one in 1997.

The Arab Spring and Its Aftermath (2011–2021)

The discussions within the Jordanian Muslim Brotherhood about whether or not to participate in elections and government continued after the internal religious debates in the early 1990s, but dealt less with the Islamic acceptability of these and more with pragmatic questions, such as the organization's interests and the extent to which it believed it could achieve its goals.[102] Although the Arab Spring was not as influential in Jordan as it had been in other countries, it did lead to many demonstrations and protests. The Muslim Brotherhood participated in these as well, but it was careful not to call for the fall of the regime, as happened in other countries, but rather for its reform.[103] The organization nevertheless adopted a confrontational attitude towards the regime in 2012–2013 by making strong demands, participating in demonstrations and boycotting the elections in 2013 again, based on the belief that this was the right moment to exert political pressure. This attitude was strengthened by the electoral victory of Muhammad Mursi and the Muslim Brotherhood in Egypt in 2012 and the Jordanian organization kept this up even when a coup ended Mursi's government in Egypt in 2013.[104]

Not everyone within the Muslim Brotherhood agreed with the organization's confrontational attitude, however. To the Jordanian regime, the 2013 elections were an attempt to show that, despite the Arab Spring, the state was still a proponent of democracy and fair elections.[105] Although it was highly questionable whether the regime actually strove for these things, the Muslim Brotherhood's refusal to participate in the elections of 2013 constituted a clear rejection of the regime. As such, the Muslim Brotherhood became isolated in its refusal to participate in a political system that it wanted to reform, the organization got into an increasingly difficult position as the Arab Spring turned out to be an ever-greater disappointment and it also came under fire regionally as the driving force behind the revolutions. To protect itself from the dangers that this might entail, one group of Muslim Brothers sought a solution in cooperation with the regime and other political actors. This led to several initiatives, including the ZamZam initiative in 2012 (which will be dealt with extensively in Chapter 7) and the founding of a new Muslim Brotherhood in 2015.[106]

The regime stimulated this division by recognizing the new Muslim Brotherhood and going along with this organization's demand to ban the old group, arguing that there could not be two organizations with the same name in Jordan and that the original Muslim Brotherhood had not adequately registered. Moreover, the state repressed the old Muslim Brotherhood: it arrested some members of the group, closed the organization's offices and forbade its activities. Under this pressure, the Jordanian Muslim Brotherhood decided to completely cut all ties with the Egyptian mother organization in 2016 – thereby giving in to an oft-heard demand in Jordan – and the IAF participated once again in the parliamentary elections of that year, in which the party won ten seats (out of a total of 130).[107] This meant that the original Muslim Brotherhood had essentially ended up as a political outcast and had more or less ceased to exist, despite its far-reaching reforms in the area of political participation. It also meant that the new, more regime-friendly version of the organization and the IAF had become the standard bearers of the Muslim Brotherhood's thought in an increasingly narrow political space.[108]

The Palestinians: Political Participation without a State

Unlike all other Muslim Brotherhoods dealt with in this book, the members of the Palestinian branch of the organization do not have a state of their own. Islam nevertheless has long roots and an important history in the land the Palestinians claim as their own: Muslims arrived there in 636 and would later build the Al-Aqsa Mosque and the Dome of the Rock in Jerusalem on the spot from which the Prophet Muhammad is said to have made his heavenly journey. Partly because of this religious importance, the area – with short interruptions in the time of the Crusades from the eleventh until the thirteenth century – would remain in Muslim hands, the final instance of this being the Ottoman Empire.[109]

The more recent history of Palestine is mostly characterized by the Palestinian-Israeli conflict. With the rise of Zionism as a result of increasing anti-Semitism and nationalism in Europe at the end of the nineteenth century, more and more Jews went to Palestine to set up a state of their own there. Because the Ottoman Empire had been on the losing side of World War I, it fell apart and, in 1920, the League of Nations (the predecessor of the United Nations) gave the mandate of Palestine to Great Britain, which was allowed to rule the territory temporarily. Yet, the British made promises to both the Jews and the Arabs in Palestine, consequently contributing to conflict between both communities. Multiple wars were fought in the context of this conflict, including in 1948, when Israel declared itself independent. At the same time, a still unresolved refugee problem emerged when the Arab population of the land fled or was expelled by Zionist troops.[110]

The refugees ended up in parts of Palestine that came under Egyptian (the Gaza Strip) or under Jordanian control (the West Bank), or fled to elsewhere in the Middle East or even further away. Throughout the years, an increasing political and national consciousness has caused them to become known as the Palestinians. The Gaza Strip and the West Bank were conquered by Israel in 1967, causing all of historical Palestine to come under Israeli rule. The Palestinians, meanwhile, were represented by the Palestine Liberation Organization (PLO), an overarching organization that was led by Harakat al-Tahrir al-Watani al-Filastini ('The Palestinian National Liberation Movement'; Fatah) from 1969 onwards, the secular group of Yasser Arafat (1929–2004), and Mahmud 'Abbas (1935). This organization was not only the most important representative of the Palestinians, but it was also a competitor of the Muslim Brotherhood almost from the beginning.[111]

Origins and Early Developments (1945–1967)

Islamist activism in Palestine did not begin with the Muslim Brotherhood. In the early 1920s, before the organization was founded in Egypt, the Syrian 'Izz al-Din al-Qassam (1882–1935)[112] travelled to Palestine to work as a teacher and preacher there. His rejection of popular forms of Islam, his criticism of established scholars and his anti-colonial views suggest that he had been influenced by nineteenth-century reformers.[113] Meanwhile, he was also engaged in armed struggle against the British mandate. This eventually cost him his life in November 1935, which, in turn, was the direct cause of a revolt against the British that lasted from 1936 to 1939.[114] Directly prior to this uprising, in 1935, the Egyptian Muslim Brotherhood visited Palestine; there was also contact during the revolt itself and the Egyptian organization made an effort to help the Arab population in the area, as we saw in Chapter 1. During World War II, the Egyptian Muslim Brother Sa'id Ramadan (1926–1995), Hasan al-Banna's son-in-law, was particularly active as a preacher in Palestine and this allowed him to prepare the ground for the founding of a new branch of the organization by the end of the war.[115]

Just like its Egyptian counterpart, the Muslim Brotherhood in Palestine concentrated on preaching, education and spreading Islam among the population, which caused the organization to grow significantly in the 1940s.[116] From the outset, however, the Muslim Brotherhood in Palestine also had a political agenda, which was aimed at regional issues, but also at resisting both the Zionists and the British.[117] The latter were worried about the growth of the organization and tried, on the one hand, to keep the Egyptian Muslim Brothers out (or to expel them), and, on the other, to limit the activities of local Muslim Brothers.[118] The organization resisted this by organizing military training camps for young members to prepare them (and the Arabs in Palestine) for a possible armed conflict with the British mandatory rulers and/or the Zionists.[119] When the British gave up the mandate in 1948 and the Zionists declared the independence of the State of Israel in May of the same year, the Muslim Brotherhood fought along with several battalions to resist this.[120]

The war of 1948 was not just lost by the Arab countries, but because it split mandatory Palestine into three separate parts – Israel, the West Bank and the Gaza Strip – the Muslim Brotherhood also broke up into multiple parts. One part continued in the West Bank, which was controlled and incorporated into its own territory by Jordan and remained under its rule in the period 1949–1967, which meant that the inhabitants of this area were Jordanian citizens. To the Muslim Brotherhood, this meant, among other things, that it could participate in parliamentary elections with its Jordanian sister organization under a single name[121] and it also organized social and educational activities in the West Bank, although it was not involved in violence against Israel.[122]

The situation was different in the Gaza Strip, which was controlled by Egypt and which was where another part of the Muslim Brotherhood in Palestine ended up after 1948. The position of the organization there basically developed alongside that of the Egyptian Muslim Brotherhood. This meant that it was equally engaged in political, social and educational activities – particularly in the refugee camps in the Gaza Strip, where it recruited many new members for the organization[123] – but that it had to do all of this under a much stricter regime.[124] Especially the repression that the Egyptian Muslim Brotherhood underwent after an attempt on the life of the Egyptian president Nasser in 1954 had repercussions for the organization in the Gaza Strip,[125] where a number of members felt compelled to flee to Saudi Arabia and other Gulf States.[126] In this context, in which the organization was quite weakened, a number of Muslim Brothers split off from the group because they wanted to wage an armed struggle against Israel – something that the Muslim Brotherhood did not consider itself capable of at that moment – and founded Fatah with this goal in mind in the late 1950s. Whereas this organization wanted a direct confrontation with Israel, the Muslim Brotherhood preferred to Islamize society first before starting its jihad, a difference in approach that quickly became a major bone of contention between the two organizations.[127]

From Quietism to Armed Struggle (1967–1987)

The issue of direct confrontation with Israel became even more important when the latter conquered the West Bank and the Gaza Strip in 1967 and the Muslim Brothers were confronted with an Israeli (instead of Egyptian or Jordanian) occupation on a daily basis. The unwillingness of the Palestinian Muslim Brotherhood to participate in an armed struggle against Israel – although it did see this as legitimate and the Jordanian branch, as we saw above, did fight against Israel – prevented the organization from getting politically involved.[128] Moreover, the war of 1967 also showed how much the Arab states had failed in the fight against Israel and in their representation of the Palestinian issue, which offered opportunities for militant, nationalist Palestinian organizations like Fatah.[129]

Despite the increasing popularity of organizations such as Fatah after 1967, the influence of Islamism in the region also rose in the same period. This was caused by the fact that, together with the Arab loss in 1967, Nasser's socialism had also been damaged as the dominant ideology in the Middle East, which led to a search for an alternative. Many people, including Palestinians, found this in Islam.[130] This was stimulated by large sums of oil money that Saudi Arabia had earned and employed to spread Islam, as well as by the Islamic Revolution in Iran in 1979, which was a source of inspiration to Islamist movements.[131] Partly as a result of these, the popularity of the Muslim Brotherhood increased, particularly in the Gaza Strip,[132] and the organization also gained greater influence among students.[133] The branches of the Muslim Brotherhood in the West Bank and the Gaza Strip were also able to unite again in the 1970s.[134] Because the Muslim Brotherhood did not engage in armed action against Israel, however, the organization – unlike Fatah and the PLO – was not repressed by Israel.[135] As such, the Muslim Brotherhood was able to organize all kinds of activities, such as nurseries, schools, mosques, sports, libraries and charities, in relative freedom.[136] Al-Mujamma' al-Islami ('The Islamic Centre'), which was founded by the Muslim Brother Ahmad Yasin (1936-2004) in 1973, played a key role in all of this. It acted as an overarching organization for the activities of the Muslim Brotherhood[137] and enjoyed the support of Israel.[138]

Yet, the Muslim Brotherhood was not well disposed towards Israel and sometimes also spoke in the same anti-Semitic terms about Jews as some early Muslim Brothers in Egypt had done.[139] The Muslim Brotherhood also believed that Israel did not have the right to exist and that the entire land belonged to the Palestinians. The difference with, for example, Fatah was, that Fatah wanted to reconquer the land on the basis of secular nationalism and wanted to do so now, while the Muslim Brotherhood portrayed the Palestinian issue as an Islamic problem that could only be solved once society as a whole was fully immersed in Islam. It criticized the PLO and Fatah for their approach to the problem, which led to tensions and sometimes even to violence between the groups.[140] Many Palestinians also criticized the Muslim Brotherhood, however, and blamed it for not doing anything against the Israeli occupation, which led the organization to lean increasingly in the direction of a combination of Islamism and nationalism and caused it to become more politically engaged, so as to respond to the criticism levelled at it.[141] Concretely, this was expressed most clearly in the weapons that Yasin gathered in the 1980s to prepare the Muslim Brotherhood for an armed struggle with Israel.[142]

The Founding of Hamas and the Peace Process (1987–1996)

By 1987, it had become clear to many Palestinians that the Israeli occupation would not voluntarily leave, that international diplomacy around the Palestinian question mostly lay dormant because of the Iran-Iraq war that demanded much attention and that the PLO had been severely weakened.[143] In this context, the intifada – an uprising against the Israeli occupation – broke out in December of that year. Palestinians took to the streets in massive numbers to protest against Israel's presence in the West Bank and the Gaza Strip. Although the Muslim Brotherhood was initially taken aback by the uprising, it also realized that it was no longer an option to retain its quietist attitude while large sections of the population were demonstrating. For that reason – and building on its more recent, actively nationalist attitude and the weapons it had acquired – the organization, led by Yasin and a small group of other Muslim Brothers, set up Harakat al-Muqawama al-Islamiyya ('The Islamic Resistance Movement'; Hamas) in December 1987.[144]

The organizational structure of Hamas, which had initially been intended as a separate organization but ended up overtaking the Muslim Brotherhood from within,[145] is essentially similar to that of the other Muslim Brotherhoods dealt with in this book. The main difference was that Hamas was organized on the basis of internal elections from the start.[146] Moreover, Yasin's early military activities gradually grew into the Kata'ib 'Izz al-Din al-Qassam ('The 'Izz al-Din al-Qassam Brigades', named after the aforementioned al-Qassam), which would later form Hamas' armed wing and, from the early 1990s, would become active in committing numerous terrorist attacks against Israelis.[147] Initially, the relationship between Hamas and Israel was still good, however, because both saw the PLO as a greater direct enemy. This did not change until it became apparent that Hamas had been directly involved in the death of two Israeli soldiers in 1989, which led Israel to break off all ties, to ban the organization and to make membership of Hamas a crime punishable by law.[148]

Thus, while Hamas continued its social, educational and charitable activities, which had also characterized the Muslim Brotherhood until 1987,[149] its practical attitude towards Israel changed. This appeared to manifest itself in the organization's charter, although this contained several anti-Semitic stereotypes that contrasted sharply with Hamas' own previous contacts with Israel.[150] It is doubtful, therefore, whether the charter was ever fully representative of Hamas' practical vision of Israel. Nevertheless, Hamas was very hostile towards Israel and highly critical of an international peace conference organized in Madrid in 1991 to solve the Arab-Israeli conflict. It described the conference as a premeditated plan to force the Palestinians to accept an unjust solution that was also illegitimate because it claimed the PLO did not really represent the Palestinian people.[151]

The conference in Madrid bore little fruit. Yet, Hamas's response to the peace process became fiercer when it turned out that the PLO and the Israeli government had held secret peace negotiations in the Norwegian capital Oslo. While the Palestinian population was positively inclined towards the Oslo Accords that resulted from these negotiations in 1993, Hamas had a different view. It considered the agreements a betrayal of the Palestinian cause and indicated it wanted to continue with the intifada.[152] Yet, there was more going on for Hamas: the Oslo Accords did not just stipulate a gradual Israeli withdrawal from the Occupied Territories and Palestinian autonomy in exchange for an end to the intifada, but they had also completely marginalized Hamas. This meant that 'Oslo' not only clashed with Hamas's view of how the conflict should be solved, but also provided a scenario in which the organization had no role to play.[153] It was for both of these reasons that Hamas resisted the peace agreements. This expressed itself in a series of suicide bombings against Israeli civilians – particularly from 25 February 1994, when an Israeli settler named Baruch Goldstein murdered 29 Palestinian civilians in Hebron – that killed over a hundred people.[154] Hamas legitimized its terrorism in various ways and multiple factors played a role in this.[155] One of these was that Hamas used the attacks to pressure Israel into more concessions[156] and to present itself to the PLO and Fatah as a political actor that could not be ignored.[157]

The pragmatism that partly underpinned Hamas' terrorist attacks also manifested itself in the development of the organization's political discourse.

Although Hamas never dropped its idea that 'all of Palestine' (Israel, the West Bank and the Gaza Strip) belonged to the Palestinians, the organization formulated a two-step solution to the conflict based on pragmatic considerations: a 'historical' solution, which would provide Palestinians with the entire land, and a 'temporary' solution, which entailed accepting a Palestinian state in the West Bank and the Gaza Strip with East Jerusalem as its capital, which more or less also represents the international consensus of a definitive solution to the conflict. To Hamas, the 'historical' solution would mean peace, while the 'temporary' solution could only take place on the basis of a *hudna* ('truce').[158] This distinction allowed the organization to seemingly hold on to its principles by not giving up the historical solution in theory, on the one hand, while providing itself with the space to remain practically relevant in a system that was based on peace agreements that Hamas rejected, on the other.[159]

Under Palestinian Self-Rule (1996–2006)

One of the consequences of the Oslo Accords was that a Palestinian National Authority (PNA) was founded in 1994. This entity was meant to fight anti-Israeli Palestinian violence while simultaneously giving concrete form to Palestinian autonomous rule, for which elections were held in 1996. In its attitude towards democracy and elections, Hamas sometimes let it be known that it preferred *shura* over 'Western' democracy,[160] but others – including Yasin – indicated that they accepted democracy.[161] Because of the close ties between Hamas and the Jordanian Muslim Brotherhood, it is possible that any discussion about participation in elections of an 'un-Islamic' state[162] had more or less been decided for Hamas by the aforementioned debate that took place in Jordan at the beginning of the 1990s. This would mean that, to Hamas, there were no real religious objections anymore to electoral participation within an 'un-Islamic' system, which may have been underlined by an internal document by Hamas from 1992 that was entirely devoid of religious arguments. This document showed that the organization had made a business-like and pragmatic analysis of the situation and was most concerned about the legitimacy that the Israeli occupation, under whose ultimate rule the elections would take place, would derive from Hamas's electoral participation.[163] Because the parliamentary elections for the PNA in 1996 emanated from the Oslo Accords and Hamas did not want to be connected to that in any way, the organization decided not to participate.[164]

Just like in Kuwait and Jordan, the open attitude towards democracy and elections did not go hand in hand with drastic reforms in the area of societal rights and freedoms in Hamas's case either. For example, Hamas saw Palestinian Christians as equal citizens who should be treated in a tolerant way, but under Islamic rule, which – among other things – meant that a Christian would not be allowed to become the head of state in any future Islamic state.[165] Hamas had similar ideas about the political rights of women,[166] whose tasks were mostly limited to the family and marriage,[167] but for whom room was increasingly created within the organization itself.[168] The organization also portrayed women who did not wear a headscarf or who smoked as immoral, which occasionally led to violence against women.[169] This was related to Hamas's interpretation of the Sharia, which was flexible, on the one hand, but could not ignore certain Koranic texts that – according to the organization – spoke for themselves, which also meant that civil liberties were always limited by a religious framework.[170]

Meanwhile, the peace process between Israel and the Palestinians had reached an impasse and against this background a new intifada broke out in September 2000.[171] This uprising turned out to be much more violent than the previous one: Hamas used dozens of suicide attacks against Israeli civilians[172] and Israel undertook large-scale military action, which resulted in many civilian casualties, and it also assassinated several leaders of Hamas.[173] This intifada was not only characterized by violence, however, but also by the crumbling of the Palestinian national infrastructure that had been built up in the 1990s. On the one hand, this was related to Israel's military actions; on the other, this happened because Yasser Arafat – the chairman of the PLO, the elected president of the PNA and the man many people saw as the personification of the Palestinian cause – died in 2004 and was succeeded by Mahmud 'Abbas the following year.[174]

In the same period, Hamas became increasingly conscious of the fact that the violence had not brought about any positive change, that it enjoyed less and less support among Palestinians and that the peace process had also begun again. This realization was manifested in the organization's offer to Israel to have a ceasefire in 2003.[175] Interestingly, Hamas did so without Israel having pulled out of the Occupied Territories, which was one of the organization's demands for such a temporary solution, as we saw above. In 2005, Hamas even decided to stop using suicide bombings altogether, announced a unilateral period of calm and Israel also withdrew from the Gaza Strip.[176] Because of Hamas' pragmatism, the organization could use the support of the people – which had earlier been in favour of confronting Israel militarily, but had turned against it – to legitimize a decision to lay down its arms.[177]

In Politics (2006–2021)

The drastically different situation in the Occupied Territories also led to new parliamentary elections for the PNA in 2006. The failure of Oslo and the parties that had been involved with this (primarily Fatah and the PLO), as well as Israel's withdrawal from the Gaza Strip, created a context in which Hamas could make the transition from a militant and social organization to a political party relatively easily.[178] The organization therefore founded the party Al-Taghyir wa-l-Islah ('Change and Reform') and participated in the elections, in which its strong campaign[179] caused it to win 74 out of a total of 132 seats.[180] This way, Hamas rose to power in one fell swoop, although this was not accepted by Fatah. The election results led to an intra-Palestinian (and sometimes violent) conflict between the two organizations that ultimately resulted in Hamas coming to power, in 2007, in the Gaza Strip, where the organization was strongest, while the West Bank remained under the control of the Fatah-dominated PNA.[181]

Hamas's rule in the Gaza Strip was not a success. Although the organization now had a powerbase, it became increasingly isolated. This was not only because of the unwillingness of Fatah to accept the election results, but also because the international community was not happy with the electoral victory of an organization that, until recently, had engaged in committing suicide attacks against Israel. The fact that Hamas had stopped these attacks, however, led to criticism from radical Islamist organizations in the Gaza Strip, which blamed Hamas for its passiveness against Israel.[182] Because of this opposition and a boycott of the Gaza Strip by the PNA and part of the international community, Hamas tried to consolidate its power in the area. It did so by creating power structures parallel to those in the West Bank and filling them with its own people, all the while adopting an increasingly authoritarian attitude towards its political opponents.[183] Apart from the rising poverty, civil liberties also increasingly came under pressure because of this.[184] Moreover, in 2008, the period of calm that Hamas had announced in 2005, and had subsequently extended, ended, which resulted in renewed fighting with Israel in 2008–2009.[185]

When the Arab Spring broke out in 2010–2011, this seemed to have few consequences for Hamas and the Gaza Strip. The organization initially took a wait-and-see approach because it did not know what was going to happen, but eventually did express its support for the uprisings.[186] This was particularly the case with Egypt, where the Muslim Brotherhood had won the elections in 2012. This result was welcomed by Hamas, which realized that there was a like-minded government in Cairo now. The coup against the Muslim Brotherhood in 2013 was therefore a major disappointment for Hamas, not least because it partly resulted in renewed Egyptian pressure on the Gaza Strip.[187] In the following years – including in 2021 – conflicts between Israel and Hamas would periodically flare up. Still, in 2017, Hamas decided to take a step that many had wanted it to make for years and that, considering its changed viewpoints, had actually come much too late: it amended its old charter. Although Hamas confirms its right to the 'entire' land from the Mediterranean Sea to the Jordan River in its new charter, it nevertheless mentions the possibility of a two-state solution (article 20) and the anti-Semitism that could be found in the old document had completely disappeared.[188]

***

Whereas the Muslim Brotherhoods in Egypt and Syria still seemed to be trapped in a mentality of repression, the Muslim Brotherhoods in Kuwait, Jordan and the Palestinian territories appear to have partly outgrown this and to have adopted the role of conventional opposition parties. This entailed an acceptance of political participation that shows that the organization is certainly not the unchanging, theocratic and anti-democratic group that some believe it is, although the Muslim Brotherhoods dealt with in this chapter have not developed to the same extent with regard to societal rights and freedoms. As for Hamas, although it still does not truly accept Israel, it does view that state as a fait accompli, which it is willing to tolerate if that is what the people want. Thus, the pragmatism that characterizes the Muslim Brotherhood regarding political participation has apparently – at least in the case of Hamas – affected its views of the Palestinian issue, which has always been very important to the organization.

5.   Power

So far, we have consistently analysed the Muslim Brotherhood as an organization (with the exception of Saudi Arabia). Yet, in a certain sense, the Muslim Brotherhood is simultaneously also a broader movement that is ideologically rooted in lay Islamism and culturally in the colonial experiences of the Arab world. This chapter deals with several groups that may not be part of the Muslim Brotherhood as an organization (anymore), but do belong to the broader movement in so far as it concerns its ideological and cultural dimensions.[1] In this context, this chapter will deal with countries where organizations that are part of the Muslim Brotherhood movement have actually gained power, namely, Sudan, Morocco and Tunisia. It is precisely because these organizations have attained concrete power that this chapter will also look at the extent to which the third approach of the Muslim Brotherhood – that the organization constitutes an international conspiracy that uses sinister ways to strive for world domination – has become a reality.

Sudan: Islamist Ideals and Political Opportunism

Just like Egypt, Sudan has a history that goes back thousands of years to the pharaonic past. With regard to Islam – which in Sudan has often had a Sufi character – the country also has a long history of indigenous sultanates that ruled the area from the sixteenth century onwards.[2] In the nineteenth century, the country was ruled by several powers, including the aforementioned ruling family from Egypt (1821–1885). This was succeeded by the Mahdiyya, a rebellious movement started by Muhammad Ahmad al-Mahdi (1844–1885), who controlled the area until the end of the nineteenth century. From 1898, Sudan was under British colonial rule until the country's independence in 1956.[3]

Origins and Early Developments (1954–1969)

Precisely because the Muslim Brotherhood had already been founded in neighbouring Egypt in 1928, it is not surprising that the Sudanese branch of this organization is also older than the state of Sudan itself. Because of Egyptians who worked in Sudan and because of a Brotherhood delegation from the country's northern neighbour, dozens of local branches of the Muslim Brotherhood were founded in Sudan in the 1940s.[4] Moreover, Harakat al-Tahrir al-Islami ('The Islamic Liberation Movement') – which was ideologically very similar to the Muslim Brotherhood, but strongly emphasized Sudanese and Sufi identity – came into existence in 1947. Because of the ideological similarities, the Sudanese Muslim Brothers and the Islamic Liberation Movement decided to join forces and officially found the Sudanese Muslim Brotherhood at a conference in 1954, but they pointed out that they were independent of the Egyptian branch,[5] although the new group was similar in its organizational structure.[6]

One of the early members of the Islamic Liberation Movement who would later have a major influence on the Muslim Brotherhood in Sudan was Hasan al-Turabi (1932–2016).[7] He joined the movement in 1951, after which it quickly became apparent that he could make a valuable contribution to the group because of his knowledge of Islam, but also that he was a polemical figure whose presence was not appreciated by everyone.[8] Other Islamists, as well as academics, have described him as a dishonest and hypocritical man who was prone to lying, but also as someone who has made an important intellectual contribution to Islamism.[9]

Al-Turabi's position within the Sudanese Muslim Brotherhood remained limited at first. Rashid al-Tahir became the General Controller of the organization[10] and – considering the independence that Sudan was about to gain – the group set up an explicitly political branch named Al-Jabha al-Islamiyya li-l-Dustur ('The Islamic Front for the Constitution'; IFC) in 1955, through which it strove for the political application of the Sharia in the country.[11] The IFC was not the only Islamist party in the country, however: in 1956, the Ansar – the movement of adherents to the nineteenth-century Mahdiyya – founded the Umma Party, with Sadiq al-Mahdi (1935–2020) as its leader.[12] Yet, in 1958, the Sudanese general Ibrahim 'Abbud staged a successful coup, after which the Muslim Brotherhood was only allowed to remain as a religious movement. After the organization was involved in the planning of a counter-coup in 1959, however, it lost its freedom after all.[13] Still, the support for the coup against 'Abbud had mostly been al-Tahir's initiative, not that of the organization as a whole. When the latter was imprisoned for his role in this affair, the organization decided to establish a collective leadership in 1962, to prevent similar incidents from happening in the future.[14]

The year 1964 would turn out to be crucial for the launch of al-Turabi's career as an Islamist leader in Sudan. In that year, he returned from his PhD research, which he conducted at the Sorbonne in Paris, and gave a speech on political freedom that contributed to a student uprising that ultimately led to a revolution against 'Abbud's regime in the same year. Partly on the basis of his contribution to this, he was elected Secretary General of the Sudanese Muslim Brotherhood[15] and of a new political organization, Jabhat al-Mithaq al-Islami ('The Islamic Charter Front'; ICF), which also encompassed non-Brotherhood Islamists, in 1964.[16] The ICF participated in the parliamentary elections in both 1965 and 1968, in which the group won only a small number of seats,[17] but was nevertheless able to use its influence to cooperate with al-Mahdi's Umma Party in the battle against communists and for an Islamic constitution.[18] The ICF's approach was not to the liking of all Muslim Brothers, however. Some members of the organization wanted a greater emphasis on *da'wa* and were against the inclusive and political strategy employed by the ICF. This difference of opinion led to such conflicts that al-Turabi was forced to give up his position as leader in 1966, yet he eventually managed to gather enough support for his candidacy again, so that he became the leader of the organization once more in 1969.[19]

From Coup to Coup (1969–1989)

Five years after the previous coup, there was another successful coup in 1969, led by colonel Ja'far al-Numayri (1930–2009). The new regime strove for a socialist, secular state based on Egypt's model under Nasser's rule, thereby taking an approach that was diametrically opposed to the Islamism advocated by al-Turabi and the ICF.[20] After the latter's political opposition to the new regime, al-Numayri had the ICF leadership (including al-Turabi) arrested and imprisoned.[21] By doing so, he basically ended the ICF, meaning that the task of being an Islamist opposition had to be done by the Muslim Brotherhood.[22] The remaining members of the opposition regrouped in London, however, by founding the National Front, in which several political groups – including the Muslim Brotherhood – joined forces.[23] Although some members of this group propagated armed struggle against the regime, al-Turabi (as well as the majority of the Muslim Brotherhood) kept striving for pragmatism.[24] Yet, a coup under the direction of al-Mahdi still took place in 1976. This failed, but it did lead al-Numayri to seek rapprochement with the National Front. On the condition that the latter would be dissolved, he also allowed the opposition – including al-Turabi – to be released from prison or to return to Sudan.[25]

When the regime started adopting a different attitude towards the Muslim Brotherhood, al-Turabi, who had not succeeded in realizing his Islamist agenda by democratic means, allied himself with al-Numayri's military dictatorship to achieve his goals after all.[26] This happened in the framework of a general process of mending relations between the regime and the Muslim Brotherhood[27] that not all members of the organization agreed with,[28] possibly in part because the policy of Islamization that this resulted in seemed primarily aimed at increasing al-Numayri's legitimacy in the eyes of the people.[29] This policy nevertheless enabled the Muslim Brothers to gain influence in several layers of society, such as through education to army officers,[30] participation in a committee that judged whether Sudan's legislation concurred with the Sharia[31] and the appointment of al-Turabi as Minister of Justice in 1979.[32]

The process of Islamization continued in the following years, particularly after 1983, when al-Numayri introduced Islamic legislation to buttress his declining popularity. Yet, the Muslim Brotherhood only played a minor role in this because al-Numayri did not want the organization to have more influence. This is why he also repressed the Muslim Brotherhood by imprisoning many of its members.[33] In addition, al-Turabi was sacked as Justice Minister.[34] Despite these measures and the hasty and ill-considered attempts to apply the Sharia – which had more to do with symbolism than with doing justice to Islamic legislation[35] – the Muslim Brotherhood supported al-Numayri's policy, even though it also criticized it.[36] When the regime was overthrown through popular pressure in 1985, many blamed the Muslim Brotherhood and al-Turabi for having supported al-Numayri for so long. Al-Turabi responded to this by founding a new, broad, Islamist organization in the form of Al-Jabha al-Islamiyya al-Qawmiyya ('The National Islamic Front'; NIF).[37] With this party, al-Turabi participated in the elections of 1986, which he personally lost, but which did result in 58 seats (on a total of 300) for the NIF.[38] In 1988, the party became part of the governing coalition under the leadership of Sadiq al-Mahdi, who appointed al-Turabi as Minister of Justice again.[39]

Al-Turabi in Power (1989–1999)

The lessons the Muslim Brotherhood had taught in the Sudanese army in the 1970s had created many supporters for the organization among officers. In 1989, one such an officer, 'Umar al-Bashir (1944), staged a coup, which resulted in Sudan coming under military rule again. Because the NIF believed that the government had pursued the wrong policies and had done little about the further application of Islamic law, it supported al-Bashir's coup.[40] This led to a period of ten years in which al-Turabi – both nationally and internationally – was at the pinnacle of his power and influence, but also lost this again.

A major step in achieving the national goals of the NIF was the new criminal code that was adopted in Sudan in 1991 and that – partly due to al-Turabi's involvement – was based on the Sharia.[41] The NIF's role was further strengthened when the group was allocated positions on several different political levels in the early 1990s.[42] Al-Turabi himself increased his role in Sudanese politics when he was elected parliamentary speaker in 1996.[43] In 1998, moreover, al-Bashir, al-Turabi and their followers formed a new political organization called Al-Mu'tamar al-Watani ('The National Congress'), of which al-Bashir became chairman and al-Turabi its Secretary General.[44] In the same year, al-Turabi also had a (limited) role in rewriting the Sudanese constitution.[45]

Internationally, al-Turabi set up Al-Mu'tamar al-Sha'bi al-'Arabi al-Islami ('The Popular Arab Islamic Congress'; PAIC) in 1991, an organization that was to function as a platform for Islamist groups from all over the world. The meetings organized by PAIC were attended by members of Hamas, but also by Osama bin Laden (1957–2011) and other future members of Al-Qaida, whose business activities in Sudan were welcomed by al-Turabi in the first half of the 1990s.[46] There were, nevertheless, major ideological differences between the latter and Bin Laden and the two men found it increasingly difficult to cooperate. In 1996, al-Turabi therefore personally strove to have Bin Laden expelled to Afghanistan.[47] Al-Turabi's influence on the actual activities of militant groups in Sudan should also not be overestimated. When, in 1995, the Egyptian President Husni Mubarak was attacked during a visit to Sudan, al-Turabi may have welcomed the attack,[48] but this was more to cover up the fact that he had not been notified of the plans to do this than as an expression of his actual support.[49] When al-Turabi tried to get rid of the culprits by giving them positions at embassies in various African countries, they saw him as a hypocrite and a traitor,[50] a conclusion that Bin Laden seemed to agree with when he described al-Turabi as a 'Machiavelli' or considered him a 'nuisance'.[51]

The words of al-Turabi's critics show that not everyone shared his views or was happy with the power that he had acquired, but this was made even clearer by other incidents in the same period. For example, when al-Turabi visited Ottawa in 1992, he was physically attacked by a man of Sudanese descent at the airport.[52] Moreover, after the publication of the new constitution in 1998, al-Turabi indicated that he wanted to turn Al-Mu'tamar al-Watani into the dominant political party of Sudan, which the leadership of the army viewed as an attempt to create a popular power base for himself and to eventually replace al-Bashir. This led to an attempt to remove him from the party.[53] Although this ultimately failed, it had become clear that there was a power struggle going on between al-Turabi and al-Bashir, which the latter won by removing al-Turabi from the position as parliamentary speaker in 1999.[54] After this loss, many of al-Turabi's followers realized that the revolution of 1989 had been a failure.[55]

Towards a Post-Turabi Era (1999–2021)

Shortly after al-Turabi had been deprived of his position as parliamentary speaker, President al-Bashir closed the PAIC in 2000.[56] In the same year, he also stripped al-Turabi of his role as Secretary General of Al-Mu'tamar al-Watani, which meant he had lost his last influential formal position. In an attempt to regain his earlier status, al-Turabi once again founded a new political party in the same year: Hizb al-Mu'tamar al-Sha'bi ('The Popular Congress Party' (also known as 'The Popular National Congress Party')).[57] Al-Bashir allowed its founding because he believed he would be able to better keep an eye on the opposition if it organized itself in the open than if it continued clandestinely.[58]

Meanwhile, a decades-long conflict had developed in Sudan between the mostly Islamic north and the Christian and animistic south. Although it clashed with his earlier Islamist policies, al-Turabi signed a 'Memorandum of understanding' with John Garang (1945–2005), the leader of the South-Sudanese separatist movement, in 2001, by which the former made himself an enemy of al-Bashir's regime.[59] As a result, al-Turabi was imprisoned twice in the period 2001–2005 and was not released until after there was a peace agreement with the south.[60] The latter indicated, however, that there was a rapprochement between the northern rulers and the southern rebels, whom al-Turabi had wanted to use as allies against the regime. Al-Turabi therefore turned against the peace agreement and stated that the unity of Sudan should be preserved. This was in vain, however: the south voted in favour of separation in 2011.[61]

Al-Turabi was arrested again in 2008 after he had expressed support for the call to the president to hand himself in to the International Criminal Court in The Hague for war crimes in Darfur, a western province in Sudan with which the regime was in conflict.[62] The same happened when he labelled the 2010 elections, which al-Bashir 'won' with 68.29 per cent of the vote, as 'fraudulent'.[63] In the following years, al-Turabi was also increasingly subjected to criticism of other parties, partly because he – as had happened before – wavered between opposition against and dialogue with the regime of al-Bashir.[64]

It is tempting to simply label al-Turabi – who died in 2016 – as a political opportunist because of all the organizations that he has founded and the

U-turns he made in order to stay politically relevant. Yet, it would not do justice to al-Turabi to leave it at that, because he has been a major source of ideological influence for Islamists inside and outside Sudan.[65] This was probably partly the case because of his major emphasis on political participation and Islamist ideas on democracy,[66] expressing a preference for *shura* over a 'Western' kind of rule by the people.[67] His most important contributions as an Islamist thinker, however, were on the Sharia, about which he has written much.[68] He stated, for example, that apostates should not be executed – this rule was supposedly meant for people who joined the enemy, not those who abandoned their faith[69] – and he ultimately also propounded the view that non-Muslims could become heads of state in a Muslim country.[70]

Al-Turabi went furthest, however, in his reformist ideas on women's rights and dealt with this subject as far back as the 1950s.[71] He criticized the abuse of women and stated that many traditions about the interaction between the sexes did not emanate from Islam, but from cultural customs. As such, he strove for equal rights and political participation for women (including with regard to the presidency),[72] was opposed to gender segregation[73] and claimed that the headscarf was only a religious duty for the wives of the Prophet Muhammad, not for other women.[74] Al-Turabi's long-term legacy regarding the Muslim Brotherhood and similar organizations inside and outside of Sudan will therefore perhaps lie in his Islamist ideals, not in his political opportunism.

Morocco: Under the Care of the Commander of the Faithful

The contemporary state of Morocco, like so many other countries analysed in this book, has a long history as a Muslim country. Although Morocco was never ruled by the Ottoman Empire, unlike many other countries in the region, it did know various Islamic dynasties, was under (French) colonial rule for decades and is overwhelmingly Sunni. Still, the Moroccan state presents Islam in its own, distinct way that constitutes a kind of middle ground between the way Saudi Arabia propagates itself as an Islamic state and the emphasis Jordan places on the prophetic descent of the Hashemite monarchy there. Before analysing Islamism in Morocco – which is ideologically and culturally, but not organizationally connected with the Muslim Brotherhood – it is therefore good to deal with the country's 'Moroccan Islam' first because this is the context in which Islamists operate.

The Creation of a 'Moroccan Islam' (1912–1961)

Although the term 'Moroccan Islam' suggests indigenous roots, the way in which the state presents the dominant religion of the land today has much to do with the French protectorate over Morocco, which began in 1912. In this period, French ethnographers in Morocco – working from a colonialist perspective – described several elements that they regarded as typical of Islam in that country, including Sufism, various forms of popular religion, an emphasis on the prophetic descent of certain families and the influence of religious scholars. The French rulers adopted this description because they viewed these things as fixed sources of authority and therefore believed that the people who adhered to them would be less susceptible to the anti-French discourse that politicians and activists striving for independence used. By establishing relations with these and labelling them collectively as 'Moroccan Islam', the French authorities did not just give a certain authenticity to Muslims who were prepared to work with them, but they also legitimized the French protectorate, which was supposedly the only one with sufficient knowledge to help the country develop itself further.[75]

In reality, Islam in Morocco was more complicated than the French ethnographers and rulers claimed. Just like elsewhere in the region, for example, the country experienced the influence of *salafi* modernist thinking, which had a strongly nationalist character in Morocco. This trend was quite critical of certain forms of Sufism, was against popular religion and – under the influence of the famous Moroccan *salafi* modernist 'Allal al-Fasi (1910–1974) – enjoyed a certain influence on politics and religion in the country.[76] In 1944, adherents to this trend founded Hizb al-Istiqlal ('The Independence Party'), which not only still exists, but was also quite popular at the time because of its share in bringing about the independence of Morocco.[77]

After Morocco became formally independent in 1956 and the former sultan was crowned King Muhammad v in 1957, the new monarch tried to give the country a clearly Islamic character by, for example, compelling schools to organize prayers and by ensuring that family law conformed to the Sharia.[78] The regime also established ties with religious scholars, but simultaneously made them subservient to the authority of the king and fragmented them by dividing them over different institutes.[79] Moreover, from the 1960s onwards, the regime invested more in Arabic (as opposed to French) and Islamic education[80] and used scholars – including al-Fasi – to condemn the socialism that was popular in the Arab world in that period.[81]

Moreover, the position of the king in this context was of one whose authority went further than that of an average monarch. Firstly, there was his position as *sharif* ('noble', descendant of the Prophet Muhammad), from which he derived a certain status and legitimacy.[82] Closely connected to this was the king's claim to the position of 'commander of the faithful', a title that – as we saw in Chapter 1 – was also used by the caliphs[83] and that was formally included in the Moroccan constitution, thereby giving the king a 'sacred and inviolable' status.[84] Finally, this position was sometimes also associated with a type of power, charisma and influence that rose above the other parties.[85]

Islamists as Opposition (1961–1997)

The Islamic character of the state was the context in which Moroccan Islamists had to function, which meant that they always had to take the religious authority of the king into account. Apart from the radical Islamist opposition (see below) and the aforementioned Hizb al-Istiqlal – which was more intellectual in nature and concentrated on religious reform and party politics – Islamism in Morocco was influenced by the writings of the early ideologues of the Muslim Brotherhood.[86] Of the two popular Islamist movements that came into existence apart from those already mentioned, this was even the case for the one that least resembled the Muslim Brotherhood, namely, that of 'Abd al-Salam Yasin (1928–2012).[87]

   Yasin's Islamism was actually a typically Moroccan phenomenon in the sense that it mirrored the claims of the monarchy by appealing to the same things that the authority of the king rests on, such as his descent from the Prophet Muhammad and a certain 'sacredness' as a Sufi sheikh.[88] In particular, his membership of the Budshishiyya Sufi order[89] and the spiritual status that he derived from this position were important to Yasin and his followers.[90] At the same time, Yasin went his own way by explicitly striving for political engagement.[91] In this capacity, he sent a letter, in 1974, to King Hasan II (1929–1999),[92] who had succeeded his father in 1961. In it, Yasin called on him to repent for his alleged sins, addressed him directly and more or less approached him as if the king was his pupil.[93] Precisely because Yasin had 'desecrated' the role of the king through his letter and, in a sense, demanded the monarch's status for himself,[94] he was forcibly admitted to a mental institution[95] and was not released until 1986.[96] In his later writings, Yasin indicated that he wanted to found a caliphate; his views on violence to achieve this goal were ambiguous.[97] As a result, the organization that he founded on the basis of his ideas in the 1980s, Al-'Adl wa-l-Ihsan ('Justice and Charity'),[98] was repressed by the Moroccan regime[99] and remains illegal.[100]

A different popular Islamist movement in Morocco was much closer to the Muslim Brotherhood and can actually be seen as the standard bearer of its ideology in the country, albeit as a result of a complex process. It started in 1967, when Al-Haraka al-Sha'biyya al-Dusturiyya al-Dimuqratiyya ('The Popular Democratic and Constitutional Movement'; 'Mouvement Populaire Démocratique et Constitutionnel'; MPDC) was founded by 'Abd al-Karim al-Khatib (1921–2008). The latter was a former member of Hizb al-Istiqlal and had good ties to the regime, but had not been politically active since the 1970s.[101]

In 1969, 'Abd al-Karim Muti' (1935) founded Jam'iyyat al-Shabiba al-Islamiyya ('The Association of Islamic Youth'; Shabiba),[102] a group that was officially recognized by the state in the early 1970s.[103] Influenced by the ideology of the Muslim Brotherhood and particularly Qutb's work,[104] Muti' used his own writings to call for the overthrow of the regime and a complete reform of society.[105] The group also spoke out fiercely against the political left and, when it was accused of fatally assaulting an editor of a socialist newspaper, the association was repressed[106] and ultimately banned in 1975.[107] Because Muti', who was in exile, continued Shabiba's radical policies, part of the group explicitly distanced itself from him and from Shabiba and, in the early 1980s, split off under the name Jam'iyyat al-Jama'a al-Islamiyya ('The Association of the Islamic Group'), with the desire to continue legally.[108]

One of this group, 'Abd al-Ilah Ibn Kiran (1954), continued Jam'iyyat al-Jama'a al-Islamiyya under the name Harakat al-Islah wa-l-Tajdid ('The Movement of Reform and Renewal'), which was officially recognized as such in 1992.[109] The group had goals that strongly resembled those of the Muslim Brotherhood, such as the revival of Islam, the application of the Sharia, charity, unity and education.[110] After the regime rejected a similar attempt by Ibn Kiran and his supporters to set up a political party[111] and an effort to join Hizb al-Istiqlal failed as well,[112] they sought closer ties with the aforementioned al-Khatib, the founder of the MPDC. The cooperation between Ibn Kiran and al-Khatib resulted in two organizations, merging a number of earlier groups: firstly, in 1996, Ibn Kiran united three Islamist groups around himself under the name Rabitat al-Mustaqbal al-Islami ('The League of the Islamist Future'), which came to be led by Ahmad al-Raysuni (1953). This group subsequently merged with Ibn Kiran's aforementioned Harakat al-Islah wa-l-Tajdid under the name Harakat al-Tawhid wa-l-Islah ('The Movement of Unity and Reform'; 'Mouvement de l'Unicité et de la Réforme'; MUR).[113] In 1996, the MUR also got a political wing in the form of the pre-existing MPDC, with al-Khatib and Ibn Kiran as secretary general and deputy secretary general, respectively. Both the broad MUR movement and the MPDC political party explicitly accepted the king as commander of the faithful, rejected violence, recognized the Maliki school of Islamic law that is dominant in Morocco and indicated that they respected Moroccan territorial integrity.[114]

The Rise and Development of the PJD (1997–2003)

Thus, both the MUR and the MPDC had learned from the earlier, radical Islamists of Shabiba (and probably also Al-'Adl wa-l-Ihsan), who had sought confrontation with the regime, by explicitly positioning themselves as subservient to the Moroccan political system and the role that the king played in it. Probably in recognition of this – but also to take the wind out of Al-'Adl wa-l-Ihsan's sails – the regime allowed Islamists to participate in the political process in 1997, through which the monarchy started sharing the monopoly on Islam, to a degree, although it should be noted that parliament did not become a source of power whose influence was comparable to that of the throne.[115] As such, the MPDC participated in the parliamentary elections of 1997, in which it won nine seats (out of a total of 325).[116] Instead of taking on the role of opposition vis-à-vis a left-wing socialist government, the MPDC mostly tried to consolidate its place in the system by giving critical support to the regime and, for example, by not drawing too much attention to the regime's election rigging, which the party itself had been a victim of.[117]

In 1998, i.e. during its first parliamentary period, the MPDC got a new name: Hizb al-'Adala wa-l-Tanmiya ('The Justice and Development Party'; 'Parti de la Justice et du Développement'; PJD).[118] This party, which was increasingly characterized by internal democracy and transparency[119] and whose members of parliament were younger than those of many other parties,[120] participated fully in the political system and also accepted the monarchy.[121] With regard to policy, the party had a broad view of the Sharia, which meant that, in practice, it did not concentrate on controversial aspects, such as corporal punishment, but rather strove to encourage conservative morals and – wherever possible – tried to apply them in society.[122]

The PJD as a political party stood on its own, but it was tied to the MUR in a relationship that is comparable to that of the Islamic Action Front and the Muslim Brotherhood in Jordan.[123] Initially, there was extensive overlap between the members of both organizations[124] and the PJD relied on the MUR's broader base – the result of its emphasis on *da'wa* and education – during electoral campaigns and for popular support.[125] The PJD was more explicitly pro-regime and pro-monarchy than the MUR – probably because of its direct political involvement and the need to make compromises that this necessarily entails – but the latter also accepted the political system in Morocco.[126] Moreover, the MUR had similarly reformist ideas. These partly were manifested in the writings of the party's leader, the aforementioned Ahmad al-Raysuni, who used his work to point to the importance of the underlying purposes of the Sharia (*maqasid al-Shari'a*), which facilitated a more flexible approach to Islamic law, one not solely focussed on the rules. One of these underlying goals, according to al-Raysuni, was the prevention of social and political unrest, which could best be realized through democracy, something the people were entitled to, according to the MUR.[127]

Such openness to reform was not limited to the PJD and the MUR, however: in 1999, King Muhammad VI (1963) succeeded his father, Hasan II, and wasted no time in starting a programme to reform his country's laws, including those pertaining to women's rights in Morocco. Just like the other Islamist groups analysed in this book, the PJD was in favour of political reforms, but was less keen on societal changes. Several Islamist groups, including the PJD, expressed their objections to the king's reforms, particularly the prohibition of polygamy and the possibility for women to marry without the interference of a male family member, which they considered to be part of a broader, secular and Western agenda that it rejected. As a result, the reforms were not adopted for the time being.[128]

The greater openness promised by the new king, which partly manifested itself in planned reforms in the area of human rights and the release of political prisoners, encouraged the PJD to adopt a more assertive position in Moroccan politics from 2000 onwards. This was given concrete form in moderate calls for constitutional reforms to limit the power of the regime and only partially successful attempts to make the electoral system more efficient.[129] In 2002, the party participated in the elections again, however. Although the PJD stood for election in more districts than in 1997 (namely, in 60 per cent of the total, compared with 43 per cent in 1997), its participation was consciously limited again so as not to win too much power, which might provoke the regime.[130] Nevertheless, it won 42 seats and it even seemed as if the PJD would become part of the governing coalition.[131] Although this did not happen in the end, it did show the political maturity of the party. The same was true of the extent to which the PJD became detached from the MUR: by raising its own money through alternative sources of income and by recruiting more people from outside the MUR, the party gradually began to stand on its own organizationally.[132]

Rising to Power Under Pressure (2003–2021)

Apart from the aforementioned groups like Al-'Adl wa-l-Ihsan, the MUR and the PJD, there were also radical Islamists in Morocco who were willing to use violence to underline their vision of drastic change. This manifested itself in Morocco in a series of terrorist attacks in Casablanca that killed 33 citizens in 2003. These attacks caused the regime to become more repressive, but it also completely retook the religious reins by monopolizing the discourse on Islam so as to prevent radical ideas from leading to such attacks again. In practice, this meant more state control over scholars and preachers and their fatwas, as well as a stronger emphasis on the religious position of the king as the 'commander of the faithful'.[133] The latter was part of the aforementioned broader campaign to propagate 'Moroccan Islam' once again and in a stricter sense. This time, however, it would not serve colonial interests, but those of the regime.[134] In addition to the king's position as 'commander of the faithful', this 'Moroccan Islam' was epitomized by three different aspects, namely, the Maliki school of Islamic law that is dominant in Morocco, the prevailing Ash'ari-trend of Islamic theology[135] and forms of Sufism tied to Moroccan orders and the tenth-century Sufi scholar Junayd.[136]

Although the PJD, the MUR and other Islamist groups had nothing to do with the attacks, the more secular part of Moroccan society blamed them for the violence because – as Islamist groups – they were viewed as having an ambivalent attitude towards terrorism. Consequently, the PJD continued on the path of trying to distance itself from the MUR in order to emphasize its independence from this more explicitly Islamist group.[137] The party also continued to participate in a limited way in local elections in 2003[138] and, moreover, was careful in national politics not to give the regime an excuse to limit its activities after the Casablanca attacks. Conversely, the regime made use of this opportunity to push through the reform of the country's family law (including women's rights), which had previously failed after the king ascended the throne, in 2003. This time, the PJD and the MUR (as well as Al-'Adl wa-l-Ihsan) did give their support. Although the PJD claimed that its changed position emanated from stronger religious guarantees in and broader consultation about the new legislation, it was simultaneously quite clear that the party realized that it would not be in its own interests to oppose the regime in this context.[139]

The PJD – which had been led by Sa'd al-Din al-'Uthmani (1956) since 2004 – participated in the elections again in 2007, in which it won 46 seats.[140] In this period, the aforementioned reformist thought, espoused by people like al-Raysuni, became increasingly widespread within the party through an emphasis on the goals (rather than the rules) of the Sharia and by making their application subject to the will of the people. Moreover, the party tended towards portraying certain issues, such as the limitation of the sale of alcohol or censoring specific books and films, as questions of morality rather than as Islamic-legal issues. Still, there were clear limits to the flexibility that the PJD was willing to display with respect to societal issues, for example with regard to women's rights or the freedom to criticize Islam. Although there are certainly people within the party who want to translate its reformist ideas about democracy into societal issues, this remains a difficult point for the PJD.[141]

The PJD's agenda of political reforms received an impulse when the Arab Spring erupted in 2011. Although this did not lead to the drastic changes that took place in other Arab countries, there were protests against the regime that built on earlier activities that had started in 2007. Yet, the PJD did not take the lead in these protests. In fact, the party used its conditional promise not to participate in the protests as a means to exert political pressure to obtain concessions from the state.[142] Despite the PJD's lack of involvement in the protests, the party – which had never been in government – perhaps represented the change that the protesters desired. This, and the PJD's populist economic agenda – rather than its socially conservative points of view – were probably the reasons for its victory in the elections of 2011, when the party won 107 seats (out of a total of 395). The PJD, which had been led by Ibn Kiran since 2008, therefore got the chance to form a government. Its coalition was sworn in in the same year, while Prime Minister Ibn Kiran assured people that their civil liberties would remain untouched.[143] Moreover, the PJD showed that this was not a unique incident or coincidence: in 2016, the party won the elections again – this time with 125 seats – after which Ibn Kiran's successor al-'Uthmani became prime minister in 2017,[144] although the PJD was wiped out in the 2021 elections, when it was reduced to a tenth of its former size.[145]

Tunisia: Accepting the Loss of Power

Tunisia – even more so than Morocco, but unlike countries such as Egypt – has a strongly developed tradition of criticism towards the role of Islam in politics that still exists today and that partly manifests itself in the views of political parties. That said, the area covered by modern-day Tunisia also has a long history as a Muslim country, going back to the seventh century and which can still be seen in, for example, the Ez-Zitouna University, the oldest

Islamic educational institute in the Arab world. Unlike Morocco, Tunisia was part of the Ottoman Empire and also came under a French protectorate from 1881, during which time the country was exposed to Islamic reformist ideas. An independence movement subsequently developed in the area, led by Habib Burqiba (Bourguiba; 1903–2000), which would eventually result in independence from the French in 1956.[146]

Bourguiba became the first president of the independent state of Tunisia and, under his rule, the country became a dictatorship.[147] To Bourguiba, Islam was not an important factor in terms of legitimizing himself and his rule, but the regime did want to have control over the religious course of the country.[148] As such, he abolished Sharia courts, banished Islam to the private sphere and gave women greater freedom and rights through legal reforms that were formalized in the Code du Status Personnel ('Code of Personal Status') of 1956.[149] Just like Morocco, Bourguiba wanted to create a national Islam, but in the case of Tunisia, this was a variation of the religion that he believed combined Islam with modernity.[150] His dismantling of the Ez-Zitouna University, his delegitimization of Sufism by claiming that their sheikhs had collaborated with the French and his criticism of Muslim scholars were highly controversial among some Tunisians, however.[151]

Origins and Early Developments (1967–1987)

The first signs of Islamic activism in Tunisia were seen after its independence, from 1967 onwards, when Islam experienced a revival in the entire region as a result of the search for an alternative to the Arab socialism of the Egyptian president Nasser. In Tunisia, this was combined with a growing opposition to Bourguiba and his societal constraints on Islam.[152] Groups of people began gathering in mosques to listen to young, politically engaged speakers, such as Rashid al-Ghannushi (1941), Ahmida al-Nayfar (1942) and 'Abd al-Fattah Muru (1948).[153] In the 1970s, these groups organized, albeit informally, into Al-Jama'a al-Islamiyya ('The Islamic Group'), which strove to present Islam as an all-encompassing ideology and also wanted to apply it in society.[154]

Al-Jama'a al-Islamiyya's activities included publishing the writings of individual thinkers, especially al-Ghannushi,[155] and from 1972 onwards it issued its own monthly magazine.[156] It recruited in schools and universities, where it regularly confronted left-wing students, both electorally and physically.[157] The movement also engaged in preaching in different areas of the country and found support among many members of Al-Jam'iyya li-l-Muhafaza 'ala l-Qur'an al-Karim ('The Association for the Preservation

of the Noble Koran'). This association had been founded by the regime to
provide a controlled outlet to Tunisians seeking to practise their religion.[158]
Meanwhile, Al-Jama'a al-Islamiyya was organized more tightly, with a
hierarchical cell structure that was supposed to protect it against general
repression by the regime and that resembled that of the Muslim Brotherhood, described in earlier chapters. Members also started paying a fixed
membership fee.[159] By 1979, the group was so well-organized that it was
able to hold a conference.[160]

Although the rise of Al-Jama'a al-Islamiyya should be viewed in the
regional and national context, as described above, there were also other
sources of influence that were important to the movement. The first of
these was the Islamic Revolution in Iran in 1979, which showed Tunisian
Islamists that ideas such as theirs could actually lead to practical changes.
To them, the revolution in Iran was a model – particularly with regard
to the Islamist discourse of the oppressed versus the oppressors that it
produced – that enabled Al-Jama'a al-Islamiyya to respond better to, for
example, left-wing students at universities.[161] When the dictatorial character
of the Iranian regime became increasingly clear, however, the movement
distanced itself from it.[162]

The Muslim Brotherhood was a second important source of influence
to Al-Jama'a al-Islamiyya. This is unsurprising considering that Tunisian
Islamists – like the PJD and its predecessors – while not officially part of the
Muslim Brotherhood organization, had the same ideological and cultural
roots.[163] This was reinforced in the 1970s, when Tunisian Islamists came
into contact with the writings of al-Banna and especially Qutb, whose
ideas they adopted.[164] Not everyone agreed with this source of influence,
however. Especially al-Nayfar believed that some Islamists uncritically
accepted the Muslim Brotherhood's arguments, that this organization had
little knowledge of the situation in Tunisia and that Islamists should focus
on the future, rather than on an idealized past. For these reasons, he and
some twenty others split off in the 1970s to found Harakat al-Taqaddum
al-Islami ('The Movement of Islamic Progress'; Mouvement du Progrès
Islamiste),[165] although this movement maintained contact with Al-Jama'a
al-Islamiyya and its successors.[166]

The remaining members of Al-Jama'a al-Islamiyya were clearly in favour
of the Muslim Brotherhood[167] and at the aforementioned conference, in
1979, it decided to change its name to Harakat al-Ittijah al-Islami ('The
Movement of the Islamic Tendency'; Mouvement de la Tendance Islamique;
MTI). The leaders of the movement came from diverse regional backgrounds,
but were mostly young, male and middle class,[168] although there were

many more women among MTI's membership than had previously been the case.[169] The MTI's organizational structure was comparable to that of the Muslim Brotherhood, mirroring its Consultation Council, Executive Council and a hierarchical cell structure.[170] The MTI's ideals concurred with those espoused by the Muslim Brotherhood: in addition to specifically Tunisian points of attention, the movement primarily stood for a revival and reform of Islam, political participation and economic improvement,[171] although there were also ideological divisions between the more pragmatic Muru and people like Salah Karkir (1948–2012), who were less willing to compromise.[172]

The Tunisian regime initially took a tolerant approach to Al-Jama'a al-Islamiyya because Bourguiba wanted to fight the leftist opposition and saw Islamists as allies in this regard,[173] a policy that was also applied to the MTI, although the president later reversed this.[174] Because of the repression that took place, dissatisfaction increased among the Tunisian people, which led some of them to start using violence against the police and the army in the city of Gafsa in early 1980. While the MTI condemned the attack (despite part of its base supporting it), the movement was still blamed for it. The suspicion that the MTI was behind the violence was reinforced when Islamist students took a university dean hostage.[175] Anticipating possible repression and making use of a political opening that the regime offered in 1981, the MTI announced in that year that it wanted to participated in the elections.[176] The movement was repressed by the regime, however, by means of arrests – including of MTI-leader al-Ghannushi. This happened again in 1984 after protests against rising food prices (the 'bread riots'), which, again, the MTI was blamed for.[177] In fact, this repression gave a boost to those MTI members who sought confrontation with the regime.[178] When the more radical Karkir became leader following al-Ghannushi's imprisonment, the movement was even said to have planned a coup for 7 November 1987. This was prevented, however, mostly because the Minister of the Interior, Zayn al-'Abidin Ibn 'Ali (Bin Ali; 1936–2019), decided to stage a coup himself that day.[179]

The Rise of Ennahda (1988–1992)

Although as Minister of the Interior, Bin Ali had been partly responsible for the repression of the MTI in previous years, as the new president, in 1988–1989, he decided to pardon thousands of exiled and imprisoned Islamists, including al-Ghannushi.[180] Under the new regime, a National Pact, stipulating relations between the state and the people, was concluded in 1988. It paid more attention to Islam than the country's previous laws had done and the pact was also supported by the MTI, which pledged – through al-Ghannushi – to renounce violence and indicated that it wanted to participate in the political system.[181] On a societal level, more space was given to Islam, for example by broadcasting prayer times on radio and television and by reopening Ez-Zitouna University.[182] Yet, President Bin Ali had no plans to substantially change the policies of his predecessors and, in fact, he even held on to them by ensuring that his regime controlled public expressions of Islam.[183]

The Islamists' success in the 1989 elections was a key reason why Bin Ali's regime opted for control of Islam in the public sphere again.[184] In 1988, the MTI changed its name to Al-Nahda ('The Renaissance'; Ennahda) – because political parties were no longer allowed to have explicitly religious references in their names – and it wanted to stand for election as such in 1989. Despite its name change, however, it was not permitted to participate and the party could only propose individual candidates who had to stand as independents. This way, Ennahda still participated in the elections and won about 15 per cent of the votes,[185] even though it claimed that the election results had been rigged and that the Islamists had actually received far more votes.[186]

The election results, which turned Ennahda into the largest opposition party in the country, constituted a valid reason for the regime to limit the space for Islamists it had previously created and to violently repress Ennahda. Preachers were arrested, lessons at Ez-Zitouna University were halted and Ennahda's magazine was banned. In response, three young Islamists set fire to the office of President Bin Ali's party in 1991, which led to the death of a doorman and seriously injured another. Ennahda was also alleged to have wanted to assassinate the president. The party condemned the arson attack[187] and the overwhelming majority of its members denied that there had been an attempted coup.[188] The violence nevertheless caused the aforementioned Muru, who had been one of the first Islamist leaders, to leave Ennahda.[189]

The regime responded to these events with mass arrests that resulted in the imprisonment of thousands of Islamists from 1992 onwards. The regime also repressed a human rights organization, censored the media, dismantled a trade union affiliated with Ennahda and arrested political opponents.[190] Because part of Ennahda – including al-Ghannushi – had already fled abroad to escape the repression,[191] this campaign in effect ended the concrete political presence of the party in Tunisia itself. This forced Ennahda to continue underground in Tunisia or to regroup in exile.

Repression and Exile (1992–2010)

For many Ennahda members, the repression did not stop once they had been locked up, but continued in prison. Indeed, this period – mirroring what had happened to Muslim Brothers in Egypt in 1954 – came to be known as 'the inquisition'. Especially in the first half of the 1990s, party members were subjected to all kinds of torture, varying from physical violence and rape to food deprivation and long periods of solitary confinement.[192] This treatment was not limited to male members of Ennahda, but was equally applied to female supporters of the party who had been imprisoned or manifested itself in limitations to and harassment of the wives of male prisoners.[193] In a bid to regain the initiative and take control of their own bodies, some detainees revolted against these measures by going on a hunger strike,[194] but others publicly renounced Ennahda.[195] When the prisoners were released at the turn of the twenty-first century, many were still subjected to frequent administrative control by the state, leading them to live unfree, stigmatized and socially marginalized lives. Consequently, many had trouble finding a job or getting married, let alone becoming involved with Islamism and politics again.[196]

Considering the situation in Tunisia in this period, it is not surprising that new developments took place within the exiled Ennahda. The members who fled under Bin Ali's regime connected with Tunisian Islamists who had already gone to European countries and together they established a parallel organizational structure for Ennahda that was centred on London, where al-Ghannushi – who had been elected leader again – lived.[197] In exile, they not only tried to keep Ennahda alive, but they also protested Tunisian policy and developed several media, including their own television channel.[198]

Al-Ghannushi also used this period in exile to revise or refine the party's ideology. This did not happen without resistance from others within Ennahda, however. While al-Ghannushi stayed in England, the more radical and Qutb-inspired Karkir lived in France. Although al-Ghannushi had previously distanced himself from Karkir, the latter continued to insist that violence against the state was allowed in some cases. Because of this, Ennahda suspended Karkir and eventually removed him from the party. These developments led to a re-evaluation of the views of the past and a formal choice against violence during a conference in Switzerland in 1995.[199] Al-Ghannushi also developed his views of democracy further, retaining his insistence on the application of the Sharia, but only if this was done in a democratic way and thus by the people themselves. In addition, he accepted a multi-party system as long as it did not marginalize religion and he became more willing to compromise in terms of his views on women's rights as they applied in Tunisia.[200] Based on this attitude, cooperation with other, non-Islamist exiles became easier and they therefore launched an initiative to reconcile with President Bin Ali in the first decade of the twenty-first century.[201]

In the same period, Tunisia itself witnessed a wave of increased religiosity. In a context in which Bin Ali's regime lost popularity, people started searching for new meaning, which they found in Islam, particularly after major incidents at the beginning of the new millennium, such as the terrorist attacks of 11 September 2001 and the American invasion of Iraq in 2003.[202] The Tunisian president, convinced that Ennahda was no longer a real threat, partly responded to this by displaying greater personal piety. At the same time, the regime kept a careful eye on religious discourse and forced women to take off their headscarves.[203] In this context, Ennahda tried to regain a role in Tunisia, including by positioning itself as a moderate alternative to the radical groups that had come to the fore in its absence.[204]

The Arab Spring and Its Aftermath (2010–2021)

As we have seen before, the Arab Spring began in Tunisia, before spreading to various countries. After the protests across the country were initially beaten down by the police and the army, Ennahda mostly stayed out of sight. It had, after all, started with the aforementioned reconciliation initiative with the regime and it was unwilling to jeopardize by participating in demonstrations that it believed would eventually be put down. Yet, when the regime weakened and ultimately collapsed and Bin Ali left the country, al-Ghannushi returned to Tunisia in January 2011, welcomed enthusiastically by thousands of supporters.[205] In the period directly after the fall of the regime, Ennahda tried to prevent people from taking revenge on the old rulers.[206] It became a legal party in the same year, after which it participated in the elections of 2011 with a detailed manifesto that made very little mention of Islam. Al-Ghannushi also emphasized in interviews that he would not participate in the presidential elections and that if his party won the parliamentary elections, people's civil liberties would remain intact.[207] Ennahda ended up winning 37 per cent of the votes in the 2011 elections, becoming the biggest party in almost every constituency[208] thanks to its major reach among people and its successful campaign.[209]

After the election victory in 2011, Ennahda decided to become part of the government in a coalition with Al-Mu'tamar min Ajl al-Jumhuriyya ('The Congress for the Republic'; Congrès pour la République; CPR) and

Al-Takattul ('The Forum'),[210] two non-Islamist parties with agendas that were very different from Ennahda's. Al-Munsif al-Marzuqi (1945), a human rights activist and the head of the CPR, became president.[211] None of the three coalition parties had much political experience and in the case of the CPR and Al-Takattul, there was also little party discipline.[212] Moreover, Ennahda obtained almost all major ministerial jobs, which the party considered only natural given that it was by far the biggest partner in the coalition. To others, however, it was a sign that it wanted to claim all power for itself, especially because they suspected al-Ghannushi of being the true ruler. Combined with a general lack of strategy and a continually bad economic situation, this caused the coalition to fall apart.[213] Meanwhile, Ennahda was being pulled in two different directions: on the one hand, the secular opposition[214] thought Ennahda was too religious and from its midst the former president Muhammad al-Baji Qa'id al-Sibsi (1926–2019) founded the secular party Nida' Tunis ('The Call of Tunisia') to counter Ennahda in 2012;[215] on the other hand, pious Islamists and Salafis in Tunisia (including the radical Salafi Ansar al-Sharia) believed the party was not Islamic enough.[216] Although Ennahda did not want to pursue the same policies as Bin Ali by repressing these people and sought to engage in dialogue, the party nevertheless felt increasingly compelled to distance itself from them.[217]

Caught between these opposing groups, which mistrusted Ennahda and, at the same time, tried to pull it in their own direction, the party felt increasingly obliged to make compromises regarding its principles and did not succeed in developing a clear strategy.[218] There were, for example, internal discussions in this period about the role of the Sharia in the new constitution. Although Ennahda initially wanted to mention this explicitly, it ultimately accepted that was not going to happen.[219] Moreover, it compromised on an earlier statement that ascribed equal but different roles to men and women in the family[220] and the party also let go of its former demand that blasphemy should be criminalized.[221] These concessions made opponents of Ennahda wonder whether the party's leaders had a secret agenda, hidden behind their pragmatic discourse, while others questioned whether Ennahda was still the Islamist party that they had voted for in 2011,[222] particularly because its leaders appeared to be more secular than its supporters.[223] Although this last point may have some validity, the concessions by Ennahda's leaders were not just rooted in political pragmatism, but also in the ideological reform that had gone on for years and which had led to a re-evaluation and re-interpretation of old concepts, particularly in al-Ghannushi's work.[224]

The difficult situation Ennahda found itself in, both in the governing coalition and in the country as a whole, reached a low point when two opposition politicians were assassinated by radical Islamists in 2013. Although Ennahda (at least as an organization) had nothing to do with this, the party was nevertheless blamed for having taken too little action against the groups that the culprits belonged to.[225] In the eyes of many Tunisians, Ennahda also ought to distinguish itself from radical Islamist groups such as Ansar al-Sharia, which is likely to have been a motivating factor for the party to take a more conciliatory stance. The protests that followed the attacks were the culmination of ongoing dissatisfaction with the government. Conscious of the experiences in Algeria, where an Islamist party saw its electoral victory taken away from it in the 1990s, and the coup against Muslim Brother Muhammad Mursi in Egypt in 2013, Ennahda therefore decided to hand over power to an interim government of technocrats in January 2014.[226] This willingness to share power and make compromises also manifested itself in the new Tunisian constitution, which was adopted in January 2014 and which showed how far Ennahda – unlike radical Islamists, for example – had compromised on the role of Islam: the text of the constitution did not contain a single reference to the Sharia.[227]

The new party, Nida' Tunis, won the parliamentary elections of 2014 with 86 (out of a total of 217) seats,[228] while Ennahda won 69 seats.[229] In order not to give the impression that it wanted to win too much, the party had refrained from participating in the presidential elections,[230] but it did enter the new coalition government, this time with Nida' Tunis.[231] By 2016, however, so many members of parliament for Nida' Tunis had quit that Ennahda became the biggest party after all. Instead of seizing its chance to translate its parliamentary majority into power, the party declared in the same year that it had definitively abandoned political Islam – which was, in fact, a confirmation of its policy of the preceding years – to continue as a party of 'Muslim democracy'.[232] This separation between the political sphere (as a party) and the religious sphere (as a movement) is a sign of political maturity that, as we have seen, was also taking place elsewhere, and that was important for the party to be able to continue independently.[233] As such, Ennahda became the biggest party again in the 2019 elections and entered a coalition government once more in February 2020. Although the current president of Tunisia, Qays Sa'id (1958) has since suspended parliament, as well as much of the constitution,[234] making the country's near future and Ennahda's role within somewhat uncertain, none of this diminishes the ideological and practical developments that the Islamist group has gone through over the decades.

***

In this chapter, we have seen three different countries in which groups that were part of the Muslim Brotherhood movement actually came to power for a longer period of time. In Sudan, al-Turabi appears to be the epitome of a plotting Muslim Brother who does everything to seize power, seemingly confirming the assertion that the organization is an international conspiracy. While this must also be seen in the context of the pragmatism of the Muslim Brotherhood, which came into existence through repression, al-Turabi's behaviour was, indeed, characterized by opportunism. Yet, this seems to be much more relevant to him personally than to his views or to his party. His reformist ideas, moreover, show that he was not necessarily an opportunist thanks to his Islamism, but independent of it.

With regard to Morocco, we saw that the PJD governed for years without dominating or imposing its will and, in Tunisia, Ennahda even voluntarily gave up power in 2014. Arguably, both the PJD and Ennahda moderated due to outside pressure. Although this did play a role, their ideological moderation was simultaneously part of a much longer process in which the more recent developments are merely the latest phase. Moreover, their moderation is, in any case, a sign of pragmatism and shows that, despite their reputation as conspirators, they are certainly prepared to make compromises, share power and even give it up.

Part III

Descendants

6. Radicals

So far in this book, we have only looked at groups that formally belong to the Muslim Brotherhood organization or are part of the ideological and cultural movement of the Muslim Brothers and strongly sympathize with the organization. This chapter deals with groups that do not belong to the Muslim Brotherhood (either as an organization or as a movement), but can be said to be its descendants because they have explicitly split off from it or have actively reacted against it. Just like Chapter 3, this chapter will deal with the first academic approach to the Muslim Brotherhood, namely, that it is a terrorist organization or that it secretly sympathizes with terrorism. In this context, six organizations will be analysed: two groups that have split off from the Muslim Brotherhood (Hizb al-Tahrir and the Palestinian Islamic Jihad); two organizations that have partial ideological roots in a radical branch of the Muslim Brotherhood (the Egyptian Al-Jama'a al-Islamiyya and Tanzim al-Jihad, which is also Egyptian); and two global networks of jihad fighters (Al-Qaida and the Islamic State) that are only indirectly tied to the Muslim Brotherhood. These descendants of the Muslim Brotherhood can all be called 'radical', not because they strive for an Islamic state, but because – unlike the Muslim Brotherhood, which takes a gradual approach – they seek a drastic overthrow of the political and social systems in which they function.

The Split-Offs: Hizb al-Tahrir and the Palestinian Islamic Jihad

From its inception, the Muslim Brotherhood has not engaged in preparing (let alone executing) revolutions against the state. Although – partly because of repression – revolutionary ideas did develop within the organization, for example in the work of the Egyptian Sayyid Qutb, they were not representative of the Muslim Brotherhood as a whole and, in due course, the organization also rejected them every time. Some members of the organization, however, disagreed with the gradual approach of the Muslim Brotherhood to such an extent that they chose to split from the group and continue independently. Two examples of this development are Hizb al-Tahrir and the Palestinian Islamic Jihad.

Origin and Development of Hizb al-Tahrir

Hizb al-Tahrir al-Islami ('The Islamic Liberation Party'; Hizb al-Tahrir) was officially founded in Jerusalem, in 1953, by Taqi al-Din al-Nabhani

(1909–1977), a Palestinian Islamist, together with others who had split from the Muslim Brotherhood.[1] The party was initially only present in Jordan and the West Bank, which was controlled by that country,[2] where it engaged in spreading pamphlets written by al-Nabhani, in which he preached an anti-colonial, pan-Islamic message and through which the party called for the resurrection of the caliphate.[3] In addition, the party organized small study groups in which supporters discussed the political-religious writings of al-Nabhani on a weekly or even a daily basis.[4] All of this was done in the context of the party's method, which encompassed three phases: the first phase consisted of building up the party through recruitment and the spreading of the message; the second phase constituted establishing contacts with the Muslim community as a whole by increasing its awareness of Hizb al-Tahrir's ideas; and the third phase was the actual implementation of Islam at the moment the *umma* was ready for it.[5]

In its early years, Hizb al-Tahrir also participated in parliamentary elections in the West Bank in 1954 and 1956, when the party won a single seat both times, albeit through independent candidates.[6] Despite this political participation in the Jordanian national parliament, Hizb al-Tahrir rejected democracy, which the party considered a Western and un-Islamic system[7] and for which al-Nabhani proposed a strongly limited form of *shura* as an alternative, one that placed the process of legislation largely in the hands of the caliph, not the people.[8] In this period, Hizb al-Tahrir also rejected the Jordanian monarchy as an instrument in the hands of the British.[9] As such, the Jordanian regime limited the party's activities and, in 1957 – after an attempted coup by supporters of Egypt's President Nasser – Hizb al-Tahrir was banned and its only member of parliament was dismissed.[10]

Meanwhile, Hizb al-Tahrir had spread to other Arab countries and believed the time was right to enter the second of its phases (interaction with the *umma*) in 1960.[11] The party turned out to be incapable of mobilizing people for a revolution, however, and concluded that security measures by governments and foreign support for Arab rulers prevented them from achieving their goals.[12] Consequently, Hizb al-Tahrir tried to stage coups in various Arab countries in the 1960s, with a view to establishing a caliphate, including in Jordan in 1968, 1969 and 1971[13] and in Iraq in 1972 and 1976.[14] None of these attempts were successful. Moreover, although the party was spread across various Arab countries, never managed to set up a large organization anywhere.[15] Moreover, al-Nabhani, who – as founder and leader – was at the top of the hierarchically organized structure of the party,[16] died in 1977[17] and was succeeded by the Palestinian 'Abd al-Qadim Zallum (1924–2003).[18]

Under the new leader's rule (and sometimes also before that), the party spread further into non-Arab Muslim countries, including Indonesia, Turkey, Pakistan and countries in Central Asia,[19] but also to non-Muslim countries such as Germany, Denmark and Sweden.[20] Because the party did not think it was feasible to set up a caliphate in these states, members of Hizb al-Tahrir in non-Muslim countries were only expected to call others to join Islam in a way that fitted the societies in which they found themselves and not to engage in political struggles.[21] In this framework, Hizb al-Tahrir was especially active in Great Britain,[22] where, in 1986, a local branch of the party was founded that primarily had supporters among British people of South Asian descent and was led by Omar Bakri Muhammad (1958), who had a Syrian background.[23] The party engaged in preaching a politically charged Islamic message, particularly amongst students.[24] Because some members of the party believed Bakri demanded too much media attention for himself, he was dismissed from Hizb al-Tahrir in 1996, after which he set up his own organization, Al-Muhajiroun, which – unlike the party – also strove for a caliphate in Great Britain, was much more positive about groups such as Al-Qaida and went looking for confrontation with others.[25]

In 2003, Zallum died and was succeeded by the Palestinian engineer 'Ata' Abu l-Rushta (1943).[26] To get rid of its reputation of being tied to the much more controversial Al-Muhajiroun, Hizb al-Tahrir distanced itself from that group to such an extent that the party and its activities were not banned after the terrorist attacks committed by radical Islamists in London on 7 July 2005.[27] Still, the party remained controversial, not just because of its views on the caliphate, but also because of its rhetoric on Jews. Although Hizb al-Tahrir claims it is only anti-Zionist, has nothing against Jews and uses 'Jew' as a synonym for 'Zionist' or 'Israeli', as also happens in the Middle East sometimes, the party also refers to Jews as 'unbelievers', which – according to some – means that the group has anti-Semitic tendencies.[28] Whatever the case may be, and despite several attempts by some countries to ban the party, Hizb al-Tahrir is currently a legal organization in the West, except in Germany.[29]

How Hizb al-Tahrir Differs From the Muslim Brotherhood

Hizb al-Tahrir's ideology strongly overlaps with the Muslim Brotherhood's on several points. The party is against socialism (but also against capitalism), for example. It also views Islam as an all-encompassing ideology that has relevance for all aspects of life and it, too, strives for the application of the Sharia in daily life and politics, although al-Nabhani had different ideas

than the Muslim Brotherhood with regard to the precise details of this.[30]
Hizb al-Tahrir's stance on the Palestinian question also strongly resembles
that of the Muslim Brothers. Like them – apart from Hamas, which is more
pragmatic on this point – the party believes that no concessions are possible
in this respect, that all of Palestine is Islamic territory, that peace negotiations about this problem will not achieve anything and that the only way
to end the conflict is jihad against Israel.[31]

At the same time, there are also ideological differences between Hizb
al-Tahrir and the Muslim Brotherhood. The latter, for example, was briefly
inspired by the Islamic Revolution in Iran in 1979, as was the case with
Ennahda. Prior to the revolution, Hizb al-Tahrir had spoken several times
to its leader, Ayatollah Ruhollah Khomeini (1902–1989), and had encouraged
him to turn his Islamic republic into a state for all Muslims, not just Shiites.[32]
Hizb al-Tahrir had presented him with its writings, which more or less
amounted to a ready-made constitution, and they also proposed him as
caliph.[33] Yet, when it became clear that the Iranian regime attached much
greater value to Shiite identity and had incorporated this in the country's
new constitution, the party became frustrated by the regime and even
claimed that the United States had secretly been behind the revolution.[34]

Thus, Hizb al-Tahrir was (and is) in favour of revolution, albeit condition-
ally. Unlike in the struggle against Israel, it does not advocate jihad to bring
about revolution. In fact, jihad as a military struggle is of little practical value
to the party,[35] precisely because it connects this to the entity that must give
permission for this, namely, the caliphate,[36] which has not been founded
yet. Hizb al-Tahrir has neither engaged in terrorism throughout its history
nor has it fought against military targets.[37] As such, the coups that Hizb
al-Tahrir strives for in Muslim countries are non-violent in nature and the
party wants to stage these with popular support by seeking *nusra* ('help')
from other actors, for example within the army, so as to remove the rulers
without causing chaos or civil war.[38]

So, although Hizb al-Tahrir does not preach or strive for violence itself, its
method of trying to stage coups sets it apart from the Muslim Brotherhood.
Whereas the latter pursues slow and gradual change, Hizb al-Tahrir wants
direct and radical solutions.[39] Moreover, the party believes the desired
outcome of all this is a caliphate, which – in Hizb al-Tahrir's view – has
become an a-historical, idealized form of government[40] whose workings
al-Nabhani deals with extensively in his writings.[41] One website affiliated
with the party even counts the days since the abolition of the Ottoman
caliphate in 1924. As such, to this day Hizb al-Tahrir considers it a duty
of all Muslims to strive for the resurrection of this form of government.[42]

Origin and Development of the Palestinian Islamic Jihad

Although Hizb al-Tahrir has always been led by Palestinians and its members view the Palestinian issue as very important, its pan-Islamic character ensures that it is actually an international organization, rather than a Palestinian one. This is not the case with the Palestinian Islamic Jihad (the Islamic Jihad). This organization was started by Fathi al-Shiqaqi (1951–1995)[43] and 'Abd al-'Aziz 'Awda (1950), two Palestinians who had studied in Egypt, where they had become acquainted with radical groups and the revolutionary ideas of Sayyid Qutb.[44] Despite the fact that there were secular groups who were engaged in an armed struggle against Israel, Islamist organizations like the Muslim Brotherhood did not do so. Yet, there were minor Islamist attempts to start a jihad against Israel in the 1970s, including by the Palestinian Hizb al-Tahrir member As'ad al-Tamimi (1924–1997).[45] Dissatisfied with the quietist policy of the Muslim Brotherhood regarding Israel, al-Shiqaqi, 'Awda and a number of other members of the organization split off. Together with other Islamists, including al-Tamimi,[46] they founded the Islamic Jihad in 1980–1981, which was geared towards armed struggle with Israel.[47]

Prior to the intifada of 1987, the new organization concentrated on several activities – which, because of its stronger presence there, mostly took place in the Gaza Strip – including controlling a number of mosques. The organization recruited new members there, but also at universities – especially the Islamic University in Gaza – at social activities held on the occasion of Islamic feasts and among Palestinian prisoners in Israeli cells.[48] The Islamic Jihad was also connected with various magazines that represented its point of view through articles written by members of the organization.[49] The Islamic Jihad's most important activity, however, was attacking Israel, precisely because this was the reason the organization was founded. In the 1980s and the early 1990s, the group was also involved in several attacks against mostly Israeli military targets (but sometimes also civilians), which it committed with knives, guns and hand grenades that the organization had been able to smuggle from neighbouring countries.[50] Israel responded to this by arresting and imprisoning various members of the Islamic Jihad.[51]

When the Palestinian intifada broke out in 1987, the Islamic Jihad participated in armed actions and strikes against the Israeli occupation from early on.[52] Yet, the Islamic Jihad remained smaller than Hamas and non-Islamist groups such as Fatah, because the organization had fewer means and, unlike Hamas, did not have a broad social network that it could employ. Moreover, both al-Shiqaqi and 'Awda were expelled to Lebanon, which deprived the Islamic Jihad of its direct leadership, but this simultaneously enabled the organization to strengthen its ties with Hizbullah, a Lebanese Shiite group that was equally hostile to Israel, and its patron Iran. In Lebanon, the Islamic Jihad also continued its recruitment of Palestinians from refugee camps there, continued its struggle against Israel and also set up a new magazine in Beirut called *Al-Mujahid*.[53]

Just like Hamas, the Islamic Jihad rejected the peace process with Israel that started in the 1990s. The organization saw the Oslo Agreements in 1993 as a plan by Israel to gain peace without giving the Palestinians an independent and viable state in return. The Islamic Jihad underlined its rejection of these accords by committing attacks against Israel, which the latter only partially had an effective answer to.[54] Meanwhile, the Islamic Jihad had a critical attitude towards the Palestinian National Authority, which – the organization claimed – was too busy fighting militant organizations and spent too little time on building a Palestinian state.[55] The Islamic Jihad itself, precisely because it offered fewer social activities and did not enjoy the broad popular base that Hamas had, has never participated in parliamentary politics within the PNA. Partly because of this, the Islamic Jihad – whose leader al-Shiqaqi was assassinated by Israel in 1995 and was replaced by Ramadan Shalah (1958–2020),[56] who was succeeded by Ziyad Nakhala (1953) in 2018 – has never really outgrown its role as Hamas's little brother.

How the Palestinian Islamic Jihad Differs from the Muslim Brotherhood

The Islamic Jihad – even more so than Hizb al-Tahrir – has clear ideological similarities with the Muslim Brotherhood. Just like the Palestinian branch of the Muslim Brotherhood and Hamas, for instance, the organization was strongly influenced by the example of 'Izz al-Din al-Qassam and his struggle against British rule over Palestine in the 1930s.[57] Also, early Muslim Brothers like al-Banna and especially Sayyid Qutb have had an important influence on the Islamic Jihad's thinking about Islam as an activist religion.[58] As such, al-Shiqaqi's ideas on democracy and non-Muslims – though less important to the Islamic Jihad than to, for instance, Hamas, because of the organization's lack of parliamentary participation – are quite similar to those of the early Muslim Brotherhood.[59]

Yet, there are also considerable ideological differences between the Islamic Jihad and the Muslim Brotherhood. As is the case with Hizb al-Tahrir, these partly pertain to Iran and the revolution that took place there in 1979. Khomeini was such a great source of inspiration to Islamic Jihad that al-Shiqaqi wrote a book about him as a model. Unlike almost all Arab countries, the organization also supported Iran in its war with Iraq and it remained loyal to Iran, even when other Islamists had already turned their backs on the revolution and the regime there.[60] As a result, the Muslim Brotherhood labelled the Islamic Jihad a 'Shiite' group, a charge the organization defended itself against, but without distancing itself from its points of view.[61]

A second important difference between the Islamic Jihad and the Muslim Brotherhood is that the latter is a transnational group with local branches in various countries, while the Islamic Jihad is a more distinctly Palestinian national organization.[62] Moreover, whereas the Muslim Brotherhood cooperates with the regimes in the Arab world and does not view them as the enemy with regard to the Palestinian question, the Islamic Jihad sees the Arab regimes as part of the problem, accusing them of constituting a protective buffer around Israel and cooperating with America.[63] In fact, it takes a rather dim view of the idea of the state in general, believing states will invariably become authoritarian and preferring a strongly Islamic civil society.[64] Furthermore, for the Muslim Brotherhood, the Palestinian question is merely one (albeit important) issue, while it is the Islamic Jihad's raison d'être.[65] Because of this Palestinian nationalism, which did not manifest itself in Hamas until later, the Islamic Jihad has traditionally had relatively warm relations with secular factions like Fatah,[66] although – unlike such factions – it strives for the goal of Palestine as an Islamic state.[67]

A third difference between the Muslim Brotherhood and the Islamic Jihad has to do with both organizations' general approach: whereas the former applies gradualism in its political policies, the latter advocates direct action and criticizes the Muslim Brotherhood's approach.[68] The Islamic Jihad did not believe that a jihad against Israel could only be waged after society had been thoroughly Islamized and prepared for this, as the Palestinian Muslim Brotherhood believed before the rise of Hamas.[69] The creation of Hamas and its active engagement in armed struggle against Israel, including through the use of suicide attacks,[70] became a source of unity to the Islamic Jihad.[71] Because of the central role that armed struggle plays in the Islamic Jihad's ideology, the organization also consciously chooses to invest less in social activities and situates itself in the middle between the old quietist Palestinian Muslim Brotherhood, on the one hand, and the revolutionary Hizb al-Tahrir, on the other.[72]

The Revolutionaries: Al-Jama'a al-Islamiyya and Tanzim al-Jihad

We have already seen in this book that many Arabs started searching for a new ideology after 1967 following the military defeat by Israel in that year, the subsequent damage that this did to Nasser's Arab socialism and that they found their alternative in Islam. We have also read that the rise of Islam was stimulated by Egypt's President al-Sadat establishing a new power base for himself, which was separate from that of his predecessor. This 'Islamization' was made concrete in the 1970s through the building of mosques, more public displays of piety and increased political space for Islam, but also through more Islamic literature and a religious media offensive. This was partly related to the oil industry in Saudi Arabia: on the one hand, labourers from the oil industry who had worked there often returned to their home countries with more religiously conservative ideas; on the other, oil profits allowed Saudi Arabia to use its state propaganda to offer a conservative discourse as an alternative to Nasser's radical ideas and the revolution in Iran.[73]

This Saudi religious influence was also noticeable in Egypt, where the agendas of Saudi Arabia and President al-Sadat essentially reinforced each other.[74] The form of Islam exported from Saudi Arabia was not the one traditionally adhered to by most Muslims in Egypt, however, but stemmed from the ideas of the aforementioned eighteenth-century reformer Ibn 'Abd al-Wahhab. The adherents to his ideas, referred to above as 'Wahhabism', the central-Arabian variant of Salafism, therefore not only ensured the growth of Islam in Egypt, but also gave it a different tinge. It is within this ideological context that Al-Jama'a al-Islamiyya ('The Islamic Group') and Tanzim al-Jihad ('The Jihad Organization') came into being in Egypt in the 1970s and the 1980s.

Origin and Development of Al-Jama'a al-Islamiyya

So far, it has become clear that the Muslim Brotherhood or its descendants often recruited or were popular among students. This was also the case for Al-Jama'a al-Islamiyya or, more precisely, for *al-jama'at al-Islamiyya* ('the Islamic groups') that they first formed at universities from the late 1960s. These religious student groups functioned independently of each other, organized religious activities, tried to encourage students to live pious lives through literature and the sale of religious clothes and also provided things such as free transport or photocopies of lectures. In the 1970s, this student activism increased, encouraged by President al-Sadat, who saw it as a counterweight to left-wing students.[75] All of this took place in the context of al-Sadat's broader policy to present himself as a pious leader and to use Islam to buttress his own legitimacy. After a while, these student groups split up, however, into a trend that focussed on the north of the country, which mostly concentrated on Cairo and Alexandria and which supported the Muslim Brotherhood,[76] and a southern trend, whose identity was partly related to the poorer and less developed status of the south of Egypt.[77] Al-Jama'a al-Islamiyya would emerge from the latter trend.[78]

Around 1973, universities not only witnessed the rise of a subculture of sorts against Nasser's Arab socialism in Egypt, but the name 'Al-Jama'a al-Islamiyya' was also used to indicate a specific exponent of this subculture.[79] The activities of this group were aimed at encouraging an Islamic lifestyle among students in the 1970s, but it was also successful in university elections.[80] Yet, the services that the group provided to students gradually transformed into *hisba* ('control'), a concept used to describe the practice of supervision and enforcement of religious norms. Initially, this was only applied within universities against students with differing views, but later the group also applied it outside the university grounds. Moreover, after a while, Al-Jama'a al-Islamiyya's *hisba* took on violent forms as the group disrupted or attacked what it saw as sources of moral corruption, such as musical performances, film screenings and off-licences. The combination of services and *hisba* that Al-Jama'a al-Islamiyya was responsible for also allowed the organization to claim parts of the public sphere and, as such, gain ground on the Muslim Brotherhood, with which the group became embroiled in a battle for influence in the mosques.[81]

In the 1970s and 1980s, Al-Jama'a al-Islamiyya also became increasingly politicized, partly because of its participation in university politics, and it began adopting positions on various issues.[82] Possibly as a result of this, the group's *hisba* activities were expanded to include the harassment of Coptic Christians, imposing the classical Islamic *jizya* on them and stealing their money. This was condoned and religiously legitimized by the spiritual leader of Al-Jama'a al-Islamiyya, 'Umar 'Abd al-Rahman (1938–2017).[83] In 1980, the group even merged with Tanzim al-Jihad, another radical Islamist organization in Egypt, which had been responsible for the murder of President Anwar al-Sadat in 1981.[84] After the assassination, Al-Jama'a al-Islamiyya split off from Tanzim al-Jihad again because neither faction could agree on the group's leadership,[85] but in the same year Al-Jama'a al-Islamiyya itself attacked military personnel in the southern Egyptian city of Asyut. This action led to most of the organization's leaders being arrested and imprisoned.[86]

By the time some of the leadership of Al-Jama'a al-Islamiyya was released in 1984, the organization had changed. In prison, a new generation of ideologically well-versed and disciplined leaders had developed that spread the group's influence beyond Egypt's south.[87] This professionalization meant that Al-Jama'a al-Islamiyya was capable of creating several pockets of influence in southern cities, but also in poorer parts of the northern city of Cairo. In these areas, the group imposed its own social norms, developed an increasingly critical anti-regime discourse and attacked tourists, police officers, Coptic Christians and prominent civilians (including politicians).[88] Because of the social services that Al-Jama'a al-Islamiyya provided and the absence of the state in the underdeveloped areas in which the organization had settled, the regime arrested many people, but simultaneously allowed the group to partly continue its activities.[89]

In this context, Al-Jama'a al-Islamiyya's violence escalated. The group set up a military wing with its own leader in 1990[90] and committed terrorist attacks against intellectuals[91] and Copts, but also against tourists – an important source of income for Egypt, in the late 1990s.[92] This wave of violence, its economic consequences and a provocative remark made to an international press agency by one of the group's leaders that Imbaba, a neighbourhood in Cairo, had become an Islamic republic, caused the state to adopt a policy of general repression of Al-Jama'a al-Islamiyya in late 1992. This resulted in some 1,500 deaths and the imprisonment of 20,000 members, sympathisers and others who were somehow connected to Al-Jama'a al-Islamiyya.[93] This dealt a blow to the group and ensured that the organization had largely been beaten by the regime in 1997.[94]

At the same time as the military repression of Al-Jama'a al-Islamiyya was occurring, the regime tried to reach an understanding with the group. In the period 1993–1996, several initiatives were launched to come to a ceasefire agreement, but each of them failed.[95] In July 1997, however, the organization's leadership announced a unilateral ceasefire. This was jeopardized by continued violence – especially an attack in the southern Egyptian city of Luxor in 1997, in which 58 tourists and four police officers were killed and that had not been approved by the leadership – but the regime nevertheless eventually accepted the ceasefire.[96] Al-Jama'a al-Islamiyya also underwent a self-imposed ideological revisionism, in which it reinterpreted its core concepts to such an extent that they remained Salafi, but were no longer radical or violent.[97] The ceasefire with the state therefore came into force in 1999.[98] Not everyone agreed with this, however, including Rifa'i Ahmad Taha (1954–2016), a prominent military leader of the group who would later join Al-Qaida in Afghanistan,[99] which we will deal with later in this chapter.

How Al-Jama'a al-Islamiyya Differs From the Muslim Brotherhood

As we saw in Chapter 3, after the 1960s, the Egyptian Muslim Brotherhood increasingly became the organization of Hasan al-Hudaybi and other members who were prepared to work within the limits that the state offered them and to try to achieve its goals gradually and without the use of violence. This obviously came at the expense of the radical, revolutionary thought that clearly existed within the organization in the 1950s and 1960s, particularly in the writings of Qutb. While the Muslim Brotherhood itself rejected the controversial aspects of Qutb's ideas, the latter increasingly found a willing audience among people outside the organization who combined it with their adopted Salafi thought.[100]

One organization that had clearly been influenced by the radical ideas from within the Muslim Brotherhood was Al-Jama'a al-Islamiyya, which appeared to have adopted Qutb's concepts of *jahiliyya* and *hakimiyya*.[101] The group rejected the Muslim Brotherhood as an organization, however, precisely because the latter had denounced Qutb's radical ideas and his interpretation of concepts like *hakimiyya*,[102] besides the fact that the Muslim Brotherhood was not Salafi and Al-Jama'a al-Islamiyya was.[103] This group also actually agreed ideologically with what Qutb had written, e.g. the fundamental opposition it created between Islam and *jahiliyya*, the idea that the sovereignty of God should also be applied at the state level, the rejection of democracy and the need for jihad against the state.[104]

Although Al-Jama'a al-Islamiyya differed from the Muslim Brotherhood because of its Salafism and its revolutionary and violent approach, the group was not primarily geared towards staging coups (even though it did support the assassination of al-Sadat in 1981), instead focussing on 'cleansing' society by means of *hisba*.[105] This concept was based on 'commanding right and forbidding wrong', which the Muslim Brotherhood also gave expression to in its own way, as we saw in Chapter 2, but Al-Jama'a al-Islamiyya did so in a much more radical and violent way. In the group's ideology and practice, *hisba* and 'forbidding wrong' were not just directed against the state, but through the combination with violence, the concept also became a revolutionary means that basically boiled down to jihad against the regime.[106] This way, Al-Jama'a al-Islamiyya partly concurred with Tanzim al-Jihad.

Origin and Development of Tanzim al-Jihad

The Egyptian Tanzim al-Jihad took shape in 1980, when – under the leadership of the radical Islamist Muhammad 'Abd al-Salam Faraj (1954–1982), a consultation council of eleven members was formed. The organization built on smaller militant groups or their offshoots, which had existed since the 1970s, including parts of Al-Jama'a al-Islamiyya. As such, Tanzim al-Jihad was more or less an umbrella organization covering radical Islamists who wanted to wage Jihad against the Egyptian regime.[107] Although, on paper, Tanzim al-Jihad had a clear structure with different branches and departments,[108] the group remained only vaguely organized, partly because the structures of the different groups that were gathered under its name overlapped and people were not always aware of each other's activities, including attacks.[109] The latter was the most important activity of the organization, for which the aforementioned radical scholar 'Umar 'Abd al-Rahman gave religious justification through his fatwas.[110] That way, Tanzim al-Jihad is said to have been involved in attacking churches, robbing jewellers – which may have helped them finance the organization – infiltrating the army and preparing plans against the regime.[111]

To execute these plans, the organization also recruited actively, with Tanzim al-Jihad's members going to local mosques in the neighbourhoods where they lived. These were often smaller mosques that were not registered with the state, which enabled an illegal organization such as Tanzim al-Jihad to recruit new members in relative freedom. The organization also gained new members through family ties and acquaintances.[112] Because a considerable part of the group consisted of older networks in Upper Egypt as well as Cairo and its surroundings (where many southerners moved to), Tanzim al-Jihad's members often came from these areas as well.[113] With regard to their social background, they were generally young, lower middle class, had a strong political awareness and were relatively highly educated. There were also a number of soldiers among Tanzim al-Jihad membership.[114]

The Egyptian regime was only partly able to repress Tanzim al-Jihad's activities. In September 1981, over 1,500 (alleged) members of the organization were arrested, but this did not break the group's back. This became abundantly clear when, on 6 October of the same year, President al-Sadat was assassinated during a military parade by a Tanzim al-Jihad sympathizer, Khalid al-Islambuli (1958–1982), who was in attendance due to his position in the army.[115] It had actually been the organization's intention to unleash a revolution through the assassination of al-Sadat and also to occupy the radio and television building in Cairo, from where the coup could be announced.[116] Although Tanzim al-Jihad launched more attacks on 6 October and there were several clashes with the army in the weeks that followed, the organization's plan to start a revolution ultimately came to naught.[117] In fact, al-Islambuli, Faraj and three others were executed, many others were imprisoned and the organization as a whole gradually disintegrated after the assassination of al-Sadat, even though remaining members of the group continued to commit attacks until the early 1990s.[118]

Perhaps more important than the developments surrounding Tanzim al-Jihad in Egyptian society were the developments taking place in prison.

There, the soldier 'Abbud al-Zumur (1948) and the physician Ayman al-Zawahiri (1951) took on the leadership of the organization, still convinced that jihad against the regime was the best strategy.[119] Meanwhile, the Soviet Union had invaded Afghanistan in 1979, which ensured that this country started attracting Arabs who wanted to wage jihad against the occupying army. This enabled members of Tanzim al-Jihad who had evaded capture or who had been released again in the 1980s to escape repression in Egypt and give a different expression to their wish to fight. The Egyptian state also allowed this, presuming that the flight of the organization's members to Afghanistan would lead to a decrease in violence in Egypt itself.[120] Al-Zawahiri (and with him Tanzim al-Jihad) would ultimately join Osama bin Laden's Al-Qaida.[121]

How Tanzim al-Jihad Differs from the Muslim Brotherhood

Some members of Tanzim al-Jihad, including Faraj, had personal ties to the Muslim Brotherhood and radicalized outside the framework of that organization when it distanced itself from violence and revolution.[122] Yet, the influence of Qutb's work went much further than personal relations such as these. Because his treatment of concepts like *jahiliyya* was imprecise, as we saw in Chapter 2, it was not clear to whom this term applied: to society as a whole or only to the regime? This lack of clarity manifested itself in the 1970s, when several radical Islamist groups in Egypt started applying these ideas.[123] According to Shukri Mustafa (1942–1978), a former member of the Muslim Brotherhood, all of society should be seen as steeped in unbelief, which implied that pious Muslims should distance themselves from it.[124] His organization, Jama'at al-Muslimin ('The Group of the Muslims'), was therefore often referred to as Al-Takfir wa-l-Hijra ('Excommunication and Migration').[125] Tanzim al-Jihad did not go this far, however, and only applied this idea to the Egyptian regime.[126]

The fact that Tanzim al-Jihad had been influenced by Qutb's work does not mean that its members simply followed where his writings seemed to lead them. Its views of the West may have been hostile[127] – just like Qutb's – and its leaders had similar views to his on relations with non-Muslims – although the organization also used actual violence against Egyptian Christians[128] – but its Salafi inclination was something not shared by Qutb. This was partly made clear by its vision of the Sharia. Whereas the Muslim Brotherhood (and Qutb) believed in a certain flexibility with regard to the Sharia and also strove for a general application of Islam, Tanzim al-Jihad's Salafi approach was much more precise about what was and what was not allowed, which meant that the organization also saw a greater discrepancy between its own ideals and the concrete reality of Egyptian politics.[129]

The organization's Salafi approach to politics was mostly manifested in Tanzim al-Jihad's views on the Egyptian state. Although its choice in favour of violence against the regime is certainly not typical of Salafis – most of whom are peaceful – its reasoning on why the regime was infidel was. In *Al-Farida al-Gha'iba* ('The Absent Duty'),[130] a book by Faraj that constituted the organization's most important ideological document, the author draws a parallel between the Mongols, who conquered large parts of the Muslim world and would also convert to Islam in the Middle Ages, and the Egyptian regime. Just as the Mongols allegedly disqualified themselves as Muslims because they did not fully apply Islamic law in their rule, so, too, did the Egyptian rulers. That is why it was important to fight the Egyptian regime through jihad ('the absent duty') – just like the Mongols had done. Although the outcome of this analysis – jihad against the regime for not applying the Sharia – strongly resembles Qutb's, Faraj distinguished his work from this Muslim Brother's by referring mostly to classical scholars, in particular Ibn Taymiyya (1263–1328), a highly appreciated and widely cited scholar among contemporary Salafis.[131]

In response to Faraj's work, the Egyptian mufti at the time, Jad al-Haqq (1917–1996), wrote an extensive religious refutation, perhaps because Faraj himself had made far-reaching religious claims with arguments and sources that Qutb had never touched upon. The mufti criticized Faraj because, according to al-Haqq, he had misunderstood Ibn Taymiyya, which meant that the parallel with the Mongols was incorrect and that the Egyptian state could definitely be considered Islamic.[132] He therefore described the members of Tanzim al-Jihad as Khawarij, a reference to the early-Islamic group that also rebelled against the ruler on the basis of religious arguments. 'Abd al-Rahman, the group's spiritual leader, dismissed this accusation entirely in his defence during the court case against Tanzim al-Jihad, however, and pointed out that the organization actually consisted of pious Muslims who, through their attack on the regime, stood up for the application of the Sharia in the country.[133] By doing so, he reaffirmed the direct, radical Salafi and violent character of Tanzim al-Jihad, which were precisely the characteristics that made the organization so different from the Muslim Brotherhood.

The Global Jihadis: Al-Qaida and the Islamic State

Several leaders of Al-Jama'a al-Islamiyya and Tanzim al-Jihad, such as Rifa'i Ahmad Taha and Ayman al-Zawahiri, had gone to Afghanistan, as we saw above. They were not the only ones, however. Chapter 3 briefly mentioned that some members of the Fighting Vanguard, which emerged from the Syrian Muslim Brotherhood, fled abroad to escape repression in Syria. Dozens of them ended up in Afghanistan.[134] Radical Islamist organizations had also revolted against their regimes in other Arab countries, chiefly Algeria. They had clearly failed in their revolutionary jihad – sometimes after years of struggle – and ultimately lost. They had also fled abroad sometimes, including to Afghanistan.[135] Where a new phenomenon came into existence, namely, global jihad. The two standard bearers of this armed struggle, which were only indirectly related to the Muslim Brotherhood and increasingly expressed criticism of that organization, were (and are) Al-Qaida and the Islamic State.

Origin and Development of Al-Qaida

Afghanistan was thus not simply a safe haven for Islamists on the run, but also the cradle of global jihad. A crucial event in the rise of this phenomenon was the invasion of Afghanistan by the Soviet Union in 1979, intended to support the communist Afghan regime in the context of the Cold War. Many Afghan and Arab Islamists saw this as an invasion of a Muslim country by a non-Muslim world power. As such, many Afghan Islamists rose up in armed resistance against this foreign occupation[136] and Afghanistan became a magnet for Arab fighters wanting to wage jihad against the Soviets.[137] In 1984, 'Abdallah 'Azzam (1941–1989),[138] a Jordanian Muslim Brother of Palestinian descent, founded the Maktab al-Khidamat ('The Services Bureau') in Peshawar, Pakistan, which he used to welcome many of these tens of thousands of Arab fighters to educate and train them for battle in Afghanistan.[139] Yet, not all Afghan and Arab fighters were Islamists, let alone revolutionaries. Many were primarily motivated by the struggle against the Soviet Union and the liberation of Afghanistan, which was the reason why several Muslim countries, such as Pakistan and Saudi Arabia – as well as the United States, which saw the Soviet Union as its Cold War rival – supported them.[140]

One of the Arab fighters who came to Afghanistan in the 1980s was Osama bin Laden, a Saudi millionaire who became wealthy off the back of his father's building enterprise. Although he would later be known as a terrorist, he had not yet become one in this period of his life. Because of his wealth, the building materials that he supplied and the influence that he had gained, his role in Afghanistan became increasingly important and he financed the Arab fighters who came to Peshawar to train with 'Azzam there.[141]

This does not mean, however, that there were no revolutionary Islamists from Arab countries in Afghanistan; there were, with al-Zawahiri as their most prominent representative. He and others gained more and more influence over Bin Laden, causing tensions between the Saudi millionaire and 'Azzam.[142] When the latter died in an attack under mysterious circumstances in 1989,[143] Bin Laden – with the help of al-Zawahiri and others – continued the work of Maktab al-Khidamat by building his own organization that had already been founded in 1988 and that would eventually become known as 'Al-Qaida' ('The Base').[144]

After the Soviet Union had withdrawn from Afghanistan in 1989, Bin Laden returned to Saudi Arabia. Like many other Saudis, he was very critical about the state's decision to allow half a million American troops into the country to defend it against a possible attack by Iraq, which had just invaded Kuwait in 1990.[145] During the 1990s, Bin Laden became increasingly critical of Saudi Arabia's policies and its alleged unwillingness to govern entirely according to Islam, including in its foreign affairs.[146] It was in this context that Bin Laden's citizenship was revoked by Saudi Arabia in 1994[147] and that he moved to Sudan, where he, al-Zawahiri and others stayed under the care of Hasan al-Turabi. There, Bin Laden expanded his international network, got involved in several attacks[148] and increasingly radicalized (with al-Zawahiri) in the direction of a struggle against the West.[149] Because of these developments, it became increasingly difficult for Sudan to provide a safe haven for Bin Laden and to reject international extradition requests. In 1996, Bin Laden and some of his supporters therefore left and went to Afghanistan again.[150]

The situation in Afghanistan had not remained stagnant after the withdrawal of the Soviets and the end of the Cold War: the country had come under the control of the Afghan jihad fighters in 1992,[151] but in 1996 the Taliban[152] rose to power, a group of originally Pakistani students who had conquered the country through force of arms and submitted it to their regime.[153] Bin Laden forged close ties with the Taliban in Afghanistan and also financed the group.[154] Under their protection, Al-Qaida became the networked organization within which radicals of aforementioned groups such as Al-Jama'a al-Islamiyya and Tanzim al-Jihad found their place.[155] As such, Al-Qaida published a declaration in 1996 in which it stated that it was going to wage jihad against America because of – among other reasons – the latter's alleged occupation of Saudi Arabia.[156] In 1998, Al-Qaida also announced Al-Jabha al-Islamiyya al-'Alamiyya li-Jihad al-Yahud wa-l-Salibiyyin ('The World Islamic Front for Jihad Against the Jews and the Crusaders')[157] in a declaration in which the organization called for a global jihad and that had also been signed by Taha and al-Zawahiri.[158] Al-Qaida reinforced these declarations through a series of attacks on American targets in several countries, including Tanzania, Kenya and Yemen,[159] as well as in America itself, on 11 September 2001.[160]

In response to the attacks in America, the United States (as part of an international coalition) launched the War on Terror, which involved the invasion of Afghanistan to drive out Al-Qaida. This attack deprived the Taliban of its power, dealt a blow to Al-Qaida and eventually led to the death of Bin Laden in 2011, but also caused the organization to fragmentation. Simultaneously, local groups outside of Afghanistan had become inspired by Al-Qaida and tried to join the organization, leading to the rise of a somewhat interconnected network of local terrorist groups that were all at least nominally part of Al-Qaida.[161] The most prominent exponents of this, which could often – though not always – be found in countries with a weak central government, were Al-Qaida in Iraq after the fall of the regime there in 2003,[162] Al-Qaida in Saudi Arabia in the same period,[163] Al-Qaida in Yemen from 2007[164] and Al-Qaida in North Africa from 2007.[165] After the beginning of the Arab Spring and the uprisings against the regime in Syria in 2011, a similar process took place in that country, where Syrian groups functioned as local branches of Al-Qaida.[166]

How Al-Qaida Differs from the Muslim Brotherhood

Despite the fact that Al-Qaida did not directly arise from the Muslim Brotherhood, there were nevertheless ideological similarities between both organizations. Not only were Al-Qaida's views on the states in the Muslim world heavily influenced by Qutb's,[167] but Bin Laden's early criticism of the Saudi regime was also clearly sympathetic to the *sahwa*, the most important representative of the Muslim Brotherhood's thought in Saudi Arabia.[168] Yet, apart from the fact that both organizations shared a broadly Islamist outlook, that was as far as the similarities went. Moreover, Qutb had not represented the Muslim Brotherhood since the 1960s and Bin Laden only spoke positively about the *sahwa* at a time when he had not yet become the radical that he would later be.

Apart from the Salafi character of Al-Qaida, it was mostly the organization's views on jihad that distinguished it from the Muslim Brotherhood. Whereas the latter had reserved this theme for the fight against non-Islamic rule of Muslim countries since the 1960s – the most prominent example being Israel – Al-Qaida did not just go along with the revolutionary thought of organizations such as Al-Jama'a al-Islamiyya and Tanzim al-Jihad, but went even further in this respect. According to Al-Qaida, an important reason why 'un-Islamic' regimes in the Arab world could not be overthrown by revolutionary Islamists was that they were supported by the West. By directly attacking Western countries, Al-Qaida would provoke a counterattack that would subsequently cause the Muslim community to side with the organization. This would result in a war of attrition that would cause Western countries – especially America – to withdraw their support for regimes in Muslim countries, which, in turn, would become weakened to such an extent that they could be overthrown by Al-Qaida after all.[169]

The armed (and terrorist) struggle against the West intended to ultimately overthrow the regimes in the Muslim world was so far removed from the much more practical, political and pragmatic method of the Muslim Brotherhood that it was not surprising that Al-Qaida expressed criticism of this organization. The current leader of Al-Qaida, al-Zawahiri, has even dedicated an entire book to the Muslim Brotherhood's supposedly bad practices, *Al-Hisad al-Murr: Al-Ikhwan al-Muslimun fi Sittin 'Amman* ('The Bitter Crop: Sixty Years of the Muslim Brotherhood').[170] In this book, he criticizes the organization for its acceptance of democracy and the rights of Christians,[171] as well as its lack of jihad and its political participation.[172] Even Hamas, the only branch of the Muslim Brotherhood that truly engages in armed jihad, is criticized by Al-Qaida for its acceptance of democracy[173] and its struggle against radical groups in the Gaza Strip.[174] It is not surprising therefore that, contrary to the idea that the Muslim Brotherhood and Al-Qaida are similar terrorist organizations, it has been suggested that the Muslim Brotherhood could serve as a pragmatic and peaceful alternative to Al-Qaida, thus depriving the latter of part of its popularity.[175]

Origin and Development of the Islamic State

Whereas Al-Qaida came into existence during the aftermath of the war in Afghanistan in the 1980s, the Islamic State (IS) developed in the years directly after the American invasion of Iraq in 2003. This war was launched after the attacks of 11 September 2001 and was based on the (incorrect) assumption that Saddam Hussein's regime had been involved in these attacks and was also developing weapons of mass destruction. The American-led international coalition that overthrew the Iraqi regime was initially successful, but also dismantled the army, the ruling party and the bureaucracy, resulting in a power vacuum that several militant groups exploited to settle in the country.[176] One of these groups was Jama'at al-Tawhid wa-l-Jihad ('The Group of [God's] Unity and Jihad'), which had already been founded in 1999[177] by the aforementioned Abu Mus'ab al-Zarqawi,[178] a radical Islamist from Jordan.[179]

The chaos that erupted in Iraq as a result of the power vacuum created a situation in which all the various sectarian groups in the country could easily be pitted against each other. This was exacerbated by the fact that Sunni Arabs had had the most power under Saddam Hussein's rule through the institutions that had now been dismantled by the international coalition. The majority Shiite population, however, could translate their demographic size into a parliamentary majority in democratic elections. The new situation after the fall of the Iraqi regime was therefore not only a blow to the old rulers, but also threatened to bring the Shiite community to power, with all the possible consequences this might have for Sunni Arabs. Al-Zarqawi played into that situation with a strongly anti-Shiite discourse and attacks directed against Shiites, thereby contributing to sectarianism in the country.[180]

Although anti-Shiite ideas were widely held among (radical) Salafis,[181] Al-Qaida's leaders were critical of al-Zarqawi's policies in this respect. In 2004, it nevertheless decided – probably because of the weakening of the organization after the war in Afghanistan of 2001 – to accept Jama'at al-Tawhid wa-l-Jihad as the Iraqi branch of Al-Qaida.[182] This new organization was responsible for attacks against Shiites and many others[183] and played an important role in the civil war that developed in Iraq in the years after 2004.[184] Al-Zarqawi would only live to see some of this, however, since he was killed by the United States in a bomb attack in 2006.[185]

An important step in the concrete founding of IS was taken after al-Zarqawi's death, when Al-Qaida in Iraq was renamed Dawlat al-'Iraq al-Islamiyya ('The Islamic State of Iraq'; ISI) in 2006. This reflected the power and influence that the organization enjoyed in the Sunni areas of the country, where the Iraqi state did not have much of either. This simultaneously started a rift between Al-Qaida and the organization that would later be known as IS: from this moment, it was not exactly clear whether ISI did or did not belong to Al-Qaida, despite the sympathy that both groups publicly expressed for each other.[186] ISI's new leaders, the Egyptian Abu Ayyub al-Masri (1968–2010) and the Iraqi Abu 'Umar al-Baghdadi (1959–2010), had a difficult job, however, considering the fact that a growing resentment against ISI's activities was developing within Sunni parts of the country. The tribes in these areas therefore started cooperating with the United States and rose up against ISI,[187] during which both al-Masri and al-Baghdadi were killed in 2010. Consequently, the organization as a whole was largely destroyed and its leadership was passed on to the Iraqi Abu Bakr al-Baghdadi (1971–2019).[188]

ISI was seriously weakened in 2010, but had not been entirely beaten. When American troops pulled out of Iraq in 2011, various members of the organization were released, which strengthened ISI. Moreover, the frustration among Sunnis – who, as had been feared, were shut out of power by the largely Shiite government of the country – was still present. Furthermore, ISI also forged ties with the Sunni tribes it had initially alienated.[189] The most important factor that gave ISI new life, however, was the Arab Spring or, more precisely, the uprisings against the Syrian regime that started in 2011 and that offered the organization the chance to expand. ISI did this by setting up a cell in Syria in the same year, which would eventually be called Jabhat al-Nusra ('The Support Front').[190] Despite the fact that Jabhat al-Nusra's leader had pledged an oath of fealty to Al-Qaida, in 2013, al-Baghdadi announced that the group in Syria would be ISI's local branch and that the organization would be called Al-Dawla al-Islamiyya fi l-'Iraq wa-l-Sham ('The Islamic State in Iraq and Syria';[191] ISIS). By doing so, the organization formally broke with Al-Qaida, after which part of Jabhat al-Nusra would continue under Al-Qaida's name, while another part joined ISIS.[192]

The new organization had not finished expanding, however. In 2014, it declared that al-Baghdadi was the new caliph and the organization received yet another name: Al-Dawla al-Islamiyya ('The Islamic State'). Dropping the explicit reference to Iraq and Syria indicated that the territorial ambitions of the organization went further than just those two countries. Various radical groups in other areas pledged fealty to IS's alleged caliphate and Muslims from all over the world have joined the organization.[193] The declaration of a caliphate by IS was not just a challenge to Iraq, Syria and the international community that had to deal with this, but it also constituted an attempt to definitively dethrone Al-Qaida as the most prominent jihad organization in the world. Both organizations therefore contested each other's legitimacy, fought each other[194] and – even after the loss of IS's territory in both Iraq and Syria and the death of al-Baghdadi in 2019 – continue as separate organizations to this day.

How the Islamic State Differs from the Muslim Brotherhood

Just like Al-Qaida, IS is a radical Salafi organization, both of which differ from the Muslim Brotherhood in this regard. Yet, the ideological differences between the latter and IS go deeper than the points on which Al-Qaida differs from the Muslim Brotherhood. First, IS, just like its predecessors under the direction of al-Zarqawi, is a clearly anti-Shiite organization, while the Muslim Brotherhood, as we have seen, is far less outspoken about this.

For example, in its magazine *Dabiq*, IS describes Shiites as an un-Islamic sect and as anti-Sunni people who make common cause with Christians.[195] Moreover, IS portrays Shiites as part of a fifth column, as conspirators who have conspired against Islam from the beginning and who are part of that religion to destroy it from within.[196] As such, according to IS, Shiites are not actually Muslims (partly because of their allegedly depraved ideas and rituals), who – in a continuation of al-Zarqawi's attacks against them – should be killed wherever they are.[197]

A second issue on which IS differs strongly from the Muslim Brotherhood (and even Al-Qaida) is its attempt to establish a caliphate. Although the model of a caliphate also played a role among the early Muslim Brothers, al-Banna viewed the exact resurrection of it as neither realistic nor desirable and this issue was, therefore, of theoretical importance to the Muslim Brotherhood at best, as we saw in Chapter 2. Even Al-Qaida, which was not against the founding of a caliphate, has never taken concrete action to achieve this. For IS, on the other hand, it was central to its ideology and it took this quite seriously, which partly manifested itself in the position of Abu Bakr al-Baghdadi, who had to fulfil the criteria of a caliph – which included that he had to be a descendant of the Prophet's Quraysh tribe.[198]

A third issue on which IS differs strongly with the Muslim Brotherhood is the use of violence. Not only does IS use violence to achieve goals – the overthrow of regimes, territorial expansion, the enforcement of the Sharia – which the Muslim Brotherhood does not support, but the type of violence that IS uses is also different (even from that used by Al-Qaida). The organization has, for example, frequently beheaded journalists, charity workers and others. It has legitimized this action on the basis of Koranic texts and has disseminated it across the world through videos.[199] The organization has also reintroduced slavery for the 'polytheist' Yazidis, a religious minority in Iraq, whose women were appropriated by IS in order to act as their wives. Although slavery had long been abolished in Muslim countries, IS reintroduced it, justifying this by citing Islamic texts and practices from the time of the Prophet Muhammad.[200]

Just like Al-Qaida, IS has been clear about its hostility towards the Muslim Brotherhood, criticizing the latter on the aforementioned points. As such, IS states that the organization has become an apostate group and calls it a 'cancer', partly because of its supposedly good ties with Shiites and Iran,[201] as well as its support for interreligious dialogue with Jews and Christians.[202] IS is also critical of the Muslim Brotherhood with respect to the issue of the caliphate. It scolds the organization for having participated in parliamentary elections, for supporting democracy and for having subscribed to supposedly un-Islamic constitutions in Muslim countries since the time of al-Banna, all of which IS entirely rejects.[203] As far as violence is concerned, IS accuses the Muslim Brotherhood of being peaceful and respecting allegedly un-Islamic human rights.[204] It also blames the organization for accepting and even praising the Egyptian regime.[205] Thus, on all these points, IS distances itself from the Muslim Brotherhood. So, although IS still has a link with the Muslim Brotherhood in a very general sense – the application of the Sharia (albeit interpreted very differently) and Islam as an all-encompassing ideology – further comparisons do not hold.

***

The organisations dealt with in this chapter all have in common that they are radical, but also that they – very general similarities notwithstanding – differ (strongly) from the Muslim Brotherhood. The split-offs Hizb al-Tahrir and the Palestinian Islamic Jihad mostly differ from the Muslim Brotherhood because they strive for a revolutionary ideal in the form of a caliphate (Hizb al-Tahrir) or an Islamic state (Islamic Jihad). Al-Jama'a al-Islamiyya and Tanzim al-Jihad do not just differ from the Muslim Brotherhood because of their Salafi character, but also because they are prepared to express their revolutionary goals by means of jihad against their own regimes instead of through parliamentary participation. Al-Qaida and IS, finally, differ on all these points with the Muslim Brotherhood and build on them by striving for a worldwide jihad and, in the case of IS, by being anti-Shiite and even wanting to found a present-day caliphate. In the context of the idea that the Muslim Brotherhood is a terrorist organization or secretly has plans in that sphere, we cannot deny that all of the aforementioned organizations have distanced themselves from the Muslim Brotherhood, be it by splitting from or openly criticizing it.

7.   Liberals

In the previous chapters, we have seen that the early Muslim Brotherhood had a particular ideology, but that, over the years, the organization has dealt with this in a flexible way and, moreover, that this flexibility (but also the original ideology itself) has garnered much criticism from radical Islamist groups. All of this suggests that the Muslim Brotherhood has truly developed. Still, one could claim that the Muslim Brotherhood's flexibility is merely an attempt to fool outsiders and does not represent any true ideological development. In other words: has the Muslim Brotherhood not secretly remained a theocratic and anti-democratic organization that has merely adjusted its ways for pragmatic reasons? This question is connected with the second position in academic debates on the Muslim Brotherhood, which will also be addressed in this chapter with regard to three phenomena that are strongly connected with today's Muslim Brothers: the *wasatiyya* ('centrism'); post-Islamism; and the Jordanian ZamZam Initiative as a concrete expression of post-Islamism. Each of these three phenomena can be called liberal because they all strive for a freer, looser interpretation of the Koran, the Sunna and the Sharia than the early Muslim Brotherhood did.

Wasatiyya: The Foundation of Reforms

The term *wasatiyya* is somewhat controversial. This is not because it is seen as negative, but precisely because it has a positive connotation and Muslims like applying it to themselves. In a general sense, it denotes the idea of the golden mean between the various religious extremes. In sura 2:143, the Koran states that God has made Muslims into a 'midmost nation' (*ummatan wasatan*), which points to its desirability and also constitutes the source of the term *wasatiyya*.[1] As such, this term is used and applied by divergent groups of Muslims, all of whom claim to strive for this balanced or centrist approach in the way they experience their faith.[2] This section, however, deals with a specific trend within Islam that, like the Muslim Brotherhood itself, is rooted in the modernist reforms of the nineteenth and the early twentieth centuries.[3] In their interpretation and vision of the Sharia, its adherents strive for a middle path between what they see as an excessively textual or literal method, on the one hand, and an approach that they believe has too little consideration for the text or Islam in general, on the other.[4]

The most important representative of the *wasatiyya* is undoubtedly the Egyptian Islamist Yusuf al-Qaradawi (1926),[5] a scholar who has not only written about *wasatiyya* for decades in his books,[6] but who has also systematized, institutionalized and popularized it since the 1990s.[7] At the same time, al-Qaradawi has long been affiliated with the Muslim Brotherhood – which he actually used to be a member of.[8] It is notable that al-Qaradawi clearly turned against Qutb's views[9] and, at one point, he was even offered the leadership of the organization.[10] His most important role in the Muslim Brotherhood, however, has been his highly influential position as an ideologue, scholar and teacher to the organization.[11]

Wasatiyya as an Approach

As mentioned, the *wasatiyya* is rooted in and, indeed, builds on the reformist ideas of earlier modernist thinkers. Central to this is that the balanced and centrist approach of the *wasatiyya* – which adherents claim was typical of the earliest Muslims – demands a process of renewal: the aforementioned *tajdid*.[12] Concretely, this should manifest itself in various ways, including via *taysir* ('easing', 'facilitation'). On the basis of Koranic verses such as sura 5:9 ([...] God does not desire to make any impediment for you [...]), al-Qaradawi states that Islam should not make life needlessly difficult for people and should try to ease their burdens, making *taysir* a religious duty. This means that if there are multiple legal options in any given case, the easiest option should be chosen; necessity makes forbidden things permissible to a certain extent and prohibition should be based on reliable sources and the individuals and contexts involved should be taken into account.[13]

A second aspect of renewal that is necessary for *wasatiyya* to flourish is the aforementioned *ijtihad*, which refers to the individual interpretation of the Koran and the Sunna, independent of earlier legal decisions in existing schools of Islamic law. In order to be able to arrive at new legal rulings, it is important to take into account the circumstances in which the texts came about, to distinguish generalities from specifics, to read all sources in light of the Koran and to change fatwas if the context changes as well.[14] Yet, such a process may open the door to all kinds of decisions that are far beyond the existing frameworks of Islamic legal thought. An important guiding light for *ijtihad* within the *wasatiyya* is therefore formed by the *qawa'id fiqhiyya* ('legal principles'): short phrases (for instance: 'Damage must be taken away' or 'Acts should be judged on the basis of intentions') that indicate general legal guidelines and that are closely connected with the aforementioned *maqasid al-Shari'a* ('the purposes of Islamic law').[15]

Al-Qaradawi uses principles like these in such a way that they constitute the basis of, but also limit, *ijtihad*. By taking these general principles as a starting point (instead of using specific rulings that have been reached earlier as one's point of departure), more Islamic legal options become available, but they are simultaneously limited so as not to go too far. This forms an important legal basis for al-Qaradawi's *wasatiyya*.[16]

To what situations exactly these means of reform are applied is strongly dependent on the concept of *maslaha* ('interest'): the area or topic in which the interests of the individual Muslim or that of the entire Muslim community lies. This term has a long history in Islamic law. The mediaeval scholar Abu Hamid al-Ghazali (c. 1058–1111) distinguished between interests for which there is a textual basis, such as the preservation of life, and interests for which this is not the case. Within this latter category, he distinguished three types of interests (in order of decreasing importance): *darurat* ('necessities'); *hajat* ('needs'); and *tahsinat* ('improvements') and *tayzinat* ('embellishments'). Whereas al-Ghazali states that laws can be adjusted in cases of *darurat* that are certain and concern the entire community, other scholars – including al-Qaradawi – build on this principle by stating that the less necessary *hajat* also legitimize the amending of laws.[17] This assumes, however, that a Muslim scholar should also have knowledge of the political and societal context in which legal rulings are drawn up. Al-Qaradawi calls this *fiqh al-waqi'* ('the jurisprudence of reality').[18]

Wasatiyya on Politics

Because al-Qaradawi has played such an important role in the development of the *wasatiyya* and has had so much influence on the Muslim Brotherhood, the theory mentioned above has been translated into political practice. Al-Qaradawi's preparedness to review Islamic tradition and to reform it on the basis of the *maslaha* of Muslims today has led to all kinds of changes. With regard to the view of the state and political participation, this has resulted in the acceptance of non-Islamic legislation as long as it does not clash with the Sharia[19] and, in a broader sense, it makes explicit the idea of an Islamic state as a civil state with an Islamic authority. The latter entails that the state is not led by scholars and that the rulers and their rule are limited by the Sharia *and* by the people.[20] Concretely, this means that the Muslim community holds the ruler to account, that the ruler serves the people and that democracy is allowed, but within the boundaries of the Sharia.[21] As such, it is not surprising that al-Qaradawi has spoken out in favour of party pluralism, political participation and parliaments.[22]

As for societal issues, al-Qaradawi and like-minded scholars have expressed views on especially the rights of non-Muslims and women. On these topics, the *wasatiyya*'s adherents state that non-Muslims should be treated as equals and – just like al-Banna – they emphasize sura 60:8 (Muslims must be friendly to non-Muslims who have not fought them).[23] Yet, unlike among early Muslim Brothers, this explicitly translates into equal rights, for example for Copts in Egyptian society.[24] Moreover, the early Muslim Brothers often spoke of non-Muslims as *dhimmi*s, while al-Qaradawi has clearly moved away from this term in his writings on this subject, to the more inclusive *muwatana* ('citizenship'), which implies an equal position for everyone.[25] Still, for al-Qaradawi, too, there are limits: he continues to excludes non-Muslims from the position of head of state in an Islamic state and he also writes that, in such a context, the majority of the members of parliament should be Muslims.[26]

Al-Qaradawi makes an important distinction between the political rights of non-Muslims and women. According to adherents of the *wasatiyya*, women can become heads of state, which means they go further than the early Muslim Brother al-Siba'i did.[27] Yet, even the discourse of the *wasatiyya* in al-Qaradawi's writings remains conservative with regard to what women are allowed to do in the daily practice of marriage and family life,[28] probably because there are many clear texts about this issue that, according to his own *wasatiyya* method, he cannot ignore. Al-Qaradawi nevertheless sees room to provide women with more rights through the means that the *wasatiyya* offers. In deciding his point of view on the covering of women's bodies, for example, he chooses precisely the legal option that is easiest for women (namely, that the face and hands do not have to be covered) and also explains this as such.[29] Al-Qaradawi also only applies the words 'managers of the affairs of women' from sura 4:34 – which can be used to keep women in a subservient role – to the family situation, thereby clearing the way for leadership positions for women outside the family, for instance in politics.[30] Al-Qaradawi supports this by using the concept of 'necessity' to point to the importance of having pious Islamic women in politics (so as not to give free reign to secular feminists), thereby further underlining their right to political participation.[31]

Hizb al-Wasat

The ideas expressed by the *wasatiyya* were not just an ideological trend, but were also translated into political practice. We have already seen this above in the way the Muslim Brotherhood in several countries was prepared to deviate from the ideas of the early leaders of the organization, especially in the arenas of the state and political participation, but it would also express itself in a new political party in Egypt named Hizb al-Wasat ('The Party of the Middle').[32] This party was rooted in the reformist trend that mostly consisted of Egyptian Muslim Brothers who had gone to university in the 1970s (and were thus not part of the old guard that had been repressed by Nasser in the 1950s). These were the people who had gained democratic and organizational experience in the professional syndicates in the 1980s and 1990s. Because of the differences between their democratic experiences in these professional organizations, on the one hand, and the organizational practices of the relatively autocratic and hierarchically led Muslim Brotherhood, on the other, they became increasingly frustrated.[33]

This frustration was exacerbated when 'Umar al-Tilmisani, the third General Guide of the Egyptian Muslim Brotherhood, died in 1986 and was succeeded by two men who had more or less been appointed, not chosen. Others were not just angry about this process, but these successors also brought people with more rigid points of view back into the organization with them, to the frustration of the more reformist, younger generation of Muslim Brothers.[34] This was also connected with ideological differences between the old guard of leaders within the organization and the younger ones: the latter clearly had different ideas about issues such as political pluralism, citizenship, women's rights and the rights of non-Muslims in Egyptian society.[35]

Because the reformist, younger members of the Muslim Brotherhood had little hope left that they would be able to shape their ideas within the framework of the organization, they decided to found Hizb al-Wasat in 1996. Although 62 out of the 74 people who had founded the party came from the Muslim Brotherhood, it also counted women and Coptic Christians among its founders.[36] The official approval of the party was rejected, however, because the Muslim Brotherhood did not have its own party in this period and Hizb al-Wasat was seen by the authorities as an attempt by the organization to get such a party accepted. The regime also claimed that the initiative did not add anything to the existing party sphere.[37] The party was rejected again, in 1998, when it tried to register once more, in a different form and with fewer members from the Muslim Brotherhood.[38]

Although there are indications that the Muslim Brotherhood was initially positively inclined towards the initiative to found a party,[39] the organization quickly became very critical of what it saw as an attempt by younger members to evade its authority. It therefore called on those Muslim Brothers involved to return to the fold, which a number of them did. The old guard also tried to regain control over the Muslim Brotherhood.[40] Despite this, Hizb al-Wasat did enjoy the explicit support of al-Qaradawi[41] and the party's ideology clearly stemmed from the ideas and views of the *wasatiyya*.[42] Moreover, the party represented a trend within the Egyptian Muslim Brotherhood that would not just disappear. Firstly, not all reformers within the organization had been involved with Hizb al-Wasat, which indicated that the party was not the only one representing the trend of renewal.[43] Secondly, repression by the state led the Muslim Brotherhood, which initially did not seem to have any intention of changing in response to Hizb al-Wasat, to move in the direction of this party in the 1990s and the beginning of the new millennium.[44] This suggests that, despite not having succeeded in participating as an official party, Hizb al-Wasat nevertheless did have some ideological influence that transcended its organizational impact.

Wasatiyya Ideas in the Muslim Brotherhood and Hizb al-Wasat

The reformist *wasatiyya* ideology can be found in the Muslim Brotherhood to some extent, but especially in Hizb al-Wasat and its views about the same political issues (the state, political participation and societal rights and freedoms) that I have analysed in this book so far. With regard to the state, it is clear that the Muslim Brotherhood subscribes to the aforementioned view of a 'civil state with an Islamic authority', which *wasatiyya* thinkers also support.[45] To the organization, this is – among other things – related to the application of the Sharia. The question is, however, who gets to decide what the Sharia entails. According to some Muslim Brothers, in a civil state this is done by the people, meaning that the contents of the Sharia are democratically decided, while others believe that this should be done by (unelected) scholars[46] or that the people should only have a say in matters on which the Sharia is silent.[47] Hizb al-Wasat seems to take the democratic point of view on this issue by emphasizing the power of the people.[48] Simultaneously, it strives for the reform of the Sharia and reduces its character to the goals of Islamic law, not its precise rulings, which offers more possibilities for reform.[49]

A second element of a civil state with an Islamic authority as viewed by the Muslim Brotherhood is closely connected with political participation. Coupled with the political practice in Egypt since the 1980s, when the Muslim Brotherhood started participating in elections, the organization has increasingly come to accept democracy and does not want to apply the Sharia in any other way than democratically. Especially to the younger and more reformist Muslim Brothers, democracy is not just a pragmatic, but also a principled choice.[50] Within this system, the Muslim Brotherhood strives to limit the power of the ruler by the people and the organization is open to Coptic members within its own party or to the foundation of a Coptic party, thereby showing its practical support for party pluralism.[51] Hizb al-Wasat feels the same about all these issues, which aligns it with the Muslim Brotherhood and the ideological trend of the *wasatiyya*.[52]

So far, we have seen that the reformist ideas of the *wasatiyya* have been translated into the ideology and political practice of the Muslim Brotherhood and Hizb al-Wasat, which partly explains how the Muslim Brotherhood was able to legitimize its policy accepting the state and political participation. As such, there seems to be little difference between the Muslim Brotherhood and Hizb al-Wasat in these two areas. The same is probably the case with regard to civil liberties such as freedom of speech, which the Muslim Brotherhood supports in principle, but also clearly wants to limit through the norms of the Sharia, ensuring that, in practice, it is circumscribed.[53]

The difference between the current Egyptian Muslim Brotherhood and Hizb al-Wasat becomes clearer when we look at their ideas about the rights of non-Muslims and those of women. With regard to the former, we can see that the Muslim Brotherhood in Egypt emphasizes equal rights for Muslims and Christians, both in religion and politics.[54] We can also see that today's Egyptian Muslim Brotherhood no longer frames the rights of Copts in terms of subservient and protected minorities, but rather in the context of citizenship.[55] Still, to the Muslim Brotherhood, this nevertheless remains limited by certain religious prescriptions, such as the idea that the leader of their ideal state should always be a Muslim, excluding Copts from the presidency.[56] This is different for Hizb al-Wasat. Not only were Copts among the founders of this party, but they were also included in the leadership of Hizb al-Wasat.[57] Precisely because this party does not tend to approach this issue as a religious one, but as a national affair, it does not see a difference between Muslims and Christians in this respect and, as such – in a perspective that goes beyond al-Qaradawi's ideas on the matter – does not raise objections to having a Coptic president of Egypt.[58]

There is also a difference between the Egyptian Muslim Brotherhood and Hizb al-Wasat with regard to women's rights. In principle, the Muslim Brotherhood has a conservative view on the issue of women in public life. Men are seen as the breadwinners, partly based on the idea that men manage the affairs of women, an idea espoused by the early Muslim Brothers and al-Qaradawi. The organization also follows al-Qaradawi in his view that the term 'managers' only applies to the family and that women are clearly allowed to hold positions of political influence.[59] Yet, like with Copts, the

Muslim Brotherhood excludes women from the presidency.[60] Again, Hizb al-Wasat makes a different choice here: although it also has a generally traditional view on women in Egyptian society[61] and has not given women any leadership positions or other prominent roles within the party,[62] Hizb al-Wasat does acknowledge that women have a right to political participation, including the presidency.[63]

Post-Islamism: Beyond the Muslim Brotherhood

The *wasatiyya* is an approach to Islam that is popular within both Hizb al-Wasat and the Muslim Brotherhood. Moreover, the greatest exponent of the *wasatiyya*, Yusuf al-Qaradawi, is the Muslim Brotherhood's most important contemporary scholar. The *wasatiyya* exudes an attitude that is essentially typical of this organization: committed, engaged and pragmatic, but simultaneously assertively Islamist and emphatic about religious norms and values. As such, the Muslim Brotherhood steers a course between secularism and radical Islamism, which is actually quite like the thinking behind the *wasatiyya*.

In a sense, this also reflects the case with so-called post-Islamism, with one exception: the name suggests that this trend – unlike the *wasatiyya* – is not Islamist (anymore). The question is, however, what this means and what is so different about post-Islamism. This is actually not so easy to answer, firstly because the two phenomena do not differ all that much in practice and, secondly, because they partly describe the same phenomenon, but from different angles. Still, it is important to deal with post-Islamism separately because it is obviously a descendant of the Muslim Brotherhood that quite clearly goes further than that organization in terms of reform, but which still has influence within the Muslim Brotherhood as a movement, including with respect to expressions of the movement that we have encountered in previous chapters.

Post-Islamism as a Concept

Before examining concrete manifestations of post-Islamism, it is important to define the meaning of the concept. In fact, there is little agreement about this term. 'Post-Islamism' was first used by the French sociologist Olivier Carré, who applied it to denote a historical period from the tenth to the nineteenth century, in which he believed Muslims separated the political-military sphere from the religious sphere.[64] In the context of the discussion that is relevant to us now, the French political scientist Olivier Roy made an important contribution to this subject by pointing out that Islamism (or 'political Islam') had more or less failed in the Muslim world. As a consequence of this, he claimed a new, post-Islamist trend had emerged, which he called 'neo-fundamentalism' and which he argued would aim much less at the state and would concentrate far more on personal piety and society.[65] Islam was thus decoupled from the state, as it were, and no longer dependent on it, which, in Roy's words, led to a type of privatization of Islam.[66] A less explicit and more specific version of this theory is that of the French political scientist Gilles Kepel, who did not so much ascribe failure to Islamism as a whole, but rather to its violent and revolutionary forms.[67]

Although we saw in the previous chapters that the Islamism of both the Muslim Brotherhood and its radical descendants has certainly not always been a success, there has nevertheless been criticism of this theory of the 'failure' of Islamism. Some have pointed out that all kinds of Islamist movements still exist – including, of course, the Muslim Brotherhood – and that they have played an important role in, for example, the Arab Spring.[68] This does not mean that post-Islamism is not a phenomenon, but rather that it has not replaced Islamism. Asef Bayat, an American expert on the Middle East, states that Islamism is closely tied to the founding of an Islamic order through the adoption of the Sharia, in which the state is an important factor. Because Islamism is so strongly connected with legislation and the imposition of this by the state, Islamists focus more on duties than on rights, according to Bayat, and, in the eyes of Islamists, people are dutiful subjects rather than fully fledged citizens.[69] To Bayat, post-Islamism, on the contrary, represents an attempt to 'fuse religiosity and rights, faith and freedom, Islam and liberty'. Adherents to this emphasize 'rights instead of duties, plurality in place of a singular authoritative voice, historicity rather than fixed scriptures, and the future instead of the past'.[70]

Taking Bayat's definition of post-Islamism as a starting point, it is important to point out that political parties in the Middle East and North Africa that show certain post-Islamist characteristics, such as the Moroccan PJD, have also been compared to Christian- and social-democratic parties in European countries. The reason for this is that both have a past in a not always democratic (religious) ideology, but have now accepted and embraced the rules of liberal democracy with continuing (though much weakened) reference to that ideology.[71] This allows us to take another look at the relationship between *wasatiyya* and post-Islamism and conclude that, whereas the first term denotes an approach to Islam or a method of dealing with the Sharia, post-Islamism refers to a possible (or even probable) practical outcome of this approach. *Wasatiyya* and post-Islamism thus do not exclude each other, but can be in line with each other.

The Application of Post-Islamism

Post-Islamist thought, as described above, has not just spread and developed within the Muslim Brotherhood as a movement and in the Arab world, but also in other parts of the Muslim world, such as Indonesia,[72] Pakistan[73] and Turkey.[74] As far as the Arab world is concerned, we have seen many of these post-Islamist elements in the Muslim Brotherhood and the organizations that are ideologically related to it, particularly with regard to the state and political participation. The academic literature also associates this with post-Islamism. Several characteristics manifested in the early history of the Muslim Brotherhood in Syria, for example, when the group was still being led by Mustafa al-Siba'i, could probably be called 'post-Islamist' now, including a clear respect for the constitution and the republican system in the country. The organization also emphasized the balance of the various powers, civil rights and free elections and – as we have already seen in Chapter 3 – it was prepared to accept a compromise with respect to the influence of Islam on the state.[75]

In a different way, we saw the same phenomenon concerning the PJD in Morocco. When the party engaged in reforms, it was pointed out that its leaders used contextualized interpretations by considering the cultural and political factors that influenced the texts. Furthermore, a flexible approach to the Sharia, the use of Islamic values[76] and the broad goals of Islamic law (instead of the much more specific rulings that flow from these) are connected with post-Islamism.[77] As such, election campaigns by the PJD are not characterized by slogans such as 'Islam is the solution', a frequent Muslim Brotherhood motto.[78] Ennahda in Tunisia also claims to have an equally broad view of the Sharia and strives for its application through concepts such as justice and freedom as the goals of Islamic law, rather than arguing in favour of specific commandments and prohibitions.[79] Moreover, Ennahda's willingness to compromise, its flexibility and its reformed points of view have shown that this is not just empty rhetoric.[80]

Yet, the Muslim Brotherhood – whether in reference to the organization or to the movement – cannot simply be called 'post-Islamist', despite having several post-Islamist features. The Egyptian Muslim Brotherhood, for instance, has seen (or caused) many of its members leave after the uprising of 2011, almost all of whom were reformists. This makes one not only suspect that there is some tension between post-Islamism and the Egyptian branch

of the Muslim Brotherhood, but also that this trend within the organization has been decimated.[81] Moreover, some have rightly pointed out that a
complete separation of political and religious activities, in which politics
is engaged in from a set of values (derived from Islam), is not a realistic
expectation for an organization like the Egyptian Muslim Brotherhood, for
whom the close connection between politics and religion is crucial.[82] The
most important manifestation of post-Islamism in Egypt is therefore probably the phenomenon of Hizb al-Wasat, with its attempts to think beyond
classical Islamism and the Muslim Brotherhood, even if it cannot be said to
be entirely post-Islamist.[83] This party, whose connection with the *wasatiyya*
is even reflected in its name, thereby shows that a group that emanates from
a centrist approach to Islam can manifest itself in post-Islamist points of
view, thus revealing the relationship between *wasatiyya* and post-Islamism.

Post-Islamism and Politics

How can post-Islamism be discerned in political points of view pertaining
to the ideological themes we saw earlier (the state, political participation
and societal rights and freedoms)? In general, it may be said that classical
terms have not been cast aside by post-Islamism, but rather are interpreted
more broadly so that they may be used as the basis of rights and freedoms
of larger groups of people. This can be seen, for example, in the Moroccan
MUR, which speaks of a 'chosen caliphate' in which the early Islamic model
of the Prophet Muhammad's successors serves as a source of inspiration
and not as a rigid blueprint – thereby making it Islamically legitimate in
the Moroccan context, but it also meets people's desire for democracy.[84]

    The same phenomenon is visible with regard to political participation
among post-Islamists in Egypt. Underpinning this is the conviction that the
idea of *hakimiyya*, as described by Qutb, is unacceptable, because it places the
entire political system in the hands of God. According to the post-Islamist
view, values and principles – such as justice – emanate from God's authority,
and on this basis people can set up their own political system. They believe
that the best way to guarantee justice, therefore, is democracy. According
to Fahmi Huwaydi (1937), a prominent Egyptian post-Islamist journalist,
justice (and countering injustice), is one of the characteristics of an Islamic
democracy. The other characteristics are: the idea that legitimate authority
lies with the people; society has responsibilities and duties that it takes
care of independently of the authorities; there is freedom and equality for
all (including non-Muslims, who act as full partners in the state); and the
Sharia is the source of legislation.[85]

The application of the Sharia in the laws of the state may not sound any different from what the early Muslim Brothers said. The difference, however, is that Egypt's post-Islamists claim that only a very small number of texts from the Koran and the Sunna are political in nature and that even those texts usually deal with values, not means. Moreover, post-Islamists make much clearer than the early Muslim Brothers did that, in their view, Islamic jurisprudence is a completely human endeavour. While they see Koranic texts as divine, the rulings based on them are not, which gives people much greater freedom to fill in the very wide framework that post-Islamists believe the Sharia provides them with. To be sure, post-Islamists still connect this entire system to the aforementioned Islamic concept of *shura*, but, unlike some early Muslim Brothers, they do not see democracy as a system that will pull them in the direction of Europe. Rather, they perceive European democracies as models to learn from.[86]

A similar post-Islamist trend could be seen in Saudi Arabia in the 1990s and in the early twenty-first century, when ex-communists, liberals, Sunnis and Shiites formed a nationalist and democratic trend that turned against religious state scholars and also pushed back against the *sahwa*.[87] By offering petitions, organizing discussions and setting up a political party of their own, Saudi post-Islamists tried to spread their ideas and get them accepted. Content-wise, they did not just call for democracy, but also for respecting human rights, a change to the ubiquitous role of religion in society and founding a constitutional monarchy in the country. Although this trend has not been very successful, its adherents were arrested by the authorities because of their ideas, which – according to Saudi standards – were highly controversial.[88]

Post-Islamist thinkers also have much to say about the rights of non-Muslims and people with different ideas. In Saudi Arabia, this does not manifest itself in Islamic-Christian relations, but rather in the ties between Sunnis and Shiites. The post-Islamist dedication to equality between these two groups does not just become apparent in the aforementioned cooperation between Sunnis and Shiites, but also in the fact that they drew up petitions together in which they called for equal rights, independent of confessional background.[89] The same phenomenon manifested itself in Egypt, where post-Islamist thinkers abandoned the concept of *dhimmi*s to describe non-Muslims and, instead, emphasized their citizenship. It is striking that, rather than following al-Qaradawi's legally argued method, Egyptian post-Islamists are often more inclined to retroactively read modern-day rights and freedoms into Islamic tradition. In this context, the aforementioned Huwaydi claims that the earliest Muslims had, in fact, initiated modern rights and freedoms, but that later generations of Muslims did not apply and act upon these as they should have.[90]

In the context of post-Islamist views on equality between Muslims and Christians, the term 'umma' is of great importance. Although this word has long been seen as indicating the (worldwide) Muslim community, post-Islamists also interpret it as pointing to the Arab-Islamic civilization or, in the case of Egyptian post-Islamists, to the Egyptian people, of which Christians are an integral part. Thus, they give meaning to the term in a way that includes, rather than excludes, Christians.[91] This is related to a reading of the verses of the Koran that are also pertinent to the *wasatiyya*, namely, that negative passages about non-Muslims should be seen in the context of hostile non-Muslims.[92] Whereas al-Banna only applied this to societal tolerance, al-Qaradawi also included political rights. Just like Hizb al-Wasat, however, post-Islamists go even further, drawing the conclusion that, from an Islamic perspective, the highest office in the land – the presidency – is open to Christians.[93]

With regard to women's rights, Egyptian post-Islamists strive for equality between men and women in principle, but do not fully follow through on this, even though they limit Koranic verses on inequality to several specific situations, such as testifying in a court case.[94] Their views are flexible, however. Several Egyptian post-Islamists state, for example, that wearing a headscarf is compulsory for Muslim women, but they also note that in situations where this is not allowed – such as at state schools in France – girls and women should give priority to education at those schools and remove their headscarves in such cases.[95] Post-Islamists in Egypt also point out that certain verses in the Koran do not apply to women in general, but specifically to the Prophet Muhammad's wives. This means that they cannot be used to keep modern-day women from working outside the home or holding public office, for example in politics.[96]

Egyptian post-Islamists have also expressed their views on civil liberties. They interpret this subject in the context of public order. Every country probably has rules about what public order means and to post-Islamists this is closely connected with Islam. As such, certain things that strongly deviate from what Muslims believe become controversial and are, perhaps, banned, precisely because they run counter to social norms. Post-Islamists consider this a very democratic element of their thought – the people, after all, decide the norms – that is simultaneously flexible, given that the ideas of the people on such issues can change.[97] In practice, this has led some post-Islamists to conclude that non-Muslims who are neither Jewish nor Christian (such as Baha'is) should not be allowed to express their beliefs in public and should limit this to the private sphere. Post-Islamists argue for the same sort of compromise concerning apostasy, which many Muslims believe should be punished with the death penalty. Egyptian post-Islamists state that Muslims who convert to a different religion should not be killed or legally punished, but rather that limits should be imposed upon them by society if they want to express their apostasy publicly, precisely because their doing so would violate societal norms.[98]

ZamZam: Post-Islamism in Practice

The academic debate on post-Islamism, as discussed in the previous section, does not just revolve around what the term means precisely, but also around how the phenomenon came into being. A number of scholars disagree with the aforementioned Roy and Kepel, who associate the origins of post-Islamism with the alleged failure of Islamism. Several academics state that the theory of the failure of Islamism presupposes that there is no continuity between Islamism and post-Islamism and that an Islamist ideology cannot change, while both are, in fact, the case.[99] As such, post-Islamism is a phenomenon that sprang naturally and organically from internal debates, experiments and experiences within local and global contexts of Islamist groups such as the Muslim Brotherhood.[100] This will be illustrated on the basis of the Jordanian post-Islamist ZamZam Initiative from 2012.

The Background to the ZamZam Initiative

The Jordanian Muslim Brotherhood has a long history of political participation, even if – as we saw above – there were differences of opinion about this within the organization. This is not the only source of disagreement among Jordanian Muslim Brothers, however. In fact, there was division within the organization in roughly five areas: whether members should primarily focus on *da'wa* or on politics; whether they should mostly concentrate on the Palestinian question or on internal Jordanian affairs; whether Brothers should primarily follow an Islamist course of action or should strive for far-reaching cooperation with others; whether members should actively 'Islamize' the Jordanian state and society or should only seek reforms within the existing framework; and whether Brothers should boycott parliamentary elections on principle or should be in favour of participation for pragmatic reasons.[101]

Given these divisions, multiple points of view can be discerned among Jordanian Muslim Brothers, including post-Islamist ones, as expressed by several members of the organization, including by Nabil al-Kufahi and Ruhayyil Gharayiba, two Muslim Brothers with a long history of service to the Jordanian organization.[102] Within the Muslim Brotherhood, there was room to express these ideas, but they were not supported by the majority of the organization's members. Hence al-Kufahi, Gharayiba and others started looking for alternative organizational platforms besides the Muslim Brotherhood that they could use to express these ideas,[103] especially because the organization, under increasing repression by King 'Abdallah II, tended increasingly towards rigid points of view regarding parliamentary participation.[104]

The divisions within the Jordanian Muslim Brotherhood were reinforced by the Arab Spring. As we saw in Chapter 4, the uprisings that started in 2010 initially led to a common position in favour of reforms in Jordan, but, as the Arab Spring floundered, they gradually also laid bare Brothers' different views about the state and political participation and differences started developing about how to deal with this.[105] During the Arab Spring, Muslim Brothers such as Gharayiba and al-Kufahi spoke out in favour of more inclusive reforms that would also get non-Islamists involved and they advocated taking a less confrontational attitude towards the state, partly because they feared eventual repercussions from the regime.[106] The search for an organizational platform to express more inclusive, post-Islamist ideas such as these, combined with the urgency of the Arab Spring, led a broad group of some 500 reformist Jordanians to set up Al-Mubadara al-Wataniyya li-l-Bina' ('The National Initiative for Building') in November 2012. Because this initiative was founded in the ZamZam Towers Hotel in Amman, it became known as the ZamZam Initiative.[107]

This was a broad project that included Jordanians of all political persuasions, including many members of the Muslim Brotherhood.[108] Despite the fact that ZamZam was not a political party – it was meant as a broad initiative alongside the Muslim Brotherhood (rather than in its stead) – and did not make any ideological claims that the organization could not agree with,[109] the Muslim Brotherhood's leaders nevertheless saw this project as a form of competition. As a result of this distrust towards ZamZam, Gharayiba and two of his fellow ZamZam supporters – the aforementioned al-Kufahi and Jamil Duhaysat – were dismissed from the Muslim Brotherhood in 2014. This affair and its aftermath led to further division and a schism within the Jordanian Muslim Brotherhood.[110] Under Gharayiba's direction, ZamZam itself ended up founding a political party after all, Hizb al-Mu'tamar al-Watani ('The National Conference Party'), which received official permission to participate in the elections of 2016, in which it won five seats.[111]

ZamZam as a Post-Islamist Example

Within the above context, Gharayiba and a number of other Jordanians launched the ZamZam Initiative in November 2012. According to a press statement released at the time, they did so because they saw the necessity of a national reformist initiative that would gather all of the country's forces to lift Jordan out of the crisis that the country found itself in at that moment.[112] To illustrate the post-Islamist way in which they sought to pursue these reforms, the translated text of the ZamZam initiative is reproduced here:

In the name of God, the Merciful, the Compassionate

The National Initiative for Building (ZamZam)

Praise belongs to God, the Lord of all Being, and the best prayer (*afdal al-salat*) and the most perfect greeting (*atamm al-taslim*) for our lord, Muhammad, for his family and all his companions.

1. Who Are We...?
A comprehensive national framework (*itar watani jami'*) that establishes a total reformist method (*manhajan islahiyyan shamilan*), participates in the building of the modern Jordanian state and the building of its awakening on the bases of development (*al-intima'*), competence (*al-kafa'a*) and justice (*al-'adala*).

2. What Do We Want...?
1. Competently establishing a project of total, Jordanian, national reform;
2. Spreading moderate thought (*al-fikr al-mu'tadil*) based on mutual tolerance (*al-tasamuh*), mercy (*al-tarahum*), cooperation (*al-ta'awun*) and understanding (*al-isti'ab*);
3. Entering the institutions of the state and the institutions of civil society (*al-mujtama' al-madani*) and strengthening the values of cooperation (*al-ta'awun*), positive participation (*al-musharaka al-ijabiyya*), freedom (*al-hurriyya*), justice (*al-'adala*) and the dignity of human beings (*karamat al-insan*);
4. Offering space to society's energy (*isti'ab taqat al-mujtama'*), realizing the aspirations and the hopes of the Jordanian people (*tahqiq tumuhat al-sha'b al-Urdunni wa-amalihi*) with effectiveness (*fa'iliyya*), realism (*waqi'iyya*) and ability (*iqtidar*);

5. Confirming the openly peaceful method (*al-manhaj al-silmi al-'alani*), based on gradual scientific and programme foundations (*al-usus al-'ilmiyya wa-l-baramijiyya al-mutadarrija*) that lead to an unshakeable national structure (*al-bina' al-watani al-rasin*);

6. Participation in the building of a tight-knit Jordanian community (*al-mujtama' al-Urdunni al-mutamasik*) and the strengthening of its comprehensive cultural and national identity (*ta'ziz hawiyyatihi l-wataniyya wa-l-thaqafiyya al-jami'*);

7. Building a productive Jordanian national economy (*al-iqtisad al-watani al-Urdunni al-muntij*), far removed from dependence (*al-tab'iyya*) on and indebtedness (*al-irtihan*) to the foreign economy.

3. Justifications (*musawwighat*) and Motives of Formation (*dawa'i l-takwin*)

1. The need for renewal in propositions (*turuhat*), means and mechanisms that result in the building of a national situation that is constructive (*banna'atan*) and effective (*fa'ilatan*) in different areas;

2. The necessity of strengthening the trust (*ta'ziz al-thiqqa*) between the active political sides in the national space (*al-mada al-watani*) and of opening the horizons (*fath afaq*) of shared labour (*al-'amal al-mushtarak*) in the different flourishing areas (*al-majalat al-nahdawiyya al-mukhtalifa*);

3. The inability of the traditional political frameworks (*al-utur al-siyasiyya al-taqlidiyya*) to provide in the aspirations and the hopes of the Jordanian people in the cultural revival (*al-nuhud al-hadari*);

4. The necessity to employ the hidden energy of society (*taqat al-mujtama' al-kamina*) and to invest it well, particularly with regard to youngsters and women;

5. The urgent need (*al-haja al-mulihha*) to offer space to discerning and positive propositions and ideas (*al-afkar wa-l-turuhat al-ijabiyya wa-l-mutamayyiza*) that are present in Jordanian society and the instigation of the pace of their fruitful performance (*tahfiz watirat ada'iha al-muthmir*);

6. The will for vehement participation (*al-isham al-hadd*) in the building of Jordan's awakening and the enhancement of its national achievements (*al-munjizat al-wataniyya*), which maintain the dignity of the Jordanian citizen (*tasunu karamat al-muwatin al-Urdunni*) and the realization of economic prosperity;

7. The presence of political aggravation (*al-ta'azzum al-siyasi*), vehement societal division (*al-inqisam al-mujtama'i al-hadd*) and the increased level of tension (*ziyadat mansub al-tawattur*) between society's elements and groups (*mukawwanat al-mujtama' wa-fi'atihi*).

4. Vision

Gathering competences (*tajmi' al-kafa'at*) and attracting the potential and the energy (*jadhb al-qudrat wa-l-taqat*) that is stored (*al-mukhtazana*) in the Jordanian people and stimulating them in the direction of optimal investment (*al-istithmar al-amthal*) of the sources and abilities of the state (*mawarid al-dawla wa-maqdiratiha*) in the process of building and revival.

5. Strategy

Activating youthful energies (*taf'il al-taqat al-shababiyya*), developing them (*tanmiyatuha*), training them (*tadribuha*) and shaping them (*ta'hiluha*); [having] an effective presence (*al-hudur al-fa'il*) in the official and non-official institutions of the state and to come out openly with the truth (*al-sad' bi-l-haqq*); confronting corruption and its tools (*al-fasad wa-l-adawatiha*) with boldness (*bi-jur'a*); enhancing the values of achievement (*al-injaz*), competence (*al-kafa'a*) and reliability (*al-amana*); and participating in the building of the great civilizational project of the community (*mashru' al-umma al-hadari al-kabir*), based on unity (*al-wahda*), strength (*al-quwwa*) and the system of the right values (*manzumat al-qiyam al-rashida*).

6. Goals and Policies

1. Participating in the building and protection (*himayatihi*) of Jordan, maintaining its safety (*hifz amnihi*), its stability (*istiqrarihi*), its abilities (*maqdiratihi*) and the future of its generations (*mustaqbal ajyalihi*);
2. Strengthening Jordan with regard to foreign hegemony (*al-haymana al-ajnabiyya*) and Zionist influence (*al-nufudh al-sahyuni*) and supporting the Palestinian project of liberation (*mashru' al-tahrir al-Filastini*);
3. Fighting corruption (*muharabat al-fasad*) in all its forms, components and elements (*bi-kull ashkalihi wa-'anasirihi wa-mukawwanatihi*);
4. Anchoring truly democratic contours (*irsa' ma'alim al-dimuqratiyya al-haqiqiyya*) and the true implementation of them (*al-mumarasa al-haqqa laha*);
5. Building a modern civil state (*al-dawla al-madaniyya al-haditha*) that takes its moral authority (*marja'iyyatuha l-qimiyya*) from Islam;
6. Strengthening the values of freedom (*al-hurriyya*), justice (*al-'adala*) and the dignity of human beings (*karamat al-insan*);
7. Dedication (*al-iltizam*) to the gradual, openly peaceful method (*al-manhaj al-silmi al-'alani al-mutadarrij*) in the realization of total national reform;

8. Enlarging the areas of mutual agreement (*masahat al-tawafuq*) between the socio-political powers (*al-quwa al-siyasiyya al-ijtima'iyya*) and the building of the system of collective values (*al-qiyam al-jam'iyya*);

9. Participating in the reshaping of the Jordanian human being (*i'adat siyaghat al-insan al-Urdunni*) in accordance with a peaceful, educational method (*manhaj tarbawi salim*) that respects the knowledge foundations (*al-usus al-'ilmiyya*) and the demands of the age (*mutatallibat al-'asr*).

10. [sic] **Means and Mechanisms**

1. Arranging lectures (*al-muhadarat*), symposia (*al-nadawat*), conferences (*al-mu'tamarat*) and cultural and educational publications (*al-isdarat al-'ilmiyya wa-l-thaqafiyya*);

2. Founding training-, study- and research centres (*marakiz al-dirasat wa-l-abhath wa-l-tadrib*);

3. Contacting effective Islamic and national personalities and offering them space in this broad framework (*fi hadha l-itar al-wasi'*);

4. Putting in place an educational, cultural method (*minhaj tarbawi thaqafi*) that strengthens the national development and preserves national identity in confronting the Zionist project and all projects of Westernization (*kull mashari' al-taghrib*) and cultural invasion (*al-ghazw al-thaqafi*);

5. Possessing effective and influential media (*wasa'il i'lamiyya mu'aththira fa'ila*) that are capable of addressing the Jordanian masses (*al-jumhur al-Urdunni*);

6. Founding a network of firm ties (*shabakat 'alaqat wathiqa*) with effective political forces (*al-quwa al-siyasiyya al-fa'ila*), Jordanian national personalities and those with responsibility (*ashab al-mas'uliyya*) who are characterized by integrity (*al-mashhud lahum bi-l-nazaha*);

7. Being effectively present in the institutions of the state, the institutions of civil society and the positive cooperation with the national and political forces in the service of the highest shared goals (*al-ahdaf al-'ulya al-mushtaraka*) of our Jordanian people;

8. Finding media that are effective, capable of serving the idea (*al-qadira 'ala khidmat al-fikra*) and express the policies of the initiatives with competence.

8. Conditions of Membership

1. An abundance of willingness to perform (*tawafur al-raghba fi l-ada'*) and the will to achieve (*iradat al-injaz*);

2. Good behaviour (*husn al-sira*) and a good reputation (*al-sum'a al-tayyiba*);

3. Dedication to the method of the initiative, its system and its general programme (*nizamiha wa-barnamijiha l-'amm*);
4. To be at least eighteen years of age;
5. The duty (*ta'bi'at*) to request membership of the initiative;
6. The pledge (*ta'ahhud*) to present or support (*taqdim aw musanada*) a new practical and knowledge-based idea (ideas) (*fikra (afkar) 'ilmiyya wa-'amaliyya jadida*) that contributes to the realization of the initiative's goals.

9. Invitation to Participation

This initiative comes with its right national intention (*bi-maqsadiha l-watani l-rashid*) to summon charitable efforts (*al-juhud al-khayyira*) and to have them meet with sincere effort (*jahd mukhlis*) for the cooperation in building Jordan and the realization of its path-breaking awakening (*tahqiq nahdatihi l-ra'ida*). So it brings together (*fa-hiya tajma'u*) and does not divide (*la tufarriqu*). It builds on (*tabni*) and does not prevent (*la tu'iqu*). It brings good news (*tubashshiru*) and does not frighten (*la tunaffiru*). It eases (*tuyassiru*) and does not make [things] difficult (*la tu'assiru*). It is not there to irritate (*li-l-munakafa*) or to distract (*li-l-mushaghala*), not to monopolize (*li-l-isti'thar*) or to exclude (*al-istib'ad*) and to remove (*al-iqsa'*), but it strives with effort (*jahidatan*) and with will (*irada*), determination (*tasmim*) and power (*quwwa*) to harmonize with the aspirations and the hopes of the Jordanian people and the realization of the elevation of its case (*rif'at sha'nihi*) in a comprehensive national framework.

In this regard, we invite all of you to participate effectively in this initiative and the spread of its ideas, to support its programme (*barnamijiha*) and its views (*tawajjuhatiha*) on the basis of development, competence, reliability, love of achievement (*hubb al-injaz*) and presenting the general service (*al-khidma al-'amma*).

Praise belongs to God, the Lord of all Being[113]

Although much of what can be found in this text is seemingly unremarkable because it is based on values shared by many, it is good to point explicitly to the importance of this initiative from a post-Islamist perspective. The text places much emphasis on rights (such as freedom, art. 2.3), emphasizes tolerance to others (art. 2.2), argues in favour of political participation and democracy (art. 2.3, 6.4), calls for peaceful reform (art. 2.5), is inclusive (art. 4) and, as a whole, has a clearly encompassing, national character. Still, the initiative is occasionally (implicitly) critical of the state (art. 3.3) and the text is pro-Palestinian and anti-Israel (art. 6.2, 10.4), as was to be expected of an initiative in which many Muslim Brothers are involved.

Perhaps the most interesting aspect about this statement, however, is the role of Islam: apart from the opening and closing formulas, there is hardly any reference to Islam and nothing is said about the application of the Sharia. The only real reference to Islam can be found in article 6.5, where the initiative calls for a 'modern civil state that takes its moral authority from Islam'. This not only differs strongly from 'the application of the Sharia', which the Muslim Brotherhood used to strive for, but it also clearly goes beyond a 'civil state with an Islamic authority' that has become dominant within the organization over the past decades. Moreover, the article does not refer to the rules or even the principles or goals of Islam, but to the 'moral authority' that is taken from that religion, which is a formula that gives a very free and broad meaning to the idea of an Islamic state and clearly underlines the post-Islamist character of the ZamZam Initiative.[114]

Although the ZamZam Initiative never became a project accepted by the masses, the party that sprang from this initiative did more or less adopt these principles.[115] First and foremost, however, it shows that an initiative that has clear roots in the Muslim Brotherhood and builds on years of ideological developments within that organization can take on a post-Islamist character. This, in turn, shows – as the *wasatiyya* also did, though to a lesser extent – that the ideological framework of the Muslim Brotherhood is not as rigid as one might expect and that the Islamist ideas underpinning the organization are open to flexible interpretations.

***

The developments that the Muslim Brotherhood has experienced in the countries in which the organization has manifested itself have not been superficial changes, but are supported by a reform of Islam that is actually ideologically supported in the form of the *wasatiyya*. As such, scholars such as al-Qaradawi have laid the ideological foundations for the Muslim Brotherhood's pragmatism. This has had consequences within the Muslim Brotherhood itself with regard to the state, political participation and societal rights and freedoms, but also outside the framework of that organization in the form of Hizb al-Wasat.

Whereas the *wasatiyya* is an approach to Islam and the legal tradition that emanates from it, post-Islamism is a term used to describe the outcomes of reformist thinking and whose contents often concur with the *wasatiyya*.

Still, the ZamZam Initiative makes clear that post-Islamists sometimes go further in their reformist zeal than al-Qaradawi and his colleagues. This shows that, despite organizational fault lines with the Muslim Brotherhood or Islamism, there is clearly a natural, organic ideological shift from Islamism towards *wasatiyya* and post-Islamism. This, in turn, demonstrates that the Muslim Brotherhood is not stuck in a fundamentalist mode, but is actually flexible, dynamic and developing with regard to ideology.

8.   Europeans

A recurring theme in this book has been the position of non-Muslims in the Muslim Brotherhood's ideal state. The organization – or, rather, the movement – of the Muslim Brotherhood has also spread beyond the Muslim world, however, including to Europe, where the group's members (just like many other Muslims) are themselves part of a religious minority. This places Muslims in an entirely new situation, as a minority in an area that, traditionally, has been considered hostile. In this chapter, therefore, we will look at, respectively, the position of Muslims in non-Muslim countries, the Muslim Brotherhood in Western European countries and the ideology of the Muslim Brotherhood there. In this context, we will also examine the extent to which we can state that the Muslim Brotherhood should be seen as an international conspiracy that secretly tries to grab power.

The Muslim Brotherhood from the Middle East to Europe

Just like Islam itself, the Muslim Brotherhood was initially so strongly connected with the Muslim world that it seemed obvious that the organization would only ever exist there. Yet, the Muslim Brotherhood – again, just like Islam itself – eventually spread to non-Muslim countries. This confronted Muslim Brothers with all kinds of new obstacles: not only were the organization's members strangers in these lands, but the political systems, the religious contexts and the cultures were quite different from what they were used to. Did this mean that they should just carry on doing what they had always done, as if nothing had changed, or should they adapt?

Muslim Minorities in Non-Muslim Countries

Although the Muslim Brotherhood is a modern organization, the question of Muslim minorities in non-Muslim countries is a subject that Muslim scholars have pondered for centuries. Early Muslim scholars divided the world into the aforementioned 'abode of Islam', where Muslims were in control, the Sharia was applied, or where they could at least live in safety, and the *dar al-harb* ('the abode of war'). In the latter area, these circumstances did not apply and Muslims were therefore at war with such a region, at least in theory. As such, the general position among early Muslim scholars was that Muslims should stay away from these areas, although there were also scholars who had different views about this. Throughout the centuries, scholars also added new categories to this strict dichotomy, thereby providing more opportunities for Muslims to settle in or travel to non-Muslim areas. This development towards a more nuanced look at those parts of the world in which Muslims were not in control was influenced by conflicts, the extent to which Muslims could profess and preach their beliefs in non-Muslim countries, the necessity to live under non-Islamic laws, trade interests and the possibilities for engaging in missionary activities.[1]

Certain classical Islamic arguments used by scholars, such as those involving trade interests, are primarily relevant at the level of states or empires, but others are also relevant for the Muslim Brotherhood, because they touch upon issues that are also important to that organization. The first issue to mention in this context is loyalty to a non-Muslim country. Mediaeval Muslim scholars rejected this notion as they believed that Muslims' loyalty should be to their faith. This became particularly relevant in the case of a jihad from the Muslim world against a non-Muslim country where Muslims lived as a minority.[2] A second, related issue is the question of whether Muslims are actually allowed to live in a non-Muslim country. As indicated above, Islamic scholars were generally against this. This position was related to the question of divided loyalty, but also to the fact that residence in non-Muslim countries implied obedience to non-Islamic legislation as well as a degree of subservience to non-Muslim rule, which they rejected. Moreover, they believed that this could lead to a strengthening of the position of non-Muslims, friendships with them, the need to live in a sinful environment and the impossibility of fully expressing Islam, including by commanding wrong and forbidding right.[3]

It is clear that classical Muslim scholars viewed the position of Muslim minorities through the prism of a conflictual relationship with non-Muslim areas, which did, indeed, often exist. The same was true for the colonial era of the nineteenth and twentieth centuries, the difference being that contacts between Muslims and non-Muslims were probably more frequent, more intense and more diverse in this period. The stance adopted by Rida, who had a major influence on al-Banna, should be seen in this light. Rida rejected the French colonial government's offer of French citizenship to Tunisians because this would not only subject them to non-Islamic laws, but it would also force them to serve in the French army, which was occupying several Muslim countries at the time.[4] That this context played a role is underlined by the fact that Rida did not object to the participation of Muslims in the Russian army in a war with Japan. Not only was the latter not a Muslim country, but Rida argued that military participation could also result in

greater protection and an enhanced social status for Muslims.[5] In line with
this, he also did not object to alliances with friendly non-Muslims,[6] did not
require Muslims to emigrate to a Muslim country if they could practise
Islam in their non-Muslim country[7] and he viewed *da'wa* as a legitimate
reason to send Muslims to Europe and to let them stay there.[8]

As colonialism influenced more and more people and 'the West' increasingly came to be seen as the enemy, the views on this subject almost certainly
hardened, too. Because of this, the early leaders of the Muslim Brotherhood
would likely have found it difficult to imagine that Muslims could live freely
and openly in non-Muslim countries. This probably explains why al-Banna
objected to the idea of Muslims becoming citizens in non-Muslim countries
and stated that emigration was a duty incumbent upon those Muslims living
in a non-Muslim country where the authorities demanded citizenship.[9] Qutb
also believed that Muslims should emigrate from a non-Muslim country if
they were unable to express their religion,[10] but went further than al-Banna
in this regard. He considered a sojourn in a non-Muslim country in and of
itself as tantamount to helping non-Muslims.[11] Moreover, building on his
ideas, as outlined in Chapter 2, Qutb also saw alliances with or settlement
in the countries of non-Muslims as a serious rejection of God's sovereignty
and his laws.[12]

The International Muslim Brotherhood

Thus, the dominant position about life as a Muslim minority was – both
among Mediaeval scholars and among modern thinkers like Rida, al-Banna
and Qutb – a negative one. Yet, despite this scepticism about Muslims in
non-Muslim countries, the idea of transnational Islamism had already
existed for a long time in the ranks of the Muslim Brotherhood, including
in al-Banna's writings. In fact, this was not surprising given that the idea of
a worldwide Muslim community was important to al-Banna and that the
Muslim Brotherhood was also rooted in a broad reformist tradition that often
had an equally pan-Islamic character.[13] Still, this dimension of the Muslim
Brotherhood is one of the most controversial aspects of the organization
because the existence of an international network appears to lend credence
to the idea that the Muslim Brotherhood is an international conspiracy.[14]

In reality, the International Muslim Brotherhood is a loose and weak
network. While it does, indeed, exist, it came about – like so much of the
Muslim Brotherhood – as a response to repression, not as the result of a
preconceived plan. Concretely, the organization's members conceived the
idea of establishing an international network that was independent of the

various states so that there was an option to fall back on if national Muslim Brotherhoods experienced repression. This way, the organization could also be continued in difficult times.[15] From the 1960s onwards, this was given concrete form with the founding of an international Executive Bureau under the guidance of the Syrian Muslim Brother 'Isam al-'Attar, with members from various Arab countries. Because of the status of Egypt as the country where the Muslim Brotherhood was founded and the mediating role that the Egyptian branch has played in conflicts between Muslim Brothers elsewhere, Cairo took over the leadership of the International Muslim Brotherhood in 1973. This happened under the direction of Mustafa Mashhur (1921–2002), the fifth General Guide of the Egyptian Muslim Brotherhood, and the organization also gained a Maktab al-Irshad al-'Amm ('General Guidance Bureau') as well as a consultation council comprising members from various countries.[16]

Although this structure appeared highly organized and the International Muslim Brotherhood had more or less the same hierarchy as the national branches of the organization, the group was, in fact, loosely organized and relatively weak. This way, the organizational structure of the International Muslim Brotherhood was formalized in 1982, with a centralized leadership in Cairo, although the members did not always abide by the organization's own formal rules.[17] Moreover, some non-Egyptian Muslim Brothers did not intend to explicitly pledge fealty to the General Guide in Egypt[18] and there was also broader criticism of what some perceived as the Egyptian desire to centralize, which caused some local branches to leave the International Muslim Brotherhood.[19] This happened most explicitly when – as we saw in Chapter 4 – the International Muslim Brotherhood distanced itself from the military coalition that liberated Kuwait from Iraqi occupation in 1990, which precipitated the Kuwaiti Muslim Brotherhood's withdrawal from the international organization.[20]

The divisions in the International Muslim Brotherhood were reinforced by internal differences about local issues in various countries where the organization had a presence. Moreover, after the terrorist attacks in America on 11 September 2001, a tendency developed within the organization to de-emphasize the Muslim Brotherhood's international character, so as not to give the impression that, like Al-Qaida, it was an international terrorist network.[21] The current state of the international organization is therefore that of an administratively weak platform that can be consulted or asked for mediation,[22] but the individual branches of the group seem to enjoy complete independence.[23] The current acting General Guide of the international Muslim Brotherhood, Ibrahim Munir, resides in London, as mentioned above, but this seems to have more to do with the weakness of the organization in Egypt than with the strength of the international organization.[24] The most important form of internationalization within the Muslim Brotherhood today appears to exist on the internet, through websites and social media, including through the R4BIA symbol (a yellow background with a hand holding up four fingers). This symbol refers to the Rabi'a al-'Adawiyya square in Cairo, where some 800 Muslim Brothers were killed by the regime in 2013, and is seen as a sign of international solidarity with the Egyptian Muslim Brotherhood.[25]

'The European Muslim Brotherhood' and Related Organizations

Mirroring the presence of Muslim minorities in non-Muslim countries, the International Muslim Brotherhood was thus born of necessity, not because its members wanted it so badly. This was also the case with the presence of the Muslim Brotherhood and related organizations in Western Europe. They not only built on long-standing colonial ties between the West and Muslim countries, but also on the large numbers of Muslims who had arrived in Western European countries since the 1950s, mainly as a result of labour migration, from former colonies or as refugees. Once there, Muslims found a situation in which Islam was a minority religion and in which the religious culture differed markedly from country to country, varying from the Anglican state church in Great Britain to the secularism of France and the various forms of subsidizing religion in Germany, Belgium and the Netherlands. These different systems, in turn, had consequences for the speed with and way in which one could receive citizenship or for societal issues such as ritual slaughter or wearing a headscarf. Yet, apart from the fact that these were all non-Muslim countries, there were obviously also significant similarities between Western European countries, such as declining numbers of church goers, freedom of religion and expression and a common (mostly negative) history with Islam.[26]

Western European Muslim Brothers fit this picture in their own way because they, too, often did not come to Europe entirely voluntarily. We have already seen that oppressed Muslim Brothers from countries such as Egypt and Syria fled to countries like Saudi Arabia and Kuwait in the 1950s and 1960s. A number of these refugees did not end up in the Gulf, however, but managed to reach Europe from various countries and in different phases.[27] This started with small numbers of Muslim Brothers who fled persecution in Egypt from the 1950s onwards and who often arrived in Europe as individual exiles.[28] Later, in the 1960s, they were joined by students who were members of the Muslim Brotherhood.[29]

These small waves of migration eventually produced organizations that were ideologically, informally and/or personally tied together and which were all part of the Muslim Brotherhood movement (not the organization) in the sense that they concurred ideologically and culturally. There has never been one overarching European Muslim Brotherhood organization, however.[30] Those Europeans who are ideologically and culturally part of the Muslim Brotherhood movement therefore often deny that they are also organizationally affiliated to this group. Although such a denial can cause conspiracy theorists to believe that Muslim Brothers are secretly plotting and that members lie about their membership of the organization, the explanation is much simpler: on the one hand, Islamists in Europe have consciously set up groups outside the organizational framework of the Muslim Brotherhood because they seek to address a broader part of the population than just their own base; on the other hand, many Muslim Brothers (and particularly those who had fled repressive regimes) still fear openly associating with that organization. In that sense, years of repression have clearly left their mark and, in such a context, a less explicit connection with the Muslim Brotherhood was perceived as being more prudent and safer.[31]

Frequently, the first Muslim Brothers in Europe initially tried to copy the cell structure of the Egyptian Muslim Brotherhood, but gradually they began adjusting to the local context by catering to the cares, wishes and needs of the Muslim communities in their new countries.[32] Precisely because Muslim Brothers had always been activists rather than thinkers or scholars and because they had always emphasized the founding of organizations, they were and are relatively well organized among migrant communities.[33] Except for money coming from the group's own members, the Muslim Brotherhood was financed by Gulf States such as Saudi Arabia[34] and later by Qatar,[35] among others.

The first overarching European organization that clearly had the character of the Muslim Brotherhood was the Islamic Council of Europe (ICE), which was founded in London in 1973, but has been inactive since the 1990s.[36] By that time, a different organization had become active, one that functioned as an umbrella group of sorts to national organizations affiliated with the Muslim Brotherhood: the Federation of Islamic Organizations in Europe (FIOE), which was founded in 1989 and is known in French as the Union des Organisations Islamiques en Europe ('Union of Islamic Organizations in Europe'; UOIE).[37] The FIOE is located in Brussels and, on the one hand, seeks to present itself as an advocate of the interests of European Muslims by fighting discrimination against them; on the other, the federation wants to stimulate Muslims to actively participate in their societies and to do so as believing Muslims.[38]

In addition to constituting an overarching organization for national groups, FIOE has also set up several Europe-wide organizations, such as the Forum of European Muslim Youth and Student Organizations (FEMYSO), which was founded in 1996. This organization, also located in Brussels, unites Muslim students and youth from various European countries and is committed to education and fighting discrimination.[39] The organization gives the impression that it is assertively Islamic by clearly presenting itself as such and shows concern for political issues in the Muslim world, such as the situation in Afghanistan and the Palestinian-Israeli conflict, but also for societal problems such as racism, which is underlined by its support for the anti-racism movement Black Lives Matter.[40] FEMYSO also maintains frequent contact with members of the European Parliament.[41]

FIOE was also involved in the founding of the European Council for Fatwa and Research (ECFR), which was established in Dublin in 1997 and is aimed at tackling precisely those issues that European Muslims struggle with.[42] A more explicitly education-oriented organization affiliated with FIOE is the European Institute of Human Sciences (EIHS), which was founded in the 1990s, is located in Paris and Lampeter (Wales) and, among other things, facilitates the training of European imams.[43] FIOE also has a women's branch, the European Forum of Muslim Women (EFOMW), which was founded in Brussels in 2006. The forum is aimed at stimulating the social, political and cultural participation of European women, to represent Muslim women in Europe and to defend the rights and interests of women.[44] In 2008, FIOE also published the *Muslims of Europe Charter*, in which the federation tried to present Islam in a positive way, advocating values such as equality, peacefulness and moderation and, moreover, it claimed to represent some 400 mosques (about 25 per cent of the total number in Europe at the time).[45]

The question is to what extent the practices of FIOE and affiliated organizations can still be said to have ties to the Muslim Brotherhood. Organizationally, it they may not be part of the group in Cairo, but what role does the Muslim Brotherhood's ideology still play for like-minded Europeans? Research by the Belgian sociologist Brigitte Maréchal has shown that al-Banna – the organization's founder – remains an important personality to European Muslim Brothers, even though there is room for criticism. Indeed, some argue that it is actually in line with al-Banna's ideas to approach things critically (including al-Banna's own views), to deal with ideas in a flexible way and to renew them whenever necessary.[46] Qutb is received rather differently. Although his exegesis of the Koran is still read, European Brothers are often critical of his work and its controversial aspects, such as the emphasis he placed on Islamic law and the far-reaching consequences he believed the Sharia's absence should have.[47] Later thinkers in the Muslim Brotherhood also have a limited influence. These include al-Siba'i, contemporary Arab like-minded scholars such as al-Qaradawi and modern-day European thinkers who are able to translate this thought to everyday Western life, such as Tariq Ramadan (1962), a Swiss philosopher and grandson of al-Banna.[48] The Muslim Brotherhood's thought thus continues to be seen as a source of inspiration by like-minded Europeans, to a certain extent, but there is no question of it being used as a blueprint for the entirely new situation that presents itself in Europe. This becomes even clearer when we look at the individual Western European countries in which Muslim Brothers have manifested themselves throughout the years.

The Muslim Brotherhood in European Countries

Just as there is no actual European Muslim Brotherhood organization, there are no groups on a national level that constitute, for example, the French branch of the Muslim Brotherhood. That said, there are certainly ideologically and culturally like-minded organizations in Western Europe that are part of the Muslim Brotherhood as a movement on a national level. Moreover, from the mid-1990s, national organizations embarked on a process in which they demanded their own autonomy, perhaps partly because of the specific circumstances they were dealing with in their own countries.[49] Even though there are similar organizations in several European countries, including Scandinavia,[50] I will limit my focus to Great Britain, France, Belgium, Germany and the Netherlands in this section.

Great Britain

As mentioned before, Muslim communities in Great Britain mostly arose as a result of the British Empire in the nineteenth century and with the arrival of guest workers in the twentieth century, with the majority of immigrants coming from the Indian subcontinent.[51] Since that time, the Muslim population of Britain has been the subject of sporadic controversies, the best-known example of which is the protests that took place in 1989 against the allegedly blasphemous book *The Satanic Verses* by the British author Salman Rushdie. Less prominent, but, in fact, far more relevant and important to British Muslims is that Islam has been institutionalized in the country: Muslims have founded their own officially recognized organizations, mosques and schools within the British system.[52] Great Britain – and particularly London – also used to be a place where many persecuted Islamists fled to, as we have seen in the chapters relating to the Muslim Brotherhoods in Saudi Arabia, Sudan and Tunisia. That was not a coincidence. Although other European countries have also served as safe havens for persecuted Islamists from the Arab world, as we will see below, London became known as 'Londonistan' in the 1990s because the city was so tolerant towards Islamists, who settled there in large numbers in that period.[53]

The above establishes the context in which exiled Muslim Brothers found themselves in the 1950s and 1960s. A prominent example of a Muslim Brother who had fled Egypt is the aforementioned Sa'id Ramadan, who came to Europe in 1954 as an exile and went to several places on the continent, including Geneva, where he set up an Islamic centre in the 1960s. Ramadan founded more such centres, where Muslim Brothers could meet and exchange ideas, including one in London in 1964.[54] This was particularly relevant to those Islamist students who had come to Great Britain from the Arab world in the 1960s and who formalized their activities by founding the Muslim Students Society (MSS) in 1961.[55] The Muslim Welfare House (MWH) was also founded in the early 1970s, to help these students find housing, to provide them with literature and to arrange places for them to pray.[56] Just like the FIOE in Brussels, these organizations were neither founded by the Muslim Brotherhood nor part of that organization, but the movement's influence on them was nevertheless clear. This became apparent, for example, through the speakers that the leaders of these organizations invited and the people who made use of the facilities, who were often Muslim Brotherhood sympathizers.[57]

The MSS and the MWH were not the only (or the biggest) Islamist student organizations in Great Britain at the time, however. There was also the Federation of Student Islamic Societies (FOSIS), which was founded in the 1960s by students of South Asian descent. Although this group had been influenced by Mawdudi – who also influenced Qutb – and therefore showed an ideological overlap with the Muslim Brotherhood, there was an important cultural difference: whereas the MSS was intended for students from Arab countries, the FOSIS was far more focussed on (the much more numerous) students with roots in South Asia.[58] As such, there was a certain overlap between the MSS and the FOSIS, but there was also some competition.[59] Moreover, under Muslim Brothers' direction, other organizations were set up in Great Britain, including the aforementioned ICE, which was founded in 1973 but enjoyed little support within British Muslim communities,[60] and the Islamic Society of Britain (ISB) and Young Muslims UK (YMUK), which were founded in 1990 and 1984, respectively. The latter would later serve as the youth wing of the ISB. Although both organizations were initially at least partly rooted in British Islamist groups with a South Asian background, the international and Arab character of the Muslim Brotherhood meant that they tended more towards that group in later years.[61]

One of the people who was closely involved with many of these activities in Great Britain was Kamal Helbawy (1939),[62] an originally Egyptian Muslim Brother who arrived in 1994 to serve as the Muslim Brotherhood's official spokesperson there.[63] After differences of opinion with the leadership of the organization in Cairo, Helbawy broke his organizational ties with the Muslim Brotherhood, left the ISB and founded the Muslim Association of Britain (MAB) in 1997. Although this group is organizationally independent of the Muslim Brotherhood, it serves as the standard bearer of the movement's ideology in Great Britain.[64] The MAB is also part of the Muslim Council of Britain (MCB), a British umbrella organization established in 1997,[65] and the pan-European FIOE.[66] Like the FIOE, the MAB has also been involved in setting up like-minded specific organizations, e.g. for youngsters (MAB Youth) and women (the Muslim Women's Society).[67]

The activities that the MAB has engaged in throughout the years vary from charity and setting up Islamic financial institutions[68] to pro-Palestinian demonstrations,[69] forming a coalition against the war in Iraq of 2003,[70] protests against the ban on headscarves at French state schools in 2004[71] and initiatives against Islamophobia and negative perceptions of Islam.[72] Yet, the strong emphasis on the Palestinian question (including the openly expressed support by some for suicide attacks against Israel) and the confrontational attitude towards the British government during the war in Iraq were not to everyone's liking within the MAB. Some members accused others of jeopardizing their good relationship with the government to gain a prominent role in demonstrations, in which the MAB cooperated with the Trotskyite Socialist Workers Party. This conflict eventually led to a division, in which part of the group split off in 2005 under the new name British Muslim Initiative (BMI), which allowed the remaining MAB to restore relations with the British government, to cooperate with the authorities and to present itself as an acceptable representative of British Muslims.[73] This undoubtedly needs to be seen in the context of the aforementioned terrorist attacks in London in 2005, committed by supporters of Al-Qaida, after which it became doubly important for British Muslim organizations not to be associated with terrorism.[74]

In all of this, the relationship of the MAB and affiliated organizations with the Muslim Brotherhood has mostly been one of ideological and cultural affinity. As such, groups such as the MSS and the MWH have published works by Muslim Brothers (either translated into English or not)[75] and there is still knowledge about and respect for al-Banna.[76] This is different with Qutb: his exegetical work is still read and his personal suffering for the Muslim Brotherhood is valued,[77] but there is also criticism of him and a certain carefulness when interpreting his work.[78] As such, Islamist organizations in Great Britain have established contacts with later leaders of the Muslim Brotherhood in Egypt and international Islamist thinkers such as Rashid al-Ghannushi and Hasan al-Turabi.[79] Younger thinkers like Tariq Ramadan also have a certain influence in Great Britain[80] and the current General Guide of the Muslim Brotherhood, Ibrahim Munir, lives in London.[81]

The UK government established a commission in 2014 to investigate the relationship between the Egyptian (or, in a broader sense, Arab) Muslim Brotherhood and ideologically affiliated groups in Great Britain. In the report published by the commission in 2015, its authors do not always distinguish between the organization in the Middle East and in Great Britain and do not seem to have incorporated the ideological developments within the Muslim Brotherhood in any extensive way. It is clear that they are critical of expressions of the Muslim Brotherhood in Great Britain, which they believe lack transparency and because of the group's apparent support for Hamas, although the commission acknowledges that the organization is against terrorism. The Muslim Brotherhood is also accused more generally of failing to distance itself sufficiently and explicitly from the controversial ideological heritage of the organization.[82]

France and Belgium

Like Great Britain, France has a long colonial history. Partly because of migration from countries that were part of the French empire, the country already had a small Muslim community at the end of the nineteenth century. This community grew after World War I and became even bigger when labourers were needed to rebuild the country after World War II. From the 1970s onwards, moreover, there was a family reunification policy, which ensured that labourers' wives and children from Muslim countries could also come to France. Because of the French colonial past and the major impact this had had on certain countries, many of these immigrants came from North African countries such as Algeria, Morocco and Tunisia, which had previously been under French rule, although official numbers are not available because recording people's ethnicity in statistics is not allowed in France.[83]

Some of the immigrants who came to France in the 1960s were Islamist political refugees and, in the following decade, many North African Islamist students joined them.[84] As in Great Britain, there was also an Islamist student organization in France, namely, L'Association des Étudiants Islamiques de France ('The Association of Islamic Students of France'; AEIF), which was founded in 1963 (but no longer exists).[85] It was founded by the Indian professor Muhammad Hamidullah (1908–2002), a scholar who enjoyed good relations with several prominent Muslim Brothers, including Sa'id Ramadan, through the latter's Islamic centre in Geneva.[86] In the late 1970s, part of this organization split off from the association, however, and founded the Groupement Islamique en France ('Islamic Group in France'; GIF).[87] This group consisted mostly of supporters of the Tunisian MTI, the precursor to Ennahda, and was more eager to address the concerns of labourers than the more intellectual AEIF. It also organized demonstrations around themes such as the Palestinian question and the Soviet invasion of Afghanistan and it enjoyed good ties with prominent Islamist scholars such as al-Qaradawi.[88] In 1983, some GIF members set up a French umbrella organization, comparable to the British MAB, the Union des Organisations Islamiques en France ('Union of Islamic Organizations in France'; UOIF).[89]

The UOIF's relationship with the Muslim Brotherhood in the Middle East is comparable to that of the British MAB: the organization has informal contacts with the Muslim Brotherhood in the Arab world and has clearly been ideologically influenced by it, but is not tied to it organizationally. (Thus, we see the distinction between the Muslim Brotherhood as a movement and as an organization again here.) The leaders of the organization have also indicated that, unlike what has often been the case in the Arab world, they are not striving to set up an Islamic state in France.[90] This willingness to adjust to a new situation has not always been the case, however. Initially, the UOIF strongly focussed on the Arab world and the organization saw little need to integrate into French society. This changed in 1989, when three French pupils were denied entry to their secondary school because they were wearing headscarves. Although the different sides eventually compromised, the UOIF became involved in the issue and used it to try to create a distinct profile of itself in France.[91] From that moment, the organization's focus shifted clearly to France and it increasingly began considering that country as its own. This change in focus was also reflected in a name change, from the Union of Islamic Organizations *in* France' (*'en France'*) to the 'Union of

Islamic Organizations *of* France ('*de France*').[92] In 2017, the UOIF changed its name again and is now called Musulmans de France ('Muslims of France').[93]

The UOIF's agenda includes activities related to foreign affairs, such as demonstrations against the Palestinian-Israeli conflict, the 2001 war in Afghanistan and the war in Iraq of 2003.[94] The organization also engages in activities related to France itself. The latter includes annual conferences in Paris,[95] an emphasis on cultivating a new generation of Muslim leaders in France[96] and standing up for Muslims' interests, such as speaking out against the publication of Rushdie's *The Satanic Verses* in 1989[97] or the ban on headscarves in French state schools in 2004. The UOIF also believed it had a role to play in curbing the widespread riots that initially occurred in response to police violence and racism in 2005, during which thousands of cars were set on fire, by unambiguously condemning them.[98] The organization's intervention had only limited success, however, partly because it was seen as being out of touch with youngsters from lower socio-economic classes.[99] In line with this charge, some also blame the UOIF for fostering close ties with the French authorities, as evidenced by, for example, its only moderately critical stance towards the headscarf ban of 2004, when the organization was careful not to criticize the government too fiercely.[100]

This criticism of the UOIF underlines the extent to which the Muslim Brotherhood movement has integrated and has become institutionalized in France. For example, the UOIF is part of umbrella organizations such as the FIOE at the European level[101] and the Conseil Français du Culte Musulman ('French Council of the Muslim Religion'; CFCM) at the national level.[102] The UOIF has also been involved in the founding of organizations for specific groups, such as youngsters (Jeunes Musulmans de France; 'Muslim Youth of France'; JMF), students (Étudiants Musulmans de France ('Muslim Students of France'; EMF)), the Palestinians (Le Comité de Bienfaisance et de Solidarité avec la Palestine ('The Committee for Charity and Solidarity with Palestine'), which later became known as the Comité de Bienfaisance et de Secours aux Palestiniens ('Charity and Relief Committee for Palestinians'; CBSP))[103] and women (Ligue Française de la Femme Musulmane ('French League of the Muslim Woman'; LFFM)).[104]

So, just like the MAB in Great Britain, the UOIF (or, nowadays, Musulmans de France) is organizationally separate from the Muslim Brotherhood in the Middle East, but to what extent is the influence of the Egyptian or Arab Muslim Brotherhood still felt in this organization? In general, one can say that the Muslim Brotherhood movement in France, represented by the UOIF and other organizations, has adapted to the French context through integration and a willingness to be fully French, without compromising the pious Islamic lifestyle that it claims to strive for. As such, the activism that has always characterized the Muslim Brotherhood is used in France to focus on specific societal or political issues that are relevant to Muslims, but especially also on personal piety combined with good citizenship.[105]

The above-mentioned attitude is evident in the themes found in French Muslim Brothers' publications, which focus on Islamic teachings, on the one hand, but also pay much attention to Islam as a lifestyle, on the other.[106] Within this framework, there is still a certain influence of and space for al-Banna's work, but there is also criticism of Qutb's radical thought, which is viewed as alien to the French context.[107] The members of the UOIF and affiliated organizations therefore seem more attracted to modern Islamist thinkers, who strive for a combination of piety and full citizenship similar to the one the Muslim Brotherhood promotes. The most important representatives among these are the theologian Tareq Oubrou (1959), who wants Islam to be integrated into French society, and the aforementioned Tariq Ramadan, who wants to use the religious means of the nineteenth-century reformers discussed above to further renew Islam in a French context.[108]

The Muslim Brotherhood in Belgium is, to a certain extent, similar to the one in France, which is perhaps not strange given that the movement in both countries has been strongly influenced by Francophone thinkers and publications. Still, the Belgian context is distinct from the French one, partly because Belgium does not have a colonial past in Muslim countries. Consequently, Islam in Belgium is mostly the result of immigration that started in the 1960s, primarily from Morocco and Turkey.[109] The institutionalization of Islam began in 1974, when Islam gained legal recognition (and, as such, theoretical equality) in Belgium. In the subsequent years, more and more Belgians became aware of the presence of Islam in their country, partly through the increasing number of mosques and the growing discussion about Islam as an alleged danger to society. As was the case in Great Britain and France, this discussion became fiercer from the late 1980s onwards following a series of incidents (surrounding headscarves and Islamic education),[110] and only increased after events such as the attacks of 11 September 2001 in the United States.

The settlement of Muslim Brothers in Belgium is rooted in the same waves of migration by political refugees and students in the 1950s and 1960s that have already been discussed in the context of Great Britain and France.[111] In Belgium, too, the initial organization of activities ran through students: in 1964, L'Union Internationale des Étudiants Musulmans ('The International Union of Muslim Students') was founded, through which Islamist students could gather at the Free University of Brussels and through which they kept in touch with like-minded organizations elsewhere in Europe, especially the AEIF in France.[112] In the 1980s, the Al-Khalil Mosque in Brussels was also part of a broader network that sympathized with the Muslim Brotherhood.[113] Just like in France, the organization's thought gained a foothold through the activism of members of the Tunisian MTI and Ennahda who had fled to Belgium.[114]

The most important institutional expression of the Muslim Brotherhood in Belgium is the Ligue Islamique Interculturelle de Belgique ('Intercultural Islamic League of Belgium'; LIIB), which was founded in 1997 and which is also affiliated with the FIOE.[115] The organization has branches in several cities in Belgium, such as Brussels, Antwerp, Liege and Ghent, but the LIIB as a whole is small.[116] Supporters of the Muslim Brotherhood movement have also been involved in pro-Palestinian charities, just like in other Western European countries.[117] Together, these groups have gone through a similar development as the French UOIF and affiliated groups, namely, a process of integration in the new society in which they find themselves, while striving to combine a pious lifestyle with full participation and citizenship in that society, with respect for the authorities.[118]

Germany and the Netherlands

While France and Belgium (partly) have the French language in common and, partly because of this, share many mutual contacts and have been influenced by the same people, this is not the case for Germany and the Netherlands. That said, Germany and the Netherlands do have a number of things in common with regard to religion: neither country has a state church or a secular system as, respectively, Great Britain and France do, although they do both have a relatively close connection between church and state. In Germany, this manifests itself in a religious tax that most Germans must pay, while in the Netherlands, this connection exists because of the strong historical ties between the monarchy and the Dutch Reformed Church; both countries – unlike Great Britain, France and Belgium – have also been strongly influenced by both Roman Catholicism and Protestantism, albeit in different ways; and, finally, both countries also have a large community of Muslims of Turkish descent, which one does not find in either Great Britain or France.

The first Muslim community in the German city that would become the centre of activities of the Muslim Brotherhood movement – Munich – did not come from Turkey, however, but from the Soviet Union. The group in question consisted of Muslims who had voluntarily served in the German

army during World War II and who, as survivors, settled in Munich, where
the community numbered about a thousand people in the 1950s.[119] It was not
until later that they were joined by many Turkish (and other) immigrants,
who mostly came to Germany as guest workers. For a long time, there was
little government interference with Muslims, but after the Islamic Revolution
in Iran in 1979, and particularly after the attacks of 11 September 2001 in the
United States, intelligence services began showing more scepticism towards
Muslims in general and Islamists in particular.[120]

In the above-mentioned context, two networks surrounding Muslim
Brothers and their sympathizers came into existence in Germany: the first
was concentrated in Munich and sprang from the activities of Sa'id Ramadan
and what later became the Islamische Gemeinschaft in Deutschland ('Islamic
Community in Germany'; IGD); the second network developed around the
Syrian Muslim Brother 'Isam al-'Attar, whom we saw in Chapter 3, from
the Bilal Mosque in Aachen. These networks – once again – began with the
arrival of students from the Arab world – some of whom were Islamists – who
had fled to Germany because of the repression they were suffering in their
home countries in the 1950s and 1960s.[121]

The first network of the Muslim Brotherhood movement came into existence when one of the Islamist students who had fled, Sa'id Ramadan, came
to Germany in the 1950s. Ramadan would later set up the Islamic centres
mentioned above, but in the 1950s he managed to get a job as a cultural
attaché at the Jordanian embassy in Bonn. Situated there, he obtained his
PhD in Islamic law at the University of Cologne in the late 1950s.[122] In the
same period, Muslim Brothers founded the Islamische Gemeinschaft in
Süddeutschland ('Islamic Community in Southern Germany'; IGSD),[123] an
organization that was closely tied to a committee that had been founded
to bring about the building of a mosque in Munich that Ramadan had also
been deeply involved in.[124] In 1964, students from the same network founded
the Muslim Studenten Vereinigung in Deutschland ('Muslim Students
Association in Germany'; MSV)[125] and four years later the building of the
mosque was completed and it was opened and presented as the Islamic
centre of Munich in 1973.[126]

The second network was concentrated around al-'Attar, who had lived
in Aachen since the late 1960s. From that city, he led the Syrian Muslim
Brotherhood in Europe.[127] This fact did not escape the attention of the
Syrian intelligence services either, however, which sent secret agents to
Germany to attack Muslim Brothers there, where, among other things,
they were responsible for the assassination of al-'Attar's wife in 1981.[128] The
Bilal Mosque in Aachen was also an important centre of Islamist activities,

particularly for Syrian Muslim Brothers who had fled the repression in their own country.[129] In 1978, an Islamic centre was founded from this mosque as well, with al-'Attar as its head.[130]

Although there were contacts between both networks, they mostly acted separately. The network in Munich was more influenced by Egyptian Muslim Brothers, while the group in Aachen directed its attention towards Syria. Still, this distinction was not absolute, which was underlined by the fact that Ghaleb Himmat (1938), who was of Syrian descent himself, took over the leadership of the mosque in Munich in 1973.[131] Under his leadership, the IGSD changed its name into IGD, thereby indicating that the organization would no longer just focus on Southern Germany, but on the entire country.[132] Today, the IGD – which renamed itself Deutsche Muslimische Gemeinschaft ('German Muslim Community'; DMG) in 2018 – influences Islamic centres through like-minded people in various cities in Germany such as Frankfurt, Stuttgart and Cologne.[133] This development partly took place under the leadership of Ibrahim El-Zayat (1968). The latter led the organization from 2002–2010, was connected through family ties with various other Islamists in Europe and, moreover, played an important role in both the MSV in Germany and the FEMYSO in Brussels.[134]

The position of El-Zayat was and is not the only way in which the IGD/ DMG is connected with other organizations. The group is also tied to the Zentralrat der Muslime in Deutschland ('Central Council of Muslims in Germany'; ZMD), which is also the case for the Islamic centre in Aachen,[135] and it is also part of the pan-European FIOE.[136] In addition, the organization has personal, historical and ideological – but not organizational – ties with the Muslim Brotherhood.[137] Yet, the influence of the IGD/DMG has remained limited because the number of Muslims in Germany that support the Muslim Brotherhood movement has always been small.[138] This is partly related to the presence of much more influential Turkish organizations in Germany, including Milli Görüş. Because this organization has an ideology similar to that of the Muslim Brotherhood, there has been much cooperation with organizations like the IGD/DMG, but the cultural division (Turkish/Arab) ensures an enduring separation between them.[139]

A very different factor that has limited the activities of the IGD/DMG is the judicial investigation that has been undertaken into the IGD because of its alleged financial malpractices, its supposed attempt to spread Islamist ideas at a school and its relationship with the Muslim Brotherhood.[140] The organization operates completely openly and legally, however, and deals with student activities, the building of mosques and speaks out via publica-tions about issues in the Muslim world and Islamic affairs in Germany and

Europe.[141] Moreover, El-Zayat has explicitly come out in favour of a German, fully integrated Islam.[142] As such, suspicions about malign relations with the 'extremist' Muslim Brotherhood or accusations against the IGD about support for or close ties with Al-Qaida terrorists – who, for example, once visited the Islamic centre in Munich – turned out to be legally untenable.[143]

The discrepancy between suspicions against the Muslim Brothers and their actual activities is even clearer in the Netherlands. Unlike in Germany, the Netherlands does have a Muslim community that is tied to the country's colonial past, namely, in Indonesia (as the Dutch East Indies) and Surinam. Yet, as is the case in other European countries, the majority of the Dutch Muslim community has its roots in the migration of guest workers from especially Morocco and Turkey since the 1970s, and who have also gone through a process of institutionalization in the Netherlands.[144] As in Germany, it can be observed that Moroccan- and Turkish-Dutch communities each have their own mosques and associations, which ensures a certain division within the Muslim community.[145] Finally, the Dutch Muslim community has also not escaped a certain antipathy from others, including in response to specific incidents (the Rushdie affair in 1989, the attacks of 11 September 2001 in the United States and the murder of Dutch film director Theo van Gogh by a radical Islamist in 2004).[146]

It is within this context that the Dutch Muslim Brotherhood operates or, rather, does not operate, since it is highly doubtful whether we can actually speak of any sort of Muslim Brotherhood in the Netherlands. The country has never hosted pioneering people such as Sa'id Ramadan or Kamal Helbawy and there is hardly any academic literature published in the Netherlands on the Muslim Brotherhood. Moreover, any literature that does exist on Muslim Brotherhood-like Islamism in the Netherlands focusses on the Turkish Milli Görüş organization, which is rooted in a different cultural tradition.[147] Reports by the Algemene Inlichtingen- en Veiligheidsdienst ('General Intelligence and Security Service'; AIVD) mention the Muslim Brotherhood infrequently, but whenever they do, it is mostly in a negative way, suggesting that the organization is a threat to democracy, but this is not usually connected with the Netherlands (or even with Europe).[148]

When reports published by the AIVD do establish a direct link between the (Middle Eastern) Muslim Brotherhood and the Netherlands, they deal with alleged individual sympathizers of the organization: some are said to have been on the boards of Islamic schools, certain Salafi imams allegedly with roots in the Muslim Brotherhood or individual adherents supposedly involved in activities such as founding mosques, setting up organizations, organizing conferences and establishing ties with politicians.[149] There are more specific assertions, however, including an alleged relationship between the Muslim Brotherhood and the Essalaam Mosque in Rotterdam, and the Wester Mosque[150] or the Blue Mosque, in Amsterdam.[151] Another concerns the ties between the Muslim Brotherhood and the Contact Groep Islam ('Contact Group Islam'; CGI) and Yahia Bouyafa, the chairperson of this group, but reports about this were later retracted when a judge ruled that Bouyafa was correct in saying that he had no relationship with the Muslim Brotherhood.[152]

Apart from these examples, Dutch Muslim Brothers – either as individuals or as organizations – are also said to have ties with European expressions of the Muslim Brotherhood, such as the Bilal Mosque in Aachen, the FIOE (which was said to have ties with the Federatie Islamitische Organisaties ('Federation of Islamic Organizations'; FIO) in the Netherlands or an organization of scholars to which al-Qaradawi also belonged.[153] It is often difficult to establish the truth of these assertions, although these examples do tie in well with what the Muslim Brotherhood is, namely, a politically engaged, activist organization that strives for influence in a peaceful and legal way, just as other politically engaged, activist organizations across the world do. These claims are made, however, in a context in which they are accompanied by the conviction that the Muslim Brotherhood cannot be trusted, because it allegedly strives for the founding of an Islamic state[154] and, moreover, is said to sympathize with and collect money for Hamas.[155]

When analysing these assertions, several remarks can be made: firstly, the claim that something or someone has 'ties' to the Muslim Brotherhood appears as an accusation in and of itself, apparently based on the belief that the organization poses a danger; secondly, there appears to be little effort to distinguish between the Muslim Brotherhood as an organization – with formal decision-making procedures, a hierarchical structure and a specific leadership – and the Muslim Brotherhood as a movement, with only a shared ideology and culture. This way, sympathies towards Islamism as a movement can easily be explained as 'proof' that someone 'belongs to the Muslim Brotherhood', which suggests membership of the organization; finally, in 2011, the AIVD itself concluded that there were only a few dozen active Muslim Brothers in the Netherlands, that they had little influence and that they were not acting illegally. It added that if the Muslim Brotherhood did gain influence, it might contribute to polarization, goals that clash with the democratic order and an 'undesirable situation' ('onwenselijke situatie').[156] This was worded so vaguely, however, that it seemed intended to cover all possible scenarios, rather than to give expression to an actual, concrete suspicion of trouble that might develop in the future.

The Changing Ideology of the Muslim Brotherhood in Europe

The Muslim Brotherhood movement in the Netherlands – unlike that in Great Britain, France and Germany, where there are networks of organizations inspired by the Muslim Brotherhood – only exists as a (small) network of individuals that sympathize with the (ideology of) the organization and who do not engage in violent or illegal activities. The fact that we can nevertheless discern negative claims about the alleged presence of this group is probably related to the idea that the ideology of the Muslim Brotherhood has not just remained the same throughout time, but also irrespective of national and continental differences. This does not do justice, however, to the debates that have taken place over the decades within the Muslim Brotherhood movement to legitimize the presence, integration and participation of Muslims in the West.

The Jurisprudence of Minorities

Building on classical Islamic ideas about Muslims outside the *dar al-Islam* and the rulings derived from these by modern scholars and thinkers within the Muslim Brotherhood, modern-day Islamist scholars have developed *fiqh al-aqalliyyat* ('the jurisprudence of minorities'). The two scholars who were responsible for the foundations of this jurisprudence in the late twentieth century were the Iraqi-American scholar Taha Jabir al-'Alwani (1935–2016) and the aforementioned al-Qaradawi.[157] While al-'Alwani was probably most influential in the United States, al-Qaradawi has enjoyed greater influence among sympathizers of the Muslim Brotherhood in Europe,[158] including through the ECFR, which also deals with *fiqh al-aqalliyyat*.[159] Through this council, all kinds of other scholars have also become involved in the jurisprudence of minorities.[160] Moreover, Tariq Ramadan's books and personal experiences as a Muslim in Europe have been influential among European Muslims, specifically in terms of the combination of piety and full citizenship.[161]

Fiqh al-aqalliyyat was created to meet the specific needs of Muslim minorities.[162] It is based on the principle that Islam is a universal religion that should therefore be applicable everywhere, including in non-Muslim countries. It thereby eliminates the old distinction between the *dar al-Islam* and the *dar al-harb*, ensuring that countries in which Muslims can exercise their religion are no longer seen as areas with which Muslims are in a (theoretical) state of war. This *'alamiyyat al-Islam* ('the universality of Islam') – to facilitate the success of Muslim communities in non-Muslim countries – subsequently allows scholars to refrain from focussing on the rules of the Sharia and instead to concentrate on its broader goals, which creates a greater legal flexibility.[163] This manifests itself specifically on the basis of the same concepts that we have already seen among the *wasatiyya* in Chapter 7, such as *ijtihad, maslaha, darura* and *taysir*.[164]

On the basis of the concepts mentioned above – which, in turn, are rooted in a longer Islamic tradition – scholars such as al-Qaradawi have given concrete form to the legitimacy of Muslims' presence in Europe. Building on the aforementioned ideas of, for example, Rida, al-'Alwani and al-Qaradawi state that *da'wa* is an important reason to legitimize (and, because of the necessity to preach Islam, perhaps even to obligate) the presence of Muslims in non-Muslim countries.[165] Muslim Brothers in Europe have adopted this idea by pointing to European countries as *dar al-da'wa* ('the abode of preaching'). This label indicates that the area is not *dar al-Islam*, because the Sharia is not applied there, but simultaneously employs *da'wa* to legitimize that Muslims are not guests in Europe, but are there to stay.[166] This message is reinforced by Tariq Ramadan, who goes further by stating that the West enables Muslims to fully live as believers and as moral beings, which he refers to as *shahada* ('confession'). Wherever that is possible, he believes, Muslims are at home and have the responsibility to live as Muslims, regardless of whether non-Muslims convert to Islam or not.[167] Hence, Europe is not *dar al-da'wa*, but *dar al-shahada* ('the abode of confession'),[168] which – to European thinkers such as Ramadan and Tareq Oubrou – means that one may be a witness of Islam by living an exemplary lifestyle, rather than actively preaching one's religion.[169]

The above reasoning cancels the classical idea that Muslims should emigrate from non-Muslim countries to Islamic territory. Al-Qaradawi contextualizes the Koranic verses and traditions that seem to command such emigration and states that they only call on Muslims to leave an area if they are being oppressed.[170] This is supported by al-Qaradawi's emphasis on Koranic verses that are said to have been revealed in Mecca, where Muslims themselves were initially a minority. By mentioning verses such as '[...] so let whosoever will believe, and let whosoever will disbelieve. [...]' (sura 18:29) and 'And if thy Lord had willed, whoever is in the earth would have believed, all of them, all together. Wouldst thou then constrain the people, until they are believers?' (sura 10:99), al-Qaradawi contends implicitly that a religiously pluralist society is God's will.[171] He also states, on the basis of the aforementioned sura 60:8, that Muslims are allowed to be friendly towards non-Muslims who do not deal with them in a hostile way.[172] Scholars such as al-Qaradawi and like-minded others therefore state that, apart from *hubb 'aqa'idi* ('creedal love', love for fellow Muslims), there is also *hubb fitri* ('innate love') on the basis of other matters, which provides the religious foundation of connectedness with non-Muslims.[173]

The above suggests that Muslims in non-Muslim countries ought to behave as good citizens, adhering to the laws of the country while simultaneously cherishing their faith and the Muslim community and trying to convert others through their own good behaviour.[174] To be able to accomplish successful citizenship of Muslims in non-Muslim countries, the practitioners of *fiqh al-aqalliyyat* make use of the means that Islamic law offers to facilitate and ease this process. As such, the ECFR (and al-Qaradawi before that) explains in a fatwa that – despite the prohibition on paying interest in Islam – taking out a mortgage is allowed because of the necessity to buy a house and to offer safety to a family.[175] Based on sura 60:8, the ECFR also allows Muslims to wish non-Muslims well on the occasion of religious holidays, such as Christmas and Easter.[176] Al-Qaradawi also consents to French girls' taking off their headscarves during classes at state schools in order to be able to get an education, which he considers a necessity.[177] Al-Qaradawi also ascribes al-Banna's opposition to citizenship for Muslims in non-Muslim countries to the influence of colonialism. Because this is no longer relevant, al-Qaradawi states that Muslims may now become citizens of the European countries in which they live if they can safeguard their legal status by doing so.[178]

The practitioners of *fiqh al-aqalliyyat* who belong to the Muslim Brotherhood movement, such as al-Qaradawi and the ECFR, therefore argue in favour of strong commitment from Muslims to the societies of their non-Muslim countries. It goes without saying that this also has consequences for the duty to wage jihad. Consequently, Muslim scholars indicate that Muslim minorities can also wage jihad in other ways than fighting, for example by donating money to charity or by boycotting the enemy's products. Their citizenship in a non-Muslim country also forbids them from going against that country, even if that state wages an aggressive war against a Muslim country,[179] although fighting in a non-Muslim army against other Muslims remained forbidden.[180] This changed, however, after the attacks of 11 September 2001 in America, when the United States led a war in Afghanistan against Al-Qaida. Scholars such as al-'Alwani, al-Qaradawi and like-minded others stated at the time that this war was a just one. Moreover, participating in the army would be less bad for the Muslim community than leaving the army.[181] Precisely because this point of view was closely tied to the alleged justice of this war, the same scholars forbade participation in the Iraq war of 2003, because they did not believe this war to have the same just character as the one in Afghanistan.[182]

Islamic scholars dealing with *fiqh al-aqalliyyat* have also created more space for Muslim minorities with regard to political participation. Al-Qaradawi states that it is not allowed to participate in an un-Islamic system in principle. Yet, resorting to the principles of the Sharia that we saw in the previous chapter, he states that there may be reasons to make an exception to this rule, such as the possibility to lessen evil or the necessity to choose the lesser of two evils, provided this does not entail cooperation with tyranny or prohibited things.[183] Political participation can also be legitimate because it helps Muslims to defend their necessary rights, even if this means pledging fealty to an un-Islamic constitution,[184] and it can also be necessary to promote justice in general – including for non-Muslims.[185]

Ideological Developments among the Muslim Brotherhood in Europe

So far, we have made a distinction between the Muslim Brotherhood as an organization and the Muslim Brotherhood as a movement, with the latter being the ideological and cultural heir of the Arab (and especially Egyptian and Syrian) organization. That this cultural, Arab factor matters became clear, for instance, in the differences with South Asian or Turkish Islamists in Great Britain and Germany, but what have European Muslim Brothers retained from the ideology of their Middle Eastern predecessors? In general, they adopted the ideology of their home countries, primarily in the initial phase of the movement's development, but the Muslim Brotherhood movement has not stopped developing ideologically, as the reforms by scholars such as al-Qaradawi and organizations like the ECFR show. These European ideological developments have partly also translated into concrete positions adopted by Islamists who together make up the Muslim Brotherhood movement in Europe.

Firstly, European Muslim Brothers have in common with their Middle Eastern predecessors that they are both rooted in *salafi* modernism. Especially Tariq Ramadan considers the Muslim Brotherhood and himself as the heirs of nineteenth-century reformers. This is connected with the shared desire to return to the Koran and the Sunna, but also manifests itself in the translation of the anti-colonialist ideas of the past to what he sees as 'resistance against political, economic and cultural colonialism to preserve the Muslim identity' and strive for unity among Muslims. The idea that the Muslim Brotherhood is part of and continues this tradition, is also shared by others associated with the European Muslim Brotherhood movement.[186] Secondly, the idea of the all-encompassing nature of Islam, which makes the religion relevant in all spheres of life, also continues to exist among European Muslim Brothers, although this does not necessarily take shape in the same way as in, for example, Egypt. This means that there is difference of opinion on how to apply this all-encompassing aspect of Islam in a European context and it is therefore difficult for some supporters of the Muslim Brotherhood to fully let go of old, unrealistic ideas like the application of the Sharia at the state level.[187]

Thirdly, to European Muslim Brothers, the belief in Islam as an all-encompassing religion means that they also adhere to a conception of what it means to be a Muslim similar to that of the Arab Muslim Brotherhood, namely, that Islam is not just a religion of rituals and books, but also a lifestyle. As such, Muslim Brothers should live pious and pure lives on the level of their own personal situation, their families and society.[188] Reforms should also, just like with the Muslim Brotherhood in the Arab world, take place gradually and peacefully.[189] A fourth aspect that European Muslim Brothers have in common with the organization in the Arab world is a strong solidarity with the Palestinians. The anti-Semitic character that this takes in the Middle East sometimes is almost entirely absent among European Muslim Brothers; still, the relationship that the conflict has with, for example, participation in the commemoration of the Holocaust – which some experience as hypocritical because of the ongoing suffering in the world and, moreover, consider an implicit show of support for Israel – remains present for some European Muslim Brothers.[190]

Strongly related to the Palestinian question is the admissibility of violence. Just like the Muslim Brotherhood in the Arab world, European Muslim Brothers see the Palestinian struggle against Israel as a defensive battle for independence against a military occupation and, as such, as fundamentally justified. The fact that Jerusalem plays a major role in Islam gives this an added dimension. Moreover, they also follow al-Qaradawi in this, who is strongly pro-Palestinian and gave his consent to armed struggle against Israel. Within this context, it is not surprising that European Muslim Brothers distance themselves from groups such as Al-Qaida and IS, but express their support for Hamas.[191] In line with this is the fact that European Muslim Brothers were often reluctant to condemn Hamas' suicide bombings in the past, precisely because to them, these were (perhaps undesirable, yet nevertheless) justified expressions of a just struggle against the military occupation of Islamic, Palestinian land.[192]

The ideological similarity with the Arab Muslim Brotherhood is probably partly a result of the fact that the founders and early leaders of the movement in Europe – Sa'id Ramadan, 'Isam al-'Attar, Kamal Helbawy and many others – were all from the Arab world and were formed there. They brought their experiences, ideas, fears, traumas, priorities and cultural sensitivities with them from their home countries and operated based on that attitude, often causing them to continue to look at Europe as if it was a strange land where they did not really belong. This is much less the case with later generations of leaders within the Muslim Brotherhood movement in European countries. They were often born in, for instance, Germany, know that country better than their predecessors, consider it their own and act accordingly.[193] This can clearly be seen in a more detailed look at the political ideas of European Muslim Brothers.

When we look at the subject of state formation we can conclude that, historically, this has had several different applications: a caliphate or various types of an Islamic state. Both hardly play a role anymore in the discourse of European Muslim Brothers. It has also long ceased to be a concrete goal to Muslim Brothers in the Middle East, but this is even more the case in European countries. Some still see the caliphate as a vague ideal, but as a concrete issue, it does not play a role. As such, groups like Hizb al-Tahrir are condemned because they still adhere to this ideal. The same essentially applies to an Islamic state. While the Muslim Brotherhood in the Arab world has started striving for a civil state with an Islamic authority over the past few decades, even this watered-down version does not play a role among European Muslim Brothers and is seen as unrealistic,[194] perhaps because the idea of a civil state is common in Europe, making the addition of an Islamic authority less necessary.

Political participation is an entirely different issue. This has been a concrete reality for the Muslim Brotherhood in the Arab world for decades in the form of parliamentary participation, but it has also found expression in a more distant past in the form of legitimizations of revolutionary violence against the state, for example by Qutb in Egypt in the 1960s. European Muslim Brothers reject revolutionary violence against the states in which they live and clearly choose the gradual policy that has almost always characterized the organization and the movement.[195] European Muslim Brothers also pair this rejection of a Qutbian jihad against the state with a reinterpretation of the concept of 'jihad'. While they still acknowledge that jihad can mean an armed struggle if it has a defensive character, such as in the Palestinians' case, they also emphasize jihad as a spiritual struggle towards reform and improvement of one's own life.[196] In addition, they emphasize – in line with classical Islamic tradition, where this is connected with commanding right and forbidding wrong,[197] but also in line with al-Qaradawi's work[198] – that jihad has a societal meaning and can boil down to promoting stability, peace, security, tolerance and social well-being.[199]

Precisely because European Muslim Brothers strive for social reform, political participation is also desirable. Given the fact that ideological obstacles to this were removed by the aforementioned scholars and Europe can be seen as *dar al-da'wa*, European Muslim Brothers have come to realize that they are going to stay in Western Europe and can invest in it politically. There is no overarching, common project to do so,[200] but supporters of the Muslim Brotherhood movement do participate in elections in the framework of existing parties sometimes, such as in Great Britain on the candidate list of the Liberal Democrats,[201] or call on Muslims to vote for certain parties.[202]

Although state formation and political participation are themes on which the Muslim Brotherhood in the Arab world has also developed, this is less the case with societal rights and freedoms, as especially Chapter 4 has shown. With regard to the relationship with non-Muslims, this was partly related to the influence of colonialism, which – in the eyes of many Muslim Brothers – gave the West (and, consequently, sometimes also Christians) a bad reputation. Among European Muslim Brothers, this idea was initially continued, emphasizing the supposed superiority of Islam and the expected decline of the West because of its alleged spiritual void.[203] As a result of greater knowledge of and experience with Europe that many Muslim Brothers have gained in the meantime, this point of view has become more nuanced. They still discern much decadence around them, but they consider themselves as partly responsible for doing something about this by investing, integrating and flourishing in European countries.[204]

For the French Muslim Brother Oubrou, *fiqh al-aqalliyyat* also means that Muslims should adhere to the laws of the non-Muslim countries in which they live. Because jurisprudence is subservient to ethical values that are also shared by non-Muslims, different religions can find common ground here, independent of their specific faith.[205] A different basis of cooperation with, for example, Christians is the idea that Muslims' caliphate can translate into a sort of stewardship on earth. This entails Muslims caring for earth in its entirety, which one can apply to the environment, but also to other human beings. Seen this way, the caliphate becomes a duty to take care of humanity, including non-Muslims. Various Muslim Brothers in Europe therefore seek cooperation with others on themes of mutual interest, for example, the promotion of human rights in Muslim countries.[206]

With regard to women's rights and civil liberties it is clear that some matters, such as men and women who are neither related nor married mixing with each other, remain controversial – and al-Banna was fiercely against it in his time – even though it happens frequently in practice.[207] Muslim Brothers continue to emphasize the necessity of wearing a headscarf and they also believe women should dress modestly.[208] In all of this – following the ECFR, whose fatwas are spread and gain authority through Muslim Brotherhood structures in Europe – the Sharia is treated in a flexible way, taking into account the context in which the texts came about as well as the context in which they are applied during interpretation. This way, they give concrete meaning to *fiqh al-aqalliyyat* and the legal means that this provides.[209] Through the increased pairing of the Sharia with individual behaviour and societal action, Muslim Brothers also create space for individual Muslims to commit to applying the Sharia in their own lives instead of striving to do so at the level of the state.[210]

***

Over the years, the Muslim Brotherhood has become international and its members have set up like-minded organizations in various European countries, where they often deny being part of the Muslim Brotherhood and always operate under different names. To some people, this is a reason to view European sympathizers of the organization as part of a worldwide conspiracy of the Muslim Brotherhood that is aimed at establishing a caliphate or an Islamic state in Europe by applying the Sharia. This chapter has shown, however, that the reality is not only more complex, but also more stubborn.

An international conspiracy presupposes a preconceived plan to come to non-Muslim countries. In reality, however, there was great hesitance among classical scholars to allow this and later scholars also had to use exceptional situations to legitimize the presence of Muslims in non-Muslim countries. In other words, this was not a preconceived plan, but a pragmatic (and sometimes reluctant) adjustment to reality. It is this adjustment that offered Muslim Brothers the chance to legitimately and lastingly escape repression in their own countries, the goal that, ultimately, underpins the founding of the International Muslim Brotherhood. The denial of belonging to the Muslim Brotherhood and European Muslim Brothers' use of other names not only has to do with the fact that they are truly organizationally independent of the group in Cairo, Damascus or Amman, but also with a fear of being associated with an organization that has already suffered so much repression.

Although adherents to the European Muslim Brotherhood movement still think and act like the original organization in the Arab world on certain points – including with regard to the controversial issue of support for Hamas's armed struggle against Israel – much has changed. The ideological developments on state formation, political participation and – to a lesser extent – societal rights and freedoms could possibly be seen as attempts by the Muslim Brotherhood to deceive non-Muslims in Europe and to appear 'moderate'. Yet, such a conclusion does not take into account the fact that this ideological development did not appear out of thin air, but 1) largely kept up with similar trends among the Muslim Brotherhood in the Arab world; 2) came about in an organic, gradual and intensely discussed way; and 3) is rooted in centuries-old discussions about the Sharia. The European Muslim Brotherhood movement is therefore not an international conspiracy, but the umpteenth attempt of this Islamist trend to employ its characteristic gradualism, caution and pragmatism to settle in a strange area to rekindle the activism that has motivated the group for almost a century.

Conclusion

The early Muslim Brotherhood was an organization that built on the Islamic reformist ideas from the nineteenth century, which challenged the political and religious authorities, but also reinterpreted Islam for and adapted it to the modern era. As an activist and populist translation of this reformist trend, the organization was highly critical of the internal politics in Egypt, where the Muslim Brotherhood was founded by Hasan al-Banna in 1928, and it tried to push for reforms through the application of the Sharia. It was simultaneously strongly anti-Western, which should be seen in the context of opposition against British colonialism in Egypt and the advent of the Arab-Israeli conflict in Palestine.

The early Muslim Brotherhood strove to establish an Islamic state, but was divided on how important the application of the Sharia was in this regard: an absolute must whose absence implied unbelief or an important condition whose lack did not immediately mean that its culprits were unbelievers? The latter point of view prevailed within the organization. The same division existed within the early organization on the issue of how such a state should be brought about: through violent revolution or through peaceful and gradual preaching and political participation? Again, the second point of view won out. The early Muslim Brotherhood was also divided on societal rights and freedoms, but less so than on the state and political participation. In general, the organization applied a flexible interpretation of the Sharia whenever affairs of human interaction were concerned. With regard to the treatment of non-Muslims, this meant religious and societal rights, but no true equality with Muslims; for women, this entailed that they were equal to men in principle, but with their own tasks, such as raising a family; the Muslim Brotherhood mostly formulated civil liberties in opposition to the limitations applied by dictatorial states, which they often exchanged with Islamically inspired limitations.

In Egypt, the experiences of the Muslim Brotherhood fluctuated between partial permission to participate in politics and repression, with the latter being the most prevalent. With the exception of the 1940s–1960s, this has ultimately not led to radicalization or terrorism from within the Muslim Brotherhood. The same applied to the Muslim Brotherhood in Syria, which was decimated in the 1980s and more or less ceased to exist in the country. After this period, the Syrian branch of the organization also stopped engaging in armed struggle against the regime, did not engage in terrorism and even explicitly rejected Islamist-inspired revolutionary violence altogether, even when a major uprising broke out against the state in 2011. Some of those oppressed in Egypt and Syria fled to Saudi Arabia, where the state presented itself as Islamic and initially offered a lot of space to the highly educated Muslim Brothers fleeing repression. The *sahwa*, a movement that paired the organization's Islamist activism with Wahhabi 'purism', was given the freedom to do so, but its members – despite never having used violence – were ultimately banned, arrested, co-opted or imprisoned after having expressed criticism of the state.

In Kuwait, on the other hand, the Muslim Brotherhood was given the possibility to participate in the political system, which the organization made use of and which caused the group to adopt a pragmatic attitude and, as such, increasingly start accepting the state and democracy; on a societal level, the organization remained more conservative with regard to its willingness to reform, however. The same could be seen in Jordan, where the Muslim Brotherhood held extensive discussions on political participation and decided to take part on ideological grounds, but went less far in reforming its views on societal questions such as women's rights and civil liberties. The Palestinian Hamas appeared to build on the Jordanian experience by choosing an entirely pragmatic (rather than ideological) approach towards political participation. These reformed points of view are also reflected in its increasing acceptance of the reality of the State of Israel, but – again – not so much in similar reforms on societal issues.

In Sudan, a new Muslim Brotherhood came into existence that was more or less independent of the organization in Egypt, but managed to gain power several times through different political parties and contributed to the application of the Sharia. Both factors were less to do with the Muslim Brotherhood, however, and more with the behaviour of Hasan al-Turabi, who – despite his important contributions as an Islamist thinker – proved to be an opportunistic political actor. In Morocco, the PJD, which – through many organizational developments – ultimately became the political standard bearer of the Muslim Brotherhood's ideology in the country, gained power in a system subservient to the guidance of the king. This did not result in the imposition of the Sharia, not even with regard to societal rights and freedoms, which this party also found difficult to reform. Ennahda in Tunisia took a direction similar to that of the PJD, but could operate without having to take the limiting framework of the regime into account. Yet, the organization took a similarly conciliatory stance that took the ideas of others into account, did not impose its own views, was open to compromise and was even willing to give up the power it had gained through free and fair elections before the end of its term.

Several groups have split off or distanced themselves from the Muslim Brotherhood throughout the years. Both Hizb al-Tahrir and the Palestinian Islamic Jihad are, in a sense, radical split-offs from the organization because, unlike the Muslim Brotherhood, both favour direct action or even (non-violent) revolution. In fact, it was partly because of the lack of revolutionary zeal on the part of the Muslim Brotherhood that they went their own way. Strongly influenced by the work of the radical Muslim Brother Sayyid Qutb, the Egyptian Al-Jama'a al-Islamiyya and Tanzim al-Jihad added a Salafi character and an armed method to this direct approach, which expressed itself in assassinations and violent social activism and which distanced them even further from the Muslim Brotherhood. Al-Qaida and IS went even further than the aforementioned organizations through their global jihad and, in the case of IS, through a strongly anti-Shiite ideology, the practical desire to set up a caliphate and what many considered to be extreme violence, all of which deviate from the ideas and practices of the Muslim Brotherhood. As such, Al-Qaida and IS are very critical of the organization.

Others have laid the foundation of the Muslim Brotherhood's willingness to reform or have gone beyond that. The *wasatiyya* is a trend whose adherents strive to find a middle way between what they see as too strong an emphasis on the texts, on the one hand, and dealing with them too loosely, on the other. To express this, they concentrate more on the underlying principles and goals of the Sharia, with which *wasatiyya* scholars such as Yusuf al-Qaradawi have laid the ideological foundations for political and, to a lesser extent, societal reforms within the Muslim Brotherhood and particularly the Egyptian Hizb al-Wasat. Related to this is post-Islamism, a way of thinking that, unlike Islamism, strongly emphasizes rights instead of duties and pluralism rather than uniformity. As such, the contents of post-Islamism closely resemble the outcomes of the *wasatiyya*, which is more of an approach to Islamic tradition and the Sharia. Elements of post-Islamism, which often emanates from Islamism itself, can therefore be found within the Muslim Brotherhood and outside of it, including in the Jordanian ZamZam Initiative from 2012, in which reform, democracy and tolerance are emphasized, but which only proposes a very limited explicit role for Islam.

The Muslim Brotherhood's activities have not remained limited to the Arab world, however. Because of repression (and so out of necessity), several of the organization's members fled and have also ended up in Europe from the 1950s and 1960s onwards. There – increasingly attuned to local needs – they have set up a number of Europe-wide organizations. These are independent of the Muslim Brotherhood organization, but they are part of the Muslim Brotherhood movement in the sense that, ideologically, they stem from the same engaged lay Islamism and are culturally rooted in the same Arab, anti-colonial experiences. In the Western European countries that have been analysed in this book, the Muslim Brotherhood has become less closely related to the Muslim Brotherhood in the Middle East, has only acted peacefully and has become increasingly integrated into the countries in which its members find themselves, although this has not stopped accusations to the contrary. This course of action has been extensively ideologically discussed and legitimized through concepts such as *fiqh al-aqalliyyat* by scholars affiliated with the Muslim Brotherhood movement. Because of this, the ideological foundation has been laid for European Muslim Brothers to combine a pious lifestyle with non-violent activism, political engagement and full citizenship in the Western European countries where they live.

Returning to the different approaches of the Muslim Brotherhood, we can state that the organization is clearly not terrorist. Historically, the Muslim Brotherhood has certainly used violence against the state in Egypt and Syria in the first few decades of its existence, but this did not emanate from its ideology as such, but was mostly due to a process of radicalization that largely took place as a result of the repression that the organization underwent. Consequently, in subsequent years, the Muslim Brotherhood has not engaged in terrorism and has, in fact, explicitly distanced itself from it, which is one of the reasons that other, radical Islamist organizations have split off from or have criticized it. There is one exception to this rule, namely Hamas. This Palestinian branch of the Muslim Brotherhood has committed dozens of suicide bombings against Israeli civilians, in which many were killed or wounded, until 2005. Since then, this organization has also fired literally thousands of rockets at Israeli civilian targets. Although these acts can easily be described as 'terrorism', they should be seen in the context of the Israeli occupation and large-scale military operations from Israel's side. Moreover, Hamas's terrorism was exclusively limited to this one conflict. Because of this – and without wanting to minimize its seriousness – it is not comparable to, for example, the international terrorism of an organization such as Al-Qaida.

The idea that the Muslim Brotherhood is a theocratic, anti-democratic and enduringly fundamentalist organization should also be criticized. Throughout the years, the Muslim Brotherhood has increasingly downplayed its demand for the founding of an Islamic state and it has also adopted increasingly liberal ideas on the application of the Sharia. Moreover, democracy has become increasingly accepted within the organization, not so much as a pragmatic step towards something else, but as a strategic and ideologically justified choice. The situation is more complicated with regard to societal rights and freedoms, however. The Muslim Brotherhood has clearly conceded far less on this point. This is probably due to the relatively clear texts in the Koran on, for example, women's rights, and because of the generally conservative social norms in the Arab world that would not allow a different attitude from the populist Muslim Brotherhood. As such, the Muslim Brotherhood does not just shape conservative social norms, but is also a product of them. The organization sometimes portrays this as a sign of the extent to which it reflects society and, therefore, as proof of its democratic credentials, but to others this remains problematic.

The claim that the Muslim Brotherhood is an international conspiracy that strives for the (violent) application of the Sharia is largely incorrect, which is probably also the reason that no serious scholar claims this to be the case. To be sure, there is cooperation between the different organizations that are affiliated or sympathize with the Muslim Brotherhood and that, moreover, also have much in common ideologically and culturally (hence 'largely'), but the movement as a whole is simply too divided, too unorganized and too uncoordinated to begin to call this a conspiracy. The plans that adherents to this idea ascribe to the Muslim Brotherhood, such as the desire to found an Islamic state or to apply the Sharia, have all been watered down to such an extent throughout the years that it does not do justice to the movement to cite early ideologues such as al-Banna (let alone Qutb) to 'prove' this theory. The fact that European organizations that make up the Muslim Brotherhood as a movement do not call themselves 'Muslim Brotherhood' is therefore not the result of cunning plans or secret agendas; this has to do with the fact that they are not actually part of the Muslim Brotherhood as an organization, with that group's controversial reputation and with the ingrained fear – based on decades of repression – to be seen and treated as Muslim Brothers. As such, attempts by Muslim Brothers to gain influence in politics, school boards and mosque councils are not examples of stealthy infiltration, but of behaviour that characterizes political parties, activists and ideological organizations all over the world. One may differ over whether this is desirable or not, but it is not a conspiracy.

So, what is the Muslim Brotherhood? This book has made clear that it is an organization that has been strongly marked by its past in the Middle East, given the enduring inspiration it derives from nineteenth-century reformers and the Islamist ideology that emanates from it, as well as the context of colonial and dictatorial traumas from which the group originated. At the same time, the Muslim Brotherhood has continually adapted – both ideologically and practically – to the new contexts in which it found itself (particularly in Europe) and has developed itself into what it is today: a pragmatic, peaceful, flexible and activist organization and – in a broader sense – a movement that strives for political and societal reforms on the basis of an Islamist ideology that it has truly and gradually adjusted throughout the years.

It is precisely because this description of today's Muslim Brotherhood is not very precise that ensures that it can incorporate different forms. One could argue, therefore, that some of the politicians mentioned in the foreword of this book are not so much fearsome exponents of a dangerous organization, but rather examples of the extent to which the Muslim Brotherhood movement has developed throughout the years. This will not reassure all the readers of this book, just like the previous chapters may not have erased all worries about the group, which was never the purpose of this book. It does show, however, that the Muslim Brotherhood is a dynamic group with an ideological, historical and cultural tradition that is too complex to reduce to simple labels or stereotypes.

Notes

Introduction

1. All quotations from the Koran were taken from A.J. Arberry, *The Koran Interpreted* (New York: Touchstone, 1955), although my verse numbering follows the more common verse numbering found in other translations. All other translations of any languages are my own.

2. For a possibly apocryphal story that supports this reading, see Martyn Frampton, *The Muslim Brotherhood and the West: A History of Enmity and Engagement* (Cambridge, MA: Belknap/Harvard University Press, 2018), 11.

3. W.J. Berridge, *Islamism in the Modern World: A Historical Approach* (London: Bloomsbury, 2019), 3.

4. François Burgat and William Dowell, *The Islamic Movement in North Africa* (Austin, TX: Center for Middle Eastern Studies, University of Texas at Austin, 1993), 39–40.

5. Berridge, *Islamism*, 4–5.

6. *Ibid.*, 5; William Shepard, 'Islam and Ideology: Towards a Typology', *International Journal of Middle East Studies* 19, no. 3 (1987): 311–314.

7. Berridge, *Islamism*, 6.

8. *Ibid.*, 5–6; Shepard, 'Islam', 314–317; *idem*, 'The Diversity of Islamic Thought: Towards a Typology', in *Islamic Thought in the Twentieth Century*, eds. Suha Taji-Farouki and Basheer M. Nafi (London and New York: I.B. Tauris, 2004), 74–80.

9. Bruce B. Lawrence, 'Muslim Fundamentalist Movements: Reflections Toward a New Approach', in *The Islamic Impulse*, ed. Barbara Freyer Stowasser (Washington, DC: Center for Contemporary Arab Studies at Georgetown University, 1987), 17–18.

10. Berridge, *Islamism*, 2; Lawrence, 'Muslim', 18–19. Choueiri states that the Arabic term '*usuli*' can be translated with 'fundamentalist' and has a long history in Islam. It is doubtful, however, whether this term has, historically, always been used to refer to the same phenomenon. See Youssef M. Choueiri, *Islamic Fundamentalism 3rd Edition: The Story of Islamist Movements* (London and New York: Continuum, 2010), 1–5.

11. Berridge, *Islamism*, 2.

12. Burgat and Dowell, *Islamic*, 19–20; Roxanne L. Euben, *Enemy in the Mirror: Islamic Fundamentalism and the Limits of Modern Rationalism* (Princeton, NJ: Princeton University Press, 1999), 16–19. This is also the approach adopted in Michael Cook, *Ancient Religions, Modern Politics: The Islamic Case in Comparative Perspective* (Princeton, NJ: Princeton University Press, 2014), 371–398. For an extensive discussion of the term 'fundamentalism' in the context of Islam, see Lawrence, 'Muslim', 15–36.

13. Joas Wagemakers, 'Making Definitional Sense of Islamism', *Orient: Deutsche Zeitschrift für Politik, Wirtschaft und Kultur des Orients* 62, no. 2 (2021): 7–13.

14. The definition of fundamentalism used by Marty and Appleby is broader and does encompass the practices of the Muslim Brotherhood. See Martin E. Marty and R. Scott Appleby, 'Introduction', in *Accounting for Fundamentalisms: The Dynamic Character of Movements*, eds. Martin E. Marty and R. Scott Appleby (Chicago, IL, and London: University of Chicago Press, 1994), 1.

15. Berridge, *Islamism*, 3–4; Shepard, 'Islam', 308.

16. Burgat and Dowell, *Islamic*, 9–10.

17. Berridge, *Islamism*, 8–9; Euben, *Enemy*, 25–48; Salwa Ismail, *Rethinking Islamist Politics: Culture, the State and Islamism* (London: I.B. Tauris, 2006), 2–11; Emad Eldin Shahin, *Political Ascent: Contemporary Islamic Movements in North Africa* (Boulder, CO: Westview, 1998), 8–10, 11–13.

18. Berridge, *Islamism*, 9–10.

19. *Ibid.*, 11–12; Olivier Roy (translation: Carol Volk), *The Failure of Political Islam* (London: I.B. Tauris, 1994), 1–7.

20. Ismail, *Rethinking*, 11–15; Susan Waltz, 'Islamist Appeal in Tunisia', *Middle East Journal* 40, no. 4 (1986): 661–665.

21. Ismail, *Rethinking*, 15.

22. Shahin, *Political*, 13–15.

23. Ismail, *Rethinking*, 15–26.

24. Social movements can be defined as social processes whose participants 'are involved in conflictual relations with clearly defined opponents', 'are linked by dense informal networks' and 'share a distinct collective identity' through which they are 'engaged in collective action'. See Donatella Della Porta and Mario Diani, *Social Movements: An Introduction* (Malden, MA: Blackwell Publishing, 2006), 20.

25. Khalil al-Anani, 'Upended Path: The Rise and Fall of Egypt's Muslim Brotherhood', *Middle East Journal* 69, no. 4 (2015): 528–529; Mohammed M. Hafez, *Why Muslims Rebel: Repression and Resistance in the Islamic World* (Boulder, CO: Lynne Rienner Publishers, 2003); Quintan Wiktorowicz (ed.), *Islamic Activism: A Social Movement Theory Approach* (Bloomington and Indianapolis, IN: Indiana University Press, 2004).

26. Farid Hafez, 'Criminalizing Muslim Civil Society in the West: The Muslim Brotherhood Allegation', *SETA Perspective* 55 (2019): 1–5.

27. Nachman Tal, *Radical Islam in Egypt and Jordan* (Brighton and Portland, OR: Sussex Academic Press, 2005), 49, 191, 205, 235.

28. Amira El-Azhary Sonbol, 'Egypt', in *The Politics of Islamic Revivalism: Diversity and Unity*, ed. Shireen Hunter (Bloomington and Indianapolis, IN: Indiana University Press, 1988), 31.

29. Daniel Pipes, 'Islamism's Unity in Tunisia', 30 October 2012, danielpipes.org/12103/islamism-unity; Jonathan Schanzer, *Hamas vs. Fatah: The Struggle for Palestine* (New York: Palgrave MacMillan, 2008), 132–135.

30. Barry Rubin, 'Comparing Three Muslim Brotherhoods', in *The Muslim Brotherhood: The Organization and Policies of a Global Islamist Movement*, ed. Barry Rubin (New York: Palgrave MacMillan, 2010), 7–18.

31. J. Millard Burr and Robert O. Collins, *Sudan in Turmoil: Hasan al-Turabi and the Islamist State* (Princeton, NJ: Markus Wiener Publishers, 2010).

32. Cynthia Farahat, 'The Muslim Brotherhood, Fountain of Islamist Violence', *Middle East Quarterly* 24, no. 2 (2017): 2.

33. Schanzer, *Hamas*, 4–5; Samuel Tadros, 'Egypt's Muslim Brotherhood After the Revolution', *Current Trends in Islamist Ideology* 12 (2011): 6, 18.

34. Uriya Shavit, 'Islamotopia: The Muslim Brotherhood's Idea of Democracy', *Azure*, no. 46 (2011): 35–62; Mariz Tadros, 'Participation not Domination: Morsi on an Impossible Mission?', in *Islamists and the Politics of the Arab Uprisings: Governance, Pluralisation and Contention*, eds. Hendrik Kraetzschmar and Paola Rivetti (Edinburgh: Edinburgh University Press, 2018), 22–31.

35. Eric Trager, 'Egypt's Looming Competitive Theocracy', *Current Trends in Islamist Ideology* 14 (2014): 27–37; *idem, Arab Fall: How the Muslim Brotherhood Won and Lost Egypt in 891 Days* (Washington, DC.: Georgetown University Press, 2016), 5.

36. 'Introduction', in *The Muslim Brotherhood in Europe*, eds. Roel Meijer and Edwin Bakker (London: Hurst & Co., 2012), 4–11; Frank Peter, 'Muslim "Double Talk" and the Ways of the Shari'a in France', in *The Muslim Brotherhood in Europe*, eds. Roel Meijer and Edwin Bakker (London: Hurst & Co., 2012), 127–148.

37. Wierd Duk and Maarten Ritman, 'Politieke islam reikt tot in ambtenarenapparaat Rotterdam', *De Telegraaf*, 16 August 2019, telegraaf.nl/nieuws/2439901/politiek-islam-reikt-tot-in-ambtenarenapparaat-rotterdam.

38. Nawaf Obaid, *The Failure of the Muslim Brotherhood in the Arab World*, (Santa Barbara, CA: Praeger Security International, 2020), x.

39. *Ibid.*, xv.

40. *Ibid.*, 121–147.

41. Sana Abed-Kotob, 'The Accommodationists Speak: Goals and Strategies of the Muslim Brotherhood of Egypt', *International Journal of Middle East Studies* 27, no. 3 (1995): 321–339; Khalil al-Anani (translation: William Joseph Ward), 'Egypt's Muslim Brotherhood: From Opposition to Power and Back Again. A Study in the Dynamics of their Rise and Fall', in *The Prospects of Political Islam in a Troubled Region: Islamists and Post-Arab Spring Challenges*, ed. Mohammed Abu Rumman (Amman: Friedrich Ebert Stiftung, 2018), 75–87; Khalil al-Anani, *Inside the Muslim Brotherhood: Religion, Identity, and Politics* (Oxford: Oxford University Press, 2016); Gehad Auda, 'The "Normalization" of the Islamic Movement in Egypt from the 1970s to the Early 1990s', in *Accounting for Fundamentalisms: The Dynamic Character of Movements*, eds. Martin E. Marty and R. Scott Appleby (Chicago, IL, and London: University of Chicago Press, 1994), 375–377, 379–381, 385–391; Hesham al-Awadi, *In Pursuit of Legitimacy: The Muslim Brothers and Mubarak, 1982–2000* (London and New York: I.B. Tauris, 2004); Ana Belén Soage and Jorge Fuentelsaz Franganillo, 'The Muslim Brothers in Egypt', in *The Muslim Brotherhood: The*

Organization and Policies of a Global Islamist Movement, ed. Barry Rubin
(New York: Palgrave MacMillan, 2010), 39–55; Leen den Besten, *De Moslimbroederschap en de utopie van islamisten* (Soesterberg: Uitgeverij Aspect,
2015); Nathan J. Brown, *When Victory is not an Option: Islamist Movements in
Arab Politics* (Ithaca, NY, and London: Cornell University Press, 2012), 86–94,
181–187; Katerina Dalacoura, *Islamist Terrorism and Democracy in the Middle
East* (Cambridge: Cambridge University Press, 2011), 130–140; Amr Elshobaki,
'The Muslim Brotherhood – Between Evangelizing and Politics: The Challenges of Incorporating the Brotherhood into the Political Process', in *Islamist Politics in the Middle East: Movements and Change*, ed. Samer S. Shehata
(London and New York: Routledge, 2012), 107–119; Olaf Farschid, 'Hizbiya:
Die Neuorientierung der Muslimbruderschaft Ägyptens in den Jahren 1984
bis 1989', *Orient: Deutsche Zeitschrift für Politik und Wirtschaft des Orients* 30,
no. 1 (1989): 53–74; Mona El-Ghobashy, 'The Metamorphosis of the Egyptian
Muslim Brothers', *International Journal of Middle East Studies* 37 (2005):
373–395; Shadi Hamid, 'Arab Islamist Parties: Losing on Purpose?', *Journal of
Democracy* 22, no. 1 (2011): 68–80; Chris Harnisch and Quinn Mecham, 'Dem-
ocratic Ideology in Islamist Opposition? The Muslim Brotherhood's "Civil
State"', *Middle Eastern Studies* 45, no. 2 (2009): 189–205; Marc Lynch, *The
Brotherhood's Dilemma* (Waltham, MA: Crown Center for Middle East Studies
at Brandeis University, 2008); Marc Lynch, 'Young Brothers in Cyberspace',
Middle East Report 245 (2007): 26–33; Roel Meijer, 'Moslim Broederschap
maakt zich op voor de democratie van morgen,' *ZemZem: Tijdschrift over het
Midden-Oosten, Noord-Afrika en islam* 1, no. 2 (2005): 56–58; Alison Pargeter,
The Muslim Brotherhood: The Burden of Tradition (London: Saqi Books, 2010),
15–60; idem, *The Muslim Brotherhood: From Opposition to Power* (London:
Saqi Books, 2010), 15–64; Carrie Rosefsky Wickham, *Mobilizing Islam: Reli-
gion, Activism, and Political Change in Egypt* (New York: Columbia University
Press, 2002); idem, *The Muslim Brotherhood: Evolution of an Islamist Move-
ment* (Princeton, NJ, and Oxford: Princeton University Press, 2013); Bruce K.
Rutherford, *Egypt after Mubarak: Liberalism, Islam, and Democracy in the
Arab World* (Princeton, NJ, and Oxford: Princeton University Press, 2008), 77-
99; Samer S. Shehata, 'Political *Da'wa*: Understanding the Muslim Brotherhood's Participation in Semi-Authoritarian Elections', in *Islamist Politics in
the Middle East: Movements and Change*, ed. Samer S. Shehata (London and
New York: Routledge, 2012), 120–145; Denis J. Sullivan and Sana Abed-Kotob,
Islam in Contemporary Egypt: Civil Society vs. the State (Boulder, CO: Lynne
Rienner Publishers, 1999), 41–70; Mohammed Zahid, *The Muslim Brotherhood and Egypt's Succession Crisis: The Politics of Liberalisation and Reform in
the Middle East* (London and New York: I.B. Tauris, 2010), 83–103, 109–127.

42.   Mohammad Suliman Abu Rumman (translation: Issam Daoud Khoury), *The
Muslim Brotherhood in the 2007 Jordanian Parliamentary Elections: A Pass-
ing 'Political Setback' or Diminished Popularity?* (Amman: Friedrich Ebert
Stiftung, 2007), 44–55; Nathan J. Brown, *Jordan and Its Islamic Movement:*

The Limits of Inclusion?, Carnegie Papers no. 74 (Washington, DC: Carnegie Endowment for International Peace, 2006); Juan José Escobar Stemmann, 'The Crossroads of Muslim Brothers in Jordan', in *The Muslim Brotherhood: The Organization and Policies of a Global Islamist Movement*, ed. Barry Rubin (New York: Palgrave MacMillan, 2010), 57–71; Hamid, 'Arab', 69–71; *idem*, 'New Democrats? The Political Evolution of Jordan's Islamists'. Paper presented at the CSIC Sixth Annual Conference 'Democracy and Development: Challenges for the Islamic World', Washington, DC, 22–23 April, 2005; *idem*, *Temptations of Power: Islamists & Illiberal Democracy in a New Middle East* (Oxford: Oxford University Press, 2014); Mansoor Moaddel, *Jordanian Exceptionalism: A Comparative Analysis of State-Religion Relations in Egypt, Iran, Jordan, and Syria* (New York: Palgrave, 2002), 33–36; Glenn E. Robinson, 'Can Islamists Be Democrats? The Case of Jordan', *Middle East Journal* 51, no. 3 (1997): 373–387; Rosefsky Wickham, *Muslim*, 204–218; Jillian Schwedler, 'A Paradox of Democracy? Islamist Participation in Elections', *Middle East Report*, no. 209 (1998): 27–28, 41; Joas Wagemakers, *The Muslim Brotherhood in Jordan* (Cambridge: Cambridge University Press, 2020); Quintan Wiktorowicz, 'Islamists, the State and Cooperation in Jordan', *Third World Quarterly* 21, no. 4 (1999): 1–16; *idem*, *The Management of Islamic Activism: Salafis, the Muslim Brotherhood, and State Power in Jordan* (New York: State University of New York Press, 2001), 93–110.

43.   Idriss al-Kanbouri, 'Morocco's Islamists: Action Outside Religion,' in *The Prospects of Political Islam in a Troubled Region: Islamists and Post-Arab Spring Challenges*, ed. Mohammed Abu Rumman (Amman: Friedrich Ebert Stiftung, 2018), 67–74; Shahin, *Political*, 166–201; Eva Wegner, *Islamist Opposition in Authoritarian Regimes: The Party of Justice and Development in Morocco* (Syracuse, NY: Syracuse University Press, 2011).

44.   Jeroen Gunning, *Hamas in Politics: Democracy, Religion, Violence* (London: Hurst & Co., 2007); Mohammed M. Hafez and Marc-André Walther, 'Hamas: Between Pragmatism and Radicalism', in *Routledge Handbook of Political Islam*, ed. Shahram Akbarzadeh (London: Routledge, 2011), 62–73; Khaled Hroub, 'Die Aktuelle Politik von Hamas: Überleben ohne Strategie', *Inamo* 8, no. 32 (2002): 16–17; *idem*, *Hamas: A Beginner's Guide* (London and Ann Arbor, MI: 2006); *idem*, 'A "New Hamas" Through Its New Documents', *Journal of Palestine Studies* 35, no. 4 (2006): 6–27; International Crisis Group, *Dealing with Hamas*, Middle East Report no. 21 (Amman and Brussels: International Crisis Group, 2004), 13–19; *idem*, *Enter Hamas: The Challenge of Political Integration*, Middle East Report no. 49 (Amman and Brussels: International Crisis Group, 2006); Menachem Klein, 'Hamas in Power', *Middle East Journal* 61, no. 3 (2007): 442–459; Jean-François Legrain, 'Hamas as a Ruling Party', in *Islamist Politics in the Middle East: Movements and Change*, ed. Samer S. Shehata (London and New York: Routledge, 2012), 183–204; Shaul Mishal, 'The Pragmatic Dimension of the Palestinian Hamas: A Network Perspective', *Armed Forces and Society* 29, no. 4 (2003): 569–589;

Shaul Mishal and Avraham Sela, *The Palestinian Hamas: Vision, Violence and Coexistence* (New York: Columbia University Press, 2000); *idem*, 'Participation without Presence: Hamas, the Palestinian Authority and the Politics of Negotiated Coexistence', *Middle Eastern Studies* 38, no. 3 (2002): 1–26; Muhammad Muslih, 'Hamas: Strategy and Tactics', in *Ethnic Conflict and International Politics in the Middle East*, ed. Leonard Binder (Gainsville, FL: University of Florida Press, 1999), 311–326; Joas Wagemakers, 'Legitimizing Pragmatism: Hamas' Framing Efforts from Militancy to Moderation and Back?', *Terrorism and Political Violence* 22 (2010): 357–377.

45. Meijer, 'Moslim', 58–61; Itzchak Weismann, 'Democratic Fundamentalism? The Practice and Discourse of the Muslim Brothers Movement in Syria', *The Muslim World* 100 (2010): 1–16.

46. Francesco Cavatorta and Fabio Merone, 'Moderation Through Exclusion? The Journey of the Tunisian *Ennahda* from Fundamentalist to Conservative Party', *Democratization* 20, no. 5 (2013): 857–875; Dalacoura, *Islamist*, 140–145; Abdul Latif al-Hanashi (translation: William Joseph Ward), 'Tunisia: The Impact of Democratic Transition on the Ennahda Party', in *The Prospects of Political Islam in a Troubled Region: Islamists and Post-Arab Spring Challenges*, ed. Mohammed Abu Rumman (Amman: Friedrich Ebert Stiftung, 2018), 53–65; Monica Marks, 'Tunisia's Islamists and the "Turkish Model"', *Journal of Democracy* 28, no. 1 (2017): 102–115; Rory McCarthy, 'Protecting the Sacred: Tunisia's Islamist Movement Ennahda and the Challenge of Free Speech', *British Journal of Middle Eastern Studies* 42, no. 4 (2015): 447–464; Shahin, *Political*, 63–111.

1.   The General Ideology of the Early Muslim Brotherhood

1.   General works on the political history of Islam and the Arab world include Patricia Crone, *God's Rule: Government and Islam* (New York: Columbia University Press, 2004); Marshall G.S. Hodgson, *The Venture of Islam: Conscience and History in a World Civilization* (3 volumes) (Chicago, IL, and London: The University of Chicago Press, 1974); Albert Hourani, *A History of the Arab Peoples* (London: Faber & Faber, 2013 [1991]); Ira M. Lapidus, *A History of Islamic Societies* (Cambridge: Cambridge University Press, 2002 [1988]).

2.   Marshall G.S. Hodgson, *The Venture of Islam: Conscience and History in a World Civilization – Vol. III: The Gunpowder Empires and Modern Times* (Chicago, IL, and London: The University of Chicago Press, 1974), 105–106.

3.   *Idem, The Venture of Islam: Conscience and History in a World Civilization – Vol. II: The Expansion of Islam in the Middle Periods* (Chicago, IL, and London: The University of Chicago Press, 1974), 214–218.

4.   A well-known example of a Sufi order whose adherents strive for both spirituality and compliance with the Sharia is the Naqshbandiyya. For more on

this, see Itzchak Weismann, *The Naqshbandiyya: Orthodoxy and Activism in a Worldwide Sufi Tradition* (London and New York: Routledge, 2007).

5. Hodgson, *Venture – Vol. II*, 218–220.

6. *Ibid.*, 220–222.

7. Basheer M. Nafi, 'The Rise of Reformist Thought and Its Challenge to Traditional Islam', in *Islamic Thought in the Twentieth Century*, eds. Suha Taji-Farouki and Basheer M. Nafi (London and New York: I.B. Tauris, 2008 [2004]), 31–33.

8. John O. Voll, *Islam: Continuity and Change in the Modern World* (Boulder, CO: Westview Press, 1994 [1982]), 25–27.

9. *Ibid.*, 31–33.

10. *Ibid.*, 33–36, 41–43, 49–51.

11. Albert Hourani, *Arabic Thought in the Liberal Age, 1798–1939* (Cambridge: Cambridge University Press, 1983 [1962]), 38–40.

12. Voll, *Islam*, 29–31.

13. *Ibid.*, 27–29, 37–41, 44–49, 51–52.

14. Choueiri, *Islamic*, 19–21; Nafi, 'Rise,' 33–35.

15. Berridge, *Islamism*, 32–42; Voll, *Islam*, 53–79.

16. For an overview of the discussion on the extent to which there was one reform movement here, see Christian Lange, 'Was There an Arab Intellectual Revival (*Nahda*) in the 17th and 18th Centuries? A Review Essay', in *Oman, Ibadism and Modernity*, eds. Abdulrahman Al Salimi and Reinhard Eisener (Hildesheim: Georg Olms Verlag, 2018), 15–24.

17. Basheer M. Nafi and Suha Taji-Farouki, 'Introduction', in *Islamic Thought in the Twentieth Century*, eds. Suha Taji-Farouki and Basheer M. Nafi (London and New York: I.B. Tauris, 2008 [2004]), 5–8, 10; Nafi, 'Rise,' 36–38, 40.

18. Simon A. Wood, *Christian Criticisms, Islamic Proofs: Rashid Rida's Modernist Defense of Islam* (Oxford: OneWorld, 2008), 17–23. See also Choueiri, *Islamic*, 41–57.

19. For more on al-Afghani, see Hourani, *Arabic*, 103–129; Nikki Keddie, 'Sayyid Jamal al-Din "al-Afghani"', in *Pioneers of Islamic Revival*, ed. Ali Rahnema (London and New York: Zed Books, 2005 [1994]), 11–29; *idem, An Islamic Response to Imperialism: Political and Religious Writings of Sayyid Jamal ad-Din 'al-Afghani'* (Berkeley, CA: University of California Press, 1983 [1968]); *idem, Sayyid Jamal Ad-Din "al-Afghani": A Political Biography* (Berkeley, CA: University of California Press, 1972).

20. For more on 'Abduh, see Hourani, *Arabic*, 130–160; Yvonne Y. Haddad, 'Muhammad Abduh: Pioneer of Islamic Reform', in *Pioneers of Islamic Revival*, ed. Ali Rahnema (London and New York: Zed Books, 2005 [1994]), 30–63.

21. The label '*salafi*' (with a small 's' and italicized) as a reference to *salafi* modernist reformers should not be confused with what we refer to as 'Salafism' (with a capital 'S') today. Although this contemporary trend has, at its core, the same approach to the Koran as earlier *salafi* reformers, unlike the nineteenth-century thinkers mentioned here, it is not aimed at modernizing Islam at all.

22.   Henri Lauzière, 'The Construction of *Salafiyya*. Reconsidering Salafism from
      the Perspective of Conceptual History', *International Journal of Middle East
      Studies* 42, no. 3 (2010): 369–389.

23.   David Dean Commins, *Islamic Reform: Politics and Social Change in Late Ot-
      toman Syria* (New York and Oxford: Oxford University Press, 1990), 79–82.

24.   John O. Voll, 'Renewal and Reform in Islamic History: *Tajdid* and *Islah*', in
      Voices of Resurgent Islam, ed. John L. Esposito (Oxford: Oxford University
      Press, 1983), 32–47.

25.   Nafi, 'Rise', 40–44.

26.   Choueiri, *Islamic*, 38.

27.   For more on Rida, see Hourani, *Arabic*, 222–244; Umar Ryad, *Islamic Reform
      and Christianity: A Critical Reading of the Works of Muhammad Rashid Rida
      and His Associates (1898–1935)* (Leiden: Brill, 2008); Wood, *Christian*.

28.   See Nafi, 'Rise', 45–47.

29.   Henri Lauzière, *The Making of Salafism: Islamic Reform in the Twentieth
      Century* (New York: Columbia University Press, 2016), 60–94.

30.   Andrew F. March, *The Caliphate of Man: Popular Sovereignty in Modern
      Islamic Thought* (Cambridge, MA: Belknap/Harvard University Press, 2019),
      41–61; Wagemakers, *Muslim*, 31–33.

31.   Marion Boulby, *The Muslim Brotherhood and the Kings of Jordan, 1945–1993*
      (Atlanta, GA: Scholars Press, 1999), 126–129.

32.   Beverley Milton-Edwards, *The Muslim Brotherhood: The Arab Spring and Its
      Future Face* (New York: Routledge, 2016), 14–15.

33.   Mehdi Sajid, 'A Reappraisal of the Role of Muhibb al-Din al-Khatib and the
      YMMA in the Rise of the Muslim Brotherhood', *Islam and Christian–Muslim
      Relations* 29, no. 2 (2018): 193–195.

34.   Dale F. Eickelman and James Piscatori, *Muslim Politics* (Princeton, NJ:
      Princeton University Press, 2004 [1996]), 25, 28.

35.   Burgat and Dowell, *Islamic*, 18–19; Shepard, 'Islam', 318–319; *idem*, 'Diversity',
      63–64.

36.   David Commins, 'Hasan al-Banna (1906–1949)', in *Pioneers of Islamic Revival*,
      ed. Ali Rahnema (London and New York: Zed Books, 2005 [1994]), 128–133;
      Gudrun Krämer, *Hasan al-Banna* (London: OneWorld Publications, 2009);
      Brynjar Lia, 'Autobiography or Fiction? Hasan al-Banna's Memoirs Revis-
      ited', *Journal of Arabic and Islamic Studies* 15 (2015): 199–226; *idem, The
      Society of the Muslim Brothers in Egypt: The Rise of an Islamic Mass Move-
      ment, 1928–1942* (Reading, UK: Ithaca Press, 1998), 22–35; Richard P. Mitchell,
      The Society of the Muslim Brothers (Oxford: Oxford University Press, 1993
      [1969]), 1–6.

37.   Lia, *Society*, 32–33.

38.   Ishak Musa Husaini, *The Moslem Brethren: The Greatest of Modern Islamic
      Movements* (Westport, CT: Hyperion Press, Inc., 1986 [1956]), 10–11.

39.   Hasan al-Banna, *Majmu'at Rasa'il al-Imam al-Shahid Hasan al-Banna* (N.P.:
      Dar al-Tawzi', 1992), 202.

40. Husaini, *Moslem*, 7, 30–31.
41. Al-Banna, *Majmu'at*, 417.
42. *Ibid.*, 379–418.
43. Husaini, *Moslem*, 4, 28.
44. *Ibid.*, 9.
45. Al-Banna, *Majmu'at*, 122.
46. Mitchell, *Society*, 216–217.
47. Husaini, *Moslem*, 25; Lia, *Society*, 35.
48. Roel Meijer, 'The Muslim Brotherhood and the Political: An Exercise in Ambiguity', in *The Muslim Brotherhood in Europe*, eds. Roel Meijer and Edwin Bakker (London: Hurst & Co. 2012), 298–308.
49. Mitchell, *Society*, 217–218.
50. *Ibid.*, 220.
51. *Ibid.*, 218–219.
52. *Ibid.*, 220–222.
53. Mitchell, *Society*, 223–224.
54. Husaini, *Moslem*, 29; Mitchell, *Society*, 214.
55. Mitchell, *Society*, 214–215.
56. Lia, *Society*, 34; Mitchell, *Society*, 212.
57. Mitchell, *Society*, 213.
58. *Ibid.*, 213–213.
59. Al-Banna, *Majmu'at*, 18.
60. *Ibid.*, 119.
61. For more on the life of Sayyid Qutb, see Sayyid Qutb (editing and translation: John Calvert and William Shepard), *A Child from the Village* (New York: Syracuse University Press, 2004); John Calvert, *Sayyid Qutb and the Origins of Radical Islamism* (New York: Columbia University Press, 2010); Charles Tripp, 'Sayyid Qutb: The Political Vision', in *Pioneers of Islamic Revival*, ed. Ali Rahnema (London and New York: Zed Books, 2005 [1994]), 155–165.
62. Yvonne Y. Haddad, 'Sayyid Qutb: Ideologue of Islamic Revival,' in *Voices of Resurgent Islam*, ed. John L. Esposito (Oxford: Oxford University Press, 1983), 76.
63. For example, the Islamic Action Front, the political party affiliated with the Muslim Brotherhood in Jordan, published its 2007 election manifesto under the title '*Na'am.. Al-Islam Huwa l-Hall*' ('Yes..., Islam Is the Solution').
64. Haddad, 'Sayyid,' 74–75.
65. Mitchell, *Society*, 233–234.
66. Commins, 'Hasan', 133.
67. Mitchell, *Society*, 232.
68. Sayyid Qutb, *Ma'alim fi l-Tariq* (Beirut and Cairo: Dar al-Shuruq, 1979 [6th edn]), 59–61, 62.
69. *Ibid.*, 62.
70. Haddad, "Sayyid", 81–83.
71. Mitchell, *Society*, 260–264.

72. *Ibid.*, 272–274.

73. *Ibid.*, 283–285.

74. Al-Banna, *Majmu'at*, 212–213.

75. Kiki M. Santing, *Imagining the Perfect Society in Muslim Brotherhood Journals: An Analysis of al-Da'wa and Liwa' al-Islam* (Berlin: De Gruyter, 2020), 330–332.

76. William L. Cleveland and Martin Bunton, *A History of the Modern Middle East* (Boulder, CO: Westview Press, 2013 [5th edn]), 180–183.

77. Frampton, *Muslim*, 13–14.

78. *Ibid.*, 16–17.

79. Al-Banna, *Majmu'at*, 150.

80. Santing, *Imagining*, 412.

81. Pargeter, *The Muslim Brotherhood: The Burden of Tradition*, 203, 205; *idem, The Muslim Brotherhood: From Opposition to Power*, 205.

82. *Idem, The Muslim Brotherhood: The Burden of Tradition*, 204; *idem, The Muslim Brotherhood: From Opposition to Power*, 206; Santing, *Imagining*, 408–410.

83. Pargeter, *The Muslim Brotherhood: The Burden of Tradition*, 204; *idem, The Muslim Brotherhood: From Opposition to Power*, 206.

84. *Idem, The Muslim Brotherhood: The Burden of Tradition*, 204–206. For more on views of the West among Islamists, see John O. Voll, 'Islamic Renewal and the "Failure of the West"', in *Religious Resurgence: Contemporary Cases in Islam, Christianity, and Judaism*, eds. Richard T. Antoun and Mary Elaine Hegland (Syracuse, NY: Syracuse University Press, 1987), 127–144.

85. Abd Al-Fattah Muhammad El-Awaisi, *The Muslim Brothers and the Palestine Question, 1928–1947* (London and New York: Tauris Academic Studies, 1998), 21–28.

86. *Ibid.*, 28–33.

87. Lia, *Society*, 235.

88. El-Awaisi, *Muslim*, 34–67, 76–89; Lia, *Society*, 237–247.

89. El-Awaisi, *Muslim*, 174–175.

90. Mitchell, *Society*, 227–228. The quotation is on page 227.

91. El-Awaisi, *Muslim*, 68–71.

92. *Ibid.*, 74–75; Lia, *Society*, 244.

93. El-Awaisi, *Muslim*, 179–182.

94. *Ibid.*, 7–8; Lia, *Society*, 244; James Toth, *Sayyid Qutb: The Life and Legacy of a Radical Islamic Intellectual* (Oxford: Oxford University Press, 2013), 280–281.

95. Mitchell, *Society*, 63–64, 75.

96. Kiki Santing, 'Conspiracy Theories and Muslim Brotherhood Antisemitism under Sadat', *Religions* 13, no. 2 (2022): 8–13; Santing, *Imagining*, 392–407; Uriya Shavit, *Islamism and the West: From 'Cultural Attack' to 'Missionary Migrant'* (London and New York: Routledge, 2014), 71–73.

97. Noha Mellor, *Voice of the Muslim Brotherhood: Da'wa, Discourse, and Political Communication* (London and New York: Routledge, 2018), 108–109.

98.   Mitchell, *Society*, 231.

99.   Santing, *Imagining*, 410–412.

100. Mitchell, *Society*, 229–230.

101. Sayyid Qutb, *Al-'Adala al-Ijtima'iyya fi l-Islam* (Cairo: Dar al-Shuruq, 2009 [17th edn]), 189. This book was also translated into English: William E. Shepard (editing and translation), *Sayyid Qutb and Islamic Activism: A Translation and Critical Analysis of* Social Justice in Islam (Leiden: Brill, 1996), 286.

102. Qutb, *Al-'Adala*, 190 (Shepard, *Sayyid*, 287).

103. See also Pargeter, *The Muslim Brotherhood: The Burden of Tradition*, 203; idem, *The Muslim Brotherhood: From Opposition to Power*, 205.

104. For more on the Islamist idea of the West as a source of a 'cultural attack', see Shavit, *Islamism*, 26–62.

105. Frampton, *Muslim*, 17–20.

106. Commins, 'Hasan', 133.

107. Shavit, *Islamism*, 108–109.

108. Qutb, *Al-'Adala*, 193 (Shepard, *Sayyid*, 292).

109. *Ibid.*, 194 (Shepard, *Sayyid*, 293).

110. Mitchell, *Society*, 224–225.

111. Qutb, *Ma'alim*, 129.

112. Frampton, *Muslim*, 19.

113. Lia, *Society*, 77.

114. *Ibid.*, 76–81. See also Frampton, *Muslim*, 33.

115. Frampton, *Muslim*, 35–37. For more on the early Muslim Brotherhood's views on jihad, see Hossam Tammam, 'The Muslim Brotherhood and Jihad', in *Twenty-First Century Jihad: Law, Society and Military Action*, eds. Elisabeth Kendall and Ewan Stein (London and New York: I.B. Tauris, 2017), 166–168.

116. 'Abd al-Qadir 'Awda, *Al-Islam wa-Awda'una al-Qanuniyya* (N.P., 1967 [1951]), 85.

117. *Ibid.*, 86.

118. Frampton, *Muslim*, 37–38.

119. 'Awda, *Al-Islam wa-Awda'una al-Qanuniyya*, 157–158.

120. El-Awaisi, *Muslim*, 135–137, 140, 152, 164.

121. Frampton, *Muslim*, 135–136.

2.   The Political Ideology of the Early Muslim Brotherhood

1.   Husaini, *Moslem*, 71.

2.   Olivier Carré and Michel Seurat, *Les frères musulmans (1928–1982)* (Paris: L'Harmattan, 2001 [1983]), 37; Ana Belén Soage, 'Hasan al-Banna and Sayyid Qutb: Continuity or Rupture?', *The Muslim World* 99 (2009): 301; Weismann, 'Democratic', 10.

3.   'Abd al-Qadir 'Awda, *Al-Islam wa-Awda'una al-Siyasiyya* (N.P., N.D.), 92–101.

4. Al-Banna, *Majmu'at*, 144; Christina Phelps Harris, *Nationalism and Revolu-tion in Egypt: The Role of the Muslim Brotherhood* (The Hague: Mouton, 1964), 162–163.
5. Al-Banna, *Majmu'at*, 145.
6. 'Awda, *Al-Islam wa-Awda'una al-Siyasiyya*, 101–109.
7. 'Abd al-Qadir 'Awda, *Al-Mal wa-l-Hukm fi l-Islam* (Dammam and Riyadh: Al-Dar al-Sa'udiyya li-l-Nashr wa-l-Tawzi', 1984 [1951]), 23–43.
8. 'Awda, *Al-Islam wa-Awda'una al-Siyasiyya*, 84–87; 'Awda, *Al-Mal*, 117–121.
9. 'Awda, *Al-Mal*, 13–19.
10. *Ibid.*, 55–82.
11. *Ibid.*, 85.
12. 'Awda, *Al-Islam wa-Awda'una al-Siyasiyya*, 81.
13. *Idem, Al-Mal*, 99.
14. *Ibid.*, 103.
15. Bélen Soage, 'Hasan,' 300–302.
16. Sullivan and Abed-Kotob, *Islam*, 46.
17. Abdelilah Belkeziz, *The State in Contemporary Islamic Thought: A Historical Survey of the Major Muslim Political Thinkers of the Modern Era* (London: I.B. Tauris, 2015), 129-31; Lia, *Society*, 204–205.
18. Belkeziz, *State*, 131.
19. Al-Banna, *Majmu'at*, 48.
20. 'Awda, *Al-Islam wa-Awda'una al-Siyasiyya*, 170–176.
21. *Ibid.*, 170.
22. *Ibid.*, 183–184.
23. *Ibid.*, 176–182.
24. Ahmad S. Moussalli, 'Hasan al-Banna's Islamist Discourse on Constitutional Rule and Islamic State', *Journal of Islamic Studies* 4, no. 3 (1993): 168, 169–170, 172; Toth, *Sayyid*, 197–198, 199–202.
25. 'Awda, *Al-Islam wa-Awda'una al-Qanuniyya*, 40–1.
26. *Ibid.*, 37–40.
27. *Ibid.*, 14–15, 54–62.
28. *Ibid.*, 63–64.
29. *Ibid.*, 25–26.
30. *Ibid.*, 31–35.
31. *Ibid.*, 67–74.
32. *Idem, Al-Islam wa-Awda'una al-Siyasiyya*, 219–222.
33. *Idem, Al-Islam wa-Awda'una al-Qanuniyya*, 146–250.
34. *Ibid.*, 154–156.
35. *Ibid.*, 92–101.
36. *Ibid.*, 101–104, 134–136.
37. Santing, *Imagining*, 306–310.
38. Seyyed Vali Reza Nasr, 'Mawdudi and the Jama'at-i Islami: The Origins, Theory and Practice of Islamic Revivalism', in *Pioneers of Islamic Revival*, ed. Ali Rahnema (London and New York: Zed Books, 2005), 111–24.

39. Charles J. Adams, 'Mawdudi and the Islamic State', in *Voices of Resurgent Islam*, ed. John L. Esposito (Oxford: Oxford University Press, 1983), 113–114.

40. For more on Mawdudi's life, see Charles J. Adams, 'The Ideology of Mawlana Mawdudi', in *South Asian Politics and Religion*, ed. Donald Eugene Smith (Princeton, NJ: Princeton University Press, 1966), 372–381; Nasr, 'Mawdudi', 99–104; Seyyed Vali Reza Nasr, *Mawdudi & and the Making of Islamic Revivalism* (Oxford: Oxford University Press, 1996).

41. For more on the linguistic origins of the term '*hakimiyya*', see Sayed Khatab, *The Power of Sovereignty: The Political and Ideological Philosophy of Sayyid Qutb* (Abingdon and New York: Routledge, 2006), 15–19.

42. Asma Afsaruddin, 'Theologizing about Democracy: A Critical Appraisal of Mawdudi's Thought', *Islam, the State, and Political Authority: Medieval Issues and Modern Concerns*, ed. Asma Afsaruddin (New York: Palgrave MacMillan, 2011), 132–133. For a critical analysis of Mawdudi's use of the term '*hakimiyya*', see *ibid.*, 139–141.

43. Adams, 'Mawdudi', 115–116.

44. Nelly Lahoud, *Political Thought in Islam: A Study in Intellectual Boundaries* (London and New York: Routledge, 2005), 52–53.

45. Belkaziz, *State*, 206–208.

46. March, *Caliphate*, 78–86.

47. Lahoud, *Political*, 53.

48. Adnan A. Musallam, *From Secularism to Jihad: Sayyid Qutb and the Foundation of Radical Islamism* (Westport, CT: Praeger Publishers, 2005), 151–152.

49. Belkaziz, *State*, 208–209.

50. Qutb, *Ma'alim*, 123.

51. Belkaziz, *State*, 209–210; Khatab, *Power*, 36–40.

52. Toth, *Sayyid*, 140.

53. Sayed Khatab, '*Hakimiyya* and *Jahiliyya* in the Thought of Sayyid Qutb', *Middle Eastern Studies* 38, no. 3 (2002): 163.

54. Haddad, 'Sayyid,' 89; Qutb, *Al-'Adala*, 80, 182 (Shepard, *Sayyid*, 112, 277).

55. Qutb, *Al-'Adala*, 80 (Shepard, *Sayyid*, 112).

56. *Idem, Ma'alim*, 91–92.

57. *Ibid.*, 92.

58. For more on this verse in the context of Islamism, see Mark S. Wagner, '*Hukm bi-ma anzala 'llah*: The Forgotten Prehistory of an Islamist Slogan', *Journal of Qur'anic Studies* 18, no. 1, (2015): 117–143.

59. This is a reference to sura 5:45 and 46, where reference is made to what appears to be the same group of people by calling them 'evildoers' and 'ungodly', respectively.

60. Sayyid Qutb, *Fi Zilal al-Qur'an*, Vol. II (Beirut and Cairo: Dar al-Shuruq, 1988 [15th edn]), 888. See also Calvert, *Sayyid*, 216.

61. Calvert, *Sayyid*, 214–215.

62. See, for example, Itzchak Weismann, 'Sa'id Hawwa and Islamic Revivalism in Ba'thist Syria', *Studia Islamica* 85, no. 1 (1997): 151–153.

63. For more on the life of al-Hudaybi, see Barbara H. E. Zollner, *The Muslim Brotherhood: Hasan al-Hudaybi and Ideology* (Abingdon and New York: 2009), 19–25.

64. For an extensive study on *Du'at La Qudat*, see *ibid.*, 64–145.

65. Hasan al-Hudaybi, *Du'at La Qudat* (Port Said: Dar al-Tawzi' wa-l-Nashr al-Islamiyya, 1977), 91.

66. *Ibid.*, 93.

67. *Ibid.*, 97.

68. *Ibid.*, 175–176.

69. *Ibid.*, 176–179.

70. *Ibid.*, 109–110. For an extensive discussion of al-Hudaybi's views on *takfir*, see Zollner, *Muslim*, 71–197; Barbara H. E. Zollner, 'Opening to Reform: Hasan al-Hudaybi's Legacy', in *The Muslim Brotherhood in Europe*, eds. Roel Meijer and Edwin Bakker (London: Hurst & Co., 2012), 277–279.

71. Al-Hudaybi, *Du'at*, 161.

72. *Ibid.*, 168.

73. *Ibid.*, 53–54.

74. *Ibid.*, 27–29, 58.

75. Al-Banna, *Majmu'at*, 212–213; Sullivan and Abed-Kotob, *Islam*, 46–47, 51–52, 59–60.

76. Al-Banna, *Majmu'at*, 213.

77. *Ibid.*, 214.

78. *Ibid.*, 146–147. See also *ibid.*, 165–169; Belkeziz, *State*, 133–136.

79. Al-Banna, *Majmu'at*, 146.

80. *Ibid.*, 147.

81. *Ibid.*, 326–327; Husaini, *Moslem*, 66–67; Mitchel, *Society*, 218–219.

82. Lia, *Society*, 203–205.

83. For an extensive study of this concept, see Michael Cook, *Commanding Right and Forbidding Wrong in Islamic Thought* (Cambridge: Cambridge University Press, 2001).

84. Moussalli, 'Hasan,' 171.

85. 'Awda, *Al-Islam wa-Awda'una al-Siyasiyya*, 130–131.

86. *Ibid.*, 179.

87. *Idem, Al-Islam wa-Awda'una al-Qanuniyya*, 15–19.

88. For an overview of the meaning and the use of *shura*, see C. E. Bosworth, Manuela Marin and A. Ayalon, 'Shura', in *Encyclopaedia of Islam: New Edition*, Vol. IX, ed. C. E. Bosworth (Leiden: E. J. Brill, 1997), 504–506.

89. Sura 3:159 ('[...] take counsel with them (*shawirhum*) in the affair [...]') and sura 42:38 ('[...] their affair being counsel (*shura*) between them [...]').

90. Al-Banna, *Majmu'at*, 319.

91. 'Awda, *Al-Islam wa-Awda'una al-Siyasiyya*, 144–145.

92. *Idem, Al-Mal*, 115–116.

93. Belkaziz, *State*, 179–189; Jens Kutscher, 'Islamic Shura, Democracy, and Online Fatwas', *CyberOrient* 5, no. 2 (2011), 50–72; Uriya Shavit, 'Is *Shura* a

Muslim Form of Democracy? Roots and Systemization of a Polemic', *Middle Eastern Studies* 46, no. 3 (2010): 349–374.

94. 'Awda, *Al-Islam wa-Awda'una al-Siyasiyya*, 152; Mariz Tadros, *The Muslim Brotherhood in Contemporary Egypt: Democracy Redefined or Confined?* (London and New York: Routledge, 2012), 65.

95. 'Awda, *Al-Mal*, 128–129. Similar views on *shura* and democracy can also be seen among leaders of the Muslim Brotherhood in Syria. See, for example, Dara Conduit, *The Muslim Brotherhood in Syria* (Cambridge: Cambridge University Press, 2019), 51–52; Weismann, 'Democratic', 7–12, but see also Conduit, *Muslim*, 146–149.

96. 'Awda, *Al-Islam wa-Awda'una al-Siyasiyya*, 145–146; *idem, Al-Mal*, 116; Tadros, *Muslim*, 62.

97. Al-Banna, *Majmu'at*, 319; Tadros, *Muslim*, 62.

98. 'Awda, *Al-Islam wa-Awda'una al-Qanuniyya*, 123.

99. M. J. Kister, 'Notes on an Account of the Shura Appointed by 'Umar b. al-Khattab', *Journal of Semitic Studies* 9 (1964): 320–326.

100. Wael B. Hallaq, 'Ahl al-Hall Wa-al-'Aqd,' in *The Oxford Encyclopedia of the Islamic World*, Vol. I, ed. John L. Esposito (Oxford: Oxford University Press, 2009), 77–78.

101. Al-Banna, *Majmu'at*, 328.

102. 'Awda, *Al-Islam wa-Awda'una al-Siyasiyya*, 154–156; Tadros, *Muslim*, 60–61.

103. 'Awda, *Al-Islam wa-Awda'una al-Siyasiyya*, 166–169.

104. E. Tyan, 'Bay'a', in *Encyclopaedia of Islam: New Edition*, Vol. I, eds. B. Lewis, Ch. Pellat and J. Schacht (Leiden: E. J. Brill, 1986), 1113–1114.

105. 'Awda, *Al-Islam wa-Awda 'una al-Qanuniyya*, 14–15, 59–60.

106. Uriya Shavit, 'The Muslim Brothers' Conception of Armed Insurrection Against an Unjust Regime', *Middle Eastern Studies* 51, no. 4 (2015): 606–607.

107. For more on the origin and meaning of *jahiliyya*, see Sayed Khatab, *The Political Thought of Sayyid Qutb: The Theory of Jahiliyya* (Abingdon and New York: Routledge, 2006), 10–43.

108. Qutb, *Zilal*, Vol. II, 891.

109. *Idem, Ma'alim*, 105.

110. Belkaziz, *State*, 203–204; Calvert, *Sayyid*, 158.

111. Calvert, *Sayyid*, 157.

112. *Ibid.*, 158; Emmanuel Sivan, *Radical Islam: Medieval Theology and Modern Politics* (New Haven, CT, and London: Yale University Press, 1985), 22–23.

113. Calvert, *Sayyid*, 217–220; Khatab, *Political*, 59–171; William Shepard, 'Sayyid Qutb's Doctrine of *Jāhiliyya*', *International Journal of Middle East Studies* 35, no. 4 (2003): 521–545; Sivan, *Radical*, 21–28; Toth, *Sayyid*, 125–135; Tripp, 'Sayyid', 171–175.

114. Fouad Ajami, 'In the Pharaoh's Shadow: Religion and Authority in Egypt', in *Islam in the Political Process*, ed. James Piscatori (Cambridge: Cambridge University Press, 1983), 22–27.

115. Belkaziz, *State*, 201; Calvert, *Sayyid*, 218–220; Khatab, *Political*, 68–72.

116. Calvert, *Sayyid*, 220, 258; Shepard, 'Sayyid', 529.
117. Compare also Qutb's use of the term *'jahiliyya'* with the application of the word *'ridda'* ('apostasy') by the Syrian Muslim Brother Sa'id Hawwa: Weismann, 'Sa'id,' 134–137. For more on Hawwa, see Itzchak Weismann, 'Sa'id Hawwa: The Making of a Radical Muslim Thinker in Modern Syria', *Middle Eastern Studies* 29, no. 4 (1993): 601–623.
118. Khatab, *Power*, 8.
119. *Ibid.*, 29–30; Sivan, *Radical*, 73;
120. Toth, *Sayyid*, 208–209.
121. *Ibid.*, 176–177.
122. Belkaziz, *State*, 212.
123. Fawaz A. Gerges, *Making the Arab World: Nasser, Qutb, and the Clash that Shaped the Middle East* (Princeton, NJ: Princeton University Press, 2018), 243–251; Sivan, *Radical*, 40–41, 42–43, 47–48, 89–90.
124. For more on the history of jihad, see Asma Afsaruddin, *Striving in the Path of God: Jihad and Martyrdom in Islamic Thought* (Oxford: Oxford University Press, 2013); Michael Bonner, *Jihad in Islamic History: Doctrines and Practice* (Princeton, NJ, and Oxford: Princeton University Press, 2006); David Cook, *Understanding Jihad* (Berkeley, CA: University of California Press, 2005).
125. Qutb, *Ma'alim*, 59, 64.
126. *Ibid.*, 64–65.
127. *Ibid.*, 59.
128. Toth, *Sayyid*, 143.
129. Qutb, *Ma'alim*, 9–10. The quotation is on page 9.
130. Calvert, *Sayyid*, 224–247; Toth, *Sayyid*, 147–150.
131. Qutb, *Al-'Adala*, 81–82 (Shepard, *Sayyid*, 113–14).
132. Zollner, 'Opening', 284.
133. *Ibid.*, 283–284.
134. *Idem, Muslim*, 122.
135. *Ibid.*, 127–128.
136. *Ibid.*, 122.
137. Al-Hudaybi, *Du'at*, 184–186.
138. *Ibid.*, 122–123; Sivan, *Radical*, 109–110.
139. Sullivan and Abed-Kotob, *Islam*, 60–65.
140. *Ibid.*, 47–50.
141. With 'societal rights and liberties', I mean legal rights and liberties related to societal affairs.
142. 'Awda, *Al-Islam wa-Awda 'una al-Qanuniyya*, 105–106; Khatab, *Political*, 116–118; Mitchell, *Society*, 236–237; Toth, *Sayyid*, 160–163.
143. Mitchell, *Society*, 237–240.
144. Tariq al-Jamil, 'Ibadah', in *The Oxford Encyclopedia of the Islamic World*, Vol. II, ed. John Esposito (Oxford: Oxford University Press, 2009), 475.
145. Khatab, *Power*, 38.

146. Sura 5:38: 'And the thief, male and female: cut off the hands of both (*fa-qta'u aydiyahuma*), as a recompense for what they have earned, and a punishment exemplary from God; God is All-mighty, All-wise'.

147. Mitchell, *Society*, 240–241.

148. Toth, *Sayyid*, 98, 203–204.

149. Zollner, *Muslim*, 102–106.

150. Mitchell, *Society*, 231.

151. Rachel M. Scott, *The Challenge of Political Islam: Non-Muslims and the Egyptian State* (Stanford, CA: Stanford University Press, 2010), 94–95.

152. For more on the position of Jews and Christians in the Muslim world, see Mark R. Cohen, *Under Crescent & Cross: The Jews in the Middle Ages* (Princeton, NJ: Princeton University Press, 2008 [1994]); Milka Levy-Rubin, *Non-Muslims in the Early Islamic Empire: From Surrender to Coexistence* (Cambridge: Cambridge University Press, 2011); Bernard Lewis, *The Jews of Islam* (Princeton, NJ: Princeton University Press, 2014 [1984]).

153. Al-Banna, *Majmu'at*, 285–286.

154. El-Awaisi, *Muslim*, 6–7; Husaini, *Moslem*, 70.

155. Scott, *Challenge*, 98–99.

156. Conduit, *Muslim*, 49–50.

157. 'Awda, *Al-Islam wa-Awda'una al-Siyasiyya*, 195.

158. Idem, *Al-Islam wa-Awda'una al-Qanuniyya*, 106–107.

159. Idem, *Al-Islam wa-Awda'una al-Siyasiyya*, 196.

160. *Ibid.*, 207.

161. Khatab, *Power*, 62.

162. Michael Ebstein, *In the Shadows of the Koran: Said* [sic] *Qutb's Views on Jews and Christians as Reflected in his Koran Commentary* (Washington, DC: Hudson Institute, 2009), 12.

163. *Ibid.*, 5–6.

164. Scott, *Challenge*, 115.

165. Mitchell, *Society*, 223.

166. Santing, *Imagining*, 344–345.

167. Mitchell, *Society*, 254–255.

168. For more on his life, see Sami Moubayed, *Under the Black Flag: An Exclusive Insight into the Inner Workings of ISIS* (London and New York: I.B. Tauris, 2015), 23–26.

169. Mustafa al-Siba'i, *Al-Mar'a bayna l-Fiqh wa-l-Qanun* (Beirut: Dar al-Warraq, 1999 [7th edn]), 13–17.

170. *Ibid.*, 17–20.

171. *Ibid.*, 23–27.

172. Santing, *Imagining*, 344; Toth, *Sayyid*, 277.

173. Mitchell, *Society*, 255; Tadros, *Muslim*, 137–138.

174. Euben, *Enemy*, 66.

175. Sura 2:282: '[...] And call in to witness two witnesses, men; or if the two be not men, then one man and two women, such witnesses as you approve of, that if one of the two women errs the other will remind her; [...]'.

176.   Berridge, *Islamism*, 170–171, al-Siba'i, *Al-Mar'a*, 27–29.

177.   Sura 4:11: 'God charges you, concerning your children: to the male the like of
        the portion of two females [...]'. See also sura 4:176: '[...] if there be brothers
        and sisters, the male shall receive the portion of two females. [...]'.

178.   Euben, *Enemy*, 66; al-Siba'i, *Al-Mar'a*, 29–32.

179.   Al-Banna, *Majmu'at*, 373–375; Euben, *Enemy*, 64.

180.   Euben, *Enemy*, 65; Mitchell, *Society*, 257; Toth, *Sayyid*, 275.

181.   Santing, *Imagining*, 338–344.

182.   Sura 4:3: 'If you fear that you will not act justly towards the orphans, marry
        such women as seem good to you, two, three, four; but if you fear you will
        not be equitable, then only one, or what your right hands own; so it is like-
        lier you will not be partial'.

183.   Mitchell, *Society*, 258; al-Siba'i, *Al-Mar'a*, 60–98; Toth, 276.

184.   Al-Siba'i, *Al-Mar'a*, 49–59, 99–118.

185.   Mitchell, *Society*, 256. See also Santing, *Imagining*, 346–349.

186.   Mitchell, *Society*, 256; al-Siba'i, *Al-Mar'a*, 148–149; Tadros, *Muslim*, 140–141;
        Toth, *Sayyid*, 278.

187.   Mitchell, *Society*, 256–257, 258; al-Siba'i, *Al-Mar'a*, 133; Tadros, *Muslim*, 139–140.

188.   Mitchell, *Society*, 258; Phelps Harris, *Nationalism*, 167; Santing, *Imagining*,
        351; al-Siba'i, *Al-Mar'a*, 137–147; Toth, *Sayyid*, 277–278.

189.   Tadros, *Muslim*, 147–149.

190.   Al-Siba'i, *Al-Mar'a*, 121–122.

191.   *Ibid.*, 124–129.

192.   *Ibid.*, 33–35.

193.   Euben, *Enemy*, 62–64; Toth, *Sayyid*, 209–210.

194.   'Awda, *Al-Islam wa-Awda'una al-Qanuniyya*, 108.

195.   *Ibid.*, 109–111; *idem, Al-Islam wa-Awda'una al-Siyasiyya*, 197–200.

196.   *Idem, Al-Islam wa-Awda'una al-Siyasiyya*, 200–201.

197.   Husaini, *Moslem*, 64, 100.

198.   'Awda, *Al-Islam wa-Awda'una al-Siyasiyya*, 199. See also Mitchell, *Society*, 249.

3.   Repression

1.   Santing, *Imagining*, 56–57.

2.   Lia, *Society*, 35–37; Mitchell, *Society*, 7–8.

3.   Lia, *Society*, 37–38; Mitchell, *Society*, 9.

4.   Neil Ketchley, Steven Brooke and Brynjar Lia, 'Who Supported the Early
        Muslim Brotherhood?', *Politics and Religion*, doi:10.1017/S1755048321000298
        (2021): 1–29; Lia, *Society*, 38–39.

5.   Lia, *Society*, 295.

6.   Zahid, *Muslim*, 70.

7.   Commins, 'Hasan', 145–149; Lia, *Society*, 109–112.

8.   Lia, *Society*, 154–156.

9. Mitchell, *Society*, 13–15.

10. *Ibid.*, 33–34.

11. Lia, *Society*, 264–265.

12. Al-Anani, *Inside*, 100–110; Lia, *Society*, 93–109, 296–299; Mitchell, *Society*, 165–180; Trager, *Arab*, 2016, 51–55.

13. Hazem Kandil, *Inside the Brotherhood* (Cambridge, UK: Polity Press, 2015), 5–118.

14. Elshobaki, 'Muslim', 109–112; Trager, *Arab*, 48–51.

15. Ella Landau-Tasseron, *Leadership and Allegiance in the Society of the Muslim Brothers* (Washington, DC: Center on Islam, Democracy, and the Future of the Muslim World at the Hudson Institute, 2010), 4–22.

16. Lia, *Society*, 177–181; Mitchell, *Society*, 30; Santing, *Imagining*, 65–66; Ahmed Abou El Zalaf, 'The Special Apparatus (al-Nizam al-Khass): The Rise of Nationalist Militancy in the Ranks of the Egyptian Muslim Brotherhood,' *Religions* 13, no. 1 (2022): 9–10.

17. Lia, *Society*, 268–270.

18. El Zalaf, 'Special', 10–13.

19. Mitchell, *Society*, 67.

20. Gerges, *Making*, 73; Mitchell, *Society*, 43–52, 58–71; Santing, *Imagining*, 70–74.

21. Mitchell, *Society*, 71–84.

22. *Ibid.*, 84–88; Santing, *Imagining*, 74–76.

23. Marie-Christine Aulas, 'State and Ideology in Republican Egypt: 1952–82', in *State and Ideology in the Middle East and Pakistan*, eds. Fred Halliday and Hamza Alavi (London: MacMillan, 1988), 134–145; Gerges, *Making*, 78–83.

24. Gerges, *Making*, 83–89.

25. *Ibid.*, 72–76.

26. Mitchell, *Society*, 101–104.

27. Gerges, *Making*, 89–99.

28. Carré and Seurat, *Frères*, 65–82; Gerges, *Making*, 112–122; Santing, *Imagining*, 95–96.

29. Gerges, *Making*, 241–243, 251–259, 263–275.

30. *Ibid.*, 141–142; Barbara Zollner, 'Prison Talk: The Muslim Brotherhood's Internal Struggle During Gamal Abdel Nasser's Persecution, 1954–1971', *International Journal of Middle East Studies* 39, no. 3 (2007): 411–433.

31. Gerges, *Making*, 276–279; Santing, *Imagining*, 101–103.

32. Aulas, 'State', 145–162; Santing, *Imagining*, 118–122.

33. Gerges, *Making*, 317–318; Santing, *Imagining*, 125–128.

34. Santing, *Imagining*, 147–150. See also Aaron Rock-Singer and Steven Brooke, 'Reading the Ads in *al-Da'wa* Magazine: Commercialism and Islamist Activism in al-Sadat's Egypt', *British Journal of Middle Eastern Studies* 47, no. 3 (2020): 444–461; Khalil al-Anani, 'Devout Neoliberalism?! Explaining Egypt's Muslim Brotherhood's Socio-Economic Perspective and Policies', *Politics and Religion* 13, no. 4 (2020): 752–755.

35. Gerges, *Making*, 315–317.

36.   John L. Esposito, *Islam and Politics* (Syracuse, NY: Syracuse University Press, 1994 [1984]), 236–237; Judith Jolen, 'The Quest for Legitimacy: The Role of Islam in the State's Political Discourse in Egypt and Jordan (1979–1996)' (PhD, Catholic University Nijmegen, 2003), 51–52, 60–70.

37.   R. Hrair Dekmejian, *Islam in Revolution: Fundamentalism in the Arab World* (Syracuse, NY: Syracuse University Press, 1995 [1985]), 79–84; Gerges, *Making*, 318–326; Ibrahim Ibrahim, 'Religion and Politics Under Nasser and Sadat, 1952–1981', in *The Islamic Impulse*, ed. Barbara Freyer Stowasser (London and Sydney: Croom Helm, 1987), 126.

38.   Pargeter, *The Muslim Brotherhood: The Burden of Tradition*, 36–37; *idem*, *The Muslim Brotherhood: From Opposition to Power*, 37; Santing, *Imagining*, 141–144.

39.   Rosefsky Wickham, *Muslim*, 30; Santing, *Imagining*, 145–146.

40.   Rosefsky Wickham, *Muslim*, 31.

41.   Gerges, *Making*, 326–328.

42.   Santing, *Imagining*, 144.

43.   Ibrahim, 'Religion', 131–132; Santing, *Imagining*, 130–131.

44.   Annette Ranko, *The Muslim Brotherhood and Its Quest for Hegemony in Egypt: State-Discourse and Islamist Counter-Discourse* (Wiesbaden: Springer, 2012), 69–70; Santing, *Imagining*, 150–152.

45.   Awadi, *Pursuit*, 51–53.

46.   *Ibid.*, 64–66.

47.   *Ibid.*, 53–55, 57–61; Santing, *Imagining*, 161–162.

48.   Awadi, *Pursuit*, 82–85; Farschid, 'Hizbiya,' 58.

49.   Awadi, *Pursuit*, 55–57; Farschid, 'Hizbiya', 53–58.

50.   Awadi, *Pursuit*, 78–82; Farschid, 'Hizbiya', 59–61; Hamid, *Temptations*, 67–70; Santing, *Imagining*, 163–173; Zahid, *Muslim*, 95–98.

51.   Awadi, *Pursuit*, 112–116; Farschid, 'Hizbiya', 61–65; Martin Forstner, 'Auf dem legalen Weg zur Macht? Zur Politischen Entwicklung der Muslimbruderschaft Ägyptens', *Orient: Deutsche Zeitschrift für Politik und Wirtschaft des Orients* 29, no. 3 (1988): 395–400; Hamid, *Temptations*, 71–77; Santing, *Imagining*, 173–180; Zahid, *Muslim*, 98–99. For more on the 1987 elections from the Muslim Brotherhood's point of view, see Kiki Santing, 'Islam and the Struggle over Political Legitimacy in Egypt: The 1987 Elections Through the Lenses of *Al-Liwa' al-Islami* and *Liwa' al-Islam*', *Global Media Journal* 10, no. 1 (2020): 1–18.

52.   Awadi, *Pursuit*, 117–122.

53.   *Ibid.*, 113, 116–117.

54.   Ranko, *Muslim*, 83–86.

55.   Awadi, *Pursuit*, 91–95, 122–123, 155–156.

56.   *Ibid.*, 95–98, 126–127, 146–147; Rosefsky Wickham, *Muslim*, 58–63; Bélen Soage and Fuentelsaz Franganillo, 'Muslim', 43–44; Zahid, *Muslim*, 105–115, 117–119, 125–127.

57.   Janine A. Clark, *Islam, Charity and Activism: Middle-Class Networks and Social Welfare in Egypt, Jordan, and Yemen* (Bloomington and Indianapolis, IN: Indiana University Press, 2004), 42–81.

58. Awadi, *Pursuit*, 142, 144.

59. *Ibid.*, 148–149. See also Gehad Auda, 'An Uncertain Response: The Islamic Movement in Egypt', in *Islamic Fundamentalisms and the Gulf Crisis*, ed. James Piscatori (Chicago, IL: American Academy of Arts and Sciences, 1991), 118–119, 125–126.

60. Awadi, *Pursuit*, 114.

61. *Ibid.*, 171–174.

62. *Ibid.*, 156–157.

63. Dekmejian, *Islam*, 183–184; Hamid, *Temptations*, 90–91; Ranko, *Muslim*, 142–148; Rutherford, *Egypt*, 86–89.

64. Hamid, *Temptations*, 91–97, 122–129.

65. Awadi, *Pursuit*, 171–172; Rosefsky Wickham, *Muslim*, 117–119, 148–150.

66. Rosefsky Wickham, *Muslim*, 63–70.

67. Awadi, *Pursuit*, 61–64.

68. Forstner, 'Weg', 400–407.

69. Rosefsky Wickham, *Muslim*, 158–160; Trager, *Arab*, 17.

70. Pargeter, *The Muslim Brotherhood: From Opposition to Power*, 212–213; *idem, Return to the Shadows: The Muslim Brotherhood and An-Nahda since the Arab Spring* (London: Saqi Books, 2016), 13–14.

71. Milton-Edwards, *Muslim*, 37–38; Pargeter, *The Muslim Brotherhood: From Opposition to Power*, 213–216; *idem, Return*, 22–26; Rosefsky Wickham, *Muslim*, 160–162; Trager, *Arab*, 19–22.

72. Pargeter, *The Muslim Brotherhood: From Opposition to Power*, 218–220; *idem, Return*, 15, 28–33.

73. Milton-Edwards, *Muslim*, 38–40; Pargeter, *Return*, 14–15, 26–27; Rosefsky Wickham, *Muslim*, 166–169.

74. Pargeter, *The Muslim Brotherhood: From Opposition to Power*, 222–224; *idem, Return*, 33–35; Rosefsky Wickham, *Muslim*, 170–172; Trager, *Arab*, 61–67.

75. Pargeter, *The Muslim Brotherhood: From Opposition to Power*, 226–227; *idem, Return*, 35–36; Rosefsky Wickham, *Muslim*, 174–176; Trager, *Arab*, 68–70.

76. Brown, *Victory*; Hamid, 'Arab', 68–80; Milton-Edwards, *Muslim*, 41–42.

77. Hamid, *Temptations*, 142–143; Pargeter, *The Muslim Brotherhood: From Opposition to Power*, 221–222; Trager, *Arab*, 61.

78. Pargeter, *The Muslim Brotherhood: From Opposition to Power*, 228–229; *idem, Return*, 38; Trager, *Arab*, 100–101.

79. Pargeter, *Return*, 40.

80. Hamid, *Temptations*, 152–154; Pargeter, *The Muslim Brotherhood: From Opposition to Power*, 231–232; *idem, Return*, 40–42; Rosefsky Wickham, *Muslim*, 178–180, 254–255; Trager, *Arab*, 127–132;

81. Hamid, *Temptations*, 154–155; Milton Edwards, *Muslim*, 44–45; Pargeter, *The Muslim Brotherhood: From Opposition to Power*, 235–236; *idem, Return*, 42–44; Rosefsky Wickham, *Muslim*, 255–257; Trager, *Arab*, 132–133.

82. Pargeter, *Return*, 50–55.

83. Roel Meijer, 'The Majority Strategy of the Muslim Brotherhood,' *Orient* 54, no. 1 (2013): 22–30.

84. Pargeter, *Return*, 56–59.

85. Elizabeth Iskander Monier and Annette Ranko, 'The Fall of the Muslim Brotherhood: Implications for Egypt', *Middle East Policy* 20, no. 4 (2013): 117.

86. Pargeter, *Return*, 66–93.

87. *Ibid.*, 96–108; Trager, *Arab*, 178–179, 182–185, 196–197, 202–203, 210–213, 221–225.

88. Khalil al-Anani, 'Rethinking the Repression-Dissent Nexus: Assessing Egypt's Muslim Brotherhood's Response to Repression since the Coup of 2013', *Democratization* 26, no. 8 (2019): 1333–1337; Trager, *Arab*, 227–229.

89. Shadi Hamid, *Islamic Exceptionalism: How the Struggle over Islam is Reshaping the World* (New York: St. Martin's Press, 2016), 106–110.

90. Erika Biagini and Lucia Ardovini, '"Struggle Is Our Way": Assessing the Egyptian Muslim Brotherhood's Relationship with Violence Post-2013', *Religions* 13, no. 2 (2022): 1–22.

91. Hamid, *Islamic*, 114–116.

92. 'Fratricidal Tendencies: The Oldest Islamist Movement is Riven by Infighting', *The Economist*, 11 December 2021, 30.

93. Stig Jarle Hansen and Rafat Faisal Al-Mohareb, 'Three Important Poles? Ennahda, Turabism, and the Egyptian Brotherhood', in *The Muslim Brotherhood Movement in the Arab Winter*, eds. Stig Jarle Hansen, Mohamed Husein Gaas and Ida Bary (Cambridge, MA: Harvard Kennedy School Belfer Center for Science and International Affairs, 2017), 29–30.

94. Cleveland and Bunton, *History*, 202–207.

95. Raymond A. Hinnebusch, 'Syria', in *The Politics of Islamic Revivalism*, ed. Shireen T. Hunter (Bloomington and Indianapolis, IN: Indiana University Press, 1988), 39–41; Michael C. Hudson, 'The Islamic Factor in Syrian and Iraqi Politics', in *Islam in the Political Process*, ed. James Piscatori (Cambridge: Cambridge University Press, 1983), 82.

96. David McDowall, *A Modern History of the Kurds* (London and New York: I.B. Tauris, 1996), 3–4.

97. Conduit, *Muslim*, 22–23.

98. *Ibid.*, 23–24; Raphaël Lefèvre, *Ashes of Hama: The Muslim Brotherhood in Syria* (Oxford: Oxford University Press, 2013), 4–11; Itzchak Weismann, 'The Politics of Popular Religion: Sufis, Salafis, and Muslim Brothers in 20th-Century Hama', *International Journal of Middle East Studies* 37, no. 1 (2005): 50–53.

99. Umar F. Abd-Allah, *The Islamic Struggle in Syria* (Berkeley, CA: Mizan Press, 1983), 88–90; Conduit, *Muslim*, 24–27; Lefèvre, *Ashes*, 11–17; Johannes Reissner, *Ideologie und Politik der Muslimbrüder Syriens: Von den Wahlen 1947 bis zum Verbot unter Adīb aš-Šišaklī 1952* (Freiburg: Klaus Schwarz Verlag, 1980), 80–96; Joshua Teitelbaum, 'The Muslim Brotherhood in Syria, 1945–1958: Founding, Social Origins, Ideology', *Middle East Journal* 65, no. 2 (2011): 215–216.

100. Abd-Allah, *Islamic*, 96–97; Teitelbaum, 'The Muslim Brotherhood in Syria, 1945–1958', 214.

101. Abd-Allah, *Islamic*, 90–91; Conduit, *Muslim*, 41; Lefèvre, *Ashes*, 23–27; Reissner, *Ideologie*, 97–100; Teitelbaum, 'The Muslim Brotherhood in Syria, 1945–1958', 216–217.

102. Abd-Allah, *Islamic*, 92; Conduit, *Muslim*, 41–45; Hanna Battatu, 'Syria's Muslim Brethren', in *State and Ideology in the Middle East and Pakistan*, eds. Fred Halliday and Hamza Alavi (London: MacMillan, 1988), 115–120.

103. Thomas Pierret, *Religion and State in Syria: The Sunni Ulama from Coup to Revolution* (Cambridge: Cambridge University Press, 2013), 168–169.

104. Teitelbaum, 'The Muslim Brotherhood in Syria, 1945–1958', 226.

105. Reissner, *Ideologie*, 102–103; Teitelbaum, 'The Muslim Brotherhood in Syria, 1945–1958', 225–226.

106. Conduit, *Muslim*, 28–29.

107. Teitelbaum, 'The Muslim Brotherhood in Syria, 1945–1958', 228–231.

108. Conduit, *Muslim*, 93.

109. *Ibid.*, 67–72; Joshua Teitelbaum, 'The Muslim Brotherhood and the "Struggle for Syria", 1947–1958: Between Accommodation and Ideology,' *Middle Eastern Studies* 40, no. 3 (2004): 136–138, 141–142, 148–149.

110. Lefèvre, *Ashes*, 30–32; Reissner, *Ideologie*, 338–354; Teitelbaum, 'The Muslim Brotherhood and the "Struggle for Syria", 1947–1958', 142–144.

111. Conduit, *Muslim*, 73; Teitelbaum, 'The Muslim Brotherhood and the "Struggle for Syria", 1947–1958,' 151.

112. Conduit, *Muslim*, 73–76.

113. For more on the origins and development of the Ba'th Party in Syria, see Nikolaos van Dam, *The Struggle for Power in Syria: Politics and Society Under Asad and the Ba'th Party* (London and New York: I.B. Tauris, 1996 [1979]).

114. Conduit, *Muslim*, 32, 76.

115. For more on Hadid, see Abd-Allah, *Islamic*, 103–107; Moubayed, *Under*, 28–29; Behnam T. Said, *Islamischer Staat: IS-Miliz, al-Qaida und die deutschen Brigaden* (München: C. H. Beck, 2014), 26–30.

116. Conduit, *Muslim*, 95–97; Lefèvre, *Ashes*, 44–46; Moubayed, *Under*, 31–32; Pierret, *Religion*, 180–182.

117. Conduit, *Muslim*, 32, 78; Lefèvre, *Ashes*, 87–96; Pargeter, *The Muslim Brotherhood: The Burden of Tradition*, 66–70; idem, *The Muslim Brotherhood: From Opposition to Power*, 71–75.

118. Conduit, *Muslim*, 107–108.

119. *Ibid.*, 33–34; Lefèvre, *Ashes*, 47–56.

120. Conduit, *Muslim*, 78–79.

121. *Ibid.*, 104–107.

122. *Ibid.*, 103–109; Lefèvre, *Ashes*, 96–101.

123. Conduit, *Muslim*, 34, 100–101; Lefèvre, *Ashes*, 101–210; Pargeter, *The Muslim Brotherhood: The Burden of Tradition*, 74–78; idem, *The Muslim Brotherhood: From Opposition to Power*, 79–83; Said, *Islamischer*, 25–26.

124. Conduit, *Muslim*, 98–99; Lefèvre, *Ashes*, 102–103.

125. Conduit, *Muslim*, 102.

126. Batatu, 'Syria's', 128–129; Conduit, *Muslim*, 101–102; Lefèvre, *Ashes*, 103–104; Moubayed, *Under*, 34–35.

127. Conduit, *Muslim*, 102–103, 109–111.

128. Carré and Seurat, *Frères*, 135–136; Conduit, *Muslim*, 35, 112–113; Moubayed, *Under*, 35.

129. Conduit, *Muslim*, 113–115; Lefèvre, *Ashes*, 109–115.

130. Abd-Allah, *Islamic*, 114–128; Dekmejian, *Islam*, 110–111; Hinnebusch, 'Syria', 45–48; Pierret, *Religion*, 189–190.

131. Conduit, *Muslim*, 115–123.

132. *Ibid.*, 123–124; Lefèvre, *Ashes*, 122–128; Moubayed, *Under*, 39–40.

133. Conduit, *Muslim*, 124; Moubayed, 40–41.

134. Conduit, *Muslim*, 130–133; *idem*, 'The Syrian Muslim Brotherhood and the Spectacle of Hama', *Middle East Journal* 70, no. 2 (2016): 211–226.

135. *Idem, Muslim*, 135–141, 143–145.

136. *Ibid.*, 37, 59, 128–130; Lefèvre, *Ashes*, 162–164.

137. Conduit, *Muslim*, 59–60; Lefèvre, *Ashes*, 70–71.

138. Conduit, *Muslim*, 81–82.

139. *Ibid.*, 37–38, 60–62; Lefèvre, *Ashes*, 171–173; Robert G. Rabil, 'The Syrian Muslim Brotherhood', in *The Muslim Brotherhood: The Organization and Policies of a Global Islamist Movement*, ed. Barry Rubin (New York: Palgrave MacMillan, 2010), 80–81.

140. Conduit, *Muslim*, 62–64; Meijer, 'Moslim', 58–61.

141. Conduit, *Muslim*, 87–88; Lefèvre, *Ashes*, 177.

142. Conduit, *Muslim*, 88–89; Lefèvre, *Ashes*, 177–178; Pargeter, *The Muslim Brotherhood: The Burden of Tradition*, 91–93; *idem, The Muslim Brotherhood: From Opposition to Power*, 96–98; Rabil, 'Syrian', 83–84;

143. Conduit, *Muslim*, 89–90; Pargeter, *The Muslim Brotherhood: The Burden of Tradition*, 93–95; *idem, The Muslim Brotherhood: From Opposition to Power*, 98–100.

144. Conduit, *Muslim*, 155–158.

145. *Ibid.*, 158-60; Aron Lund, *Struggling to Adapt: The Muslim Brotherhood in a New Syria* (Washington, DC: Carnegie Endowment for International Peace, 2013), 15–17.

146. Conduit, *Muslim*, 160, 163; Lefèvre, *Ashes*, 187–188.

147. Conduit, *Muslim*, 161–169.

148. *Ibid.*, 169–171; Lefèvre, *Ashes*, 189–190.

149. Conduit, *Muslim*, 189–198.

150. *Ibid.*, 176–178, 185–188.

151. *Ibid.*, 173–176.

152. *Ibid.*, 200–221; Lund, *Struggling*, 17–21.

153. Esposito, *Islam*, 108–114; James P. Piscatori, 'Ideological Politics in Sa'udi Arabia', in *Islam in the Political Process*, ed. James P. Piscatori (Cambridge: Cambridge University Press, 1983), 59–63.

154. For more on the history of Saudi Arabia, see David E. Long, *The Kingdom of Saudi Arabia* (Gainesville, FL: University Press of Florida, 1997); Christine

Moss Helms, *The Cohesion of Saudi Arabia: Evolution of Political Identity* (London: Croom Helm, 1981); Tim Niblock, *Saudi Arabia: Power, Legitimacy and Survival* (Abingdon and New York: Routledge, 2006); Madawi Al-Rasheed, *A History of Saudi Arabia* (Cambridge: Cambridge University Press, 2002); Alexei Vassiliev, *The History of Saudi Arabia* (London: Saqi Books, 2000); R. Bayly Winder, *Saudi Arabia in the Nineteenth Century* (London: MacMillan/St. Martin's Press, 1965).

155.   For more on Salafism, see Martijn de Koning, Joas Wagemakers and Carmen Becker, *Salafisme: Utopische idealen in een weerbarstige praktijk* (Almere: Parthenon, 2014); Roel Meijer (ed.), *Global Salafism: Islam's New Religious Movement* (London: Hurst & Co., 2009); Bernard Rougier (ed.), *Qu'est-ce que le salafisme?* (Paris: Presses Universitaires de France, 2008); Behnam T. Said and Hazim Fouad (ed.), *Salafismus: Auf der Suche nach dem wahren Islam* (Freiburg, Basel and Vienna: Herder, 2014).

156.   For more on Wahhabism and its character in the history of Saudi Arabia, see Muhammad Al Atawneh, *Wahhabi Islam Facing the Challenges of Modernity: Dar al-Ifta in the Modern Saudi State* (Leiden and Boston, MA: Brill, 2010); David Commins, *Islam in Saudi Arabia* (London and New York: I.B. Tauris, 2015); David Commins, *The Wahhabi Mission and Saudi Arabia* (London and New York: I.B. Tauris, 2005); Nabil Mouline, *Les clercs de l'islam: Autorité religieuse et pouvoir politique en Arabie Saoudite, XVIIIe–XXIe siècle* (Paris: Presses Universitaires de France, 2011); Guido Steinberg, *Religion und Staat in Saudi-Arabien: Die wahhabitischen Gelehrten, 1902–1943* (Würzburg: Ergon Verlag, 2002).

157.   For overviews of Islamist groups and activities in Saudi Arabia, see Abdulaziz O. Sager, 'Political Opposition in Saudi Arabia', in *Saudi Arabia in the Balance: Political Economy, Society, Foreign Affairs*, eds. Paul Aarts and Gert Nonneman (London: Hurst & Co., 2005), 234–270; International Crisis Group, *Saudi Arabia Backgrounder: Who are the Islamists?*, Middle East Report no. 31 (Amman: International Crisis Group, 2004).

158.   The Saudi *sahwa* should not be confused with the more general Islamic revival in the Arab world since the 1960s that is also referred to as such. See Stéphane Lacroix, *Les islamistes saoudiens: Une insurrection manquée* (Paris: Presses Universitaires de France, 2010), 64–65.

159.   *Ibid.*, 66–74.

160.   Gilles Kepel, *The War for Muslim Minds: Islam and the West* (Cambridge, MA, and London: Belknap/Harvard University Press, 2004), 171–172; Lacroix, *Islamistes*, 50–51.

161.   Kepel, *War*, 172; Lacroix, *Islamistes*, 54–58; Lefèvre, *Ashes*, 95–96; Mouline, *Clercs*, 190.

162.   Kepel, *War*, 172–174; Lacroix, *Islamistes*, 52–64.

163.   Kepel, *War*, 174–177; Lacroix, *Islamistes*, 54, 65–70, 84–86; Madawi Al-Rasheed, *Contesting the Saudi State: Islamic Voices from a New Generation* (Cambridge: Cambridge University Press, 2007), 72–77.

164. Sager, 'Political', 243.

165. Lacroix, *Islamistes*, 49–50.

166. *Ibid.*, 77–87.

167. *Ibid.*, 90–95. For more on this religious infrastructure, see Al Atawneh, *Wahhabi*; Mouline, *Clercs*.

168. Robert Lacey, *Inside the Kingdom: Kings, Clerics, Modernists, Terrorists, and the Struggle for Saudi Arabia* (London: Viking, 2009), 3–5.

169. For more on the background of Juhayman and his followers, see James Buchan, 'The Return of the Ikhwan', in *The House of Saud: The Rise and Rule of the Most Powerful Dynasty in the Arab World*, David Holden and Richard Johns (New York: Holt, Rhinehart and Winston, 1981), 513–522; Thomas Hegghammer and Stéphane Lacroix, "Rejectionist Islamism in Saudi Arabia: The Story of Juhayman al-'Utaybi Revisited', *International Journal of Middle East Studies* 39, no. 1 (2007): 103–122; Florian Peil, 'Die Besetzung der Großen Moschee von Mekka 1979', *Orient: Deutsche Zeitschrift für Politik, Wirtschaft und Kultur des Orients* 47, no. 3 (2006): 388–393, 394–398.

170. Dekmejian, *Islam*, 134–136; Peil, 'Besetzung', 398–405.

171. Buchan, 'Return', 522–526; Dekmejian, *Islam*, 136–137; Yaroslav Trofimov, *The Siege of Mecca: The 1979 Uprising at Islam's Holiest Shrine* (New York: Anchor Books, 2007).

172. Toby Craig Jones, 'Religious Revivalism and Its Challenge to the Saudi Regime', in *Religion and Politics in Saudi Arabia: Wahhabism and the State*, eds. Mohammed Ayoob and Hasan Kosebalaban (Boulder, CO, and London: Lynne Rienner, 2009), 110–111; Niblock, *Saudi*, 83–85; Gwenn Okruhlik, 'Making Conversation Permissible: Islamism and Reform in Saudi Arabia', in *Islamic Activism: A Social Movement Theory Approach*, ed. Quintan Wiktorowicz (Bloomington and Indianapolis, IN: Indiana University Press, 2004, 254–255.

173. Lacroix, *Islamistes*, 174–177; Al-Rasheed, *Contesting*, 59–65.

174. Kepel, *War*, 182–184; Lacroix, *Islamistes*, 177–179. For an extensive discussion of this book, see Daniel Lav, *Radical Islam and the Revival of Medieval Theology* (Cambridge: Cambridge University Press, 2012), 86–119.

175. Joshua Teitelbaum, *Holier than Thou: Saudi Arabia's Islamic Opposition* (Washington, DC: The Washington Institute for Near East Policy, 2000), 26.

176. Mordechai Abir, *Saudi Arabia: Government, Society and the Gulf Crisis* (London and New York: Routledge, 1993), 174, 178–179; Teitelbaum, *Holier*, 26–28.

177. Toby Jones, 'The Clerics, the Sahwa and the Saudi State', *Strategic Insights* 4, no. 3, March 2005; Gwenn Okruhlik, 'Networks of Dissent: Islamism and Reform in Saudi Arabia', Social Science Research Council, ssrc.org/sept11/essays/okruhlik_text_only.htm, 10 May 2007.

178. Dekmejian, *Islam*, 144; *idem*, 'The Liberal Impulse in Saudi Arabia', *Middle East Journal* 57, no. 3 (2003): 402–404; Gudrun Krämer, 'Good Counsel to the King: The Islamist Opposition in Saudi Arabia, Jordan, and Morocco', in *Middle East Monarchies: The Challenge of Modernity*, ed. Joseph Kostiner (Boulder, CO: Lynne Rienner Publishers, 2000), 263.

179. Dekmejian, *Islam*, 144; Lacroix, *Islamistes*, 191–196.

180. Dekmejian, *Islam*, 146–148.

181. Lacroix, *Islamistes*, 206–209.

182. For more on al-Mas'ari, see Mamoun Fandy, *Saudi Arabia and the Politics of Dissent* (New York: Palgrave, 1999), 121–126.

183. For more on al-Faqih, see *ibid.*, 151–159.

184. Lacroix, *Islamistes*, 201–206.

185. For more on al-'Awda, see Fandy, *Saudi*, 89–113.

186. For more on al-Hawali, see *ibid.*, 61–87.

187. Lacroix, *Islamistes*, 197–201; Teitelbaum, *Holier*, 28–32.

188. Kepel, *War*, 175–177.

189. Teitelbaum, *Holier*, 28–29.

190. Daryl Champion, *The Paradoxical Kingdom: Saudi Arabia and the Momentum of Reform* (New York: Columbia University Press, 2003), 221–224; Dekmejian, *Islam*, 142–144; *idem*, 'The Rise of Political Islamism in Saudi Arabia', *Middle East Journal* 48, no. 4 (1994): 630–633; Lacroix, *Islamistes*, 214–219.

191. Champion, *Paradoxical*, 224–225; Dekmejian, *Islam*, 144–146; *idem*, 'Rise', 633–635; Lacroix, *Islamistes*, 219–223.

192. This name can also be translated as 'The Committee for the Defence of Sharia Rights'.

193. Fandy, *Saudi*, 118–121; Lacroix, *Islamistes*, 224–226; Teitelbaum, *Holier*, 49–51.

194. Dekmejian, *Islam*, 149–150.

195. Lacroix, *Islamistes*, 238–242.

196. *Ibid.*, 246–250.

197. Dekmejian, *Islam*, 149.

198. Kepel, *War*, 185; Lacroix, *Islamistes*, 242–244.

199. Teitelbaum, *Holier*, 56–57.

200. *Ibid.*, 51.

201. Lacroix, *Islamistes*, 226–227; Al-Rasheed, *Contesting*, 86–87; Al-Rasheed, *History*, 177–180.

202. Fandy, *Saudi*, 126–127.

203. *Ibid.*, 135–140; Teitelbaum, *Holier*, 51–55, 60–63.

204. Fandy, *Saudi*, 140–142. The literal translation of this movement is 'Islamic Movement for Reform in the Land of the Two Holy Places'.

205. *Ibid.*, 159–163, 167–173.

206. *Idem*, 'CyberResistance: Saudi Opposition between Globalization and Localization', *Comparative Studies in Society and History* 41, no. 1 (1999): 136–137; *idem*, *Saudi*, 150–151.

207. *Idem*, 'CyberResistance', 145–146; Al-Rasheed, *History*, 180–183; Teitelbaum, *Holier*, 63–65.

208. Champion, *Paradoxical*, 227; Fandy, 'CyberResistance', 135–136; *idem*, *Saudi*, 128–129.

209. Joshua Teitelbaum, 'Dueling for *Da'wa*: State vs. Society on the Saudi Internet', *Middle East Journal* 56, no. 2 (2002): 226–227.

210.   See islah.co.
211.   Lacroix, *Islamistes*, 255–259.
212.   Al-Rasheed, *Contesting*, 77–81.
213.   *Ibid.*, 81–86.
214.   Lacroix, *Islamistes*, 245.
215.   Kepel, *War*, 188–190; Al-Rasheed, *Contesting*, 88–91, 95–101.
216.   Al-Rasheed, *Contesting*, 91–95.
217.   'Saudi Arabia: Prominent Reformist Cleric Faces Death Penalty for
       His Peaceful Activism', Amnesty International, amnesty.org/en/latest/
       news/2019/07/saudi-arabia-prominent-reformist-cleric-faces-death-sen-
       tence-for-his-peaceful-activism/, 26 July 2019.

4.   Participation

1.   Luciano Zaccara, Courtney Freer and Hendrik Kraetzschmar, 'Kuwait's Is-
      lamist Proto-Parties and the Arab Uprisings: Between Opposition, Pragma-
      tism and the Pursuit of Cross-Ideological Cooperation', in *Islamists and the
      Politics of the Arab Uprisings: Governance, Pluralisation and Contention*, eds.
      Hendrik Kraetzschmar and Paola Rivetti (Edinburgh: Edinburgh University
      Press, 2018), 182–204.
2.   Courtney Freer, *Rentier Islamism: The Influence of the Muslim Brotherhood
      in Gulf Monarchies* (Oxford: Oxford University Press, 2018), 29–31; Carine
      Lahoud-Tatar, *Islam et politique au Koweït* (Paris: Presses Universitaires de
      France, 2011), 5–13, 42–43.
3.   Freer, *Rentier*, 31–32.
4.   Brown, *Victory*, 103–104.
5.   Freer, *Rentier*, 46–47.
6.   *Ibid.*, 47; Lahoud-Tatar, *Islam*, 52–53; Falah Abdullah al-Mdaires, *Islamic
      Extremism in Kuwait: From the Muslim Brotherhood to al-Qaeda and Other
      Islamist Political Groups* (New York: Routledge, 2010), 11.
7.   Brown, *Victory*, 104–105; Courtney Freer, 'Exclusion-Moderation in the Gulf
      Context: Tracing the Development of Pragmatic Islamism in Kuwait', *Middle
      Eastern Studies* 54, no. 1 (2018): 6; *idem, Rentier*, 47; Lahoud-Tatar, *Islam*,
      53–54; al-Mdaires, *Islamic*, 12.
8.   Rosefsky Wickham, *Muslim*, 199.
9.   Freer, *Rentier*, 48–51; Lahoud-Tatar, *Islam*, 54–59; Mdaires, *Islamic*, 13–19.
10.   Freer, *Rentier*, 51–52. See also Lacroix, *Islamistes*, 81–82, on how this organi-
      zation was influenced by Islamist refugees from Saudi Arabia.
11.   Lahoud-Tatar, *Islam*, 61.
12.   *Ibid.*, 64.
13.   Freer, *Rentier*, 52–53.
14.   *Idem*, 'Exclusion', 7; *idem, Rentier*, 53.
15.   *Idem, Rentier*, 53.

16. Brown, *Victory*, 106.

17. Lahoud-Tatar, *Islam*, 66–70.

18. *Ibid.*, 62, 70.

19. Mdaires, *Islamic*, 128–142.

20. Freer, *Rentier*, 70.

21. Brown, *Victory*, 108; Freer, *Rentier*, 70; al-Mdaires, *Islamic*, 119.

22. Freer, *Rentier*, 74–77.

23. *Idem*, 'Exclusion', 7; Rosefsky Wickham, *Muslim*, 200–201.

24. Freer, 'Exclusion', 7–8; *idem, Rentier*, 77–78.

25. Cleveland and Bunton, *History*, 445–454.

26. Freer, 'Exclusion', 8; *idem, Rentier*, 78–79.

27. *Idem, Rentier*, 79; Mdaires, *Islamic*, 37–38.

28. Freer, *Rentier*, 82–84; Lahoud-Tatar, *Islam*, 212–213, 214–217.

29. Lahoud-Tatar, *Islam*, 217; Mdaires, *Islamic*, 38.

30. Freer, *Rentier*, 84–85; Rosefsky Wickham, *Muslim*, 219–220.

31. Al-Mdaires, *Islamic*, 38.

32. Lahoud-Tatar, *Islam*, 165–166.

33. Brown, *Victory*, 108–109.

34. Lahoud-Tatar, *Islam*, 169–171.

35. Al-Mdaires, *Islamic*, 39–40.

36. Freer, *Rentier*, 85–87.

37. *Idem*, 'Exclusion', 8–9.

38. Brown, *Victory*, 110; Freer, *Rentier*, 86; Lahoud-Tatar, *Islam*, 167–169.

39. Al-Mdaires, *Islamic*, 41–42; Rosefsky Wickham, *Muslim*, 223–224.

40. Rosefsky Wickham, *Muslim*, 221.

41. Freer, 'Exclusion', 9–10; *idem, Rentier*, 109–113; al-Mdaires, *Islamic*, 44.

42. Brown, *Victory*, 111; Freer, *Rentier*, 109–110; Rosefsky Wickham, *Muslim*, 224.

43. Lahoud-Tatar, *Islam*, 219. See also Rosefsky Wickham, *Muslim*, 225.

44. Freer, *Rentier*, 110; Rosefsky Wickham, *Muslim*, 227.

45. Freer, 'Exclusion', 10–11; *idem, Rentier*, 113–115.

46. Freer, *Rentier*, 145–146, 147–149.

47. *Idem*, 'Exclusion', 14–15; *idem, Rentier*, 141–144, 147.

48. *Idem, Rentier*, 149.

49. Rosefsky Wickham, *Muslim*, 229–230.

50. For more on this, see, for example, Yoav Alon, *The Making of Jordan: Tribes Colonialism and the Modern State* (London and New York: I.B. Tauris, 2009); *idem, The Shaykh of Shaykhs: Mithqal al-Fayiz and Tribal Leadership in Modern Jordan* (Stanford, CA: Stanford University Press, 2016); Andrew Shryock, *Nationalism and the Genealogical Imagination: Oral History and Textual Authority in Tribal Jordan* (Berkeley and Los Angeles, CA: University of California Press, 1997).

51. Muhammad Abu Rumman and Hasan Abu Haniyya, *Al-Hall al-Islami fi l-Urdunn: Al-Islamiyyun wa-l-Dawla wa-Rihanat al-Dimuqratiyya wa-l-Amn* (Amman: Friedrich Ebert Stiftung, 2012), 25–27.

52.   *Ibid.*, 38–53.

53.   Naseer H. Aruri, *Jordan: A Study in Political Development (1921–1965)* (The Hague: Martinus Nijhoff, 1972), 74–88.

54.   Boulby, *Muslim*, 127–128.

55.   *Ibid.*, 39–46.

56.   *Ibid.*, 46–48.

57.   Mary C. Wilson, *King Abdullah, Britain and the Making of Jordan* (Cambridge: Cambridge University Press, 1987), 207–215.

58.   Abu Rumman and Abu Haniyya, *Al-Hall*, 67.

59.   Hassan Abu Hanieh (translation: Mohammad Abu Risheh), *The Muslim Brotherhood in Jordan: A Religious-Political Crisis in the National Context* (Amman: Konrad Adenauer Stiftung, 2016), 170–174; Boulby, *Muslim*, 73–77; Denis Engelleder, *Die islamistische Bewegung in Jordanien und Palästina, 1945–1989* (Wiesbaden: Harrassowitz Verlag, 2002), 103–111, 114–120.

60.   Boulby, *Muslim*, 80–90; Wiktorowicz, *Management*, 83–92.

61.   Clark, *Islam*, 82–83, 91–114; Janine Astrid Clark, 'Patronage, Prestige, and Power: The Islamic Center Charity Society's Political Role within the Muslim Brotherhood', in *Islamist Politics in the Middle East: Movements and Change*, ed. Samer S. Shehata (London and New York: Routledge, 2012), 73–80.

62.   Thomas Hegghammer, "Abdallah 'Azzam and Palestine,' *Die Welt des Islams* 53, nos. 3–4 (2013): 367–376; *idem, The Caravan: Abdallah Azzam and the Rise of Global Jihad* (Cambridge: Cambridge University Press, 2020), 47–65.

63.   Boulby, *Muslim*, 50–54.

64.   Joas Wagemakers, 'Foreign Policy as Protection: The Jordanian Muslim Brotherhood as a Political Minority During the Cold War', in *Muted Minorities: Ethnic, Religious and Political Groups in (Trans)Jordan, 1921–2016*, eds. Idir Ouahes and Paolo Maggiolini (London: Palgrave, 2021), 185–198.

65.   Clark, *Islam*, 87.

66.   Ellen M. Lust-Okar, 'The Decline of Jordanian Political Parties: Myth or Reality?', *International Journal of Middle East Studies* 33 (2001): 558.

67.   Robert B. Satloff, *Troubles on the East Bank: Challenges to the Domestic Stability of Jordan* (New York, Westport, CT, and London: Praeger/Washington, DC: The Center for Strategic and International Studies at Georgetown University, 1986), 40–48, 55–58; Lawrence Tal, 'Dealing with Radical Islam: The Case of Jordan', *Survival* 37, no. 3 (1995): 143.

68.   Anne Marie Baylouny, 'Militarizing Welfare: Neo-liberalism and Jordanian Policy', *Middle East Journal* 62, no. 2 (2008): 291–293; Rex Brynen, 'Economic Crisis and Post-Rentier Democratization in the Arab World: The Case of Jordan', *Canadian Journal of Political Science/Revue canadienne de science politique* 25, no. 1 (1992): 83–93; Anne Mariel Peters and Pete W. Moore, 'Beyond Boom and Bust: External Rents, Durable Authoritarianism, and Institutional Adaptation in the Hashemite Kingdom of Jordan', *Studies in Comparative International Developments* 44 (2009): 270–274; Kathrine Rath, 'The Process of Democratization in Jordan', *Middle Eastern Studies* 30, no. 3

(1994): 536–540; Curtis R. Ryan, *Jordan in Transition: From Hussein to Abdullah* (Boulder, CO: Lynne Rienner, 2002), 52–53; *idem*, 'Peace, Bread and Riots: Jordan and the International Monetary Fund', *Middle East Policy* 6, no. 2 (1998): 55–57; Hamed El-Said and Jane Harrigan, 'Economic Reform, Social Welfare, and Instability: Jordan, Egypt, Morocco, and Tunisia, 1983–2004', *Middle East Journal* 68, no. 1 (2014): 101–105.

69.   Kamel S. Abu Jaber and Schirin H. Fathi, 'The 1989 Jordanian Parliamentary Elections', *Orient: Deutsche Zeitschrift für Politik und Wirtschaft des Orients* 31, no. 1 (1990): 67–86; Curtis R. Ryan, 'Jordan and the Rise and Fall of the Arab Cooperation Council', *Middle East Journal* 52, no. 3 (1998): 393–394.

70.   Marc Lynch, *State Interests and Public Spheres: The International Politics of Jordan's Identity* (New York: Columbia University Press, 1999), 81–99.

71.   Russell E. Lucas, 'Deliberalization in Jordan', *Journal of Democracy* 14, no. 1 (2003): 137–144; Glenn E. Robinson, 'Defensive Democratisation in Jordan', *International Journal of Middle East Studies* 30, no. 3 (1998): 387–410; Ranjit Singh, 'Liberalisation or Democratisation? The Limits of Political Reform and Civil Society in Jordan', in *Jordan in Transition: 1990–2000*, ed. George Joffé (London: Hurst & Co., 2002), 75–82.

72.   Boulby, *Muslim*, 102–114; Hanna Y. Freij and Leonard C. Robinson, 'Liberalization, the Islamists, and the Stability of the Arab State: Jordan as a Case Study', *The Muslim World* 86, no. 1 (1996): 10; Curtis R. Ryan, 'Elections and Parliamentary Democratization in Jordan', *Democratization* 5, no. 4 (1998): 177–180.

73.   Boulby, *Muslim*, 141–145; Ryan, *Jordan in Transition*, 24–25; Sabah El-Said, *Between Pragmatism and Ideology: The Muslim Brotherhood in Jordan, 1989–1994* (Washington, DC: Washington Institute for Near Eastern Policy, 1995), 2.

74.   Hamid, *Temptations*, 78–80.

75.   Boulby, *Muslim*, 147–148.

76.   Abla M. Amawi, 'The 1993 Elections in Jordan', *Arab Studies Quarterly* 16, no. 3 (1994): 16–17; Frédéric Charillon and Alain Mouftard, 'Jordanie: Les élections du 8 novembre 1993 et le processus de paix', *Monde arabe/Maghreb-Machrek*, no. 144 (1994): 45–46; Hamid, *Temptations*, 103–104; Ryan, *Jordan in Transition*, 26–27; Schwedler, 'Paradox', 28.

77.   Wagemakers, *Muslim*, 167–175.

78.   Jillian Schwedler, *Faith in Moderation: Islamist Parties in Jordan and Yemen* (Cambridge: Cambridge University Press, 2006), 163–164; Wagemakers, *Muslim*, 175–181.

79.   Wagemakers, *Muslim*, 206–210.

80.   Janine A. Clark and Jillian Schwedler, 'Who Opened the Window? Women's Activism in Islamist Parties', *Comparative Politics* 35, no. 3 (2003): 300–308.

81.   Rosefsky Wickham, *Muslim*, 211–212. For more on the position of women in the Jordanian Muslim Brotherhood's thought, see Lisa Taraki, 'Islam is the Solution: Jordanian Islamists and the Dilemma of the "Modern Woman"',

British Journal of Sociology 46, no. 4, (1995): 643–661; *idem*, 'Jordanian Islamists and the Agenda for Women: Between Discourse and Practice', *Middle Eastern Studies* 32, no. 1 (1996): 140–158; Wagemakers, *Muslim*, 214–222.

82. Rosefsky Wickham, *Muslim*, 208–211; Wagemakers, *Muslim*, 224–230.

83. Abu Hanieh, *Muslim*, 174–178; Shadi Hamid, 'The Islamic Action Front in Jordan', in *The Oxford Handbook of Islam and Politics*, eds. John L. Esposito and Emad el-Din Shahin (Oxford: Oxford University Press, 2013), 544–557.

84. Beverley Milton-Edwards, 'Façade Democracy in Jordan', *British Journal of Middle Eastern Studies* 20, no. 2 (1993): 198.

85. Hamid, *Temptations*, 104–105; Ryan, 'Elections', 182; *idem, Jordan in Transition*, 27–28.

86. Avi Shlaim, *Lion of Jordan: The Life of King Hussein in War and Peace* (New York: Alfred A. Knopf, 2008), 555–557.

87. Ryan, *Jordan in Transition*, 29.

88. Laurie A. Brand, 'The Effects of the Peace Process on Political Liberalization in Jordan', *Journal of Palestine Studies* 28, no. 2 (1999): 59–64.

89. Hamid, *Temptations*, 109–110; Ryan, 'Elections', 183–193; *idem, Jordan in Transition*, 30–40.

90. Randa Habib (translation: Miranda Tell), *Hussein and Abdullah: Inside the Jordanian Royal Family* (London: Saqi, 2010), 201–204.

91. King Abdullah II of Jordan, *Our Last Best Chance: The Pursuit of Peace in a Time of Peril* (London: Viking, 2011), 198–199.

92. Habib, *Hussein*, 204–205.

93. Wagemakers, *Muslim*, 106–107.

94. Clark, 'Patronage', 73.

95. Jillian Schwedler, 'Don't Blink: Jordan's Democratic Opening and Closing', *Middle East Report Online*, 2002, merip.org/mero/mero070302.

96. Hamid, *Temptations*, 130.

97. Curtis R. Ryan and Jillian Schwedler, 'Return to Democratization or New Hybrid Regime? The 2003 Elections in Jordan', *Middle East Report* 11, no. 2 (2004): 146.

98. For an extensive analysis of the IAF's performance in the elections of 2007, see Abu Rumman, *Muslim*.

99. Wagemakers, *Muslim*, 108–109.

100. Jillian Schwedler, 'Jordan's Islamists Lose Faith in Moderation', *Foreign Policy*, 2010, foreignpolicy.com/2010/06/30/jordans-islamists-lose-faith-in-moderation/#.

101. Ellen Lust and Sami Hourani, 'Jordan Votes: Election or Selection?', *Journal of Democracy* 22, no. 2 (2011): 119–129.

102. Wagemakers, *Muslim*, 181–183.

103. Jacob Amis, 'The Jordanian Brotherhood in the Arab Spring', *Current Trends in Islamist Ideology* 14 (2013): 38–57; Curtis R. Ryan, *Jordan and the Arab Uprisings: Regime Survival and Politics Beyond the State* (New York: Columbia University Press, 2018), 19–42.

104. Joas Wagemakers, 'Between Exclusivism and Inclusivism: The Jordanian Muslim Brotherhood's Divided Responses to the "Arab Spring"', *Middle East Law and Governance* 12, no. 1 (2020): 47–53; *idem, Muslim*, 109–111.

105. Morten Valbjørn, 'The 2013 Parliamentary Elections in Jordan: Three Stories and Some General Lessons', *Mediterranean Politics* 18, no. 2 (2013): 311–317.

106. Curtis R. Ryan, 'One Society of Muslim Brothers in Jordan or Two?', *Middle East Report Online*, 2015, merip.org/one-society-muslim-brothers-jordan-or-two; Wagemakers, 'Between', 53–8; *idem, Muslim*, 111–113.

107. Wagemakers, *Muslim*, 113–116.

108. For detailed analyses of how the Muslim Brotherhood in Jordan imploded, see Abdulgani Bozkurt and Muhammed Ünalmış, 'Partnership and Rescue Party and the Transformation of Political Opposition in Jordan', *Religions* 13, no. 3 (2022): 5–13; Joas Wagemakers, 'Things Fall Apart: The Disintegration of the Jordanian Muslim Brotherhood', *Religions* 12, no. 12 (2021): 1–17.

109. Nels Johnson, *Islam and the Politics of Meaning in Palestinian Nationalism* (London: Kegan Paul International, 1982), 9–11.

110. The literature on the Palestinian-Israeli conflict is huge. One book that tries to describe the entire conflict is, for example, Benny Morris, *Righteous Victims: A History of the Zionist-Arab Conflict, 1881–2001* (New York: Vintage Books, 2001 [1999]).

111. For more on Palestinian nationalism and the PLO, see Amal Jamal, *The Palestinian National Movement: Politics of Contention, 1967–2005* (Bloomington, IN: Indiana University Press, 2005); Baruch Kimmerling and Joel Migdal, *The Palestinian People: A History* (Cambridge, MA: Harvard University Press, 2003); Cheryl A. Rubenberg, *The Palestinians: In Search of a Just Peace* (Boulder, CO: Lynne Rienner, 2003); Yezid Sayigh, *Armed Struggle and the Search for State: The Palestinian National Movement, 1949–1993* (Oxford: Oxford University Press, 1997).

112. For more on al-Qassam, see Mark Sanagan, 'Teacher, Preacher, Soldier, Martyr: Rethinking 'Izz al-Din al-Qassam', *Die Welt des Islams* 53, nos. 3–4 (2013): 315–352.

113. Beverley Milton-Edwards, *Islamic Politics in Palestine* (London and New York: I.B. Tauris, 1996), 13–14; *idem, Muslim*, 64.

114. Beverley Milton-Edwards and Stephen Farrell, *Hamas* (Cambridge and Malden, MA: Polity Press, 2010), 26–31; Milton-Edwards, *Islamic*, 18–23.

115. Ziad Abu-Amr, *Islamic Fundamentalism in the West Bank and Gaza: Muslim Brotherhood and Islamic Jihad* (Bloomington and Indianapolis, IN: Indiana University Press, 1994), 1–3; El-Awaisi, *Muslim*, 150–155; Khaled Hroub, *Hamas: Political Thought and Practice* (Washington, DC: Institute for Palestine Studies, 2000), 14–17.

116. El-Awaisi, *Muslim*, 155–156; Milton-Edwards, *Islamic*, 40.

117. El-Awaisi, *Muslim*, 157–158.

118. *Ibid.*, 164–166.

119. *Ibid.*, 166–171.

120. Abu-Amr, *Islamic*, 3–4; Hroub, *Hamas*, 18–19.

121. Abu-Amr, *Islamic*, 4–6.

122. *Ibid.*, 4; Hroub, *Hamas*, 20; Mohammed K. Shadid, 'The Muslim Brotherhood Movement in the West Bank and Gaza', *Third World Quarterly* 10, no. 2 (1988): 660–661.

123. Milton-Edwards, *Islamic*, 43–46.

124. Abu-Amr, *Islamic*, 7–9; Hroub, *Hamas*, 23–25; Milton-Edwards, *Islamic*, 46–47.

125. Milton-Edwards, *Islamic*, 47–55.

126. Abu-Amr, *Islamic*, 9–10.

127. Hroub, *Hamas*, 25–29.

128. Abu-Amr, *Islamic*, 10; Hroub, *Hamas*, 29–32.

129. Milton-Edwards, *Islamics*, 73–75, 84–90.

130. Shadid, 'Muslim,' 662–663.

131. Abu-Amr, *Islamic*, 11–12.

132. *Ibid.*, 20–22.

133. *Ibid.*, 16–18; Milton-Edwards, *Islamic*, 108–114; Mishal and Sela, *Palestinian*, 23–26; Azzam Tamimi, *Hamas: A History from Within* (Northampton, MA: Olive Branch Press, 2007), 39–42.

134. Abu-Amr, *Islamic*, 10–11.

135. *Ibid.*, 14; Ze'ev Schiff and Ehud Ya'ari (translation: Ina Friedman), *Intifada: The Inside Story of the Palestinian Uprising That Changed the Middle East Equation* (New York: Touchstone/Simon & Schuster, 1991 [1989]), 223–225.

136. Abu-Amr, *Islamic*, 14–16; Shadid, 'Muslim', 670–674.

137. Abu-Amr, *Islamic*, 16; Milton-Edwards, *Islamic*, 101–102; *idem* and Farrell, *Hamas*, 39–41.

138. Hillel Frisch, 'Hamas: The Palestinian Muslim Brotherhood', in *The Muslim Brotherhood: The Organization and Policies of a Global Islamist Movement*, ed. Barry Rubin (New York: Palgrave/MacMillan, 2010), 90; Milton-Edwards, *Islamic*, 101, 105, 128–129.

139. Abu-Amr, *Islamic*, 26.

140. *Ibid.*, 23–52.

141. *Ibid.*, 36–38; Paola Caridi (translation: Andrea Teti), *Hamas: From Resistance to Government* (New York: Seven Stories Press, 2012 [2009]), 60–62.

142. Zaki Chehab, *Inside Hamas: The Untold Story of the Militant Islamic Movement* (New York: Nation Books, 2007), 21–22; Milton-Edwards, *Islamic*, 115; Schiff and Ya'ari, *Intifada*, 220–221.

143. Abu-Amr, *Islamic*, 53–59.

144. *Ibid.*, 59–66; Chehab, *Inside*, 23–26; Hroub, *Hamas*, 36–41.

145. Mishal and Sela, *Palestinian*, 37.

146. Gunning, *Hamas*, 98–107; Mishal and Sela, *Palestinian*, 173.

147. Chehab, *Inside*, 31–33, 39–68; Milton-Edwards and Farrell, *Hamas*, 110–133.

148. Milton-Edwards, *Islamic*, 151–153.

149. Caridi, *Hamas*, 71–85; Hroub, *Hamas*, 233–242; Michael Irving Jensen (translation: Sally Laird), *The Political Ideology of Hamas: A Grassroots Perspective*

(London and New York: I.B. Tauris, 2010 [2009]), 47–139; Matthew Levitt, *Hamas: Politics, Charity, and Terrorism in the Service of Jihad* (New Haven, CT, and London: Yale University Press, 2006); Milton-Edwards and Farrell, *Hamas*, 157–181; Sara Roy, *Hamas and Civil Society in Gaza: Engaging in the Islamist Social Sector* (Princeton, NJ, and Oxford: Princeton University Press, 2011), 51–225.

150. For English translations of Hamas' charter, see Hroub, *Hamas*, 267–291; Mishal and Sela, *Palestinian*, 175–199. For analyses of the charters, see Abu-Amr, *Islamic*, 80–83; Caridi, *Hamas*, 99–108; Hroub, *Hamas*, 52–54; Mishal and Sela, *Palestinian*, 43–46; Tamimi, *Hamas*, 150–156.

151. Milton-Edwards, *Islamic*, 155–160; Andrea Nüsse, *Muslim Palestine: The Ideology of Hamas* (Abingdon: RoutledgeCurzon, 1998), 129–137.

152. Nüsse, *Muslim*, 145–153.

153. Milton-Edwards, *Islamic*, 161–162.

154. Dalacoura, *Islamist*, 71–74; Hroub, *Hamas*, 242–251; Milton-Edwards, *Islamic*, 166–170; Nüsse, *Muslim*, 164–166.

155. Gunning, *Hamas*, 198–203.

156. Tamimi, *Hamas*, 161–162.

157. Gunning, *Hamas*, 215–220; Mishal and Sela, *Palestinian*, 68–71.

158. Hroub, *Hamas*, 59–63, 69–84; Tamimi, *Hamas*, 156–159.

159. Mishal and Sela, *Palestinian*, 108–110.

160. Milton-Edwards, *Islamic*, 165–166;

161. Hroub, *Hamas*, 210–211.

162. For more on Hamas' views on an Islamic state, see Gunning, *Hamas*, 57–62, 64–74.

163. Mishal and Sela, *Palestinian*, 121–131; *idem*, 'Participation', 1–26.

164. Caridi, *Hamas*, 120–126; Hroub, *Hamas*, 224–229; Mishal and Sela, *Palestinian*, 131–138; Milton-Edwards and Farrell, *Hamas*, 82–83; Nüsse, *Muslim*, 161–163.

165. Gunning, *Hamas*, 62–63; Hroub, *Hamas*, 133–139.

166. Gunning, *Hamas*, 62.

167. Hroub, *Hamas*, 234.

168. Caridi, *Hamas*, 90–97.

169. Milton-Edwards and Farrell, *Hamas*, 188–192.

170. Gunning, *Hamas*, 74–81.

171. Tamimi, *Hamas*, 198–199.

172. Frisch, 'Hamas', 94–96.

173. Caridi, *Hamas*, 161–165.

174. *Ibid.*, 165–170.

175. *Ibid.*, 150–159.

176. *Ibid.*, 172–173, 181–183; Tamimi, *Hamas*, 211–213.

177. Wagemakers, 'Legitimizing', 365–369.

178. Tavishi Bhasin and Maia Carter Hallward, 'Hamas as a Political Party: Democratization in the Palestinian Territories', *Terrorism and Political Violence* 25, no. 1 (2013): 78–80.

179. Manal A. Jamal, 'Beyond *Fateh* Corruption and Mass Discontent: *Hamas, the Palestinian Left and the 2006 Legislative Elections'*, *British Journal of Middle East Studies* 40, no. 3 (2013): 283–93.

180. Caridi, *Hamas*, 173–180, 183–190; Frisch, 'Hamas', 96–99; Milton-Edwards and Farrell, *Hamas*, 245–259; Tamimi, *Hamas*, 217–221.

181. Benedetta Berti, 'Non-State Actors as Providers of Governance: The Hamas Government in Gaza between Effective Sovereignty, Centralized Authority, and Resistance', *Middle East Journal* 69, no. 1 (2015): 12–15; Caridi, *Hamas*, 199–258; Frisch, 'Hamas', 99–101; Legrain, 'Hamas', 190–192; Milton-Edwards and Farrell, *Hamas*, 260–294; Beverley Milton-Edwards, 'The Ascendance of Political Islam: Hamas and Consolidation in the Gaza Strip', *Third World Quarterly* 29, no. 8 (2008): 1585–1589.

182. International Crisis Group, *Radical Islam in Gaza*, Middle East Report no. 104 (Brussels: International Crisis Group, 2011); Beverley Milton-Edwards, 'Islamist Versus Islamist: Rising Challenge in Gaza', *Terrorism and Political Violence* 26, no. 2 (2014): 259–276.

183. Berti, 'Non-State', 15–20, 26; Milton-Edwards, 'Ascendance', 1591–1597.

184. Berti, 'Non-State', 27–29.

185. Caridi, *Hamas*, 265–277; Milton-Edwards and Farrell, *Hamas*, 298–302.

186. For more on Hamas and the Arab Spring, see Basem Ezbidi, '"Arab Spring": Weather Forecast for Palestine', *Middle East Policy* 20, no. 3 (2013): 99–110; International Crisis Group, *Light at the End of Their Tunnels? Hamas & the Arab Uprisings*, ICG Middle East Report no. 129 (Brussels: International Crisis Group, 2012); Frode Løvlie and Are Knudsen, 'Hamas and the Arab Spring', *Middle East Policy* 20, no 3 (2013): 56–59; Beverley Milton-Edwards, 'Hamas and the Arab Spring: Strategic Shifts?', *Middle East Policy* 20, no. 3 (2013): 60–72; Valentina Napolitano, 'Hamas and the Syrian Uprising: A Difficult Choice', *Middle East Policy* 20, no. 3 (2013): 73–85; Dag Tuastad, 'Hamas-PLO Relations Before and After the Arab Spring', *Middle East Policy* 20, no. 3 (2013): 86–98.

187. Milton-Edwards, *Muslim*, 69–75.

188. For an English translation of the 2017 charter, see middleeasteye.net/news/hamas-2017-document-full.

5. Power

1.   See Stig Jarle Hansen and Mohamed Husein Gaas, 'The Ideological Arena of the Wider Muslim Brotherhood', in *The Muslim Brotherhood Movement in the Arab Winter*, eds. Stig Jarle Hansen, Mohamed Husein Gaas and Ida Bary (Cambridge, MA: Harvard Kennedy School Belfer Center for Science and International Affairs), 2017, 7–19.

2.   Mustafa A. Abdelwahid, *The Rise of the Islamic Movement in Sudan (1945–1989)* (New York: Edwin Mellen Press, 2008), 57–60; Abdelwahab El-Affendi,

Turabi's Revolution: Islam and Power in Sudan (London: Grey Seal Books, 1991), 23–26.

3. Abdelwahid, *Rise*, 60–65; Berridge, *Islamism*, 149–150; John L. Esposito and John O. Voll, *Islam and Democracy* (Oxford: Oxford University Press, 1996), 78–83; John L. Esposito, 'Sudan', in *The Politics of Islamic Revivalism*, ed. Shireen T. Hunter (Bloomington and Indianapolis: IN: Indiana University Press, 1988), 187–189.

4. Abdelwahid, *Rise*, 82–84; El-Affendi, *Turabi's Revolution*, 46–48.

5. Abdelwahid, *Rise*, 85–88; El-Affendi, *Turabi's Revolution*, 48, 52–53; Berridge, *Islamism*, 151; Esposito and Voll, *Islam*, 88.

6. Abdelwahid, *Rise*, 170–172; El-Affendi, *Turabi's Revolution*, 67–68;

7. For more on the life and thought of al-Turabi, see W.J. Berridge, *Hasan al-Turabi: Islamist Politics and Democracy in Sudan* (Cambridge: Cambridge University Press, 2017), 26–48; Joyce M. Davis, *Between Jihad and Salaam: Profiles in Islam*, (New York: St. Martin's Griffin, 1999 [1997]), 1–28; John L. Esposito and John O. Voll, *Makers of Contemporary Islam* (Oxford: Oxford University Press, 2001), 118–149.

8. Berridge, *Hasan*, 36–37.

9. *Ibid.*, 1–16.

10. Abdelwahid, *Rise*, 88; El-Affendi, *Al-Turabi's Revolution*, 53–54.

11. Abdelwahid, *Rise*, 88–90; El-Affendi, *Turabi's Revolution*, 57–59; Esposito and Voll, *Islam*, 88.

12. Gilles Kepel, *Jihad: The Trail of Political Islam* (Cambridge, MA: Belknap/Harvard University Press, 2002), 177.

13. Abdelwahid, *Rise*, 91; El-Affendi, *Turabi's Revolution*, 60–62; Gabriel R. Warburg, 'Muslim Brotherhood in Sudan', in *The Oxford Encyclopedia of the Islamic World*, Vol. IV, ed. John L. Esposito (Oxford: Oxford University Press, 2009), 175, 177.

14. Abdelwahid, *Rise*, 91; El-Affendi, *Turabi's Revolution*, 62.

15. Berridge, *Hasan*, 51–52; Esposito and Voll, *Islam*, 89.

16. Abdelwahid, *Rise*, 94; El-Affendi, *Turabi's Revolution*, 74–77; Esposito and Voll, *Islam*, 90; Abdel Salam Sidahmed, 'Sudan: Ideology and Pragmatism', in *Islamic Fundamentalism*, eds. Abdel Salam Sidahmed and Anoushiravan Ehteshami (Boulder, CO: Westview Press, 1996), 181.

17. Abdelwahid, *Rise*, 94–96; El-Affendi, *Turabi's Revolution*, 76–77, 84–85; Berridge, *Hasan*, 71.

18. Abdelwahid, *Rise*, 95; El-Affendi, *Turabi's Revolution*, 79–84.

19. Abdelwahid, *Rise*, 97; Berridge, *Hasan*, 54–57.

20. Alexander S. Cudsi, 'Islam and Politics in the Sudan', in *Islam in the Political Process*, ed. James Piscatori (Cambridge: Cambridge University Press, 1983), 45; Esposito, 'Sudan', 190.

21. Berridge, *Hasan*, 58–59.

22. Abdelwahid, *Rise*, 97–98.

23. *Ibid.*, 98; Esposito, *Islam*, 263–264; *idem*, 'Sudan', 190; Warburg, 'Muslim', 175–176.

24. Warburg, 'Muslim', 176.
25. Abdelwahid, *Rise*, 99–100; El-Affendi, *Turabi's Revolution*, 109–110; Berridge, *Hasan*, 63; Esposito, 'Sudan', 191–192.
26. Berridge, *Hasan*, 64–65.
27. Abdelwahid, *Rise*, 100–101; El-Affendi, *Turabi's Revolution*, 112–115.
28. Cudsi, 'Islam', 49–50.
29. Esposito, *Islam*, 265–269; *idem*, 'Sudan', 195–199.
30. Warburg, 'Muslim', 177.
31. Berridge, *Hasan*, 66.
32. El-Affendi, *Turabi's Revolution*, 115–116; Berridge, *Hasan*, 66.
33. El-Affendi, *Turabi's Revolution*, 126–130; Sidahmed, 'Sudan', 184.
34. Berridge, *Hasan*, 67.
35. *Idem, Islamism*, 153.
36. *Idem, Hasan*, 67–70.
37. Abdelwahid, *Rise*, 104–106.
38. *Ibid.*, 106–107; El-Affendi, *Turabi's Revolution*, 139–143; Berridge, *Hasan*, 71–72; Esposito, 'Sudan', 200–201.
39. Berridge, *Hasan*, 74–75.
40. Abdelwahid, *Rise*, 108; Berridge, *Hasan*, 84.
41. Yehudit Ronen, 'The Rise and Fall of Hasan Abdallah al-Turabi: A Unique Chapter in Sudan's Political History (1989–99)', *Middle Eastern Studies* 50, no. 6 (2014): 995.
42. Peter Woodward, 'Sudan: Islamic Radicals in Power', in *Political Islam: Revolution, Radicalism or Reform?*, ed. John L. Esposito (Boulder, CO: Lynne Rienner Publishers, 1997), 101.
43. Ronen, 'Rise', 997.
44. *Ibid.*, 999.
45. Berridge, *Hasan*, 107.
46. *Ibid.*, 179–182; Burr and Collins, *Sudan*, 56–63, 69–75, 137–139, 166–174.
47. Berridge, *Hasan*, 183–184.
48. Burr and Collins, *Sudan*, 190.
49. Berridge, *Hasan*, 103–104.
50. *Ibid.*, 105.
51. *Ibid.*, 183.
52. Burr and Collins, *Sudan*, 98–99; Ronen, 'Rise', 996.
53. Berridge, *Hasan*, 108–111; Ronen, 'Rise', 999–1000.
54. Ronen, 'Rise', 1000.
55. Berridge, *Hasan*, 77.
56. Burr and Collins, *Sudan*, 272.
57. Berridge, *Hasan*, 295–297.
58. Ronen, 'Rise', 1001.
59. Berridge, *Hasan*, 269, 298.
60. *Ibid.*, 298–299; Ronen, 'Rise', 1001.
61. Berridge, *Hasan*, 289–290.

62. *Ibid.*, 299; Ronen, 'Rise', 1001–1002.

63. Ronen, 'Rise', 1002.

64. Berridge, *Hasan*, 302.

65. See, for example, Wagemakers, *Muslim*, 20.

66. Berridge, *Hasan*, 244–268; El-Affendi, *Turabi's Revolution*, 158–162.

67. Ahmad S. Moussalli, 'Hasan al-Turabi's Islamist Discourse on Democracy and *Shura*', *Middle Eastern Studies* 30, no. 1 (1994): 57–61.

68. Berridge, *Hasan*, 225–236; Moussalli, 'Hasan', 53–55.

69. Berridge, *Hasan*, 237–238.

70. El-Affendi, *Turabi's Revolution*, 176; Berridge, *Hasan*, 241.

71. El-Affendi, *Turabi's Revolution*, 173–174.

72. Berridge, *Islamism*, 173.

73. Abdelwahid, *Rise*, 140–148.

74. Warburg, 'Muslim', 181.

75. Edmund Burke III, *The Ethnographic State: France and the Invention of Moroccan Islam* (Oakland, CA: University of California Press, 2014), 170–176; Nina ter Laan, 'Dissonant Voices: Islam-Inspired Music in Morocco and the Politics of Religious Sentiments' (PhD, Radboud University Nijmegen, 2016), 51–52.

76. Malika Zeghal, *Les islamistes Marocaines: Le défi à la monarchie* (Paris: Éditions La Découverte, 2005), 41–51.

77. Sarah J. Feuer, *Regulating Islam: Religion and the State in Contemporary Morocco and Tunisia* (Cambridge: Cambridge University Press, 2018), 32–36.

78. Burgat and Dowell, *Islamic*, 168–169.

79. Zeghal, *Islamistes*, 33–39.

80. Feuer, *Regulating*, 57–66; Zeghal, *Islamistes*, 83–91.

81. Zeghal, *Islamistes*, 95–98.

82. Dekmejian, *Islam*, 208–209; Feuer, *Regulating*, 28–29; Zeghal, *Islamistes*, 31, 33.

83. Zeghal, *Islamistes*, 9–11.

84. Feuer, *Regulating*, 30.

85. Krämer, 'Good', 275; Zeghal, *Islamistes*, 15.

86. Shahin, *Political*, 172; Wegner, *Islamist*, 19.

87. Henry Munson, Jr., 'Morocco', in *The Politics of Islamic Revivalism*, ed. Shireen T. Hunter (Bloomington and Indianapolis: IN: Indiana University Press, 1988), 138–139; Wegner, *Islamist*, 27–28.

88. Zeghal, *Islamistes*, 11–12, 15–16. For more on Yasin's life, see Munson, Jr., 'Morocco', 135–138; Zeghal, *Islamistes*, 119–125.

89. Henri Lauzière, 'Post-Islamism and the Religious Discourse of 'Abd al-Salam Yasin', *International Journal of Middle East Studies* 37 (2005): 244–250; *idem*, 'The Religious Dimension of Islamism: Sufism, Salafism, and Politics in Morocco', in *Islamist Politics in the Middle East: Movements and Change*, ed. Samer S. Shehata (New York: Routledge, 2012), 94–97; Shahin, *Political*, 193; Zeghal, *Islamistes*, 125–128.

90. Zeghal, *Islamistes*, 175–177.

91. *Ibid.*, 128–133.

92.   Burgat and Dowell, *Islamic*, 166–167; Wegner, *Islamist*, 28; Zeghal, *Islamistes*, 115–116, 135–137.

93.   Zeghal, *Islamistes*, 136, 138–153.

94.   *Ibid.*, 159–162.

95.   Burgat and Dowell, *Islamic*, 167; Wegner, *Islamist*, 28; Zeghal, *Islamistes*, 137–138.

96.   Burgat and Dowell, *Islamic*, 178.

97.   Vish Sakthivel, *Al-Adl wal-Ihsan: Inside Morocco's Islamist Challenge* (Washington, DC: Washington Institute for Near East Policy, 2015), 13; Zeghal, *Islamistes*, 165–170.

98.   Burgat and Dowell, *Islamic*, 179; Zeghal, *Islamistes*, 163–164.

99.   Burgat and Dowell, *Islamic*, 180.

100.   Sakthivel, *Al-Adl*, 17.

101.   Zeghal, *Islamistes*, 213–214.

102.   For more on the organizational structure of Shabiba, see Esen Kirdiş, *The Rise of Islamic Political Movements and Parties: Morocco, Turkey and Jordan* (Edinburgh: Edinburgh University Press, 2021 [2019]), 61.

103.   Burgat and Dowell, *Islamic*, 170–171; Dekmejian, *Islam*, 209–210; Feuer, *Regulating*, 36; Munson, Jr., 'Morocco', 133; Shahin, *Political*, 181–184; Zeghal, *Islamistes*, 193, 198.

104.   Rosefsky Wickham, *Muslim*, 202; Wegner, *Islamist*, 21.

105.   Shahin, *Political*, 184–186.

106.   Burgat and Dowell, *Islamic*, 171–172; Munson, Jr., 'Morocco', 133–135; Shahin, *Political*, 186–187; Wegner, *Islamist*, 22; Zeghal, *Islamistes*, 197–199.

107.   Rosefsky Wickham, *Muslim*, 202; Shahin, *Political*, 187–188.

108.   Burgat and Dowell, *Islamic*, 176; Rosefsky Wickham, *Muslim*, 202–203; Shahin, *Political*, 188–190; Wegner, *Islamist*, 23; Zeghal, *Islamistes*, 204–205.

109.   Wegner, *Islamist*, 223; Zeghal, *Islamistes*, 212.

110.   Wegner, *Islamist*, 224.

111.   Rosefsky Wickham, *Muslim*, 203; Shahin, *Political*, 191–192; Wegner, *Islamist*, 26; Zeghal, *Islamistes*, 213.

112.   Wegner, *Islamist*, 26; Zeghal, *Islamistes*, 213.

113.   Rosefsky Wickham, *Muslim*, 203; Wegner, *Islamist*, 21, 24; Zeghal, *Islamistes*, 214.

114.   Zeghal, *Islamistes*, 215.

115.   *Ibid.*, 188–190, 210–211, 244.

116.   Wegner, *Islamist*, 27; Zeghal, *Islamistes*, 220–221.

117.   Wegner, *Islamist*, 74–76, 96–103.

118.   Rosefsky Wickham, *Muslim*, 203; Wegner, *Islamist*, 35; Zeghal, *Islamistes*, 211, 215.

119.   Wegner, *Islamist*, 35–44.

120.   *Ibid.*, 51–52.

121.   Zeghal, *Islamistes*, 12–13, 211–212.

122.   *Ibid.*, 236–241.

123.   Ashraf Nabih El Sherif, 'Institutional and Ideological Re-Construction of the Justice and Development Party (PJD): The Question of Democratic Islamism in Morocco', *The Middle East Journal* 66, no. 4 (2012): 661–663.

124. Zeghal, *Islamistes*, 216.

125. Eva Wegner and Miquel Pellicer, 'Islamist Moderation without Democratization: The Coming of Age of the Moroccan Party of Justice and Development?', *Democratization* 16, no. 1 (2009): 162; Wegner, *Islamist*, 57–59.

126. Zeghal, *Islamistes*, 218, 232–233.

127. *Ibid.*, 229–231, 234.

128. Wegner, *Islamist*, 87; Zeghal, *Islamistes*, 248–251.

129. Wegner, *Islamist*, 76–82.

130. Rosefsky Wickham, *Muslim*, 230, 233–234.

131. Wegner, *Islamist*, 105–106; Zeghal, *Islamistes*, 224–227.

132. Wegner and Pellicer, 'Islamist', 161–167; Wegner, *Islamist*, 59–64.

133. Zeghal, *Islamistes*, 20, 247–248, 297–303.

134. Bradley Davis, 'Educator of the Faithful: The Power of Moroccan Islam', *Current Trends in Islamist Ideology* 25 (2020): 100–102; Ann Marie Wainscott, *Bureaucratizing Islam: Morocco and the War on Terror* (Cambridge: Cambridge University Press, 2017), 70–73.

135. Wainscott, *Bureaucratizing*, 73–78.

136. Lauzière, 'Religious', 100; Wainscott, *Bureaucratizing*, 78–81.

137. Lauzière, 'Religious', 97–99; Wegner, *Islamist*, 64–69.

138. Miqual Pellicer and Eva Wegner, 'The Justice and Development Party in Moroccan Local Politics', *Middle East Journal* 69, no. 1 (2015): 32–50.

139. Rosefsky Wickham, *Muslim*, 234–236; Wegner, *Islamist*, 83–89; Zeghal, *Islamistes*, 252–254.

140. Rosefsky Wickham, *Muslim*, 242–243; Wegner, *Islamist*, 92–93, 115–119.

141. Rosefsky Wickham, *Muslim*, 236–242. For an extensive treatment of the PJD's inclusion of women in its own party ranks, see Katarina Škrabáková, 'Islamist Women as Candidates in Elections: A Comparison of the Party of Justice and Development in Morocco and the Muslim Brotherhood in Egypt', *Die Welt des Islams* 57 (2017): 329–359.

142. Matt Buehler, 'The Threat to "Un-Moderate": Moroccan Islamists and the Arab Spring', *Middle East Law and Governance* 5 (2013): 241–257; Mohammed Masbah, 'Rise and Endurance: Moderate Islamists and Electoral Politics in the Aftermath of the "Moroccan Spring"', in *Islamists and the Politics of the Arab Uprisings: Governance Pluralisation and Contention*, eds. Hendrik Kraetzschmar and Paola Rivetti (Edinburgh: Edinburgh University Press, 2018), 130–131.

143. Rosefsky Wickham, *Muslim*, 244–245; El Sherif, 'Institutional', 679–682.

144. For an extensive analysis on how the party managed to stay in power after 2011 and 2017, see Masbah, 'Rise', 136–143.

145. 'Morocco Elections: Islamists Suffer Losses as Liberal Parties Gain Ground', *The Guardian*, 9 September 2021, www.theguardian.com/world/2021/sep/09/islamists-suffer-losses-as-liberal-parties-gain-ground-in-morocco-elections; 'Out of Power', *The Economist*, 18 September 2021, 33.

146. Anne Wolf, *Political Islam in Tunisia: The History of Ennahda* (London: Hurst & Co, 2017), 11–25.

147.   *Ibid.*, 31.
148.   Feuer, *Regulating*, 106–109.
149.   Milton-Edwards, *Muslim*, 113–115.
150.   Anne Wolf, 'An Islamist "Renaissance"? Religion and Politics in Post-Revolutionary Tunisia', *Journal of North African Studies* 18, no. 4 (2013): 561.
151.   *Idem, Political*, 27–30.
152.   *Ibid.*, 33–34.
153.   Rory McCarthy, *Inside Tunisia's al-Nahda: Between Politics and Preaching* (Cambridge: Cambridge University Press, 2018), 14–15.
154.   *Ibid.*, 21; Wolf, *Political*, 32–36.
155.   For more on al-Ghannushi, see François Burgat, *Face to Face with Political Islam* (London and New York: I.B. Tauris, 2003), 28–37; Davis, *Between*, 81–105; Esposito and Voll, *Makers*, 91–117; Azzam S. Tamimi, *Rachid Ghannouchi: A Democrat within Islamism* (Oxford: Oxford University Press, 2001).
156.   Shahin, *Political*, 77–78.
157.   McCarthy, *Inside*, 27–33; Wolf, *Political*, 42–45.
158.   McCarthy, *Inside*, 21; Wolf, *Political*, 37.
159.   Wolf, *Political*, 37.
160.   *Idem*, 'Islamist', 562.
161.   Burgat and Dowell, *Islamic*, 185; McCarthy, *Inside*, 42; Shahin, *Political*, 82–84; Wolf, *Political*, 48–49.
162.   Wolf, *Political*, 50.
163.   Pargeter, *The Muslim Brotherhood: From Opposition to Power*, 237–238; *idem, Return*, 184.
164.   McCarthy, *Inside*, 128; Shahin, *Political*, 77, 79; Wolf, *Political*, 40.
165.   Norma Salem, 'Tunisia', in *The Politics of Islamic Revivalism*, ed. Shireen T. Hunter (Bloomington and Indianapolis: IN: Indiana University Press, 1988), 163–164; Shahin, *Political*, 79–80; Wolf, *Political*, 45–47.
166.   Wolf, *Political*, 47–48.
167.   *Ibid.*, 50.
168.   Shahin, *Political*, 92–95.
169.   Waltz, 'Islamist', 655.
170.   Shahin, *Political*, 90–92.
171.   Salem, 'Tunisia', 162–163; Shahin, *Political*, 86–87.
172.   Wolf, *Political*, 53.
173.   *Ibid.*, 38–40.
174.   Feuer, *Regulating*, 116–117.
175.   Burgat and Dowell, *Islamic*, 193; Wolf, 'Islamist', 563–564; Wolf, *Political*, 56–57.
176.   McCarthy, *Inside*, 40, 43; Salem, 'Tunisia', 161; Waltz, 'Islamist', 653; Wolf, *Political*, 54–56.
177.   McCarthy, *Inside*, 44–45, 52, 59–60; Shahin, *Political*, 87–90; Wolf, *Political*, 57–61.
178.   Wolf, *Political*, 61–62.

179. Pargeter, *Return*, 189–190; Wolf, *Political*, 63–66.
180. Feuer, *Regulating*, 117; McCarthy, *Inside*, 62; Shahin, *Political*, 100; Wolf, *Political*, 66–67.
181. Feuer, *Regulating*, 110, 117; McCarthy, *Inside*, 62; Shahin, *Political*, 100; Wolf, *Political*, 67–68.
182. Shahin, *Political*, 99–100.
183. Feuer, *Regulating*, 159.
184. Wolf, 'Islamist', 562.
185. Feuer, *Regulating*, 117; McCarthy, *Inside*, 62, 64; Shahin, *Political*, 100–101; Wolf, *Political*, 69–71.
186. Pargeter, *Return*, 190.
187. Feuer, *Regulating*, 117–118; Shahin, *Political*, 101–102; Wolf, *Political*, 73–75.
188. Wolf, *Political*, 75–76.
189. Shahin, *Political*, 102; Wolf, 'Islamist', 564; *idem, Political*, 76–77.
190. Feuer, *Regulating*, 118; Shahin, *Political*, 103; Anne Wolf, *Political*, 74–76.
191. Feuer, *Regulating*, 118; Shahin, *Political*, 101.
192. McCarthy, *Inside*, 69–77; Wolf, *Political*, 80–83.
193. McCarthy, *Inside*, 90–94; Wolf, *Political*, 83–86.
194. McCarthy, *Inside*, 84–89.
195. *Ibid.*, 77–78.
196. *Ibid.*, 98–102.
197. Wolf, *Political*, 86–89.
198. *Ibid.*, 89–93.
199. *Ibid.*, 93–95.
200. *Ibid.*, 97–98. For more on al-Ghannushi's views on democracy, see March, *Caliphate*, 152–200; Tamimi, *Rachid*, 30–104, 182–199. For more on his views on women's rights, see Muhammad Mahmoud, 'Women and Islamism: The Case of Rashid al-Ghannushi of Tunisia', in *Islamic Fundamentalism*, eds. Abdel Salam Sidahmed and Anoushiravan Ehteshami (Boulder, CO: Westview Press, 1996), 249–265.
201. Wolf, *Political*, 98–106.
202. *Ibid.*, 108–110.
203. *Ibid.*, 110–114.
204. *Ibid.*, 114–126.
205. McCarthy, *Inside*, 123; Pargeter, *Return*, 193–194; Wolf, *Political*, 129–131.
206. Wolf, *Political*, 132–133.
207. Pargeter, *Return*, 194–197.
208. McCarthy, *Inside*, 136; Wolf, *Political*, 133–134.
209. Pargeter, *Return*, 197–198.
210. The full name of Al-Takattul is Al-Takattul al-Dimuqrati min Ajl al-'Amal wa-l-Hurriyyat ('The Democratic Forum for Labour and Freedoms').
211. Hamid, *Temptations*, 197; Pargeter, *Return*, 185, 200; Wolf, *Political*, 134.
212. Wolf, *Political*, 134–135.
213. Pargeter, *Return*, 201–211.

214. The secular opposition in Tunisia itself sometimes made use of religion, too, however. For more on secular Tunisian parties and their use of Islam, see Anne Wolf, 'Secular Forms of Politicised Islam in Tunisia: The Constitutional Democratic Rally and Nida' Tunis', in *Islamists and the Politics of the Arab Uprisings: Governance, Pluralisation and Contention*, eds. Hendrik Kraetzschmar and Paola Rivetti (Edinburgh: Edinburgh University Press, 2018), 205–220.

215. Wolf, *Political*, 153.

216. Francesco Cavatorta, 'The Complexity of Tunisian Islamism: Conflicts and Rivalries Over the Role of Religion in Politics', in *Islamists and the Politics of the Arab Uprisings: Governance, Pluralisation and Contention*, eds. Hendrik Kraetzschmar and Paola Rivetti (Edinburgh: Edinburgh University Press, 2018), 248–254.

217. Cavatorta, 'Complexity', 252; Pargeter, *Return*, 223–228; Wolf, 'Islamist', 566–567; *idem, Political*, 143–153.

218. Pargeter, *Return*, 214–216.

219. Hamid, *Temptations*, 197–198; Pargeter, *Return*, 216–221; Wolf, *Political*, 138–140.

220. Pargeter, *Return*, 222–223; Wolf, *Political*, 140–142.

221. McCarthy, 'Protecting', 455–463; Pargeter, *Return*, 221–222; Wolf, *Political*, 142–143.

222. Hamid, *Temptations*, 197–198.

223. *Idem, Islamic*, 184–191; Pargeter, *Return*, 228–229.

224. Cavatorta and Merone, 'Moderation', 859–862, 865–870; *idem*, 'Post-Islamism, Ideological Evolution and "la *tunisianité*" of the Tunisian Islamist Party al-Nahda', *Journal of Political Ideologies* 20, no. 1 (2015): 31–38.

225. McCarthy, *Inside*, 131; Milton-Edwards, *Muslim*, 124–125; Pargeter, *Return*, 214, 229–230, 233.

226. Feuer, *Regulating*, 186; Monica Marks, 'Did Egypt's Coup Teach Ennahda to Cede Power?', paper for the workshop 'Transnational Diffusion and Cooperation in the Middle East and North Africa' in Hamburg, 8–9 June 2016; McCarthy, *Inside*, 131; Pargeter, *Return*, 230–232, 234–237.

227. For more on the road to the new constitution, see Sami Zemni, 'From Revolution to *Tunisianité*: Who is the Tunisian People? Creating Hegemony Through Compromise', *Middle East Law and Governance* 8, nos. 2–3 (2016): 141–149.

228. McCarthy, *Inside*, 141; Wolf, *Political*, 157.

229. McCarthy, *Inside*, 137–141; Pargeter, *Return*, 237–238; Wolf, *Political*, 158.

230. McCarthy, *Inside*, 143; Wolf, *Political*, 158.

231. Milton-Edwards, *Muslim*, 128; Wolf, *Political*, 158–159.

232. Cavatorta, 'Complexity', 244–247; Wolf, *Political*, 160–162.

233. Roel Meijer, 'Islamisme en de Arabische Lente', *ZemZem: Tijdschrift over het Midden-Oosten, Noord-Afrika en islam* 16, no. 2 (2020): 67–76.

234. 'Arab Democracy's Fading Start', *The Economist*, 31 July 2021, 23–24; 'Fiddling While Carthage Burns', *The Economist*, 2 October 2021, 29–30.

6. Radicals

1. Boulby, *Muslim*, 53; Engelleder, *Islamistische*, 49–51; Reza Pankhurst, *Hizb ut-Tahrir: The Untold Story of the Liberation Party* (London: Hurst & Co., 2016), 51–60; Suha Taji-Farouki, 'Hizb al-Tahrir al-Islami,' in *The Oxford Encyclopedia of the Islamic World*, Vol. II, ed. John L. Esposito (Oxford: Oxford University Press, 2009), 423.

2. Engelleder, *Islamistische*, 51–52.

3. Milton-Edwards, *Islamic*, 65.

4. *Ibid.*, 66-7; Pankhurst, *Hizb*, 63.

5. Zeyno Baran, *Hizb ut-Tahrir: Islam's Political Insurgency* (Washington, DC: The Nixon Center, 2004), 20–23; International Crisis Group, *Radical Islam in Central Asia: Responding to Hizb ut-Tahrir*, ICG Asia Report no. 58, 30 June 2003, 5–6; Jean-François Mayer, *Hizb ut-Tahrir – The Next Al-Qaida, Really?* (Geneva: PSIO, 2004), 16–17, 22; Pankhurst, *Hizb*, 73.

6. Engelleder, *Islamistische*, 52; Milton-Edwards, *Islamic*, 69; Pankhurst, *Hizb*, 76–77, 85.

7. Baran, *Hizb*, 19; International Crisis Group, *Radical*, 6.

8. Suha Taji-Farouki, 'Islamic State Theories and Contemporary Realities', in *Islamic Fundamentalism*, eds. Abdel Salam Sidahmed and Anoushiravan Ehteshami (Boulder, CO: Westview Press, 1996), 41–43.

9. Pankhurst, *Hizb*, 86.

10. Engelleder, *Islamistische*, 52, 54–55; Milton-Edwards, *Islamic*, 69–70; Pankhurst, *Hizb*, 83, 86.

11. Pankhurst, *Hizb*, 105.

12. *Ibid.*, 120.

13. Engelleder, *Islamistische*, 95; Pankhurst, *Hizb*, 133–142.

14. Pankhurst, *Hizb*, 151–152, 162.

15. Taji-Farouki, 'Hizb', 423.

16. Baran, *Hizb*, 24–27; Engelleder, *Islamistische*, 111–114, 120–121.

17. Pankhurst, *Hizb*, 166.

18. *Ibid.*, 172.

19. Baran, *Hizb*, 35–36, 42–43, 77–91; International Crisis Group, *Radical*, 11, 12–13, 14–43; Pankhurst, *Hizb*, 207–208, 211–213, 218–219.

20. Baran, *Hizb*, 38–42; International Crisis Group, *Radical*, 11; Elisa Orofino, *Hizb ut-Tahrir and the Caliphate: Why the Group is Still Appealing to Muslims in the West* (London and New York: 2020).

21. Pankhurst, *Hizb*, 206.

22. Baran, *Hizb*, 38–42; International Crisis Group, *Radical*, 11.

23. Sadek Hamid, *Sufis, Salafis and Islamists: The Contested Ground of British Islamic Activism* (London: I.B. Tauris, 2016), 41.

24. *Ibid.*, 42–45.

25. Baran, *Hizb*, 53–64; Hamid, *Sufis*, 42, 45–47. For more on Al-Muhajiroun, see also Quintan Wiktorowicz, *Radical Islam Rising: Muslim Extremism in the West* (London: Rowman & Littlefield, 2005).

26.   Baran, *Hizb*, 17; International Crisis Group, *Radical*, 3.

27.   Taji-Farouki, 'Hizb', 424.

28.   Baran, *Hizb*, 28–29; Suha Taji-Farouki, 'Islamists and the Threat of *Jihad*: Hizb al-Tahrir and al-Muhajiroun on Israel and the Jews', *Middle Eastern Studies* 36, no. 4 (2000): 24–28.

29.   Pankhurst, *Hizb*, 4, 225–227, 232–233.

30.   Taji-Farouki, 'Hizb', 424.

31.   Engelleder, *Islamistische*, 125–128; Taji-Farouki, 'Islamists', 28–30.

32.   Pankhurst, *Hizb*, 185–189.

33.   Engelleder, *Islamistische*, 96–97.

34.   Pankhurst, *Hizb*, 191–193.

35.   Mayer, *Hizb*, 17–19.

36.   International Crisis Group, *Radical*, 8.

37.   *Ibid.*, 9.

38.   *Ibid.*, 7–8, 9.

39.   Mayer, *Hizb*, 14; Milton-Edwards, *Islamic*, 65.

40.   Hamid, *Sufis*, 35.

41.   Taji-Farouki, 'Islamic', 43–46.

42.   Mayer, *Hizb*, 15–16.

43.   For more on al-Shiqaqi, see Erik Skare, *A History of Palestinian Islamic Jihad: Faith, Awareness and Revolution in the Middle East* (Cambridge: Cambridge University Press, 2021), 14–17.

44.   Abu-Amr, *Islamic*, 91, 94, 101; Iyad Barghouti, 'Islamist Movements in Historical Palestine', in *Islamic Fundamentalism*, eds. Abdel Salam Sidahmed and Anoushiravan Ehteshami (Boulder, CO: Westview Press, 1996), 169; Meir Hatina, *Islam and Salvation in Palestine* (Tel Aviv: The Moshe Dayan Center for Middle Eastern and African Studies at Tel Aviv University, 2001), 23–26; Milton-Edwards, *Islamic*, 118, but see also Skare, *History*, 51–52.

45.   Abu-Amr, *Islamic*, 91–92; Engelleder, *Islamistische*, 70–71; Hatina, *Islam*, 33–34.

46.   Baran, *Hizb*, 53; Pankhurst, *Hizb*, 91.

47.   Abu-Amr, *Islamic*, 92–95; Skare, *History*, 22–24, 33.

48.   Abu-Amr, *Islamic*, 95–96; Hatina, *Islam*, 28–29, 30; Skare, *History*, 62–64.

49.   Abu-Amr, *Islamic*, 103–104; Hatina, *Islam*, 29; Skare, *History*, 64–65.

50.   Abu-Amr, *Islamic*, 96, 107, 107–108; Engelleder, *Islamistische*, 71; Hatina, *Islam*, 35–37; Milton-Edwards, *Islamic*, 121–123, 139–141, 141–142; Skare, *History*, 90–94; Tamimi, *Hamas*, 50.

51.   Abu-Amr, *Islamic*, 107; Hatina, *Islam*, 35, 37–38.

52.   Abu-Amr, *Islamic*, 114–115; Hatina, *Islam*, 39.

53.   Hatina, *Islam*, 39–44; Skare, *History*, 104–111.

54.   Hatina, *Islam*, 85–88; Milton-Edwards, *Islamic*, 171–173.

55.   Hatina, *Islam*, 92–95.

56.   *Ibid.*, 102–106; Milton-Edwards, *Islamic*, 170–171; Skare, *History*, 153–157.

57.   Abu-Amr, *Islamic*, 98–100; Milton-Edwards, *Islamic*, 205.

58. Abu-Amr, *Islamic*, 97–98; Barghouti, 'Islamist', 169; Milton-Edwards, *Islamic*, 198, 202–205.

59. Hatina, *Islam*, 96–99.

60. Abu-Amr, *Islamic*, 100–101, 102, 123–125; Barghouti, 'Islamist', 169; Hatina, *Islam*, 53–57, 107–113; Skare, *History*, 129–136.

61. Abu-Amr, *Islamic*, 123, 124; Hatina, *Islam*, 77.

62. Abu-Amr, *Islamic*, 103; Skare, *History*, 42–48.

63. Abu-Amr, *Islamic*, 122–123; Hatina, *Islam*, 77–78.

64. Erik Skare, 'Controlling the State in the Political Theory of Hamas and Palestinian Islamic Jihad', *Religions* 12, no. 11 (2021): 2–5.

65. Abu-Amr, *Islamic*, 104–105; Barghouti, 'Islamist', 169; Hatina, *Islam*, 26, 48–50, 76–77; Milton-Edwards, *Islamic*, 116–117; Tamimi, *Hamas*, 43–44.

66. Abu-Amr, *Islamic*, 109, 111–112, 114; Hatina, *Islam*, 35, 64–65, 73–76; Milton-Edwards, *Islamic*, 141.

67. Abu-Amr, *Islamic*, 105; Hatina, *Islam*, 26.

68. Abu-Amr, *Islamic*, 120–121.

69. *Ibid.*, 101–102, 103, 106–107; Hatina, *Islam*, 51–53; Milton-Edwards, *Islamic*, 206–208.

70. Abu-Amr, *Islamic*, 102.

71. Hatina, *Islam*, 80; Skare, *History*, 94.

72. Hatina, *Islam*, 31, 32–33.

73. Kepel, *Jihad*, 69–75.

74. Gerges, *Making*, 328–333.

75. Dalacoura, *Islamist*, 112–113; Kepel, *Muslim*, 132–134; Roel Meijer, 'Commanding Right and Forbidding Wrong as a Principle of Social Action: The Case of the Egyptian al-Jama'a al-Islamiyya', in *Global Salafism: Islam's New Religious Movement*, ed. Roel Meijer (London: Hurst & Co., 2009), 191–192; *idem*, 'The Egyptian Jama'a al-Islamiyya as a Social Movement', in *Social Movements, Mobilization, and Contestation in the Middle East and North Africa*, eds. Joel Beinin and Frédéric Vairel (Stanford, CA: Stanford University Press, 2011), 148–149.

76. For more on these supporters, see Pargeter, *The Muslim Brotherhood: The Burden of Tradition*, 36–46; *idem*, *The Muslim Brotherhood: From Opposition to Power*, 37–47.

77. For more on the southern roots of this trend, see Mamoun Fandy, 'Egypt's Islamic Group: Regional Revenge?', *Middle East Journal* 48, no. 4 (1994): 607–625; James Toth, 'Islamism in Southern Egypt: A Case Study of a Radical Religious Movement', *International Journal of Middle East Studies* 35, no. 4 (2003): 552–566.

78. Sullivan and Abed-Kotob, *Islam*, 82–83.

79. Meijer, 'Egyptian', 149.

80. Kepel, *Muslim*, 141–145.

81. Meijer, 'Egyptian', 149–150, 152.

82. *Ibid.*, 150–151.

83. *Idem*, 'Commanding', 197.

84. *Ibid.*, 197–198; *idem*, 'Egyptian', 152–153.

85. Auda, '"Normalization"', 400.

86. Sullivan and Abed-Kotob, *Islam*, 83.

87. Meijer, 'Egyptian', 153–154.

88. Dalacoura, *Islamist*, 115; Mohammed M. Hafez and Quintan Wiktorowicz, 'Violence as Contention in the Egyptian Islamic Movement', in *Islamic Activism: A Social Movement Theory Approach*, ed. Quintan Wiktorowicz (Bloomington and Indianapolis, IN: Indiana University Press, 2004), 72; Kepel, *Jihad*, 282–283, 285–286, 290–291.

89. Hafez and Wiktorowicz, 'Violence', 76–77; Kepel, *Jihad*, 283–284.

90. Hafez, *Why*, 131–132.

91. Kepel, *Jihad*, 287–288.

92. Dalacoura, *Islamist*, 115; Hafez and Wiktorowicz, 'Violence', 72; Kepel, *Jihad*, 288–289; Sullivan and Abed-Kotob, *Islam*, 86; Zuhur, *Egypt*, 1973.

93. Meijer, 'Egyptian', 158.

94. Hafez and Quintan Wiktorowicz, 'Violence', 77–80; Hafez, *Why*, 82–88; Kepel, *Jihad*, 291, 294–295, 297–298; Meijer, 'Commanding', 207–208; Sullivan and Abed-Kotob, *Islam*, 86–89.

95. Hafez, *Why*, 132–135; Meijer, 'Egyptian', 158–159.

96. Hafez, *Why*, 135–137; Kepel, *Jihad*, 297.

97. For more on this ideological revisionism, see Omar Ashour, 'Post-Jihadism and the Ideological Revisions of Armed Islamists', in *Contextualising Jihadi Ideology*, eds. Jeeval Deol and Zaheer Kazmi (London: Hurst & Co., 2012), 123–143; Fawaz A. Gerges, *The Far Enemy: Why Jihad Went Global* (Cambridge: Cambridge University Press, 2005), 200–228; *Initiative to Stop the Violence: Mubādarat Waqf al-'Unf: Sadat's Assassins and the Renunciation of Political Violence* (New Haven, CT, and London: Yale University Press, 2015); Meijer, 'Commanding', 210–217.

98. Dalacoura, *Islamist*, 116.

99. Gerges, *Far*, 155–158.

100. Dekmejian, *Islam*, 84–88; Toth, 'Islamism', 550.

101. Kepel, *Muslim*, 155–156; Meijer, 'Commanding', 194; *idem*, 'Egyptian', 151.

102. Meijer, 'Commanding', 196; *idem*, 'Egyptian', 152.

103. *Idem*, 'Egyptian', 152.

104. Hafez, *Why*, 175–182.

105. Meijer, 'Egyptian', 153.

106. *Ibid.*, 157.

107. Hamied N. Ansari, 'The Islamic Militants in Egyptian Politics', *International Journal of Middle East Studies* 16 (1984): 126; Auda, '"Normalization"', 382; Jeffrey T. Kenney, *Muslim Rebels: Kharijites and the Politics of Extremism in Egypt* (Oxford: Oxford University Press, 2006), 135; Gilles Kepel, *Muslim Extremism in Egypt: The Prophet and Pharaoh* (Berkeley and Los Angeles, CA: University of California Press, 2003 [1984]), 205–207; Sullivan and Abed-Kotob, *Islam*, 78–79; Sherifa Zuhur, *Egypt: Security, Political, and Islamist Challenges* (Carlisle, PA: Strategic Studies Institute, 2007), 60.

108. Dekmejian, *Islam*, 91–93; Sullivan and Abed-Kotob, *Islam*, 79.

109. Auda, "'Normalization'", 382–383.

110. Ansari, 'Islamic', 126; Auda, "'Normalization'", 382; Malika Zeghal, 'Religion and Politics in Egypt: The Ulema of Al-Azhar, Radical Islam, and the State (1952–1994)', *International Journal of Middle East Studies* 31, no. 3 (1999): 391–393.

111. Ansari, 'Islamic', 126–128.

112. *Ibid.*, 127–129.

113. *Ibid.*, 130–133; Kepel, *Muslim*, 215–216, 219.

114. Ansari, 'Islamic', 133–135; Kepel, *Muslim*, 216–217, 221.

115. Ansari, 'Islamic', 128–130; Auda, "'Normalization'", 383; Kenney, *Muslim*, 134–135; Kepel, *Muslim*, 191–192, 210–213.

116. Sullivan and Abed-Kotob, *Islam*, 80–81.

117. Kepel, *Muslim*, 213–214; Zuhur, *Egypt*, 61.

118. Auda, "'Normalization'", 400–401; Saad Eddin Ibrahim, 'Egypt's Islamic Activism in the 1980s', *Third World Quarterly* 10, no. 2 (1988): 650–651; Sullivan and Abed-Kotob, *Islam*, 81–82.

119. Dalacoura, *Islamist*, 114.

120. Auda, "'Normalization'", 398.

121. Zuhur, *Egypt*, 66–67, 75

122. Ansari, 'Islamic', 135.

123. Kepel, *Muslim*, 56–57.

124. Ajami, 'Pharaoh's Shadow', 27–30; Nazih Ayubi, *Political Islam: Religion and Politics in the Arab World* (London and New York: Routledge, 1991), 143; Kepel, *Muslim*, 71–72, 74–75.

125. For more on this group, see Saad Eddin Ibrahim, 'Anatomy of Egypt's Militant Islamic Groups: Methodological Note and Preliminary Findings', *International Journal of Middle East Studies* 12 (1980): 423–453; Saad Eddin Ibrahim, 'Egypt's Islamic Militants', *MERIP Reports* 103 (1982): 5–14; Kenney, *Muslim*, 125–127.

126. Ayubi, *Political*, 142–143; Sullivan and Abed-Kotob, *Islam*, 79.

127. Gerges, *Far*, 47–49.

128. Kepel, *Muslim*, 207–210.

129. Ansari, 'Islamic', 136.

130. For a translation of this text, see Johannes J.G. Jansen, *The Neglected Duty: The Creed of Sadat's Assassins and Islamic Resurgence in the Middle East* (New York: MacMillan, 1986), 159–234.

131. Ansari, 'Islamic', 136–138; Dekmejian, *Islam*, 94–95; Gerges, *Far*, 44–46; Johannes J.G. Jansen, 'The Creed of Sadat's Assassins: The Contents of "The Forgotten Duty" Analysed', *Die Welt des Islams* 25 (1985): 1–30; *idem*, *Neglected*, 1–34; Kenney, *Muslim*, 135–136; Kepel, *Muslim*, 192–204; Rachel Scott, 'An "Official" Islamic Response to the Egyptian Al-Jihad Movement', *Journal of Political Ideologies* 8, no. 1 (2003): 45–50; Sivan, *Radical*, 127–129; Sullivan and Abed-Kotob, *Islam*, 79–80.

132. Ansari, 'Islamic', 138–139; Jansen, *Neglected*, 53–60; Scott, "'Official'", 50–55.

133. Kenney, *Muslim*, 137–139.

134. Conduit, *Muslim*, 145–151; Lefèvre, *Ashes*, 141. The most prominent, Abu Mus'ab al-Suri (b. 1958), became an important Al-Qaida strategist later. See Moubayed, *Under*, 50–55; Said, *Islamischer*, 35–41. For more on him, see Brynjar Lia, *Architect of Global Jihad: The Life of Al-Qaida Strategist Abu Mus'ab al-Suri* (London: Hurst & Co., 2007).

135. Gerges, *Far*, 151–158.

136. Kepel, *Jihad*, 140–144; Barnett R. Rubin, 'Arab Islamists in Afghanistan', in *Political Islam: Revolution, Radicalism or Reform?*, ed. John L. Esposito (Boulder, CO: Lynne Rienner Publishers, 1997), 182–187.

137. Peter L. Bergen, *Holy War, Inc.: Inside the Secret World of Osama Bin Laden* (New York: Touchstone, 2002 [2001]), 51–53; Kepel, *Jihad*, 136–139.

138. For more on 'Azzam, see Hegghammer, "Abdallah', 353–387; *idem, Caravan*; Moubayed, *Under*, 42–50; Jed Lea-Henry, 'The Life and Death of Abdullah Azzam', *Middle East Policy* 25, no. 1 (2018): 64–79.

139. Bergen, *Holy*, 54–56, 57–59; Jason Burke, *Al-Qaeda: The True Story of Radical Islam* (London and New York: I.B. Tauris, 2006 [2003]), 72–77; Rohan Gunaratna, *Inside Al-Qaeda: Global Network of Terror* (New York: Berkley Books, 2003 [2002]), 24–27; Kepel, *Jihad*, 144–148.

140. Gerges, *Far*, 80–84.

141. Abdel Bari Atwan, *The Secret History of al Qaeda* (New York: Columbia University Press, 2006), 43–44; Bergen, *Holy*, 53–54, 59–62; Gunaratna, *Inside*, 23–24, 26–28.

142. Gunaratna, *Inside*, 30–32.

143. Hegghammer, *Caravan*, 436–449.

144. Atwan, *Secret*, 44; Burke, *Al-Qaeda*, 1–2, 3–4.

145. Atwan, *Secret*, 45–46; Bergen, *Holy*, 80–81; Gerges, *Far*, 145–150; Gunaratna, *Inside*, 36–37; Kepel, *Jihad*, 316.

146. Fandy, *Saudi*, 186–187.

147. Atwan, *Secret*, 47; Gunaratna, *Inside*, 45.

148. Gunaratna, *Inside*, 47–51.

149. Atwan, *Secret*, 50; Gerges, *Far*, 143; Gunaratna, *Inside*, 33–36.

150. Atwan, *Secret*, 50–51; Bergen, *Holy*, 94; Gerges, *Far*, 107–109; Gunaratna, *Inside*, 51–52.

151. Kepel, *Jihad*, 300.

152. For more on the Taliban, see Antonio Giustozzi, *Koran, Kalashnikov, and Laptop: The Neo-Taliban Insurgency in Afghanistan* (New York: Columbia University Press, 2008); M.J. Gohari, *The Taliban: Ascent to Power* (Oxford: Oxford University Press, 1999); William Maley (ed.), *Fundamentalism Reborn? Afghanistan and the Taliban* (Washington Square, NY: New York University Press, 2001 [1998]); Peter Marsden, *The Taliban: War and Religion in Afghanistan* (London and New York: Zed Books, 2002); Ahmed Rashid, *Taliban: Militant Islam, Oil and Fundamentalism in Central Asia* (New Haven, CO, and London: Yale University Press, 2000).

153. Gunaratna, *Inside*, 52–53; Kepel, *Jihad*, 223–232.

154. Gunaratna, *Inside*, 54.

155. Gerges, *Far*, 170–177.

156. For the text of this declaration, see Gilles Kepel and Jean-Pierre Milleli (ed.) Pascale Ghazaleh (translation), *Al Qaeda in Its Own Words* (Cambridge, MA, and London: Belknap/Harvard University Press, 2008), 47–50; Bruce Lawrence (ed.), James Howarth (translation), *Messages to the World: The Statements of Osama bin Laden* (London and New York: Verso, 2005), 23–30.

157. For the text of this message, see Kepel and Milleli (eds.), *Al Qaeda*, 53–56; Lawrence (ed.), *Messages*, 58–62.

158. Atwan, *Secret*, 54; Bergen, *Holy*, 98–99; Gunaratna, *Inside*, 60–63; Kepel, *Jihad*, 319–320.

159. Bergen, *Holy*, 108–129; Kepel, *Jihad*, 320–321.

160. Gunaratna, *Inside*, 67–68; Kepel, *Jihad*, 321–322.

161. Dalacoura, *Islamist*, 47.

162. Mohammed M. Hafez, *Suicide Bombers in Iraq: The Strategy and Ideology of Martyrdom* (Washington, DC: United States Institute of Peace, 2007).

163. Thomas Hegghammer, *Jihad in Saudi Arabia: Violence and Pan-Islamism Since 1979* (Cambridge: Cambridge University Press, 2010), 99–226.

164. Gregory D. Johnsen, *The Last Refuge: Yemen, Al-Qaeda, and America's War in Arabia* (New York: W.W. Norton & Co., 2013).

165. Jean-Pierre Filiu, 'The Local and Global Jihad of al-Qa'ida in the Islamic Maghrib', *Middle East Journal* 63, no. 2 (2009): 213–226; Guido Steinberg and Isabelle Werenfels, 'Between the "Near" and the "Far" Enemy: Al-Qaeda in the Islamic Maghreb', *Mediterranean Politics* 12, no. 3 (2007): 407–413.

166. Charles Lister, *The Syrian Jihad: Al-Qaeda, the Islamic State and the Evolution of an Insurgency* (Oxford: Oxford University Press, 2015), 51–218.

167. Berridge, *Islamism*, 210.

168. See, for example, Lawrence (ed.), *Messages*, 8, 26.

169. Atwan, *Secret*, 220–222; Burke, *Al-Qaeda*, 164–166; Gerges, *Far*, 56–67; Gunaratna, *Inside*, 119.

170. For a partial translation of this text, see Kepel and Milleli (ed.), *Al Qaeda*, 171–181.

171. Gerges, *Far*, 111–114.

172. Meir Hatina, 'Redeeming Sunni Islam: Al-Qa'ida's Polemic against the Muslim Brethren', *British Journal of Middle Eastern Studies* 39, no. 1 (2012): 104–105.

173. Sagi Polka, 'Hamas as a *Wasati* (Literally: Centrist) Movement: Pragmatism within the Boundaries of the *Sharia*', *Studies in Conflict & Terrorism* 42, no. 7 (2019): 692–694.

174. Jean-Pierre Filiu, 'The Brotherhood vs. Al-Qaeda: A Moment of Truth?', *Current Trends in Islamist Ideology* 9 (2009), 18–25.

175. Marc Lynch, 'Islam Divided Between *Salafi-jihad* and the *Ikhwan*', *Studies in Conflict & Terrorism* 33, no. 6 (2010): 467–487.

176. Fawaz A. Gerges, *ISIS: A History* (Princeton, NJ: Princeton University Press, 2016), 68–69.

177. Aaron Y. Zelin, 'The War Between ISIS and al-Qaeda for Supremacy of the Global Jihadist Movement', Research Notes no. 20 (Washington, DC: Washington Institute for Near East Policy, 2014), 1–2.

178. For more on al-Zarqawi, see Joby Warrick, *Black Flags: The Rise of ISIS* (New York: Doubleday, 2015), 15–220.

179. Gerges, *ISIS*, 63–68; Lister, *Syrian*, 262; Said, *Islamischer*, 41–42, 44–47; Jessica Stern and J.M. Berger, *ISIS: The State of Terror* (New York: HarperCollins Publishers, 2015), 17–19; Michael Weiss and Hassan Hassan, *ISIS: Inside the Army of Terror* (New York: Regan Arts, 2015), 13–26.

180. Gerges, *ISIS*, 71–72; Moubayed, *Under*, 91; Loretta Napoleoni, *Insurgent Iraq: Al Zarqawi and the New Generation* (New York: Seven Stories Press, 2005), 157–167; Stern and Berger, *ISIS*, 20–21; Weiss and Hassan, *ISIS*, 28–30.

181. See, for example, Bernard Haykel, 'Jihadis and the Shi'a', in *Self-Inflicted Wounds: Debates and Divisions within al-Qa'ida and Its Periphery*, eds. Assaf Moghadam and Brian Fishman (West Point, NY: Combating Terrorism Center, 2010), 202–223; Susanne Olsson, 'Shia as Internal Others: A Salafi Rejection of the "Rejectors"', *Islam and Christian-Muslim Relations* 28, no. 4 (2017): 416–424; Guido Steinberg, 'Jihadi-Salafism and the Shi'is: Remarks about the Intellectual Roots of Anti-Shi'ism', in *Global Salafism: Islam's New Religious Movement*, ed. Roel Meijer (London: Hurst & Co., 2007), 107–125.

182. Gerges, *ISIS*, 72–81; Lister, *Syrian*, 265–266; Stern and Berger, *ISIS*, 21; Weiss and Hassan, *ISIS*, 34; Zelin, 'War', 2–3.

183. Gerges, *ISIS*, 84–91.

184. Napoleoni, *Insurgent*, 169–178.

185. Gerges, *ISIS*, 91–93; Stern and Berger, *ISIS*, 25–26; Weiss and Hassan, *ISIS*, 61–62.

186. Gerges, *ISIS*, 93–96; Lister, *Syrian*, 266–267; William F. McCants, *The ISIS Apocaplyse: The History, Strategy, and Doomsday Vision of the Islamic State* (New York: St. Martin's Press, 2015), 15–19; Said, *Islamischer*, 66–67; Weiss and Hassan, *ISIS*, 62–64; Zelin, 'War', 3.

187. Weiss and Hassan, *ISIS*, 68–81.

188. Gerges, *ISIS*, 96–98; McCants, *ISIS*, 31–45; Lister, *Syrian*, 270; Said, *Islamischer*, 67–68; Weiss and Hassan, *ISIS*, 114–117.

189. Gerges, *ISIS*, 119–128; Weiss and Hassan, *ISIS*, 270.

190. Gerges, *ISIS*, 175–187; Lister, *Syrian*, 51–81; Moubayed, *Under*, 70–78; Said, *Islamischer*, 56–64; Weiss and Hassan, *ISIS*, 149–152.

191. The Arabic word 'Sham' actually means 'Levant', the area that encompasses today's Lebanon, Syria, Israel, the Palestinian territories and Jordan. This is why ISIS is also called 'ISIL' sometimes.

192. Gerges, *ISIS*, 187–194; Lister, *Syrian*, 122–127, 139–149; McCants, *ISIS*, 89–95; Moubayed, *Under*, 117–120; Stern and Berger, *ISIS*, 42–44; Weiss and Hassan, *ISIS*, 182–187; Zelin, 'War', 4–6.

193. Gerges, *ISIS*, 226–231; Lister, *Syrian*, 236–241; Stern and Berger, *ISIS*, 44–47.

194. Gerges, *ISIS*, 232–259; Lister, *Syrian*, 229–231, 240; McCants, *ISIS*, 95–97, 128–131; Said, *Islamischer*, 81–98; Stern and Berger, *ISIS*, 177–198.

195. 'Know Your Enemy: Who Were the Safawiyyah?', *Dabiq* 13 (1437 Rabi' al-Akhir [January/February 2016]): 10–12.

196. 'The Rafidah: From Ibn Saba' to the Dajjal', *Dabiq* 13 (1437 Rabi' al-Akhir [January/February 2016]): 33–34.

197. *Ibid.*, 35–37, 41–43, 45.

198. Gerges, *ISIS*, 28; McCants, *ISIS*, 121–128; Joas Wagemakers, 'De ideologische onderbouwing van de Islamitische Staat', *ZemZem: Tijdschrift over het Midden-Oosten, Noord-Afrika en islam* 10, no. 2 (2014): 8–10.

199. Stern and Berger, *ISIS*, 120–125; Wagemakers, 'Ideologische', 11–12.

200. McCants, *ISIS*, 111–114; Stern and Berger, *ISIS*, 215–217; Wagemakers, 'Ideologische', 10–11.

201. 'The Murtadd Brotherhood', *Dabiq* 14 (Rajab 1437 [April/May 2016]): 29–31.

202. *Ibid.*, 31–33.

203. *Ibid.*, 33–36.

204. *Ibid.*, 36–38.

205. *Ibid.*, 38–40.

7. Liberals

1. Dekmejian, *Islam*, 213; Bettina Gräf, 'The Concept of *Wasatiyya* in the Work of Yusuf al-Qaradawi', in *Global Mufti: The Phenomenon of Yusuf al-Qaradawi*, eds. Bettina Gräf and Jakob Skovgaard-Petersen (New York: Columbia University, 2009), 215; Uriya Shavit, *Shari'a and Muslim Minorities: The Wasati and Salafi Approaches to Fiqh al-Aqalliyyat al-Muslima* (Oxford: Oxford University Press, 2015), 24.

2. Shavit, *Shari'a*, 16–17.

3. *Ibid.*, 17–18.

4. Gräf, 'Concept', 223; Shavit, *Shari'a*, 25, 39; Mahmud El-Wereny, 'Reichweite und Instrumente islamrechtlicher Normenfindung in der Moderne: Yusuf al-Qaradawis *igtihad*-Konzept', *Die Welt des Islams* 58 (2018): 80–82.

5. For an interview with al-Qaradawi, see Davis, *Between*, 219–234.

6. Gräf, 'Concept', 218–223.

7. Shavit, *Shari'a*, 17, 18–19, 22–24.

8. Ana Belén Soage, 'Yusuf al-Qaradawi: The Muslim Brothers' Favorite Ideological Guide', in *The Muslim Brotherhood: The Organization and Policies of a Global Islamist Movement*, ed. Barry Rubin (New York: Palgrave MacMillan, 2010), 20.

9. Husam Tammam, 'Yusuf al-Qaradawi and the Muslim Brothers: The Nature of a Special Relationship', in *Global Mufti: The Phenomenon of Yusuf*

al-Qaradawi, eds. Bettina Gräf and Jakob Skovgaard-Petersen (New York: Columbia University, 2009), 69–71.

10.   Belén Soage, 'Yusuf,' 20; Tammam, 'Yusuf', 71–73.

11.   Belén Soage, 'Yusuf', 21; Polka, 'Hamas', 685–686; Tammam, 'Yusuf', 57–65.

12.   Shavit, *Shari'a*, 27–29.

13.   *Ibid.*, 29–31.

14.   *Ibid.*, 32–33. For a discussion of the more technical details behind this, see El-Wereny, 'Reichweite', 77–80, 82–98.

15.   For the historical role of these legal principles, see Felicitas Opwis, 'New Trends in Islamic Legal Theory: *Maqasid al-Shari'a* as a New Source of Law?', *Die Welt des Islams* 57 (2017): 11–14; Ron Shaham, 'Legal Maxims (*Qawa'id fiqhiyya*) in Yusuf al-Qaradawi's Jurisprudence and Fatwas', *Journal of the American Oriental Society* 140, no. 2 (2020): 435–438.

16.   Shaham, 'Legal', 439–448.

17.   Shavit, *Shari'a*, 33–39; see also Armando Salvatore, 'Qaradawi's *Maslaha*: From Ideologue of the Islamic Awakening to Sponsor of Transnational Public Islam', in *Global Mufti: The Phenomenon of Yusuf al-Qaradawi*, eds. Bettina Gräf and Jakob Skovgaard-Petersen (New York: Columbia University Press, 2009), 240–246.

18.   Raymond William Baker, *Islam Without Fear: Egypt and the New Islamists* (Cambridge, MA, and London: Harvard University Press, 2003), 181–183.

19.   Rutherford, *Egypt*, 106–108.

20.   *Ibid.*, 127.

21.   *Ibid.*, 109–113, 117–121; *idem*, 'What Do Egypt's Islamists Want? Moderate Islam and the Rise of Islamic Constitutionalism', *Middle East Journal* 60, no. 4 (2006): 713–714.

22.   Rutherford, 'What', 714–716.

23.   Shavit, *Shari'a*, 48–49.

24.   Rutherford, *Egypt*, 116; *idem*, 'What', 718–719.

25.   Roel Meijer, 'The Political, Politics, and Political Citizenship in Modern Islam', in *The Middle East in Transition: The Centrality of Citizenship*, eds. Nils A. Butenschon and Roel Meijer (Cheltenham: Edward Elgar Publishing, 2018), 197; David H. Warren and Christine Gilmore, 'One Nation Under God? Yusuf al-Qaradawi's Changing Fiqh of Citizenship in the Light of the Islamic Legal Tradition', *Contemporary Islam* 8 (2014): 225–235; *idem*, 'Rethinking Neo-Salafism Through an Emerging Fiqh of Citizenship: The Changing Status of Minorities in the Discourse of Yusuf al-Qaradawi and the "School of the Middle Way"', *New Middle Eastern Quick Studies* 2 (2012): 1–7.

26.   Ovamir Anjum, 'Dhimmi Citizens: Non-Muslims in the New Islamist Discourse', *ReOrient* 2, no. 1 (2016): 43–44; Rutherford, *Egypt*, 116.

27.   Rutherford, *Egypt*, 115–116; *idem*, 'What', 717–718; Shavit, *Shari'a*, 45–46.

28.   Barbara Freyer Stowasser, 'Yusuf al-Qaradawi on Women', in *Global Mufti: The Phenomenon of Yusuf al-Qaradawi*, eds. Bettina Gräf and Jakob Skovgaard-Petersen (New York: Columbia University, 2009), 184.

29.   *Ibid.*, 192.

30.   *Ibid.*, 203.

31.   *Ibid.*, 204.

32.   There is also a similar party in Jordan. For more on this, see Rosefsky Wickham, *Muslim*, 214–218.

33.   Meijer, 'Moslim', 56; Rosefsky Wickham, *Muslim*, 58–68; Joshua Stacher, 'Post-Islamist Rumblings in Egypt: The Emergence of the Wasat Party', *Middle East Journal* 56, no. 3 (2002): 418–422.

34.   Belén Soage and Fuentelsaz Franganillo, 'Muslim', 48–49; Pargeter, *The Muslim Brotherhood: The Burden of Tradition*, 46–50; *idem, The Muslim Brotherhood: From Opposition to Power*, 47–51; Zahid, *Muslim*, 91–92.

35.   Belén Soage and Fuentelsaz Franganillo, 'Muslim', 49.

36.   Hamid, *Temptations*, 98–99; Rosefsky Wickham, *Muslim*, 81; Stacher, 'Post-Islamist', 422.

37.   Hamid, *Temptations*, 100; Pargeter, *The Muslim Brotherhood: The Burden of Tradition*, 51; *idem, The Muslim Brotherhood: From Opposition to Power*, 51; Rosefsky Wickham, *Muslim*, 82; Stacher, 'Post-Islamist', 422.

38.   Hamid, *Temptations*, 101; Rosefsky Wickham, *Muslim*, 82–83; Stacher, 'Post-Islamist', 422–423.

39.   Hamid, *Temptation*, 100.

40.   Pargeter, *The Muslim Brotherhood: The Burden of Tradition*, 51; *idem, The Muslim Brotherhood: From Opposition to Power*, 51; Rosefky Wickham, *Muslim*, 81, 93–95.

41.   Pargeter, *The Muslim Brotherhood: The Burden of Tradition*, 51; *idem, The Muslim Brotherhood: From Opposition to Power*, 51.

42.   Baker, *Islam*, 192–196, 198–199, 200; Shavit, *Shari'a*, 21–22; Stacher, 'Post-Islamist', 417–418.

43.   Pargeter, *The Muslim Brotherhood: The Burden of Tradition*, 52–53; *idem, The Muslim Brotherhood: From Opposition to Power*, 52–53.

44.   Rosefsky Wickham, *Muslim*, 95–101, 104–107.

45.   Moataz El Fegiery, *A Tyranny of the Majority? Islamists' Ambivalence About Human Rights* (Madrid: Fride, 2010), 4–7.

46.   Harnisch and Mecham, 'Democratic', 197–198.

47.   Rutherford, 'What', 721–722.

48.   Rosefsky Wickham, *Muslim*, 83.

49.   *Idem*, 'The Path to Moderation: Strategy and Learning in the Formation of Egypt's *Wasat* Party', *Comparative Politics* 36, no. 2 (2004): 208–209; Stacher, 'Post-Islamist', 426.

50.   Harnisch and Mecham, 'Democratic', 190–196, 201–202.

51.   Rutherford, 'What', 722–725.

52.   Stacher, 'Post-Islamist', 424–425.

53.   El Fegiery, *Tyranny*, 12–13; Harnisch and Quinn Mecham, 'Democratic', 200–201; Rutherford, 'What', 725. Civil liberties (and especially freedom of speech) is probably the area on which Islamists, including reformists

among them, are least prone to concessions. See, for example, Wagemakers, *Muslim*, 222–230. Hence it is unlikely that Hizb al-Wasat will be very different in this respect.

54. El Fegiery, *Tyranny*, 10–12; Rutherford, 'What', 725–726.

55. Jakob Skovgaard-Petersen, 'Brothers and Citizens: The Second Wave of Islamic Constitutional Thinking and the Concept of Citizenship', in *The Crisis of Citizenship in the Arab World*, eds. Roel Meijer and Nils Butenschon (Leiden: Brill, 2017), 326.

56. El Fegiery, *Tyranny*, 12; Harnisch and Mecham, 'Democratic', 199–200; Skovgaard-Petersen, 'Brothers', 326, 328–330.

57. Meijer, 'Moslim', 58; Stacher, 'Post-Islamist', 427–428.

58. Hamid, *Temptations*, 98.

59. El Fegiery, *Tyranny*, 9–10.

60. *Ibid.*, 10; Rutherford, 'What', 725

61. Rosefsky Wickham, 'Path', 221–222.

62. Stacher, 'Post-Islamist', 429.

63. Hamid, *Temptations*, 98; Shavit, *Shari'a*, 45–46; Stacher, 'Post-Islamist', 430.

64. Abdul Ghani Imad, 'The Failure of Political Islam: Ideological Delusions and Sociological Realities', in *Post-Islamism: A New Phase or Ideological Delusions?*, ed. Mohammad Abu Rumman (Amman: Friedrich Ebert Stiftung/Centre for Strategic Studies, 2018), 70, 74; Hassan Abu Hanieh, 'From Islamism to Post-Islamism: An Examination of Concepts and Theses', in *Post-Islamism: A New Phase or Ideological Delusions?*, ed. Mohammad Abu Rumman (Amman: Friedrich Ebert Stiftung/Centre for Strategic Studies, 2018), 27–28; Luz Gómez, '"Post-Islamism": Lessons from Arab Revolutions', in *Post-Islamism: A New Phase or Ideological Delusions?*, ed. Mohammad Abu Rumman (Amman: Friedrich Ebert Stiftung/Centre for Strategic Studies, 2018), 58.

65. Roy, *Failure*; idem, *Globalized Islam: The Search for a New Umma* (New York: Columbia University Press, 2004), 3, 4, 58–61.

66. *Idem, Globalized*, 97–99.

67. Kepel, *Jihad*, 361–376.

68. Burgat, *Face*, 180–183; Cavatorta and Merone, 'Post-Islamism', 29–30.

69. Asef Bayat, 'Post-Islamism at Large', in *Post-Islamism: The Changing Face of Political Islam*, ed. Asef Bayat (Oxford: Oxford University Press), 4, 5.

70. *Ibid.*, 8.

71. Brown, *Victory*, 34–44.

72. Noorhaidi Hasan, 'Post-Islamist Politics in Indonesia', in *Post-Islamism: The Changing Face of Political Islam*, ed. Asef Bayat (Oxford: Oxford University Press, 2013), 157–182.

73. Humeira Iqtidar, 'Post-Islamist Strands in Pakistan: Islamist Spin-Offs and Their Contradictory Trajectories', in *Post-Islamism: The Changing Face of Political Islam*, ed. Asef Bayat (Oxford: Oxford University Press, 2013), 257–276.

74. Ihsan Dagi, 'Post-Islamism à la Turca', in *Post-Islamism: The Changing Face of Political Islam*, ed. Asef Bayat (Oxford: Oxford University Press, 2013), 71–108; Uğur Kömeçoğlu, 'Islamism, Post-Islamism, and Civil Islam', *Current Trends in Islamist Ideology* 16 (2014): 16–32; Cihan Tuğal, 'Islam and the Retrenchment of Turkish Conservatism', in *Post-Islamism: The Changing Face of Political Islam*, ed. Asef Bayat (Oxford: Oxford University Press, 2013), 109–133.

75. Thomas Pierret, 'Syria's Unusual "Islamic Trend": Political Reformists, the Ulema, and Democracy', in *Post-Islamism: The Changing Face of Political Islam*, ed. Asef Bayat (Oxford: Oxford University Press, 2013), 324–326.

76. Sami Zemni, 'Moroccan Post-Islamism: Emerging Trend or Chimera?', in *Post-Islamism: The Changing Face of Political Islam*, ed. Asef Bayat (Oxford: Oxford University Press, 2013), 151.

77. Rachid Mouqtadir, 'Transformations in the Moroccan Islamist Experience', in *Post-Islamism: A New Phase or Ideological Delusions?*, ed. Mohammad Abu Rumman (Amman: Friedrich Ebert Stiftung/Centre for Strategic Studies, 2018), 116.

78. *Ibid.*, 122, 124.

79. Cavatorta and Merone, 'Post-Islamism', 33, 35.

80. *Ibid.*, 31–32; McCarthy, 'Protecting', 449–451.

81. Robbert A.F.L. Woltering, 'Post-Islamism in Distress? A Critical Evaluation of the Theory in Islamist-Dominated Egypt (11 February 2011–3 July 2013)', *Die Welt des Islams* 54 (2014): 111–113.

82. Khalil al-Anani, '"Posts": The Muslim Brotherhood as a Model', in *Post-Islamism: A New Phase or Ideological Delusions?*, ed. Mohammad Abu Rumman (Amman: Friedrich Ebert Stiftung/Centre for Strategic Studies, 2018), 103–106.

83. Stacher, 'Post-Islamists', 416–417, 432.

84. Zemni, 'Moroccan', 145.

85. Baker, *Islam*, 171, 174, 175, 177.

86. *Ibid.*, 174, 176.

87. Stéphane Lacroix, 'Between Islamists and Liberals: Saudi Arabia's New "Islamo-Liberal" Reformists', *Middle East Journal* 58, no. 3 (2004): 346; *idem*, 'Saudi Arabia and the Limits of Post-Islamism', in *Post-Islamism: The Changing Face of Political Islam*, ed. Asef Bayat (Oxford: Oxford University Press, 2013), 283–284.

88. *Idem*, 'Saudi', 278–283; *idem*, 'Islamo-Liberal Politics in Saudi Arabia', in *Saudi Arabia in the Balance: Political Economy, Society, Foreign Affairs*, eds. Paul Aarts and Gerd Nonneman (London: Hurst & Co., 2005), 42–56.

89. *Idem*, 'Between', 360.

90. Anjum, 'Dhimmi', 35–37, 42–43, 44–46; Scott, *Challenge*, 125–132, 139–145. It is important to point out here that some authors, including Scott and Baker, more or less treat al-Qaradawi as if he is a post-Islamist whose reasonings are the same as those of people like Huwaydi. Because of his far more legal and technical approach (as well as partly because of his actual points of view), I do not think this is correct. See also Anjum, 'Dhimmi', 34.

91. Anjum, 'Dhimmi', 37 39, 40–42, Baker, *Islam*, 108–109, 165–168; Scott, *Challenge*, 132–139.

92. Scott, *Challenge*, 149–150.

93. *Ibid.*, 150–152.

94. Baker, *Islam*, 99.

95. *Ibid.*, 98.

96. *Ibid.*, 104–105.

97. Scott, *Challenge*, 152–156.

98. *Ibid.*, 158–160.

99. Burgat, *Face*, 180–183; Cavatorta and Merone, 'Post-Islamism', 32.

100. Bayat, 'Post-Islamism', 8, 25–26, 29.

101. Wagemakers, *Muslim*, 117–119.

102. Mohammad Abu Rumman and Neven Bondokji (translation: William Joseph Ward), *From Caliphate to Civil State: The Young Face of Political Islam in Jordan After the Arab Spring* (Amman: Friedrich Ebert Stiftung, 2018), 80–82; Wagemakers, *Muslim*, 199–201.

103. Abu Rumman and Bonokji, *Caliphate*, 82; Nabil al-Kofahi, 'The Zamzam Initiative: Causes, Goals and Prospects', in *The Prospects of Political Islam in a Troubled Region: Islamists and Post-Arab Spring Challenges*, ed. Mohammed Abu Rumman (Amman: Friedrich Ebert Stiftung, 2018), 146–147.

104. Wagemakers, *Muslim*, 112–113.

105. Hassan al-Barari, 'Post-Islamism in the Jordanian Context', in *Post-Islamism: A New Phase or Ideological Delusions?*, ed. Mohammad Abu Rumman (Amman: Friedrich Ebert Stiftung/Center for Strategic Studies, 2018), 218–219; Wagemakers, 'Between', 35–60.

106. Abu Rumman and Neven Bondokji, *Caliphate*, 83–84; Tareq al-Naimat, 'Zamzam and the Jordanian Brotherhood', *Sada: Analysis on Arab Reform* (Washington, DC: Carnegie Endowment for International Peace, 2014); Wagemakers, 'Between', 56–57.

107. Abu Rumman and Bondokji, *Caliphate*, 79–80; Wagemakers, *Muslim*, 111–112.

108. Abu Rumman and Bondokji, *Caliphate*, 84; al-Naimat, 'Zamzam'.

109. Brian Katulis, Hardin Lang and Mokhtar Awad, *Jordan in the Eye of the Storm* (Washington, DC: Center for American Progress, 2014), 12.

110. Abu Hanieh, *Muslim*, 58–63, 95–98; Wagemakers, *Muslim*, 112–116; *idem*, 'Things', 7–13.

111. Abu Rumman and Bondokji, *Caliphate*, 86–92.

112. Press statement of the National Initiative for Building, obtained from Ruhayyil Gharayiba and in possession of the author, no date.

113. Text of the National Initiative for Building (ZamZam), obtained from Ruhayyil Gharayiba and in possession of the author, no date. The translation from the Arabic is the author's.

114. Abu Rumman and Bondokji, *Caliphate*, 85–88; al-Kofahi, 'Zamzam', 147–148.

115. Al-Kofahi, 'ZamZam', 149–152.

8. Europeans

1. Basheer M. Nafi, 'Fatwa and War: On the Allegiance of the American Muslim Soldiers in the Aftermath of September 11', *Islamic Law & Society* 11, no. 1 (2004): 83–86; Shavit, *Shari'a*, 100–101.

2. Andrew F. March, *Islam and Liberal Citizenship: The Search for an Overlapping Consensus* (Oxford: Oxford University Press, 2009), 113–117.

3. *Ibid.*, 103–113.

4. *Ibid.*, 115; Shavit, *Shari'a*, 192–193. For the text of the fatwa in which Rida said these things, see Alan Verskin, *Oppressed in the Land? Fatwas on Muslims Living under Non-Muslim Rule from the Middle Ages to the Present* (Princeton, NJ: Markus Wiener Publishers, 2013), 115–117.

5. March, *Islam*, 192–194; Shavit, *Shari'a*, 227.

6. March, *Islam*, 229.

7. *Ibid.*, 171–172; Shavit, *Shari'a*, 102. For the text of this fatwa, see Verskin, *Oppressed*, 118–127.

8. Shavit, *Shari'a*, 102–103.

9. *Ibid.*, 197.

10. March, *Islam*, 106–107.

11. *Ibid.*, 111; Qutb, *Zilal*, Vol. II, 732–723.

12. March, *Islam*, 129–130.

13. Milton-Edwards, *Muslim*, 163–165; Pargeter, *The Muslim Brotherhood: The Burden of Tradition*, 99; idem, *The Muslim Brotherhood: From Opposition to Power*, 106.

14. Pargeter, *The Muslim Brotherhood: The Burden of Tradition*, 96–98; idem, *The Muslim Brotherhood: From Opposition to Power*, 103–106.

15. Lahoud-Tatar, *Islam*, 213; Milton-Edwards, *Muslim*, 165, 166; Pargeter, *The Muslim Brotherhood: The Burden of Tradition*, 99; idem, *The Muslim Brotherhood: From Opposition to Power*, 106–107.

16. Lahoud-Tatar, *Islam*, 213–214; Pargeter, *The Muslim Brotherhood: The Burden of Tradition*, 99–102, 104–106; idem, *The Muslim Brotherhood: From Opposition to Power*, 107–109, 111–113.

17. Steven Brooke, 'The Muslim Brotherhood in Europe and the Middle East: The Evolution of a Relationship', in *The Muslim Brotherhood in Europe*, eds. Roel Meijer and Edwin Bakker (London: Hurst & Co. 2012), 30–31; Pargeter, *The Muslim Brotherhood: The Burden of Tradition*, 105–106, 106–107; idem, *The Muslim Brotherhood: From Opposition to Power*, 113–114, 114–115.

18. Dekmejian, *Islam*, 218; Pargeter, *The Muslim Brotherhood: The Burden of Tradition*, 102; idem, *The Muslim Brotherhood: From Opposition to Power*, 109.

19. Pargeter, *The Muslim Brotherhood: The Burden of Tradition*, 108–114; idem, *The Muslim Brotherhood: From Opposition to Power*, 115–117.

20. Lahoud-Tatar, *Islam*, 214–215; Pargeter, *The Muslim Brotherhood: The Burden of Tradition*, 117–124; idem, *The Muslim Brotherhood: From Opposition to Power*, 120–128.

21.   Pargeter, *The Muslim Brotherhood: The Burden of Tradition*, 124, 125–127,
       129–131; *idem, The Muslim Brotherhood: From Opposition to Power*, 127–130,
       132–134.
22.   Pargeter, *The Muslim Brotherhood: The Burden of Tradition*, 131–132; *idem*,
       The Muslim Brotherhood: From Opposition to Power, 134–135.
23.   Conduit, *Muslim*, 134–135.
24.   *The Economist*, 'Fratricidal', 30.
25.   Milton-Edwards, *Muslim*, 169–174. The symbol itself (the four fingers and
       the in the name) is a play on words. The Arabic word *rabi'a* refers not only
       to the square, but also means 'fourth'.
26.   P.S. van Koningsveld, *Sprekend over de islam en de moderne tijd* (Utrecht:
       Teleac/Amsterdam: Prometheus, 1992), 78–80; Roy, *Globalized*, 100–101.
27.   Brigitte Maréchal, 'The Historical and Contemporary Sociology of the Eu-
       ropean Muslim Brotherhood Movement and Its Logics of Action', *Journal of
       Muslims in Europe* 4 (2015): 230.
28.   *Idem, Les frères musulmans en Europe: Racines et discours* (Paris: Presses
       Universitaires de France, 2009), 49–50; Pargeter, *The Muslim Brotherhood:
       The Burden of Tradition*, 102–103; *idem, The Muslim Brotherhood: From Op-
       position to Power*, 109–110.
29.   Amel Boubekeur, 'Political Islam in Europe', in *European Islam: Challenges
       for Society and Public Policy* (Brussels: Centre for European Policy Studies,
       2007), 17–18; Maréchal, *Frères*, 50–51.
30.   Dunja Larise, *State and Civil Society as Defined by the Muslim Brothers in Eu-
       rope* (EUI Working Papers, MWP 2011/23, 2001), 10–11; Brigitte Maréchal, 'The
       European Muslim Brothers' Quest to Become a Social (Cultural) Movement',
       in *The Muslim Brotherhood in Europe*, eds. Roel Meijer and Edwin Bakker
       (London: Hurst & Co., 2012), 91–92; *idem*, 'Historical', 224–225, 254–256;
       Anne Sofie Roald, 'Democratisation and Secularisation in the Muslim
       Brotherhood: The International Dimension', in *The Muslim Brotherhood in
       Europe*, eds. Roel Meijer and Edwin Bakker (London: Hurst & Co., 2012), 81;
       Lorenzo Vidino, 'The European Organization of the Muslim Brotherhood:
       Myth or Reality?', in *The Muslim Brotherhood in Europe*, eds. Roel Meijer and
       Edwin Bakker (London: Hurst & Co., 2012), 56–57, 58–59, 61–62; *idem*, 'The
       Muslim Brotherhood in Europe', in *The Muslim Brotherhood: The Organiza-
       tion and Policies of a Global Islamist Movement*, ed. Barry Rubin (New York:
       Palgrave MacMillan, 2010), 110–111; *idem, The New Muslim Brotherhood in the
       West* (New York: Columbia University Press, 2010), 30.
31.   Pargeter, *The Muslim Brotherhood: The Burden of Tradition*, 134–136; *idem*,
       The Muslim Brotherhood: From Opposition to Power, 137–139.
32.   Maréchal, *Frères*, 51–52; *idem*, 'European', 90.
33.   *Idem, Frères*, 68–69; Vidino, 'Muslim', 108.
34.   Pargeter, *The Muslim Brotherhood: The Burden of Tradition*, 103–104; *idem*,
       The Muslim Brotherhood: From Opposition to Power, 110–111; Vidino, 'Euro-
       pean', 60; *idem*, 'Muslim', 107–108; *idem, New*, 47–48.

35. Vidino, 'European', 60–61; *idem, New*, 48.

36. *Idem*, 'European', 53–54, 57.

37. Boubekeur, 'Political', 22; Maréchal, *Frères*, 56; *idem*, 'Historical', 225, 243; Sara Silvestri, 'Moderate Islamist Groups in Europe: The Muslim Brothers', in *Political Islam: Context versus Ideology*, ed. Khaled Hroub (London: Saqi, 2010), 268–269; Vidino, 'European', 57, 58.

38. Silvestri, 'Moderate', 270–274; Vidino, 'European', 64–67.

39. Maréchal, *Frères*, 58, 260; Silvestri, 'Moderate', 275–276; Guido Steinberg, 'The Muslim Brotherhood in Germany', in *The Muslim Brotherhood: The Organization and Policies of a Global Islamist Movement*, ed. Barry Rubin (New York: Palgrave MacMillan, 2010), 157.

40. FEMYSO's website is femyso.org.

41. Lorenzo Vidino, *The Closed Circle: Joining and Leaving the Muslim Brotherhood in the West* (New York: Columbia University Press, 2020), 94; *idem, New*, 51; *idem*, 'European', 57.

42. Boubekeur, 'Political', 23; Brooke, 'Muslim', 39–40; Larise, *State*, 16; Maréchal, *Frères*, 56; *idem*, 'Historical', 243–244; Silvestri, 'Moderate', 280–283. Institutes that are somewhat comparable and more or less like-minded, but not directly affiliated with the FIOE include the International Union of Muslim Scholars and the Islamic Institute for Development and Research. See Maréchal, *Frères*, 60.

43. Dina Lisnyansky, 'From Da'wa in Europe to European Da'wa: The Muslim Brotherhood and the Salafiyya in France and Britain', *The Journal for Interdisciplinary Middle Eastern Studies* 1 (2017): 87–89; Maréchal, 'Historical', 243; Silvestri, 'Moderate', 278–280.

44. Silvestri, 'Moderate', 274.

45. Larise, *State*, 17; Maréchal, *Frères*, 70–71; *idem*, 'European', 99–106; *idem*, 'Historical', 244–245; Silvestri, 'Moderate', 283–284. For the text of the *Charter*, see itstime.it/Approfondimenti/muslims_of_europe_charter.pdf.

46. Maréchal, *Frères*, 84–87, 88–89, 113, 152–153, 157–158.

47. *Ibid.*, 91–103.

48. *Ibid.*, 104–132, 134–136, 142–146.

49. *Idem*, 'Historical', 246–248.

50. Roald, 'Democratisation', 79–83.

51. Dilwar Hussain, 'United Kingdom', in *Yearbook of Muslims in Europe*, Vol. VI, eds. Jørgen S. Nielsen, Samim Akgönül, Ahmet Alibašic and Egdunas Račius (Leiden: Brill, 2014), 625–627.

52. *Ibid.*, 630–637.

53. David Rich, 'The Very Model of a British Muslim Brotherhood', in *The Muslim Brotherhood: The Organization and Policies of a Global Islamist Movement*, ed. Barry Rubin (New York: Palgrave MacMillan, 2010), 119–120.

54. Maréchal, *Frères*, 52; Pargeter, *The Muslim Brotherhood: The Burden of Tradition*, 102, 151–152; *idem, The Muslim Brotherhood: From Opposition to Power*, 109–110, 154.

55. Innes Bowen, 'The Muslim Brotherhood In Britain', in *The Muslim Brother-hood in Europe*, eds. Roel Meijer and Edwin Bakker (London: Hurst & Co., 2012), 111; Hamid, *Sufis*, 19; Maréchal, *Frères*, 53; *idem*, 'Historical', 225, 233; Pargeter, *The Muslim Brotherhood: The Burden of Tradition*, 150–151; *idem*, *The Muslim Brotherhood: From Opposition to Power*, 152–153; Rich, 'Very', 118.

56. Bowen, 'Muslim', 112; Maréchal, *Frères*, 52; *idem*, 'Historical', 231; Pargeter, *The Muslim Brotherhood: The Burden of Tradition*, 151; *idem*, *The Muslim Brotherhood: From Opposition to Power*, 154; Vidino, *Closed*, 45–46.

57. Pargeter, *The Muslim Brotherhood: The Burden of Tradition*, 152; *idem*, *The Muslim Brotherhood: From Opposition to Power*, 154155.

58. Bowen, 'Muslim', 111–112, 125; Maréchal, *Frères*, 53; Rich, 'Very', 118.

59. Rich, 'Very', 118–119.

60. Vidino, *New*, 32–33.

61. Bowen, 'Muslim', 112–114; Hamid, *Sufis*, 22–23, 25–26, 27; Maréchal, *Frères*, 57; *idem*, 'Historical', 252; Rich, 'Very', 120–121.

62. For more on Helbawy's life and career, see Vidino, *Closed*, 33–56.

63. Rich, 'Very', 121.

64. Bowen, 'Muslim', 115; Martyn Frampton and Shiraz Maher, 'Between "Engage-ment" and a "Values-Led" Approach: Britain and the Muslim Brotherhood from 9/11 to the Arab Spring', in *The West and the Muslim Brotherhood After the Arab Spring*, ed. Lorenzo Vidino (N.P.: Al Mesbar Studies & Research Center/Foreign Policy Research Institute, 2013), 38–40; Pargeter, *The Muslim Brotherhood: The Burden of Tradition*, 156–159; *idem*, *The Muslim Brotherhood: From Opposition to Power*, 159–161; Rich, 'Very', 121–122; Vidino, *New*, 140–141.

65. Bowen, 'Muslim', 117; Maréchal, 'Historical', 240; Rich, 'Very', 122; Vidino, *New*, 141.

66. Boubekeur, 'Political', 22; Vidino, *New*, 140–141.

67. Maréchal, 'Historical', 239–240.

68. *Idem*, *Frères*, 57.

69. *Idem*, 'Historical', 241; Damon Perry, *The Global Muslim Brotherhood in Britain: Non-Violent Islamist Extremism and the Battle of Ideas* (London and New York: 2019), 59; Rich, 'Very', 122–124. For more on pro-Palestinian activi-ties among British Islamic and Islamist organizations, see: Damon L. Perry, *The Islamic Movement in Britain* (London: International Centre for the Study of Radicalisation, 2020), 49–68.

70. Bowen, 'Muslim', 118; Maréchal, 'Historical', 242; Vidino, *New*, 141–142.

71. Maréchal, 'Historical', 240; Silvestri, 'Moderate', 274–275.

72. Perry, *Global*, 55–59. See also *idem*, *Islamic*, 81–95.

73. Bowen, 'Muslim', 120–121.

74. Hamid, *Sufis*, 29–30.

75. Maréchal, *Frères*, 62–65.

76. *Ibid.*, 82, 83, 87.

77. Pargeter, *The Muslim Brotherhood: The Burden of Tradition*, 152–153; *idem*, *The Muslim Brotherhood: From Opposition to Power*, 155.

78. Bowen, 'Muslim', 122; Maréchal, *Frères*, 99, 102, 150.

79. Bowen, 'Muslim" 113–114; Pargeter, *The Muslim Brotherhood: The Burden of Tradition*, 154; *idem, The Muslim Brotherhood: From Opposition to Power*, 156.

80. Maréchal, *Frères*, 134, 142.

81. *The Economist*, 'Fratricidal', 30.

82. *Muslim Brotherhood Review: Main Findings* (London, 2015): assets.publishing.service.gov.uk/government/uploads/system/uploads/attachment_data/file/486948/53163_Muslim_Brotherhood_Review_-_PRINT.pdf.

83. Jean-François Daguzan, 'France and Islamist Movements: A Long Non-Dialogue', in *The West and the Muslim Brotherhood After the Arab Spring*, ed. Lorenzo Vidino (N.P.: Al Mesbar Studies & Research Center/Foreign Policy Research Institute, 2013), 102–103.

84. Samir Amghar, 'Europe Puts Islamists to the Test: The Muslim Brotherhood (France, Belgium and Switzerland)', *Mediterranean Politics* 13, no. 1 (2008): 69–70.

85. Boubekeur, 'Political', 18; Maréchal, *Frères*, 53.

86. Pargeter, *The Muslim Brotherhood: The Burden of Tradition*, 136–137; *idem, The Muslim Brotherhood: From Opposition to Power*, 140.

87. Maréchal, *Frères*, 53; *idem*, 'Historical', 237.

88. Pargeter, *The Muslim Brotherhood: The Burden of Tradition*, 137–138; *idem, The Muslim Brotherhood: From Opposition to Power*, 140–141.

89. Amghar, 'Europe', 68–69, 70; Boubekeur, 'Political', 22; Farhad Khosrokhavar, 'The Muslim Brotherhood in France', in *The Muslim Brotherhood: The Organization and Policies of a Global Islamist Movement*, ed. Barry Rubin (New York: Palgrave MacMillan, 2010), 138; Maréchal, *Frères*, 53; *idem*, 'Historical', 237; Pargeter, *The Muslim Brotherhood: The Burden of Tradition*, 138–139; *idem, The Muslim Brotherhood: From Opposition to Power*, 141–142.

90. Pargeter, *The Muslim Brotherhood: The Burden of Tradition*, 143–147; *idem, The Muslim Brotherhood: From Opposition to Power*, 146–150.

91. Boubekeur, 'Political', 22–23; Pargeter, *The Muslim Brotherhood: The Burden of Tradition*, 139–141; *idem, The Muslim Brotherhood: From Opposition to Power*, 142–144.

92. Pargeter, *The Muslim Brotherhood: The Burden of Tradition*, 141–142; *idem, The Muslim Brotherhood: From Opposition to Power*, 144.

93. See musulmansdefrance.fr/notre-histoire/.

94. Khosrokhavar, 'Muslim', 138–139.

95. Boubekeur, 'Political', 23; Maréchal, 'Historical', 241.

96. Pargeter, *The Muslim Brotherhood: The Burden of Tradition*, 142; *idem, The Muslim Brotherhood: From Opposition to Power*, 144–145.

97. Boubekeur, 'Political', 23.

98. Khosrokhavar, 'Muslim', 139.

99. Brooke, 'Muslim', 34; Lisnyansky, 'Da'wa', 83–84.

100. Pargeter, *The Muslim Brotherhood: The Burden of Tradition*, 134, 147–148; *idem, The Muslim Brotherhood: From Opposition to Power*, 137, 150; Vidino, 'Muslim',108–109.

101. Boubekeur, 'Political', 22.
102. Khosrokhavar, 'Muslim', 138; Maréchal, *Frères*, 58; *idem*, 'Historical', 241.
103. Khosrokhavar, 'Muslim', 138; Maréchal, *Frères*, 55, 57; *idem*, 'Historical', 238–239.
104. Khosrokhavar, 'Muslim', 138; Maréchal, 'Historical', 240.
105. Amghar, 'Europe', 72–75.
106. Maréchal, *Frères*, 62.
107. *Ibid.*, 81–82, 100–102, 150.
108. *Ibid.*, 136–146.
109. Jan Rath, Rinus Penninx, Kees Groenendijk and Astrid Meijer, *Nederland en zijn islam: Een ontzuilde samenleving reageert op het ontstaan van een geloofsgemeenschap* (Amsterdam: Het Spinhuis, 1996), 191.
110. *Ibid.*, 191–192.
111. Amghar, 'Europe', 64.
112. Maréchal, *Frères*, 54.
113. *Ibid.*, 55; *idem*, 'Historical', 237.
114. Amghar, 'Europe', 70.
115. Boubekeur, 'Political', 22, 24.
116. Maréchal, 'Historical', 238.
117. *Idem*, *Frères*, 57.
118. Amghar, 'Europe', 72–76; Boubekeur, 'Political', 24.
119. Stefan Meining, 'The Islamic Community in Germany: An Organisation under Observation', in *The Muslim Brotherhood in Europe*, eds. Roel Meijer and Edwin Bakker (London: Hurst & Co., 2012), 215–216.
120. Guido Steinberg, 'Germany and the Muslim Brotherhood', in *The West and the Muslim Brotherhood After the Arab Spring*, ed. Lorenzo Vidino (N.P.: Al Mesbar Studies & Research Center/Foreign Policy Research Institute, 2013), 86.
121. Meining, 'Islamic', 216; Steinberg, 'Germany', 87; *idem*, 'Muslim', 149.
122. Meining, 'Islamic', 217; Steinberg, 'Germany', 87; *idem*, 'Muslim', 149; Vidino, *New*, 28.
123. Maréchal, *Frères*, 55.
124. Meining, 'Islamic', 216–217; Pargeter, *The Muslim Brotherhood: The Burden of Tradition*, 160–161; *idem*, *The Muslim Brotherhood: From Opposition to Power*, 163; Vidino, *New*, 29–30.
125. Meining, 'Islamic', 218–219.
126. *Ibid.*, 220–221.
127. Maréchal, 'Historical', 233; Pargeter, *The Muslim Brotherhood: The Burden of Tradition*, 161; *idem*, *The Muslim Brotherhood: From Opposition to Power*, 163–164; Weismann, 'Sa'id', 615.
128. Steinberg, 'Germany', 87–88, 89; *idem*, 'Muslim', 151–152.
129. Maréchal, *Frères*, 55; *idem*, 'Historical', 237; Pargeter, *The Muslim Brotherhood: The Burden of Tradition*, 162; *idem*, *The Muslim Brotherhood: From Opposition to Power*, 164.

130. Steinberg, 'Germany', 88–89.

131. Pargeter, *The Muslim Brotherhood: The Burden of Tradition*, 161; *idem, The Muslim Brotherhood: From Opposition to Power*, 163; Steinberg, 'Muslim', 149.

132. Meining, 'Islamic', 223; Pargeter, *The Muslim Brotherhood: The Burden of Tradition*, 162; *idem, The Muslim Brotherhood: From Opposition to Power*, 164; Steinberg, 'Germany', 87.

133. Steinberg, 'Muslim', 150.

134. Pargeter, *The Muslim Brotherhood: The Burden of Tradition*, 163–164; *idem, The Muslim Brotherhood: From Opposition to Power*, 166–167; Steinberg, 'Muslim', 157.

135. Steinberg, 'Germany', 89; *idem*, 'Muslim', 152.

136. Boubekeur, 'Political', 22; Meining, 'Islamic', 210, 219.

137. Meining, 'Islamic', 210–211; Pargeter, *The Muslim Brotherhood: The Burden of Tradition*, 165–167; *idem, The Muslim Brotherhood: From Opposition to Power*, 168–170; Steinberg, 'Muslim', 150.

138. Pargeter, *The Muslim Brotherhood: The Burden of Tradition*, 164; *idem, The Muslim Brotherhood: From Opposition to Power*, 167.

139. *Idem, The Muslim Brotherhood: The Burden of Tradition*, 164–165; *idem, The Muslim Brotherhood: From Opposition to Power*, 167–168; Steinberg, 'Muslim', 154–155.

140. Pargeter, *The Muslim Brotherhood: The Burden of Tradition*, 170–171; *idem, The Muslim Brotherhood: From Opposition to Power*, 172–174.

141. Meining, 'Islamic', 218–219, 225–259.

142. Pargeter, *The Muslim Brotherhood: The Burden of Tradition*, 168–169; *idem, The Muslim Brotherhood: From Opposition to Power*, 170–172.

143. Meining, 'Islamic', 229–231.

144. For more on the institutionalisation of Islam in the Netherlands, see Nico Landman, *Van mat tot minaret: De institutionalisering van de islam in Nederland* (Amsterdam: vu Uitgeverij, 1992); Rath *et al.*, *Nederland*, 1–185.

145. For more on the forms of Islam adhered to by Dutch people of Turkish descent, see Thijl Sunier, *Islam in beweging: Turkse jongeren en islamitische organisaties* (Amsterdam: Het Spinhuis, 1996). For more on the forms of Islam adhered to by Dutch people of Moroccan descent, see Martijn de Koning, *Zoeken naar een 'zuivere' islam: Geloofsbeleving en identiteitsvorming van jonge Marokkaans-Nederlandse moslims* (Amsterdam: Uitgeverij Bert Bakker, 2008); Ruud Strijp, *Om de moskee: Het religieuze leven van Marokkaanse migranten in een Nederlandse provinciestad* (Amsterdam: Thesis Publishers, 1998).

146. De Koning, *Zoeken*, 16–18.

147. Edwin Bakker, 'The Public Image of the Muslim Brotherhood in the Netherlands', in *The Muslim Brotherhood in Europe*, eds. Roel Meijer and Edwin Bakker (London: Hurst & Co., 2012), 176, 179–180.

148. *Ibid.*, 172–174.

149. *Ibid.*, 171, 174, 175.

150.   *Ibid.*, 176–177, 181, 183; Roel Meijer, 'Political Islam According to the Dutch', in *The West and the Muslim Brotherhood After the Arab Spring*, ed. Lorenzo Vidino (N.P.: Al Mesbar Studies & Research Center/Foreign Policy Research Institute, 2013), 72, 74.

151.   Bakker, 'Public', 180.

152.   *Ibid.*, 181–183; Meijer, 'Political', 73–74.

153.   Bakker, 'Public', 180–181, 184.

154.   Meijer, 'Political', 72, 74.

155.   Bakker, 'Public', 178–179; Meijer, 'Political', 73.

156.   See aivd.nl/actueel/nieuws/2011/04/12/geen-directe-dreiging-vanuit-moslimbroederschap-in-nederland.

157.   Tauseef Ahmad Parray, 'The Legal Methodology of *"Fiqh al-Aqalliyyat"* and Its Critics: An Analytical Study', *Journal of Muslim Minority Affairs* 32, no. 1 (2012): 90–91; Shavit, *Shari'a*, 82–84.

158.   Brooke, 'Muslim', 41–43.

159.   Maréchal, Historical', 243–244.

160.   Shavit, *Shari'a*, 84–87.

161.   Brooke, 'Muslim', 43–44.

162.   Parray, 'Legal', 91–92.

163.   *Ibid.*, 89–90; Shavit, *Shari'a*, 106–108.

164.   Parray, 'Legal', 93–100; Shavit, *Shari'a*, 96–98.

165.   March, *Islam*, 173–174; Shavit, *Shari'a*, 98–100, 108–110.

166.   Pargeter, *The Muslim Brotherhood: The Burden of Tradition*, 141–142; *idem*, *The Muslim Brotherhood: From Opposition to Power*, 144; Rich, 'Very', 119; Vidino, 'European', 54–55; *idem*, 'Muslim', 106–107. For an analysis of how this point of view fits in a longer history of Islamist thinking about the West, see Shavit, *Islamism*, especially 142–158.

167.   March, *Islam*, 174–176; Shavit, *Shari'a*, 113.

168.   Rich, 'Very', 132.

169.   Cédric Baylocq, 'The Autonomisation of the Muslim Brotherhood in Europe: *Da'wa, Mixité* and Non-Muslims', in *The Muslim Brotherhood in Europe*, eds. Roel Meijer and Edwin Bakker (London: Hurst & Co., 2012), 153.

170.   Shavit, *Shari'a*, 110–111.

171.   March, *Islam*, 213–215.

172.   Uriya Shavit, 'Can Muslims Befriend Non-Muslims? Debating *al-Wala' wa-l-Bara'* (Loyalty and Disavowal) in Theory and Practice', *Islam and Christian-Muslim Relations* 25, no. 1 (2014): 78–80; *idem, Shari'a*, 131.

173.   March, *Islam*, 223.

174.   Shavit, *Shari'a*, 112.

175.   *Ibid.*, 141–147.

176.   *Ibid.*, 170–173.

177.   *Ibid.*, 242–244.

178.   *Ibid.*, 197.

179.   March, *Islam*, 189.

180. Shavit, *Shari'a*, 227–279.

181. Nafi, 'Fatwa', 91–95; Shavit, *Shari'a*, 229–231. For the text of the fatwa on this issue, see Nafi, 'Fatwa', 78–80.

182. Shavit, *Shari'a*, 231–233.

183. March, *Islam*, 252–253.

184. Shavit, *Shari'a*, 211.

185. March, *Islam*, 249.

186. Maréchal, *Frères*, 184–190, 261–266. The words quoted are on page 263.

187. Amghar, 'Europe', 71; Maréchal, *Frères*, 169, 253–257.

188. Maréchal, *Frères*, 163–165, 173–175.

189. *Ibid.*, 181–184.

190. *Ibid.*, 260–261.

191. Perry, *Global*, 130–133; *idem, Islamic*, 23–26.

192. Bowen, 'Muslim', 119, 121; Rich, 'Very', 124, 130; Vidino, *New*, 87–89.

193. Pargeter, *The Muslim Brotherhood: The Burden of Tradition*, 172–176; *idem, The Muslim Brotherhood: From Opposition to Power*, 174–178; Steinberg, 'Muslim', 153.

194. Maréchal, *Frères*, 239–246; Perry, *Islamic*, 14.

195. Bowen, 'Muslim', 116; Maréchal, *Frères*, 246–251; Rich, 'Very', 130.

196. Maréchal, *Frères*, 193–197.

197. Cook, *Commanding*, 38–39.

198. Perry, *Global*, 128–129, 129–130; *idem, Islamic*, 22.

199. Maréchal, *Frères*, 192–193, 195; Perry, *Global*, 129–130; *idem, Islamic*, 22–23.

200. Maréchal, *Frères*, 233–235.

201. Bown, 'Muslim', 123–124.

202. Pargeter, *The Muslim Brotherhood: The Burden of Tradition*, 159; *idem, The Muslim Brotherhood: From Opposition to Power*, 162.

203. Maréchal, *Frères*, 215–220.

204. *Ibid.*, 221–226.

205. Baylocq, 'Autonomisation', 159–160; Khosrokhavar, 'Muslim', 143–144.

206. Maréchal, *Frères*, 226–230.

207. Baylocq, 'Autonomisation', 154–157.

208. Maréchal, *Frères*, 200–201.

209. *Ibid.*, 205–214.

210. *Ibid.*, 179–180.

Bibliography

Primary Sources

Arberry, A.J. *The Koran Interpreted*. New York: Touchstone, 1955.

'Awda, 'Abd al-Qadir. *Al-Islam wa-Awda'una al-Qanuniyya*. N.P., 1967 [1951].

———. *Al-Islam wa-Awda'una al-Siyasiyya*. N.P., N.D.

———. *Al-Mal wa-l-Hukm fi l-Islam*. Dammam and Riyadh: Al-Dar al-Sa'udiyya li-l-Nashr wa-l-Tawzi', 1984 [1951].

Banna, Hasan al-. *Majmu'at Rasa'il al-Imam al-Shahid Hasan al-Banna*. N.P.: Dar al-Tawzi', 1992.

Hudaybi, Hasan al-. *Du'at La Qudat*. Port Said: Dar al-Tawzi' wa-l-Nashr al-Islamiyya, 1977.

'Know Your Enemy: Who Were the Safawiyyah?' *Dabiq* 13 (1437 Rabi' al-Akhir [January/February 2016]): 10–12.

Qutb, Sayyid (editing and translation: John Calvert and William Shepard). *A Child from the Village*. New York: Syracuse University Press, 2004.

———. *Al-'Adala al-Ijtima 'iyya fi l-Islam*. Cairo: Dar al-Shuruq, 2009 [17th edn].

———. *Fi Zilal al-Qur'an* (6 volumes). Beirut and Cairo: Dar al-Shuruq, 1988 [15th edn].

———. *Ma'alim fi l-Tariq*. Beirut and Cairo: Dar al-Shuruq, 1979 [6th edn].

Shepard, William E. (ed. and transl.). *Sayyid Qutb and Islamic Activism: A Translation and Critical Analysis of* Social Justice in Islam. Leiden: Brill, 1996.

Siba'i, Mustafa al-. *Al-Mar'a bayna l-Fiqh wa-l-Qanun*. Beirut: Dar al-Warraq, 1999 [7th edn].

'The Murtadd Brotherhood'. *Dabiq* 14 (Rajab 1437 [April/May 2016]): 28–43.

'The Rafidah: From Ibn Saba' to the Dajjal'. *Dabiq* 13 (1437 Rabi' al-Akhir [January/February 2016]): 32–45.

Secondary Sources

Abd-Allah, Umar F. *The Islamic Struggle in Syria*. Berkeley, CA: Mizan Press, 1983.

Abdelwahid, Mustafa A. *The Rise of the Islamic Movement in Sudan (1945–1989)*. New York: Edwin Mellen Press, 2008.

Abed-Kotob, Sana. 'The Accommodationists Speak: Goals and Strategies of the Muslim Brotherhood of Egypt'. *International Journal of Middle East Studies* 27, no. 3 (1995): 321–339.

Abir, Mordechai. *Saudi Arabia: Government, Society and the Gulf Crisis*. London and New York: Routledge, 1993.

Abu Hanieh, Hassan (transl. Mohammad Abu Risheh). *The Muslim Brotherhood in Jordan: A Religious-Political Crisis in the National Context*. Amman: Konrad Adenauer Stiftung, 2016.

———. 'From Islamism to Post-Islamism: An Examination of Concepts and Theses'. In *Post-Islamism: A New Phase or Ideological Delusions?*, edited by Mohammad Abu Rumman, 23–56. Amman: Friedrich Ebert Stiftung/Centre for Strategic Studies, 2018.

Abu Jaber, Kamel S. and Schirin H. Fathi. 'The 1989 Jordanian Parliamentary Elections'. *Orient: Deutsche Zeitschrift für Politik und Wirtschaft des Orients* 31, no. 1 (1990): 67–86.

Abu Rumman, Mohammad and Neven Bondokji (translation: William Joseph Ward). *From Caliphate to Civil State: The Young Face of Political Islam in Jordan After the Arab Spring*. Amman: Friedrich Ebert Stiftung, 2018.

Abu Rumman, Muhammad and Hasan Abu Haniyya. *Al-Hall al-Islami fi l-Urdunn. Al-Islamiyyun wa-l-Dawla wa-Rihanat al-Dimuqratiyya wa-l-Amn*. Amman: Friedrich Ebert Stiftung, 2012.

Abu Rumman, Mohammad Suliman (translation: Issam Daoud Khoury). *The Muslim Brotherhood in the 2007 Jordanian Parliamentary Elections: A Passing 'Political Setback' or Diminished Popularity?* Amman: Friedrich Ebert Stiftung, 2007.

Abu-Amr, Ziad. *Islamic Fundamentalism in the West Bank and Gaza: Muslim Brotherhood and Islamic Jihad*. Bloomington and Indianapolis, IN: Indiana University Press, 1994.

Adams, Charles J. 'Mawdudi and the Islamic State'. In *Voices of Resurgent Islam*, edited by John L. Esposito, 99–133. Oxford: Oxford University Press, 1983.

Adams, Charles J. 'The Ideology of Mawlana Mawdudi'. In *South Asian Politics and Religion*, edited by Donald Eugene Smith, 371–397. Princeton, NJ: Princeton University Press, 1966.

Affendi, Abdelwahab El-. *Turabi's Revolution: Islam and Power in Sudan*. London: Grey Seal Books, 1991.

Afsaruddin, Asma. 'Theologizing about Democracy: A Critical Appraisal of Mawdudi's Thought', *Islam, the State, and Political Authority: Medieval Issues and Modern Concerns*, edited by Asma Afsaruddin, 131–154. New York: Palgrave MacMillan, 2011.

———. *Striving in the Path of God: Jihad and Martyrdom in Islamic Thought*. Oxford: Oxford University Press, 2013.

Ajami, Fouad. 'In the Pharaoh's Shadow: Religion and Authority in Egypt'. In *Islam in the Political Process*, edited by James Piscatori, 12–35. Cambridge: Cambridge University Press, 1983.

Alon, Yoav. *The Making of Jordan: Tribes Colonialism and the Modern State*. London and New York: I.B. Tauris, 2009.

———. *The Shaykh of Shaykhs: Mithqal al-Fayiz and Tribal Leadership in Modern Jordan*. Stanford, CA: Stanford University Press, 2016.

Amawi, Abla M. 'The 1993 Elections in Jordan'. *Arab Studies Quarterly* 16, no. 3 (1994): 15–27.

Amghar, Samir. 'Europe Puts Islamists to the Test: The Muslim Brotherhood (France, Belgium and Switzerland)'. *Mediterranean Politics* 13, no. 1 (2008): 63–77.

Amis, Jacob. 'The Jordanian Brotherhood in the Arab Spring'. *Current Trends in Islamist Ideology* 14 (2013): 38–57.

Anani, Khalil al- (transl. William Joseph Ward). 'Egypt's Muslim Brotherhood: From Opposition to Power and Back Again. A Study in the Dynamics of their Rise and Fall'. In *The Prospects of Political Islam in a Troubled Region: Islamists and Post-Arab Spring Challenges*, edited by Mohammed Abu Rumman, 75–87. Amman: Friedrich Ebert Stiftung, 2018.

———. '"Posts": The Muslim Brotherhood as a Model'. In *Post-Islamism: A New Phase or Ideological Delusions?*, edited by Mohammad Abu Rumman, 91–106. Amman: Friedrich Ebert Stiftung/Centre for Strategic Studies, 2018.

———. 'Devout Neoliberalism?! Explaining Egypt's Muslim Brotherhood's Socio-Economic Perspective and Policies'. *Politics and Religion* 13, no. 4 (2020): 748–767.

———. 'Rethinking the Repression-Dissent Nexus: Assessing Egypt's Muslim Brotherhood's Response to Repression since the Coup of 2013'. *Democratization* 26, no. 8 (2019): 1329–1341.

———. 'Upended Path: The Rise and Fall of Egypt's Muslim Brotherhood'. *Middle East Journal* 69, no. 4 (2015): 527–543.

———. *Inside the Muslim Brotherhood: Religion, Identity, and Politics*. Oxford: Oxford University Press, 2016.

Anjum, Ovamir. 'Dhimmi Citizens: Non-Muslims in the New Islamist Discourse'. *ReOrient* 2, no. 1 (2016): 31–50.

Ansari, Hamied N. 'The Islamic Militants in Egyptian Politics'. *International Journal of Middle East Studies* 16 (1984): 123–144.

'Arab Democracy's Fading Start'. *The Economist*, 31 July 2021, 23–24.

Aruri, Naseer H. *Jordan: A Study in Political Development (1921–1965)*. The Hague: Martinus Nijhoff, 1972.

Ashour, Omar. 'Post-Jihadism and the Ideological Revisions of Armed Islamists'. In *Contextualising Jihadi Ideology*, edited by Jeeval Deol and Zaheer Kazmi, 123–143. London: Hurst & Co., 2012.

Atawneh, Muhammad Al. *Wahhabi Islam Facing the Challenges of Modernity: Dar al-Ifta in the Modern Saudi State*. Leiden and Boston, MA: Brill, 2010.

Atwan, Abdel Bari. *The Secret History of al Qaeda*. New York: Columbia University Press, 2006.

Auda, Gehad. 'An Uncertain Response: The Islamic Movement in Egypt'. In *Islamic Fundamentalisms and the Gulf Crisis*, edited by James Piscatori, 109–130. Chicago, IL: American Academy of Arts and Sciences, 1991.

———. 'The "Normalization" of the Islamic Movement in Egypt from the 1970s to the Early 1990s'. In *Accounting for Fundamentalisms: The Dynamic Character of Movements*, edited by Martin E. Marty and R. Scott Appleby, 374–412. Chicago, IL, and London: University of Chicago Press, 1994.

Aulas, Marie-Christine. 'State and Ideology in Republican Egypt: 1952–82'. In *State and Ideology in the Middle East and Pakistan*, edited by Fred Halliday and Hamza Alavi, 133–166. London: MacMillan, 1988.

Awadi, Hesham al-. *In Pursuit of Legitimacy: The Muslim Brothers and Mubarak, 1982–2000*. London and New York: I.B. Tauris, 2004.

Awaisi, Abd Al-Fattah Muhammad El-. *The Muslim Brothers and the Palestine Question, 1928–1947*. London and New York: Tauris Academic Studies, 1998.

Ayubi, Nazih. *Political Islam: Religion and Politics in the Arab World*. London and New York: Routledge, 1991.

Azhary Sonbol, Amira El-. 'Egypt'. In *The Politics of Islamic Revivalism: Diversity and Unity*, edited by Shireen Hunter, 23–38. Bloomington and Indianapolis, IN: Indiana University Press, 1988.

Baker, Raymond William. *Islam Without Fear: Egypt and the New Islamists*. Cambridge, MA, and London: Harvard University Press, 2003.

Bakker, Edwin. 'The Public Image of the Muslim Brotherhood in the Netherlands'. In *The Muslim Brotherhood in Europe*, edited by Roel Meijer and Edwin Bakker, 169–188. London: Hurst & Co., 2012.

Baran, Zeyno. *Hizb ut-Tahrir: Islam's Political Insurgency*. Washington, DC: The Nixon Center, 2004).

Barari, Hassan al-. 'Post-Islamism in the Jordanian Context'. In *Post-Islamism: A New Phase or Ideological Delusions?*, edited by Mohammad Abu Rumman, 212–225. Amman: Friedrich Ebert Stiftung/Center for Strategic Studies, 2018.

Barghouti, Iyad. 'Islamist Movements in Historical Palestine'. In *Islamic Fundamentalism*, edited by Abdel Salam Sidahmed and Anoushiravan Ehteshami, 163–177. Boulder, CO: Westview Press, 1996.

Battatu, Hanna. 'Syria's Muslim Brethren'. In *State and Ideology in the Middle East and Pakistan*, edited by Fred Halliday and Hamza Alavi, 112–132. London: MacMillan, 1988.

Bayat, Asef. 'Post-Islamism at Large'. In *Post-Islamism: The Changing Face of Political Islam*, edited by Asef Bayat, 3–32. Oxford: Oxford University Press.

Baylocq, Cédric. 'The Autonomisation of the Muslim Brotherhood in Europe: *Da'wa*, *Mixité* and Non-Muslims'. In *The Muslim Brotherhood in Europe*, edited by Roel Meijer and Edwin Bakker, 149–168. London: Hurst & Co., 2012.

Baylouny, Anne Marie. 'Militarizing Welfare: Neo-Liberalism and Jordanian Policy'. *Middle East Journal* 62, no. 2 (2008): 277–303.

Belén Soage, Ana and Jorge Fuentelsaz Franganillo. 'The Muslim Brothers in Egypt'. In *The Muslim Brotherhood: The Organization and Policies of a Global Islamist Movement*, edited by Barry Rubin, 39–55. New York: Palgrave MacMillan, 2010).

Belén Soage, Ana. 'Hasan al-Banna and Sayyid Qutb: Continuity or Rupture?' *The Muslim World* 99 (2009): 294–311.

———. 'Yusuf al-Qaradawi: The Muslim Brothers' Favorite Ideological Guide'. In *The Muslim Brotherhood: The Organization and Policies of a Global Islamist Movement*, edited by Barry Rubin, 19–37. New York: Palgrave MacMillan, 2010.

Belkeziz, Abdelilah. *The State in Contemporary Islamic Thought: A Historical Survey of the Major Muslim Political Thinkers of the Modern Era*. London: I.B. Tauris, 2015.

Bergen, Peter L. *Holy War, Inc.: Inside the Secret World of Osama Bin Laden*. New York: Touchstone, 2002 [2001].

Berridge, W.J. *Hasan al-Turabi: Islamist Politics and Democracy in Sudan*. Cambridge: Cambridge University Press, 2017.

———. *Islamism in the Modern World: A Historical Approach*. London: Bloomsbury, 2019.

Berti, Benedetta. 'Non-State Actors as Providers of Governance: The Hamas Government in Gaza between Effective Sovereignty, Centralized Authority, and Resistance'. *Middle East Journal* 69, no. 1 (2015): 9–31.

Besten, Leen den. *De Moslimbroederschap en de utopie van islamisten*. Soesterberg: Uitgeverij Aspect, 2015.

Bhasin, Tavishi and Maia Carter Hallward. 'Hamas as a Political Party: Democratization in the Palestinian Territories'. *Terrorism and Political Violence* 25, no. 1 (2013): 75–93.

Biagini, Erika, and Lucia Ardovini. '"Struggle Is Our Way": Assessing the Egyptian Muslim Brotherhood's Relationship with Violence Post-2013'. *Religions* 13, no. 2 (2022): 1–22.

Bonner, Michael. *Jihad in Islamic History: Doctrines and Practice*. Princeton, NJ, and Oxford: Princeton University Press, 2006.

Bosworth, C. E., Manuela Marin and A. Ayalon. 'Shura'. In *Encyclopaedia of Islam: New Edition*, Vol. IX, edited by C. E. Bosworth, 504–506. Leiden: E. J. Brill, 1997.

Boubekeur, Amel. 'Political Islam in Europe'. In *European Islam: Challenges for Society and Public Policy*. Brussels: Centre for European Policy Studies, 2007.

Boulby, Marion. *The Muslim Brotherhood and the Kings of Jordan, 1945–1993*. Atlanta, GA: Scholars Press, 1999.

Bowen, Innes. 'The Muslim Brotherhood in Britain'. In *The Muslim Brotherhood in Europe*, edited by Roel Meijer and Edwin Bakker, 111–126. London: Hurst & Co., 2012.

Bozkurt, Abdulgani, and Muhammed Ünalmış. 'Partnership and Rescue Party and the Transformation of Political Opposition in Jordan'. *Religions* 13, no. 3 (2022): 1–26.

Brand, Laurie A. 'The Effects of the Peace Process on Political Liberalization in Jordan'. *Journal of Palestine Studies* 28, no. 2 (1999): 52–67.

Brooke, Steven. 'The Muslim Brotherhood in Europe and the Middle East: The Evolution of a Relationship'. In *The Muslim Brotherhood in Europe*, edited by Roel Meijer and Edwin Bakker, 27–49. London: Hurst & Co. 2012.

Brown, Nathan J. *Jordan and Its Islamic Movement: The Limits of Inclusion?* Carnegie Papers no. 74. Washington, DC: Carnegie Endowment for International Peace, 2006.

———. *When Victory is not an Option: Islamist Movements in Arab Politics*. Ithaca, NY, and London: Cornell University Press, 2012.

Brynen, Rex. 'Economic Crisis and Post-Rentier Democratization in the Arab World: The Case of Jordan'. *Canadian Journal of Political Science/Revue canadienne de science politique* 25, no. 1 (1992): 69–97.

Buchan, James. 'The Return of the Ikhwan'. In *The House of Saud: The Rise and Rule of the Most Powerful Dynasty in the Arab World*, David Holden and Richard Johns, 513–522. New York: Holt, Rhinehart and Winston, 1981.

Buehler, Matt. 'The Threat to "Un-Moderate": Moroccan Islamists and the Arab Spring'. *Middle East Law and Governance* 5 (2013): 231–257.

Burgat, François and William Dowell. *The Islamic Movement in North Africa*. Austin, TX: Center for Middle Eastern Studies, University of Texas at Austin, 1993.

Burgat, François. *Face to Face with Political Islam*. London and New York: I.B. Tauris, 2003.

Burke III, Edmund. *The Ethnographic State: France and the Invention of Moroccan Islam*. Oakland, CA: University of California Press, 2014.

Burke, Jason. *Al-Qaeda: The True Story of Radical Islam*. London and New York: I.B. Tauris, 2006 [2003].

Burr, J. Millard and Robert O. Collins. *Sudan in Turmoil: Hasan al-Turabi and the Islamist State*. Princeton, NJ: Markus Wiener Publishers, 2010.

Calvert, John. *Sayyid Qutb and the Origins of Radical Islamism*. New York: Columbia University Press, 2010.

Caridi, Paola (transl. Andrea Teti). *Hamas: From Resistance to Government*. New York: Seven Stories Press, 2012 [2009].

Carré, Olivier and Michel Seurat. *Les frères musulmans (1928–1982)*. Paris: L'Harmattan, 2001 [1983].

Cavatorta, Francesco. 'The Complexity of Tunisian Islamism: Conflicts and Rivalries Over the Role of Religion in Politics'. In *Islamists and the Politics of the Arab Uprisings: Governance, Pluralisation and Contention*, edited by Hendrik Kraetzschmar and Paola Rivetti, 243–257. Edinburgh: Edinburgh University Press, 2018.

Cavatorta, Francesco and Fabio Merone. 'Moderation Through Exclusion? The Journey of the Tunisian *Ennahda* from Fundamentalist to Conservative Party'. *Democratization* 20, no. 5 (2013): 857–875.

———. 'Post-Islamism, Ideological Evolution and "la *tunisianité*" of the Tunisian Islamist Party *al-Nahda*'. *Journal of Political Ideologies* 20, no. 1 (2015): 27–42.

Champion, Daryl. *The Paradoxical Kingdom: Saudi Arabia and the Momentum of Reform*. New York: Columbia University Press, 2003.

Charillon, Frédéric and Alain Mouftard. 'Jordanie. Les élections du 8 novembre 1993 et le processus de paix'. *Monde arabe/Maghreb-Machrek*, no. 144 (1994): 40–54.

Chehab, Zaki. *Inside Hamas: The Untold Story of the Militant Islamic Movement*. New York: Nation Books, 2007.

Choueiri, Youssef M. *Islamic Fundamentalism: The Story of Islamist Movements*. London and New York: Continuum, 2010.

Clark, Janine A. and Jillian Schwedler. 'Who Opened the Window? Women's Activism in Islamist Parties'. *Comparative Politics* 35, no. 3 (2003): 293–312.

Clark, Janine A.. *Islam, Charity and Activism: Middle-Class Networks and Social Welfare in Egypt, Jordan, and Yemen*. Bloomington and Indianapolis, IN: Indiana University Press, 2004.

———. 'Patronage, Prestige, and Power: The Islamic Center Charity Society's Political Role within the Muslim Brotherhood'. In *Islamist Politics in the Middle East: Movements and Change*, edited by Samer S. Shehata, 68–87. London and New York: Routledge, 2012.

Cleveland, William L. and Martin Bunton. *A History of the Modern Middle East*. Boulder, CO: Westview Press, 2013 [5th edn].

Cohen, Mark R. *Under Crescent & Cross: The Jews in the Middle Ages*. Princeton, NJ: Princeton University Press, 2008 [1994].

Commins, David. *Islamic Reform: Politics and Social Change in Late Ottoman Syria*. New York and Oxford: Oxford University Press, 1990.

———. 'Hasan al-Banna (1906–1949)'. In *Pioneers of Islamic Revival*, edited by Ali Rahnema, 125–153. London and New York: Zed Books, 2005 [1994].

———. *Islam in Saudi Arabia*. London and New York: I.B. Tauris, 2015.

———. *The Wahhabi Mission and Saudi Arabia*. London and New York: I.B. Tauris, 2005.

Conduit, Dara. 'The Syrian Muslim Brotherhood and the Spectacle of Hama'. *Middle East Journal* 70, no. 2 (2016): 211–226.

———. *The Muslim Brotherhood in Syria*. Cambridge: Cambridge University Press, 2019.

Cook, David. *Understanding Jihad*. Berkeley, CA: University of California Press, 2005.

Cook, Michael. *Ancient Religions, Modern Politics: The Islamic Case in Comparative Perspective*. Princeton, NJ: Princeton University Press, 2014.

———. *Commanding Right and Forbidding Wrong in Islamic Thought*. Cambridge: Cambridge University Press, 2001.

Crone, Patricia. *God's Rule: Government and Islam*. New York: Columbia University Press, 2004.

Cudsi, Alexander S. 'Islam and Politics in the Sudan'. In *Islam in the Political Process*, edited by James Piscatori, 36–55. Cambridge: Cambridge University Press, 1983.

Dagi, Ihsan. 'Post-Islamism à la Turca'. In *Post-Islamism: The Changing Face of Political Islam*, edited by Asef Bayat, 71–108. Oxford: Oxford University Press, 2013.

Daguzan, Jean-François. 'France and Islamist Movements: A Long Non-Dialogue'. In *The West and the Muslim Brotherhood After the Arab Spring*, edited by Lorenzo Vidino, 101–113. N.P.: Al Mesbar Studies & Research Center/Foreign Policy Research Institute, 2013.

Dalacoura, Katerina. *Islamist Terrorism and Democracy in the Middle East*. Cambridge: Cambridge University Press, 2011.

Dam, Nikolaos van. *The Struggle for Power in Syria: Politics and Society Under Asad and the Ba'th Party*. London and New York: I.B. Tauris, 1996 [1979].

Davis, Bradley. 'Educator of the Faithful: The Power of Moroccan Islam'. *Current Trends in Islamist Ideology* 25 (2020): 93–115.

Davis, Joyce M. *Between Jihad and Salaam: Profiles in Islam*. New York: St. Martin's Griffin, 1999 [1997].

Dekmejian, R. Hrair. 'The Rise of Political Islamism in Saudi Arabia'. *Middle East Journal* 48, no. 4 (1994): 627–643.

———. *Islam in Revolution: Fundamentalism in the Arab World*. Syracuse, NY: Syracuse University Press, 1995 [1985].

———. 'The Liberal Impulse in Saudi Arabia'. *Middle East Journal* 57, no. 3 (2003): 400–413.

Della Porta, Donatella and Mario Diani. *Social Movements: An Introduction*. Malden, MA: Blackwell Publishing, 2006 [1999].

Duk, Wierd and Maarten Ritman. 'Politieke islam reikt tot in ambtenarenapparaat Rotterdam'. *De Telegraaf*, 16 August 2019 (telegraaf.nl/nieuws/2439901/politiek-islam-reikt-tot-in-ambtenarenapparaat-rotterdam).

Ebstein, Michael. *In the Shadows of the Koran: Said* [sic] *Qutb's Views on Jews and Christians as Reflected in his Koran Commentary*. Washington, DC: Hudson Institute, 2009.

Eickelman, Dale F. and James Piscatori. *Muslim Politics*. Princeton, NJ: Princeton University Press, 2004 [1996].

Elshobaki, Amr. 'The Muslim Brotherhood: Between Evangelizing and Politics: The Challenges of Incorporating the Brotherhood into the Political Process'. In *Islamist Politics in the Middle East: Movements and Change*, edited by Samer S. Shehata, 107–119. London and New York: Routledge, 2012.

Engelleder, Denis. *Die islamistische Bewegung in Jordanien und Palästina, 1945–1989*. Wiesbaden: Harrassowitz Verlag, 2002.

Escobar Stemmann, Juan José. 'The Crossroads of Muslim Brothers in Jordan'. In *The Muslim Brotherhood: The Organization and Policies of a Global Islamist Movement*, edited by Barry Rubin, 57–71. New York: Palgrave MacMillan, 2010.

Esposito, John L. and John O. Voll. *Islam and Democracy*. Oxford: Oxford University Press, 1996.

———. *Makers of Contemporary Islam*. Oxford: Oxford University Press, 2001.

Esposito, John L. *Islam and Politics*. Syracuse, NY: Syracuse University Press, 1994 [1984].

———. 'Sudan'. In *The Politics of Islamic Revivalism*, edited by Shireen T. Hunter, 187–203. Bloomington and Indianapolis: IN: Indiana University Press, 1988.

Euben, Roxanne L. *Enemy in the Mirror: Islamic Fundamentalism and the Limits of Modern Rationalism*. Princeton, NJ: Princeton University Press, 1999.

Ezbidi, Basem. '"Arab Spring": Weather Forecast for Palestine'. *Middle East Policy* 20, no. 3 (2013): 99–110.

Fandy, Mamoun. 'CyberResistance: Saudi Opposition between Globalization and Localization'. *Comparative Studies in Society and History* 41, no. 1 (1999): 124–147.

———. 'Egypt's Islamic Group: Regional Revenge?' *Middle East Journal* 48, no. 4 (1994): 607–625.

———. *Saudi Arabia and the Politics of Dissent*. New York: Palgrave, 1999.

Farahat, Cynthia. 'The Muslim Brotherhood, Fountain of Islamist Violence'. *Middle East Quarterly* 24, no. 2 (2017).

Farschid, Olaf. 'Hizbiya. Die Neuorientierung der Muslimbruderschaft Ägyptens in den Jahren 1984 bis 1989'. *Orient: Deutsche Zeitschrift für Politik und Wirtschaft des Orients* 30, no. 1 (1989): 53–74.

Fegiery, Moataz El. *A Tyranny of the Majority? Islamists' Ambivalence About Human Rights*. Madrid: Fride, 2010.

Feuer, Sarah J. *Regulating Islam: Religion and the State in Contemporary Morocco and Tunisia*. Cambridge: Cambridge University Press, 2018.

'Fiddling While Carthage Burns'. *The Economist*, 2 October 2021, 29–30.

Filiu, Jean-Pierre. 'The Brotherhood vs. Al-Qaeda: A Moment of Truth?' *Current Trends in Islamist Ideology* 9 (2009), 18–25.

———. 'The Local and Global Jihad of al-Qa'ida in the Islamic Maghrib'. *Middle East Journal* 63, no. 2 (2009): 213–226.

Forstner, Martin. 'Auf dem legalen Weg zur Macht? Zur Politischen Entwicklung der Muslimbruderschaft Ägyptens'. *Orient: Deutsche Zeitschrift für Politik und Wirtschaft des Orients* 29, no. 3 (1988): 386–422.

Frampton, Martyn and Shiraz Maher. 'Between "Engagement" and a "Values-Led" Approach: Britain and the Muslim Brotherhood from 9/11 to the Arab Spring'. In *The West and the Muslim Brotherhood After the Arab Spring*, edited by Lorenzo Vidino, 32–55. N.P.: Al Mesbar Studies & Research Center/Foreign Policy Research Institute, 2013.

Frampton, Martyn. *The Muslim Brotherhood and the West: A History of Enmity and Engagement.* Cambridge, MA: Belknap/Harvard University Press, 2018.

'Fratricidal Tendencies: The Oldest Islamist Movement is Riven by Infighting'. *The Economist*, 11 December 2021, 30.

Freer, Courtney. 'Exclusion-Moderation in the Gulf Context: Tracing the Development of Pragmatic Islamism in Kuwait'. *Middle Eastern Studies* 54, no. 1 (2018): 1–21.

———. *Rentier Islamism: The Influence of the Muslim Brotherhood in Gulf Monarchies.* Oxford: Oxford University Press, 2018.

Freij, Hanna Y. and Leonard C. Robinson. 'Liberalization, the Islamists, and the Stability of the Arab State: Jordan as a Case Study'. *The Muslim World* 86, no. 1 (1996): 1–32.

Freyer Stowasser, Barbara. 'Yusuf al-Qaradawi on Women'. In *Global Mufti: The Phenomenon of Yusuf al-Qaradawi*, edited by Bettina Gräf and Jakob Skovgaard-Petersen, 181–211. New York: Columbia University, 2009.

Frisch, Hillel. 'Hamas: The Palestinian Muslim Brotherhood'. In *The Muslim Brotherhood: The Organization and Policies of a Global Islamist Movement*, edited by Barry Rubin, 89–102. New York: Palgrave/MacMillan, 2010.

Gerges, Fawaz A. *ISIS: A History.* Princeton, NJ: Princeton University Press, 2016.

———. *Making the Arab World: Nasser, Qutb, and the Clash that Shaped the Middle East.* Princeton, NJ: Princeton University Press, 2018.

———. *The Far Enemy: Why Jihad Went Global.* Cambridge: Cambridge University Press, 2005.

Ghobashy, Mona El-. 'The Metamorphosis of the Egyptian Muslim Brothers'. *International Journal of Middle East Studies* 37 (2005): 373–395.

Giustozzi, Antonio. *Koran, Kalashnikov, and Laptop: The Neo-Taliban Insurgency in Afghanistan.* New York: Columbia University Press, 2008.

Gohari, M.J. *The Taliban: Ascent to Power.* Oxford: Oxford University Press, 1999.

Gómez, Luz. '"Post-Islamism": Lessons from Arab Revolutions'. In *Post-Islamism: A New Phase or Ideological Delusions?*, edited by Mohammad Abu Rumman, 57–68. Amman: Friedrich Ebert Stiftung/Centre for Strategic Studies, 2018.

Gräf, Bettina. 'The Concept of *Wasatiyya* in the Work of Yusuf al-Qaradawi'. In *Global Mufti: The Phenomenon of Yusuf al-Qaradawi*, edited by Bettina Gräf and Jakob Skovgaard-Petersen, 213–238. New York: Columbia University, 2009.

Gunaratna, Rohan. *Inside Al-Qaeda: Global Network of Terror.* New York: Berkley Books, 2003 [2002].

Gunning, Jeroen. *Hamas in Politics: Democracy, Religion, Violence.* London: Hurst & Co., 2007.

Habib, Randa (transl. Miranda Tell). *Hussein and Abdullah: Inside the Jordanian Royal Family.* London: Saqi, 2010.

Haddad, Yvonne Y. 'Muhammad Abduh: Pioneer of Islamic Reform'. In *Pioneers of Islamic Revival*, edited by Ali Rahnema, 30–63. London and New York: Zed Books, 2005 [1994].

———. 'Sayyid Qutb: Ideologue of Islamic Revival'. In *Voices of Resurgent Islam*, edited by John L. Esposito, 67–98. Oxford: Oxford University Press, 1983.

Hafez, Farid. 'Criminalizing Muslim Civil Society in the West: The Muslim Brotherhood Allegation'. *SETA Perspective* 55 (2019): 1–5.

Hafez, Mohammed M. and Marc-André Walther. 'Hamas: Between Pragmatism and Radicalism'. In *Routledge Handbook of Political Islam*, edited by Shahram Akbarzadeh, 62–73. London: Routledge, 2011.

Hafez, Mohammed M. and Quintan Wiktorowicz. 'Violence as Contention in the Egyptian Islamic Movement'. In *Islamic Activism: A Social Movement Theory Approach*, edited by Quintan Wiktorowicz, 61–88. Bloomington and Indianapolis, IN: Indiana University Press, 2004.

Hafez, Mohammed M. *Suicide Bombers in Iraq: The Strategy and Ideology of Martyrdom.* Washington, DC: United States Institute of Peace, 2007.

———. *Why Muslims Rebel: Repression and Resistance in the Islamic World.* Boulder, CO: Lynne Rienner Publishers, 2003.

Hallaq, Wael B. 'Ahl al-Hall Wa-al-'Aqd'. In *The Oxford Encyclopedia of the Islamic World*, Vol. I, edited by John L. Esposito, 77–78. Oxford: Oxford University Press, 2009.

Hamid, Sadek. *Sufis, Salafis and Islamists: The Contested Ground of British Islamic Activism.* London: I.B. Tauris, 2016.

Hamid, Shadi. 'Arab Islamist Parties: Losing on Purpose?' *Journal of Democracy* 22, no. 1 (2011): 68–80.

———. 'New Democrats? The Political Evolution of Jordan's Islamists'. Paper presented for the CSIC Sixth Annual Conference 'Democracy and Development: Challenges for the Islamic World'. Washington, DC, 22–23 April 2005.

———. 'The Islamic Action Front in Jordan'. In *The Oxford Handbook of Islam and Politics*, edited by John L. Esposito and Emad el-Din Shahin, 544–557. Oxford: Oxford University Press, 2013.

———. *Islamic Exceptionalism: How the Struggle over Islam is Reshaping the World*. New York: St. Martin's Press, 2016.

———. *Temptations of Power: Islamists & Illiberal Democracy in a New Middle East*. Oxford: Oxford University Press, 2014.

Hanashi, Abdul Latif al- (transl. William Joseph Ward). 'Tunisia: The Impact of Democratic Transition on the Ennahda Party'. In *The Prospects of Political Islam in a Troubled Region: Islamists and Post-Arab Spring Challenges*, edited by Mohammed Abu Rumman (Amman: Friedrich Ebert Stiftung, 2018), 53–65.

Hansen, Stig Jarle and Mohamed Husein Gaas. 'The Ideological Arena of the Wider Muslim Brotherhood'. In *The Muslim Brotherhood Movement in the Arab Winter*, edited by Stig Jarle Hansen, Mohamed Husein Gaas and Ida Bary, 7–19 Cambridge, MA: Harvard Kennedy School Belfer Center for Science and International Affairs, 2017.

Hansen, Stig Jarle and Rafat Faisal Al-Mohareb. 'Three Important Poles? Ennahda, Turabism, and the Egyptian Brotherhood'. In *The Muslim Brotherhood Movement in the Arab Winter*, edited by Stig Jarle Hansen, Mohamed Husein Gaas and Ida Bary, 20–40. Cambridge, MA: Harvard Kennedy School Belfer Center for Science and International Affairs, 2017.

Harnisch, Chris and Quinn Mecham. 'Democratic Ideology in Islamist Opposition? The Muslim Brotherhood's "Civil State"'. *Middle Eastern Studies* 45, no. 2 (2009): 189–205.

Hasan, Noorhaidi. 'Post-Islamist Politics in Indonesia'. In *Post-Islamism: The Changing Face of Political Islam*, edited by Asef Bayat, 157–182. Oxford: Oxford University Press, 2013.

Hatina, Meir. 'Redeeming Sunni Islam: Al-Qa'ida's Polemic against the Muslim Brethren'. *British Journal of Middle Eastern Studies* 39, no. 1 (2012): 101–113.

———. *Islam and Salvation in Palestine*. Tel Aviv: The Moshe Dayan Center for Middle Eastern and African Studies at Tel Aviv University, 2001.

Haykel, Bernard. 'Jihadis and the Shi'a'. In *Self-Inflicted Wounds: Debates and Divisions within al-Qa'ida and Its Periphery*, edited by Assaf Moghadam and Brian Fishman, 202–223. West Point, NY: Combating Terrorism Center, 2010.

Hegghammer, Thomas and Stéphane Lacroix. 'Rejectionist Islamism in Saudi Arabia: The Story of Juhayman al-'Utaybi Revisited'. *International Journal of Middle East Studies* 39, no. 1 (2007): 103–122.

Hegghammer, Thomas. "Abdallah 'Azzam and Palestine'. *Die Welt des Islams* 53, nos. 3–4 (2013): 353–387.

———. *Jihad in Saudi Arabia: Violence and Pan-Islamism Since 1979*. Cambridge: Cambridge University Press, 2010.

———. *The Caravan: Abdallah Azzam and the Rise of Global Jihad*. Cambridge: Cambridge University Press, 2020.

Hinnebusch, Raymond A. 'Syria'. In *The Politics of Islamic Revivalism*, edited by Shireen T. Hunter, 39–56. Bloomington and Indianapolis: IN: Indiana University Press, 1988.

Hodgson, Marshall G.S. *The Venture of Islam: Conscience and History in a World Civilization* (3 volumes). Chicago, IL, and London: The University of Chicago Press, 1974.

Hourani, Albert. *A History of the Arab Peoples* (London: Faber & Faber, 2013 [1991]).

———. *Arabic Thought in the Liberal Age, 1798–1939*. Cambridge: Cambridge University Press, 1983 [1962].

Hroub, Khaled. 'A "New Hamas" Through Its New Documents'. *Journal of Palestine Studies* 35, no. 4 (2006): 6–27.

———. 'Die Aktuelle Politik von Hamas. Überleben ohne Strategie'. *Inamo* 8, no. 32 (2002): 15–17.

———. *Hamas: A Beginner's Guide*. London and Ann Arbor, MI: 2006.

———. *Hamas: Political Thought and Practice*. Washington, DC: Institute for Palestine Studies, 2000.

Hudson, Michael C. 'The Islamic Factor in Syrian and Iraqi Politics'. In *Islam in the Political Process*, edited by James Piscatori, 73–97. Cambridge: Cambridge University Press, 1983.

Husaini, Ishak Musa. *The Moslem Brethren: The Greatest of Modern Islamic Movements*. Westport, CT: Hyperion Press, Inc., 1986 [1956].

Hussain, Dilwar. 'United Kingdom'. In *Yearbook of Muslims in Europe*, Vol. VI, edited by Jørgen S. Nielsen, Samim Akgönül, Ahmet Alibašic and Egdunas Račius, 625–648. Leiden: Brill, 2014.

Ibrahim, Ibrahim. 'Religion and Politics Under Nasser and Sadat, 1952–1981'. In *The Islamic Impulse*, edited by Barbara Freyer Stowasser, 121–134. London and Sydney: Croom Helm, 1987.

Ibrahim, Saad Eddin. 'Anatomy of Egypt's Militant Islamic Groups: Methodological Note and Preliminary Findings'. *International Journal of Middle East Studies* 12 (1980): 423–453.

———. 'Egypt's Islamic Activism in the 1980s'. *Third World Quarterly* 10, no. 2 (1988): 632–657.

———. 'Egypt's Islamic Militants'. *MERIP Reports* 103 (1982): 5–14.

Imad, Abdul Ghani Imad. 'The Failure of Political Islam: Ideological Delusions and Sociological Realities'. In *Post-Islamism: A New Phase or Ideological Delusions?*, edited by Mohammad Abu Rumman, 69–87. Amman: Friedrich Ebert Stiftung/ Centre for Strategic Studies, 2018.

Initiative to Stop the Violence: Mubādarat Waqf al-'Unf: Sadat's Assassins and the Renunciation of Political Violence. New Haven, CT, and London: Yale University Press, 2015.

International Crisis Group. *Dealing with Hamas*. Middle East Report no. 21. Amman and Brussels: International Crisis Group, 2004.

———. *Enter Hamas: The Challenge of Political Integration*. Middle East Report no. 49. Amman and Brussels: International Crisis Group, 2006.

———. *Light at the End of Their Tunnels? Hamas & the Arab Uprisings*. ICG Middle East Report no. 129. Brussels: International Crisis Group, 2012.

———. *Radical Islam in Central Asia: Responding to Hizb ut-Tahrir*. ICG Asia Report no. 58, 30 June 2003.

———. *Radical Islam in Gaza*. Middle East Report no. 104. Brussels: International Crisis Group, 2011.

———. *Saudi Arabia Backgrounder: Who are the Islamists?* Middle East Report no. 31. Amman: International Crisis Group, 2004.

'Introduction'. In *The Muslim Brotherhood in Europe*, edited by Roel Meijer and Edwin Bakker, 1–23. London: Hurst & Co., 2012.

Iqtidar, Humeira. 'Post-Islamist Strands in Pakistan: Islamist Spin-Offs and Their Contradictory Trajectories'. In *Post-Islamism: The Changing Face of Political Islam*, edited by Asef Bayat, 257–276. Oxford: Oxford University Press, 2013.

Iskander Monier, Elizabeth and Annette Ranko. 'The Fall of the Muslim Brotherhood: Implications for Egypt'. *Middle East Policy* 20, no. 4 (2013): 111–123.

Ismail, Salwa. *Rethinking Islamist Politics: Culture, the State and Islamism*. London: I.B. Tauris, 2006.

Jamal, Amal. *The Palestinian National Movement: Politics of Contention, 1967–2005*. Bloomington, IN: Indiana University Press, 2005.

Jamal, Manal A. 'Beyond *Fateh* Corruption and Mass Discontent: *Hamas*, the Palestinian Left and the 2006 Legislative Elections'. *British Journal of Middle East Studies* 40, no. 3 (2013): 273–294.

Jamil, Tariq. "Ibadah'. In *The Oxford Encyclopedia of the Islamic World*, Vol. II, edited by John Esposito, 475–476. Oxford: Oxford University Press, 2009.

Jansen, Johannes J.G. 'The Creed of Sadat's Assassins: The Contents of "The Forgotten Duty" Analysed', *Die Welt des Islams* 25 (1985): 1–30

———. *The Neglected Duty: The Creed of Sadat's Assassins and Islamic Resurgence in the Middle East*. New York: MacMillan, 1986.

Jensen, Michael Irving (transl. Sally Laird). *The Political Ideology of Hamas: A Grassroots Perspective*. London and New York: I.B. Tauris, 2010 [2009].

Johnsen, Gregory D. *The Last Refuge: Yemen, Al-Qaeda, and America's War in Arabia*. New York: W.W. Norton & Co., 2013.

Johnson, Nels. *Islam and the Politics of Meaning in Palestinian Nationalism*. London: Kegan Paul International, 1982.

Jolen, Judith. 'The Quest for Legitimacy: The Role of Islam in the State's Political Discourse in Egypt and Jordan (1979–1996)'. PhD, Catholic University Nijmegen, 2003.

Jones, Toby Craig. 'Religious Revivalism and Its Challenge to the Saudi Regime'. In *Religion and Politics in Saudi Arabia: Wahhabism and the State*, edited by Mohammed Ayoob and Hasan Kosebalaban, 109–120. Boulder, CO, and London: Lynne Rienner, 2009.

———. 'The Clerics, the Sahwa and the Saudi State'. *Strategic Insights* 4, no. 3, March 2005.

Kanbouri, Idriss al-. 'Morocco's Islamists: Action Outside Religion'. In *The Prospects of Political Islam in a Troubled Region: Islamists and Post-Arab Spring Challenges*, edited by Mohammed Abu Rumman, 67–74. Amman: Friedrich Ebert Stiftung, 2018.

Kandil, Hazem. *Inside the Brotherhood*. Cambridge, UK: Polity Press, 2015.

Katulis, Brian, Hardin Lang and Mokhtar Awad, *Jordan in the Eye of the Storm*. Washington, DC: Center for American Progress, 2014.

Keddie, Nikki. 'Sayyid Jamal al-Din "al-Afghani"'. In *Pioneers of Islamic Revival*, edited by Ali Rahnema, 11–29. London and New York: Zed Books, 2005 [1994].

———. *An Islamic Response to Imperialism: Political and Religious Writings of Sayyid Jamal ad-Din "al-Afghani"*. Berkeley, CA: University of California Press, 1983 [1968].

———. *Sayyid Jamal Ad-Din "al-Afghani": A Political Biography*. Berkeley, CA: University of California Press, 1972.

Kenney, Jeffrey T. *Muslim Rebels: Kharijites and the Politics of Extremism in Egypt*. Oxford: Oxford University Press, 2006.

Kepel, Gilles and Jean-Pierre Milleli (ed.), Pascale Ghazaleh (transl.). *Al Qaeda in Its Own Words*. Cambridge, MA, and London: Belknap/Harvard University Press, 2008.

Kepel, Gilles. *Jihad: The Trail of Political Islam*. Cambridge, MA: Belknap/Harvard University Press, 2002.

———. *Muslim Extremism in Egypt: The Prophet and Pharaoh*. Berkeley and Los Angeles, CA: University of California Press, 2003 [1984].

———. *The War for Muslim Minds: Islam and the West*. Cambridge, MA, and London: Belknap/Harvard University Press, 2004.

Ketchley, Neil, Steven Brooke and Brynjar Lia. 'Who Supported the Early Muslim Brotherhood?' *Politics and Religion*, doi:10.1017/S1755048321000298 (2021): 1–29.

Khatab, Sayed. '*Hakimiyya* and *Jahiliyya* in the Thought of Sayyid Qutb'. *Middle Eastern Studies* 38, no. 3 (2002): 145–170.

————. *The Political Thought of Sayyid Qutb: The Theory of* Jahiliyya. Abingdon, UK, and New York: Routledge, 2006.

————. *The Power of Sovereignty: The Political and Ideological Philosophy of Sayyid Qutb*. Abingdon, UK, and New York: Routledge, 2006.

Khosrokhavar, Farhad. 'The Muslim Brotherhood in France'. In *The Muslim Brotherhood: The Organization and Policies of a Global Islamist Movement*, edited by Barry Rubin, 137–147. New York: Palgrave MacMillan, 2010.

Kimmerling, Baruch and Joel Migdal. *The Palestinian People: A History*. Cambridge, MA: Harvard University Press, 2003.

King Abdullah II of Jordan. *Our Last Best Chance: The Pursuit of Peace in a Time of Peril*. London: Viking, 2011.

Kirdiş, Esen. *The Rise of Islamic Political Movements and Parties: Morocco, Turkey and Jordan*. Edinburgh: Edinburgh University Press, 2021 [2019].

Kister, M. J. 'Notes on an Account of the Shura Appointed by 'Umar b. al-Khattab'. *Journal of Semitic Studies* 9 (1964): 320–326.

Klein, Menachem. 'Hamas in Power'. *Middle East Journal* 61, no. 3 (2007): 442–459.

Kofahi, Nabil al-. 'The Zamzam Initiative: Causes, Goals and Prospects'. In *The Prospects of Political Islam in a Troubled Region: Islamists and Post-Arab Spring Challenges*, edited by Mohammed Abu Rumman, 143–152. Amman: Friedrich Ebert Stiftung, 2018.

Kömeçoğlu, Uğur. 'Islamism, Post-Islamism, and Civil Islam'. *Current Trends in Islamist Ideology* 16 (2014): 16-–2.

Koning, Martijn de, Joas Wagemakers and Carmen Becker. *Salafisme: Utopische idealen in een weerbarstige praktijk*. Almere: Parthenon, 2014.

Koning, Martijn de. *Zoeken naar een 'zuivere' islam. Geloofsbeleving en identiteitsvorming van jonge Marokkaans-Nederlandse moslims*. Amsterdam: Uitgeverij Bert Bakker, 2008.

Koningsveld, P.S. van. *Sprekend over de islam en de moderne tijd*. Utrecht: Teleac/Amsterdam: Promctheus, 1992.

Krämer, Gudrun. 'Good Counsel to the King: The Islamist Opposition in Saudi Arabia, Jordan, and Morocco'. In *Middle East Monarchies: The Challenge of Modernity*, edited by Joseph Kostiner, 257–287. Boulder, CO: Lynne Rienner Publishers, 2000.

————. *Hasan al-Banna*. London: OneWorld Publications, 2009.

Kutscher, Jens. 'Islamic Shura, Democracy, and Online Fatwas'. *CyberOrient* 5, no. 2 (2011), 50–72.

Laan, Nina ter. 'Dissonant Voices: Islam-Inspired Music in Morocco and the Politics of Religious Sentiments'. PhD, Radboud University Nijmegen, 2016.

Lacey, Robert. *Inside the Kingdom: Kings, Clerics, Modernists, Terrorists, and the Struggle for Saudi Arabia*. London: Viking, 2009.

Lacroix, Stéphane. 'Between Islamists and Liberals: Saudi Arabia's New "Islamo-Liberal" Reformists'. *Middle East Journal* 58, no. 3 (2004): 345–365.

———. 'Islamo-Liberal Politics in Saudi Arabia'. In *Saudi Arabia in the Balance: Political Economy, Society, Foreign Affairs*, edited by Paul Aarts and Gerd Nonneman, 35–56. London: Hurst & Co., 2005.

———. 'Saudi Arabia and the Limits of Post-Islamism'. In *Post-Islamism: The Changing Face of Political Islam*, edited by Asef Bayat, 277–297. Oxford: Oxford University Press, 2013.

———. *Les islamistes saoudiens: Une insurrection manquée*. Paris: Presses Universitaires de France, 2010.

Lahoud, Nelly. *Political Thought in Islam: A Study in Intellectual Boundaries*. London and New York: Routledge, 2005.

Lahoud-Tatar, Carine. *Islam et politique au Koweït*. Paris: Presses Universitaires de France, 2011.

Landau-Tasseron, Ella. *Leadership and Allegiance in the Society of the Muslim Brothers*. Washington, DC: Center on Islam, Democracy, and the Future of the Muslim World at the Hudson Institute, 2010.

Landman, Nico. *Van mat tot minaret: De institutionalisering van de islam in Nederland*. Amsterdam: VU Uitgeverij, 1992.

Lange, Christian. 'Was There an Arab Intellectual Revival (*Nahda*) in the 17th and 18th Centuries? A Review Essay'. In *Oman, Ibadism and Modernity*, edited by Abdulrahman Al Salimi and Reinhard Eisener, 15–24. Hildesheim: Georg Olms Verlag, 2018.

Lapidus, Ira M. *A History of Islamic Societies*. Cambridge: Cambridge University Press, 2002 [1988].

Larise, Dunja. *State and Civil Society as Defined by the Muslim Brothers in Europe*. EUI Working Papers, MWP 2011/23, 2001.

Lauzière, Henri. 'Post-Islamism and the Religious Discourse of 'Abd al-Salam Yasin'. *International Journal of Middle East Studies* 37 (2005): 241–261.

———. 'The Construction of *Salafiyya*: Reconsidering Salafism from the Perspective of Conceptual History'. *International Journal of Middle East Studies* 42, no. 3 (2010): 369–389.

———. 'The Religious Dimension of Islamism: Sufism, Salafism, and Politics in Morocco'. In *Islamist Politics in the Middle East: Movements and Change*, edited by Samer S. Shehata, 88–106. New York: Routledge, 2012.

———. *The Making of Salafism: Islamic Reform in the Twentieth Century*. New York: Columbia University Press, 2016.

Lav, Daniel. *Radical Islam and the Revival of Medieval Theology*. Cambridge: Cambridge University Press, 2012.

Lawrence, Bruce (editing), James Howarth (translation). *Messages to the World: The Statements of Osama bin Laden*. London and New York: Verso, 2005.

Lawrence, Bruce B. 'Muslim Fundamentalist Movements: Reflections Toward a New Approach'. In *The Islamic Impulse*, edited by Barbara Freyer Stowasser, 15–36. Washington, DC: Center for Contemporary Arab Studies at Georgetown University, 1987.

Lea-Henry, Jed. 'The Life and Death of Abdullah Azzam'. *Middle East Policy* 25, no. 1 (2018): 64–79.

Lefèvre, Raphaël. *Ashes of Hama: The Muslim Brotherhood in Syria*. Oxford: Oxford University Press, 2013.

Legrain, Jean-François. 'Hamas as a Ruling Party'. In *Islamist Politics in the Middle East: Movements and Change*, edited by Samer S. Shehata, 183–204. London and New York: Routledge, 2012.

Levitt, Matthew. *Hamas: Politics, Charity, and Terrorism in the Service of Jihad*. New Haven, CT, and London: Yale University Press, 2006.

Levy-Rubin, Milka. *Non-Muslims in the Early Islamic Empire: From Surrender to Coexistence*. Cambridge: Cambridge University Press, 2011.

Lewis, Bernard. *The Jews of Islam*. Princeton, NJ: Princeton University Press, 2014 [1984].

Lia, Brynjar. 'Autobiography or Fiction? Hasan al-Banna's Memoirs Revisited'. *Journal of Arabic and Islamic Studies* 15 (2015): 199–226.

———. *Architect of Global Jihad: The Life of Al-Qaida Strategist Abu Mus'ab al-Suri*. London: Hurst & Co., 2007.

———. *The Society of the Muslim Brothers in Egypt: The Rise of an Islamic Mass Movement, 1928–1942*. Reading, UK: Ithaca Press, 1998.

Lisnyansky, Dina. 'From Da'wa in Europe to European Da'wa: The Muslim Brotherhood and the Salafiyya in France and Britain'. *The Journal for Interdisciplinary Middle Eastern Studies* 1 (2017): 79–103.

Lister, Charles. *The Syrian Jihad: Al-Qaeda, the Islamic State and the Evolution of an Insurgency*. Oxford: Oxford University Press, 2015.

Long, David E. *The Kingdom of Saudi Arabia*. Gainesville, FL: University Press of Florida, 1997.

Løvlie, Frode and Are Knudsen. 'Hamas and the Arab Spring'. *Middle East Policy* 20, no 3 (2013): 56–59.

Lucas, Russell E. 'Deliberalization in Jordan'. *Journal of Democracy* 11, no. 1 (2003): 137–144.

Lund, Aron. *Struggling to Adapt: The Muslim Brotherhood in a New Syria*. Washington, DC: Carnegie Endowment for International Peace, 2013.

Lust, Ellen and Sami Hourani. 'Jordan Votes: Election or Selection?' *Journal of Democracy* 22, no. 2 (2011): 119–129.

Lust-Okar, Ellen M. 'The Decline of Jordanian Political Parties: Myth or Reality?' *International Journal of Middle East Studies* 33 (2001): 545–569.

Lynch, Marc. 'Islam Divided Between *Salafi-jihad* and the *Ikhwan*'. *Studies in Conflict & Terrorism* 33, no. 6 (2010): 467–487.

———. 'Young Brothers in Cyberspace'. *Middle East Report* 245 (2007): 26–33.

———. *State Interests and Public Spheres: The International Politics of Jordan's Identity*. New York: Columbia University Press, 1999.

———. *The Brotherhood's Dilemma*. Waltham, MA: Crown Center for Middle East Studies at Brandeis University, 2008.

Mahmoud, Muhammad. 'Women and Islamism: The Case of Rashid al-Ghannushi of Tunisia'. In *Islamic Fundamentalism*, edited by Abdel Salam Sidahmed and Anoushiravan Ehteshami, 249–265. Boulder, CO: Westview Press, 1996.

Maley, William (ed.). *Fundamentalism Reborn? Afghanistan and the Taliban*. Washington Square, NY: New York University Press, 2001 [1998].

March, Andrew F. *Islam and Liberal Citizenship: The Search for an Overlapping Consensus*. Oxford: Oxford University Press, 2009.

———. *The Caliphate of Man: Popular Sovereignty in Modern Islamic Thought*. Cambridge, MA: Belknap/Harvard University Press, 2019.

Maréchal, Brigitte. 'The European Muslim Brothers' Quest to Become a Social (Cultural) Movement'. In *The Muslim Brotherhood in Europe*, edited by Roel Meijer and Edwin Bakker, 89–110. London: Hurst & Co., 2012.

———. 'The Historical and Contemporary Sociology of the European Muslim Brotherhood Movement and Its Logics of Action'. *Journal of Muslims in Europe* 4 (2015): 223–257.

———. *Les frères musulmans en Europe: Racines et discours*. Paris: Presses Universitaires de France, 2009.

Marks, Monica. 'Did Egypt's Coup Teach Ennahda to Cede Power?' Paper presented at the workshop 'Transnational Diffusion and Cooperation in the Middle East and North Africa' in Hamburg, 8–9 June 2016.

———. 'Tunisia's Islamists and the "Turkish Model"'. *Journal of Democracy* 28, no. 1 (2017): 102–115.

Marsden, Peter. *The Taliban: War and Religion in Afghanistan*. London and New York: Zed Books, 2002.

Marty, Martin E. and R. Scott Appleby. 'Introduction'. In *Accounting for Fundamentalisms: The Dynamic Character of Movements*, edited by Martin E. Marty and R. Scott Appleby, 1–9. Chicago, IL, and London: University of Chicago Press, 1994.

Masbah, Mohammed. 'Rise and Endurance: Moderate Islamists and Electoral Politics in the Aftermath of the "Moroccan Spring"'. In *Islamists and the Politics of the Arab Uprisings: Governance Pluralisation and Contention*, edited by Hendrik Kraetzschmar and Paola Rivetti, 127–148. Edinburgh: Edinburgh University Press, 2018.

Mayer, Jean-François. *Hizb ut-Tahrir: The Next Al-Qaida, Really?* Genève: PSIO, 2004.

McCants, William F. *The ISIS Apocaplyse: The History, Strategy, and Doomsday Vision of the Islamic State*. New York: St. Martin's Press, 2015.

McCarthy, Rory. 'Protecting the Sacred: Tunisia's Islamist Movement Ennahda and the Challenge of Free Speech'. *British Journal of Middle Eastern Studies* 42, no. 4 (2015): 447–464.

———. *Inside Tunisia's al-Nahda: Between Politics and Preaching*. Cambridge: Cambridge University Press, 2018.

McDowall, David. *A Modern History of the Kurds*. London and New York: I.B. Tauris, 1996.

Mdaires, Falah Abdullah al-. *Islamic Extremism in Kuwait: From the Muslim Brotherhood to al-Qaeda and Other Islamist Political Groups*. New York: Routledge, 2010.

Meijer, Roel (editing). *Global Salafism: Islam's New Religious Movement*. London: Hurst & Co., 2009.

———. 'Commanding Right and Forbidding Wrong as a Principle of Social Action: The Case of the Egyptian al-Jama'a al-Islamiyya'. In *Global Salafism: Islam's New Religious Movement*, edited by Roel Meijer, 189–220. London: Hurst & Co., 2009.

———. 'Islamisme en de Arabische Lente'. *ZemZem: Tijdschrift over het Midden-Oosten, Noord-Afrika en islam* 16, no. 2 (2020): 67–76.

———. 'Moslim Broederschap maakt zich op voor de democratie van morgen'. *ZemZem: Tijdschrift over het Midden-Oosten, Noord-Afrika en islam* 1, no. 2 (2005): 53–61, 124–125.

———. 'Political Islam According to the Dutch'. In *The West and the Muslim Brotherhood After the Arab Spring*, edited by Lorenzo Vidino, 68–85. N.P.: Al Mesbar Studies & Research Center/Foreign Policy Research Institute, 2013.

———. 'The Egyptian Jama'a al-Islamiyya as a Social Movement'. In *Social Movements, Mobilization, and Contestation in the Middle East and North Africa*, edited by Joel Beinin and Frédéric Vairel, 143–162. Stanford, CA: Stanford University Press, 2011.

———. 'The Majority Strategy of the Muslim Brotherhood'. *Orient: Deutsche Zeitschrift für Politik, Wirtschaft und Kultur des Orients* 54, no. 1 (2013): 22–30.

———. 'The Muslim Brotherhood and the Political: An Exercise in Ambiguity'. In *The Muslim Brotherhood in Europe*, edited by Roel Meijer and Edwin Bakker, 295–320. London: Hurst & Co. 2012.

———. 'The Political, Politics, and Political Citizenship in Modern Islam' In *The Middle East in Transition: The Centrality of Citizenship*, edited by Nils A. Butenschon and Roel Meijer, 179–202. Cheltenham Glos: Edward Elgar Publishing, 2018.

Meining, Stefan. 'The Islamic Community in Germany: An Organisation under Observation'. In *The Muslim Brotherhood in Europe*, edited by Roel Meijer and Edwin Bakker, 209–233. London: Hurst & Co., 2012.

Mellor, Noha. *Voice of the Muslim Brotherhood: Da'wa, Discourse, and Political Communication*. London and New York: Routledge, 2018.

Milton-Edwards, Beverley and Stephen Farrell. *Hamas*. Cambridge and Malden, MA: Polity Press, 2010.

Milton-Edwards, Beverley. 'Façade Democracy in Jordan'. *British Journal of Middle Eastern Studies* 20, no. 2 (1993): 191–203.

———. 'Hamas and the Arab Spring: Strategic Shifts?' *Middle East Policy* 20, no. 3 (2013): 60–72.

———. 'Islamist Versus Islamist: Rising Challenge in Gaza'. *Terrorism and Political Violence* 26, no. 2 (2014): 259–276.

———. 'The Ascendance of Political Islam: Hamas and Consolidation in the Gaza Strip'. *Third World Quarterly* 29, no. 8 (2008): 1585–1599.

———. *Islamic Politics in Palestine*. London and New York: I.B. Tauris, 1996.

———. *The Muslim Brotherhood: The Arab Spring and Its Future Face*. New York: Routledge, 2016.

Mishal, Shaul and Avraham Sela. 'Participation without Presence: Hamas, the Palestinian Authority and the Politics of Negotiated Coexistence'. *Middle Eastern Studies* 38, no. 3 (2002): 1–26.

———. *The Palestinian Hamas: Vision, Violence and Coexistence*. New York: Columbia University Press, 2000.

Mishal, Shaul. 'The Pragmatic Dimension of the Palestinian Hamas: A Network Perspective'. *Armed Forces and Society* 29, no. 4 (2003): 569–589.

Mitchell, Richard P. *The Society of the Muslim Brothers*. Oxford: Oxford University Press, 1993 [1969].

Moaddel, Mansoor. *Jordanian Exceptionalism: A Comparative Analysis of State-Religion Relations in Egypt, Iran, Jordan, and Syria*. New York: Palgrave, 2002.

Morris, Benny. *Righteous Victims: A History of the Zionist-Arab Conflict, 1881–2001*. New York: Vintage Books, 2001 [1999].

Moss Helms, Christine. *The Cohesion of Saudi Arabia: Evolution of Political Identity*. London: Croom Helm, 1981.

Moubayed, Sami. *Under the Black Flag: An Exclusive Insight into the Inner Workings of ISIS*. London and New York: I.B. Tauris, 2015.

Mouline, Nabil. *Les clercs de l'islam. Autorité religieuse et pouvoir politique en Arabie Saoudite, XVIIIe–XXIe siècle*. Paris: Presses Universitaires de France, 2011.

Mouqtadir, Rachid. 'Transformations in the Moroccan Islamist Experience'. In *Post-Islamism: A New Phase or Ideological Delusions?*, edited by Mohammad Abu Rumman, 107–138. Amman: Friedrich Ebert Stiftung/Centre for Strategic Studies, 2018.

Moussalli, Ahmad S. 'Hasan al-Banna's Islamist Discourse on Constitutional Rule and Islamic State'. *Journal of Islamic Studies* 4, no. 3 (1993): 161–174.

———. 'Hasan al-Turabi's Islamist Discourse on Democracy and *Shura*'. *Middle Eastern Studies* 30, no. 1 (1994): 52–63.

Munson, Jr., Henry. 'Morocco'. In *The Politics of Islamic Revivalism*, edited by Shireen T. Hunter, 133–147. Bloomington and Indianapolis: IN: Indiana University Press, 1988.

Musallam, Adnan A. *From Secularism to Jihad: Sayyid Qutb and the Foundation of Radical Islamism*. Westport, CT: Praeger Publishers, 2005.

Muslih, Muhammad. 'Hamas: Strategy and Tactics'. In *Ethnic Conflict and International Politics in the Middle East*, edited by Leonard Binder, 307–331. Gainsville, FL: University of Florida Press, 1999.

Muslim Brotherhood Review: Main Findings. London: assets.publishing.service.gov.uk/government/uploads/system/uploads/attachment_data/file/486948/53163_Muslim_Brotherhood_Review_-_PRINT.pdf, 2015.

Nafi, Basheer M. 'Fatwa and War: On the Allegiance of the American Muslim Soldiers in the Aftermath of September 11'. *Islamic Law & Society* 11, no. 1 (2004): 78–113.

———. 'The Rise of Reformist Thought and Its Challenge to Traditional Islam'. In *Islamic Thought in the Twentieth Century*, edited by Suha Taji-Farouki and Basheer M. Nafi, 28–60. London and New York: I.B. Tauris, 2008 [2004].

Nafi, Basheer M. and Suha Taji-Farouki. 'Introduction'. In *Islamic Thought in the Twentieth Century*, edited by Suha Taji-Farouki and Basheer M. Nafi, 1–27. London and New York: I.B. Tauris, 2008 [2004].

Naimat, Tareq al-. 'Zamzam and the Jordanian Brotherhood'. *Sada: Analysis on Arab Reform*. Washington, DC: Carnegie Endowment for International Peace, 2014.

Napoleoni, Loretta. *Insurgent Iraq: Al Zarqawi and the New Generation*. New York: Seven Stories Press, 2005.

Napolitano, Valentina. 'Hamas and the Syrian Uprising: A Difficult Choice'. *Middle East Policy* 20, no. 3 (2013): 73–785.

Nasr, Seyyed Vali Reza. 'Mawdudi and the Jama'at-i Islami: The Origins, Theory and Practice of Islamic Revivalism'. In *Pioneers of Islamic Revival*, edited by Ali Rahnema, 98–124. London and New York: Zed Books, 2005.

———. *Mawdudi & the Making of Islamic Revivalism*. Oxford: Oxford University Press, 1996.

Niblock, Tim. *Saudi Arabia: Power, Legitimacy and Survival*. Abingdon, UK, and New York: Routledge, 2006.

Nüsse, Andrea. *Muslim Palestine: The Ideology of Hamas*. Abingdon, UK: RoutledgeCurzon, 1998.

Obaid, Nawaf. *The Failure of the Muslim Brotherhood in the Arab World*. Santa Barbara, CA: Praeger Security International, 2020.

Okruhlik, Gwenn. 'Making Conversation Permissible: Islamism and Reform in Saudi Arabia'. In *Islamic Activism: A Social Movement Theory Approach*, edited by Quintan Wiktorowicz, 250–269. Bloomington and Indianapolis, IN: Indiana University Press, 2004.

———. 'Networks of Dissent: Islamism and Reform in Saudi Arabia'. Social Science Research Council, ssrc.org/sept11/essays/okruhlik_text_only.htm, 10 May 2007.

Olsson, Susanne. 'Shia as Internal Others: A Salafi Rejection of the "Rejectors"'. *Islam and Christian-Muslim Relations* 28, no. 4 (2017): 409–430.

Opwis, Felicitas. 'New Trends in Islamic Legal Theory: *Maqasid al-Shari'a* as a New Source of Law?' *Die Welt des Islams* 57 (2017): 7–32.

Orofino, Elisa. *Hizb ut-Tahrir and the Caliphate: Why the Group is Still Appealing to Muslims in the West.* London and New York: 2020.

'Out of Power.' *The Economist*, 18 September 2021, 33.

Pankhurst, Reza. *Hizb ut-Tahrir: The Untold Story of the Liberation Party.* London: Hurst & Co., 2016.

Pargeter, Alison. *Return to the Shadows: The Muslim Brotherhood and An-Nahda since the Arab Spring.* London: Saqi Books, 2016.

———. *The Muslim Brotherhood: From Opposition to Power.* London: Saqi Books, 2010.

———. *The Muslim Brotherhood: The Burden of Tradition.* London: Saqi Books, 2010.

Parray, Tauseef Ahmad. 'The Legal Methodology of *"Fiqh al-Aqalliyyat"* and Its Critics: An Analytical Study'. *Journal of Muslim Minority Affairs* 32, no. 1 (2012): 88–107.

Peil, Florian. 'Die Besetzung der Großen Moschee von Mekka 1979'. *Orient: Deutsche Zeitschrift für Politik, Wirtschaft und Kultur des Orients* 47, no. 3 (2006): 387–408.

Pellicer, Miqual and Eva Wegner. 'The Justice and Development Party in Moroccan Local Politics'. *Middle East Journal* 69, no. 1 (2015): 32–50.

Perry, Damon. *The Global Muslim Brotherhood in Britain: Non-Violent Islamist Extremism and the Battle of Ideas.* London and New York: 2019.

———. *The Islamic Movement in Britain.* London: International Centre for the Study of Radicalisation, 2020.

Peter, Frank. 'Muslim "Double Talk" and the Ways of the Shari'a in France'. In *The Muslim Brotherhood in Europe*, edited by Roel Meijer and Edwin Bakker, 127–148. London: Hurst & Co., 2012.

Peters, Anne Mariel and Pete W. Moore. 'Beyond Boom and Bust: External Rents, Durable Authoritarianism, and Institutional Adaptation in the Hashemite Kingdom of Jordan'. *Studies in Comparative International Developments* 44 (2009): 256–285.

Phelps Harris, Christina. *Nationalism and Revolution in Egypt: The Role of the Muslim Brotherhood.* The Hague: Mouton, 1964.

Pierret, Thomas. 'Syria's Unusual "Islamic Trend": Political Reformists, the Ulema, and Democracy'. In *Post-Islamism: The Changing Face of Political Islam*, edited by Asef Bayat, 321–341. Oxford: Oxford University Press, 2013.

———. *Religion and State in Syria: The Sunni Ulama from Coup to Revolution.* Cambridge: Cambridge University Press, 2013.

Pipes, Daniel. 'Islamism's Unity in Tunisia'. www.danielpipes.org/12103/islamism-unity, 30 October 2012.

Piscatori, James P. 'Ideological Politics in Sa'udi Arabia'. In *Islam in the Political Process*, edited by James P. Piscatori, 56–72. Cambridge: Cambridge University Press, 1983.

Polka, Sagi. 'Hamas as a *Wasati* (Literally: Centrist) Movement: Pragmatism within the Boundaries of the *Sharia*'. *Studies in Conflict & Terrorism* 42, no. 7 (2019): 683–713.

Quintan Wiktorowicz (ed.). *Islamic Activism: A Social Movement Theory Approach.* Bloomington and Indianapolis, IN: Indiana University Press, 2004.

Rabil, Robert G. 'The Syrian Muslim Brotherhood'. In *The Muslim Brotherhood: The Organization and Policies of a Global Islamist Movement*, edited by Barry Rubin, 73–88. New York: Palgrave MacMillan, 2010.

Ranko, Annette. *The Muslim Brotherhood and its Quest for Hegemony in Egypt: State-Discourse and Islamist Counter-Discourse.* Wiesbaden: Springer, 2012.

Rasheed, Madawi Al-. *A History of Saudi Arabia.* Cambridge: Cambridge University Press, 2002.

———. *Contesting the Saudi State: Islamic Voices from a New Generation.* Cambridge: Cambridge University Press, 2007.

Rashid, Ahmed. *Taliban: Militant Islam, Oil and Fundamentalism in Central Asia.* New Haven, CO, and London: Yale University Press, 2000.

Rath, Jan, Rinus Penninx, Kees Groenendijk and Astrid Meijer. *Nederland en zijn islam: Een ontzuilde samenleving reageert op het ontstaan van een geloofsgemeenschap.* Amsterdam: Het Spinhuis, 1996.

Rath, Kathrine. 'The Process of Democratization in Jordan'. *Middle Eastern Studies* 30, no. 3 (1994): 530–557.

Reissner, Johannes. *Ideologie und Politik der Muslimbrüder Syriens. Von den Wahlen 1947 bis zum Verbot unter Adīb aš-Šīšaklī 1952.* Freiburg: Klaus Schwarz Verlag, 1980.

Reuters. 'Morocco elections: Islamists Suffer Losses as Liberal Parties Gain Ground'. *The Guardian* (theguardian.com/world/2021/sep/09/islamists-suffer-losses-as-liberal-parties-gain-ground-in-morocco-elections), 9 September 2021.

Rich, David. 'The Very Model of a British Muslim Brotherhood'. In *The Muslim Brotherhood: The Organization and Policies of a Global Islamist Movement*, edited by Barry Rubin, 117–136. New York: Palgrave MacMillan, 2010.

Roald, Anne Sofie. 'Democratisation and Secularisation in the Muslim Brotherhood: The International Dimension'. In *The Muslim Brotherhood in Europe*, edited by Roel Meijer and Edwin Bakker, 71–88. London: Hurst & Co., 2012.

Robinson, Glenn E. 'Can Islamists be Democrats? The Case of Jordan'. *Middle East Journal* 51, no. 3 (1997), 373–387.

———. 'Defensive Democratisation in Jordan'. *International Journal of Middle East Studies* 30, no. 3 (1998): 387–410.

Rock-Singer, Aaron and Steven Brooke. 'Reading the Ads in *al-Da'wa* Magazine: Commercialism and Islamist Activism in al-Sadat's Egypt'. *British Journal of Middle Eastern Studies* 47, no. 3 (2020): 444–461.

Ronen, Yehudit. 'The Rise and Fall of Hasan Abdallah al-Turabi: A Unique Chapter in Sudan's Political History (1989–99)'. *Middle Eastern Studies* 50, no. 6 (2014): 992–1005.

Rosefsky Wickham, Carrie. 'The Path to Moderation: Strategy and Learning in the Formation of Egypt's *Wasat* Party'. *Comparative Politics* 36, no. 2 (2004): 205–228.

———. *Mobilizing Islam: Religion, Activism, and Political Change in Egypt.* New York: Columbia University Press, 2002.

———. *The Muslim Brotherhood: Evolution of an Islamist Movement.* Princeton, NJ, and Oxford: Princeton University Press, 2013.

Rougier, Bernard (ed.). *Qu'est-ce que le salafisme?* Paris: Presses Universitaires de France, 2008.

Roy, Olivier (transl. Carol Volk). *The Failure of Political Islam.* London: I.B. Tauris, 1994.

———. *Globalized Islam: The Search for a New Umma.* New York: Columbia University Press, 2004.

Roy, Sara. *Hamas and Civil Society in Gaza: Engaging in the Islamist Social Sector.* Princeton, NJ, and Oxford: Princeton University Press, 2011.

Rubenberg, Cheryl A. *The Palestinians: In Search of a Just Peace.* Boulder, CO: Lynne Rienner, 2003.

Rubin, Barnett R. 'Arab Islamists in Afghanistan'. In *Political Islam: Revolution, Radicalism or Reform?*, edited by John L. Esposito, 179–206. Boulder, CO: Lynne Rienner Publishers, 1997.

Rubin, Barry. 'Comparing Three Muslim Brotherhoods'. In *The Muslim Brotherhood: The Organization and Policies of a Global Islamist Movement*, edited by Barry Rubin, 7–18. New York: Palgrave MacMillan, 2010.

Rutherford, Bruce K. 'What Do Egypt's Islamists Want? Moderate Islam and the Rise of Islamic Constitutionalism'. *Middle East Journal* 60, no. 4 (2006): 707–731.

———. *Egypt after Mubarak: Liberalism, Islam, and Democracy in the Arab World.* Princeton, NJ, and Oxford: Princeton University Press, 2008.

Ryad, Umar. *Islamic Reform and Christianity: A Critical Reading of the Works of Muhammad Rashid Rida and His Associates (1898–1935).* Leiden: Brill, 2008.

Ryan, Curtis R. 'Elections and Parliamentary Democratization in Jordan'. *Democratization* 5, no. 4 (1998): 176–196.

———. 'Jordan and the Rise and Fall of the Arab Cooperation Council'. *Middle East Journal* 52, no. 3 (1998): 386–401.

---. 'One Society of Muslim Brothers in Jordan or Two?' *Middle East Report Online* (merip.org/one-society-muslim-brothers-jordan-or-two), 2015.

---. 'Peace, Bread and Riots: Jordan and the International Monetary Fund'. *Middle East Policy* 6, no. 2 (1998): 54–66.

---. *Jordan and the Arab Uprisings: Regime Survival and Politics Beyond the State.* New York: Columbia University Press, 2018.

---. *Jordan in Transition: From Hussein to Abdullah.* Boulder, CO: Lynne Rienner, 2002.

Ryan, Curtis R. and Jillian Schwedler. 'Return to Democratization or New Hybrid Regime? The 2003 Elections in Jordan'. *Middle East Report* 11, no. 2 (2004): 138–151.

Sager, Abdulaziz O. 'Political Opposition in Saudi Arabia'. In *Saudi Arabia in the Balance: Political Economy, Society, Foreign Affairs*, edited by Paul Aarts and Gert Nonneman, 234–270. London: Hurst & Co., 2005.

Said, Behnam T. and Hazim Fouad (eds.). *Salafismus. Auf der Suche nach dem wahren Islam.* Freiburg, Bazel and Wenen: Herder, 2014.

Said, Behnam T. *Islamischer Staat. IS-Miliz, al-Qaida und die deutschen Brigaden.* München: C. H. Beck, 2014.

Said, Hamed El- and Jane Harrigan. 'Economic Reform, Social Welfare, and Instability: Jordan, Egypt, Morocco, and Tunisia, 1983–2004'. *Middle East Journal* 68, no. 1 (2014): 99–121.

Said, Sabah El-. *Between Pragmatism and Ideology: The Muslim Brotherhood in Jordan, 1989–1994.* Washington, DC: Washington Institute for Near Eastern Policy, 1995.

Sajid, Mehdi. 'A Reappraisal of the Role of Muhibb al-Din al-Khatib and the YMMA in the Rise of the Muslim Brotherhood'. *Islam and Christian–Muslim Relations* 29, no. 2 (2018): 193–213.

Sakhtivel, Vish. *Al-Adl wal-Ihsan: Inside Morocco's Islamist Challenge.* Washington, DC: Washington Institute for Near East Policy, 2015.

Salem, Norma. 'Tunisia'. In *The Politics of Islamic Revivalism*, edited by Shireen T. Hunter, 148–170. Bloomington and Indianapolis: IN: Indiana University Press, 1988.

Salvatore, Armando. 'Qaradawi's *Maslaha*: From Ideologue of the Islamic Awakening to Sponsor of Transnational Public Islam'. In *Global Mufti: The Phenomenon of Yusuf al-Qaradawi*, edited by Bettina Gräf and Jakob Skovgaard-Petersen, 239–250. New York: Columbia University Press, 2009.

Sanagan, Mark. 'Teacher, Preacher, Soldier, Martyr: Rethinking 'Izz al-Din al-Qassam'. *Die Welt des Islams* 53, nos. 3–4 (2013): 315–352.

Santing, Kiki. 'Conspiracy Theories and Muslim Brotherhood Antisemitism under Sadat'. *Religions* 13, no. 2 (2022): 1–16.

———. 'Islam and the Struggle over Political Legitimacy in Egypt: The 1987 Elections Through the Lenses of *Al-Liwa' al-Islami* and *Liwa' al-Islam'*. *Global Media Journal* 10, no. 1 (2020): 1–18.

———. *Imagining the Perfect Society in Muslim Brotherhood Journals: An Analysis of al-Da'wa and Liwa' al-Islam*. Berlin: De Gruyter, 2020.

Satloff, Robert B. *Troubles on the East Bank: Challenges to the Domestic Stability of Jordan*. New York, Westport, CT, and London: Praeger/Washington, DC: The Center for Strategic and International Studies at Georgetown University, 1986.

'Saudi Arabia: Prominent Reformist Cleric Faces Death Penalty for His Peaceful Activism'. Amnesty International (amnesty.org/en/latest/news/2019/07/saudi-arabia-prominent-reformist-cleric-faces-death-sentence-for-his-peaceful-activism/), 26 July 2019.

Sayigh, Yezid. *Armed Struggle and the Search for State: The Palestinian National Movement, 1949–1993*. Oxford: Oxford University Press, 1997.

Schanzer, Jonathan. *Hamas vs. Fatah: The Struggle for Palestine*. New York: Palgrave MacMillan, 2008.

Schiff, Ze'ev and Ehud Ya'ari (transl. Ina Friedman). *Intifada: The Inside Story of the Palestinian Uprising that Changed the Middle East Equation*. New York: Touchstone/Simon & Schuster, 1991 [1989].

Schwedler, Jillian. 'A Paradox of Democracy? Islamist Participation in Elections'. *Middle East Report*, no. 209 (1998): 25–29, 41.

———. 'Don't Blink: Jordan's Democratic Opening and Closing'. *Middle East Report Online* (merip.org/mero/mero070302), 2002.

———. 'Jordan's Islamists Lose Faith in Moderation'. *Foreign Policy* (foreignpolicy.com/2010/06/30/jordans-islamists-lose-faith-in-moderation/#) 2010.

———. *Faith in Moderation: Islamist Parties in Jordan and Yemen*. Cambridge: Cambridge University Press, 2006.

Scott, Rachel M. *The Challenge of Political Islam: Non-Muslims and the Egyptian State*. Stanford, CA: Stanford University Press, 2010.

———. 'An "Official" Islamic Response to the Egyptian Al-Jihad Movement'. *Journal of Political Ideologies* 8, no. 1 (2003): 39–61.

Shadid, Mohammed K. 'The Muslim Brotherhood Movement in the West Bank and Gaza'. *Third World Quarterly* 10, no. 2 (1988): 658–682.

Shaham, Ron. 'Legal Maxims (*Qawa'id fiqhiyya*) in Yusuf al-Qaradawi's Jurisprudence and Fatwas'. *Journal of the American Oriental Society* 140, no. 2 (2020): 435–453.

Shahin, Emad Eldin. *Political Ascent: Contemporary Islamic Movements in North Africa*. Boulder, CO: Westview, 1998.

Shavit, Uriya. 'Can Muslims Befriend Non-Muslims? Debating *al-Wala' wa-l-Bara'* (Loyalty and Disavowal) in Theory and Practice'. *Islam and Christian-Muslim Relations* 25, no. 1 (2014): 67–88.

———. 'Is *Shura* a Muslim Form of Democracy? Roots and Systemization of a Polemic'. *Middle Eastern Studies* 46, no. 3 (2010): 349–374.

———. 'Islamotopia: The Muslim Brotherhood's Idea of Democracy'. *Azure*, no. 46 (2011): 35–62.

———. 'The Muslim Brothers' Conception of Armed Insurrection Against an Unjust Regime'. *Middle Eastern Studies* 51, no. 4 (2015): 600–617.

———. *Islamism and the West: From 'Cultural Attack' to 'Missionary Migrant'.* London and New York: Routledge, 2014.

———. *Shari'a and Muslim Minorities: The* Wasati *and* Salafi *Approaches to* Fiqh al-Aqalliyyat al-Muslima. Oxford: Oxford University Press, 2015.

Shehata, Samer S. 'Political *Da'wa*: Understanding the Muslim Brotherhood's Participation in Semi-Authoritarian Elections'. In *Islamist Politics in the Middle East: Movements and Change*, edited by Samer S. Shehata, 120–145. London and New York: Routledge, 2012.

Shepard, William. 'Islam and Ideology: Towards a Typology.' *International Journal of Middle East Studies* 19, no. 3 (1987): 307–336.

———. 'Sayyid Qutb's Doctrine of *Jāhiliyya*'. *International Journal of Middle East Studies* 35, no. 4 (2003): 521–545.

———. 'The Diversity of Islamic Thought: Towards a Typology'. In *Islamic Thought in the Twentieth Century*, edited by Suha Taji-Farouki and Basheer M. Nafi, 61–103. London and New York: I.B. Tauris, 2004.

Sherif, Ashraf Nabih El. 'Institutional and Ideological Re-Construction of the Justice and Development Party (PJD): The Question of Democratic Islamism in Morocco'. *The Middle East Journal* 66, no. 4 (2012): 660–682.

Shlaim, Avi. *Lion of Jordan: The Life of King Hussein in War and Peace.* New York: Alfred A. Knopf, 2008.

Shryock, Andrew. *Nationalism and the Genealogical Imagination: Oral History and Textual Authority in Tribal Jordan.* Berkeley and Los Angeles, CA: University of California Press, 1997.

Sidahmed, Abdel Salam. 'Sudan: Ideology and Pragmatism'. In *Islamic Fundamentalism*, edited by Abdel Salam Sidahmed and Anoushiravan Ehteshami, 179–198. Boulder, CO: Westview Press, 1996.

Silvestri, Sara. 'Moderate Islamist Groups in Europe: The Muslim Brothers'. In *Political Islam: Context versus Ideology*, edited by Khaled Hroub, 265–285. London: Saqi, 2010.

Singh, Ranjit. 'Liberalisation or Democratisation? The Limits of Political Reform and Civil Society in Jordan'. In *Jordan in Transition: 1990–2000*, edited by George Joffé, 66–90. London: Hurst & Co., 2002.

Sivan, Emmanuel. *Radical Islam: Medieval Theology and Modern Politics.* New Haven and London: Yale University Press, 1985.

Skare, Erik. 'Controlling the State in the Political Theory of Hamas and Palestinian Islamic Jihad'. *Religions* 12, no. 11 (2021): 1–12.

———. *A History of Palestinian Islamic Jihad: Faith, Awareness and Revolution in the Middle East*. Cambridge: Cambridge University Press, 2021.

Skovgaard-Petersen, Jakob. 'Brothers and Citizens: The Second Wave of Islamic Constitutional Thinking and the Concept of Citizenship'. In *The Crisis of Citizenship in the Arab World*, edited by Roel Meijer and Nils Butenschon, 320–337. Leiden: Brill, 2017.

Škrabáková, Katarina. 'Islamist Women as Candidates in Elections: A Comparison of the Party of Justice and Development in Morocco and the Muslim Brotherhood in Egypt'. *Die Welt des Islams* 57 (2017): 329–359.

Stacher, Joshua. 'Post-Islamist Rumblings in Egypt: The Emergence of the Wasat Party'. *Middle East Journal* 56, no. 3 (2002): 415–432.

Steinberg, Guido and Isabelle Werenfels. 'Between the "Near" and the "Far" Enemy: Al-Qaeda in the Islamic Maghreb'. *Mediterranean Politics* 12, no. 3 (2007): 407–413.

Steinberg, Guido. 'Germany and the Muslim Brotherhood'. In *The West and the Muslim Brotherhood After the Arab Spring*, edited by Lorenzo Vidino, 86–100. N.P.: Al Mesbar Studies & Research Center/Foreign Policy Research Institute, 2013.

———. 'Jihadi-Salafism and the Shi'is: Remarks about the Intellectual Roots of Anti-Shi'ism'. In *Global Salafism: Islam's New Religious Movement*, edited by Roel Meijer, 107–125. London: Hurst & Co., 2007.

———. 'The Muslim Brotherhood in Germany'. In *The Muslim Brotherhood: The Organization and Policies of a Global Islamist Movement*, edited by Barry Rubin, 149–160. New York: Palgrave MacMillan, 2010.

———. *Religion und Staat in Saudi-Arabien: Die wahhabitischen Gelehrten, 1902–1943*. Würzburg: Ergon Verlag, 2002.

Stern, Jessica and J.M. Berger. *ISIS: The State of Terror*. New York: HarperCollins Publishers, 2015.

Strijp, Ruud. *Om de moskee: Het religieuze leven van Marokkaanse migranten in een Nederlandse provinciestad*. Amsterdam: Thesis Publishers, 1998.

Sullivan, Denis J. and Sana Abed-Kotob. *Islam in Contemporary Egypt: Civil Society vs. the State*. Boulder, CO: Lynne Rienner Publishers, 1999.

Sunier, Thijl *Islam in beweging: Turkse jongeren en islamitische organisaties*. Amsterdam: Het Spinhuis, 1996.

Tadros, Mariz. *The Muslim Brotherhood in Contemporary Egypt: Democracy Redefined or Confined?* London and New York: Routledge, 2012.

———. 'Participation not Domination: Morsi on an Impossible Mission?' In *Islamists and the Politics of the Arab Uprisings: Governance, Pluralisation and Contention*, edited by Hendrik Kraetzschmar and Paola Rivetti, 17–35. Edinburgh: Edinburgh University Press, 2018.

Tadros, Samuel. 'Egypt's Muslim Brotherhood After the Revolution'. *Current Trends in Islamist Ideology* 12 (2011): 5–20.

Taji-Farouki, Suha. 'Hizb al-Tahrir al-Islami'. In *The Oxford Encyclopedia of the Islamic World*, Vol. II, edited by John L. Esposito, 423–426. Oxford: Oxford University Press, 2009.

———. 'Islamic State Theories and Contemporary Realities'. In *Islamic Fundamentalism*, edited by Abdel Salam Sidahmed and Anoushiravan Ehteshami, 35–50. Boulder, CO: Westview Press, 1996.

———. 'Islamists and the Threat of *Jihad*: Hizb al-Tahrir and al-Muhajiroun on Israel and the Jews'. *Middle Eastern Studies* 36, no. 4 (2000): 21–46.

Tal, Lawrence. 'Dealing with Radical Islam: The Case of Jordan'. *Survival* 37, no. 3 (1995): 139–56.

Tal, Nachman. *Radical Islam in Egypt and Jordan*. Brighton, UK, and Portland, OR: Sussex Academic Press, 2005.

Tamimi, Azzam S. *Rachid Ghannouchi: A Democrat within Islamism*. Oxford: Oxford University Press, 2001.

———. *Hamas: A History from Within*. Northampton, MA: Olive Branch Press, 2007.

Tammam, Hossam. 'The Muslim Brotherhood and Jihad'. In *Twenty-First Century Jihad: Law, Society and Military Action*, edited by Elisabeth Kendall and Ewan Stein, 164–175. London and New York: I.B. Tauris, 2017.

Tammam, Husam. 'Yusuf al-Qaradawi and the Muslim Brothers: The Nature of a Special Relationship'. In *Global Mufti: The Phenomenon of Yusuf al-Qaradawi*, edited by Bettina Gräf and Jakob Skovgaard-Petersen, 55–83. New York: Columbia University, 2009.

Taraki, Lisa. 'Islam is the Solution: Jordanian Islamists and the Dilemma of the "Modern Woman"'. *British Journal of Sociology* 46, no. 4, (1995): 643–661.

———. 'Jordanian Islamists and the Agenda for Women: Between Discourse and Practice'. *Middle Eastern Studies* 32, no. 1 (1996): 140–158.

Teitelbaum, Joshua. 'Dueling for *Da'wa*: State vs. Society on the Saudi Internet'. *Middle East Journal* 56, no. 2 (2002): 222–239.

———. 'The Muslim Brotherhood and the "Struggle for Syria", 1947–1958: Between Accommodation and Ideology'. *Middle Eastern Studies* 40, no. 3 (2004): 134–158.

———. 'The Muslim Brotherhood in Syria, 1945–1958: Founding, Social Origins, Ideology'. *Middle East Journal* 65, no. 2 (2011): 213–233.

———. *Holier than Thou: Saudi Arabia's Islamic Opposition*. Washington, DC: The Washington Institute for Near East Policy, 2000.

Toth, James. 'Islamism in Southern Egypt: A Case Study of a Radical Religious Movement'. *International Journal of Middle East Studies* 35, no. 4 (2003): 547–572.

———. *Sayyid Qutb: The Life and Legacy of a Radical Islamic Intellectual*. Oxford: Oxford University Press, 2013.

Trager, Eric. 'Egypt's Looming Competitive Theocracy'. *Current Trends in Islamist Ideology* 14 (2014): 27–37.

———. *Arab Fall: How the Muslim Brotherhood Won and Lost Egypt in 891 Days.* Washington, DC: Georgetown University Press, 2016.

Tripp, Charles. 'Sayyid Qutb: The Political Vision'. In *Pioneers of Islamic Revival*, edited by Ali Rahnema, 154–183. London and New York: Zed Books, 2005 [1994].

Trofimov, Yaroslav. *The Siege of Mecca: The 1979 Uprising at Islam's Holiest Shrine.* New York: Anchor Books, 2007.

Tuastag, Dag. 'Hamas-PLO Relations Before and After the Arab Spring'. *Middle East Policy* 20, no. 3 (2013): 86–98.

Tuğal, Cihan. 'Islam and the Retrenchment of Turkish Conservatism'. In *Post-Islamism: The Changing Face of Political Islam*, edited by Asef Bayat, 109–133. Oxford: Oxford University Press, 2013.

Tyan, E. 'Bay'a'. In *Encyclopaedia of Islam: New Edition*, Vol. I, edited by B. Lewis, Ch. Pellat and J. Schacht, 1113–1114. Leiden: E. J. Brill, 1986.

Valbjørn, Morten. 'The 2013 Parliamentary Elections in Jordan: Three Stories and Some General Lessons'. *Mediterranean Politics* 18, no. 2 (2013): 311–317.

Vassiliev, Alexei. *The History of Saudi Arabia.* London: Saqi Books, 2000.

Verskin, Alan. *Oppressed in the Land? Fatwas on Muslims Living under Non-Muslim Rule from the Middle Ages to the Present.* Princeton, NJ: Markus Wiener Publishers, 2013.

Vidino, Lorenzo. 'The European Organization of the Muslim Brotherhood: Myth or Reality?' In *The Muslim Brotherhood in Europe*, edited by Roel Meijer and Edwin Bakker, 51–69. London: Hurst & Co., 2012.

———. 'The Muslim Brotherhood in Europe'. In *The Muslim Brotherhood: The Organization and Policies of a Global Islamist Movement*, edited by Barry Rubin, 105–116. New York: Palgrave MacMillan, 2010.

———. *The Closed Circle: Joining and Leaving the Muslim Brotherhood in the West.* New York: Columbia University Press, 2020.

———. *The New Muslim Brotherhood in the West.* New York: Columbia University Press, 2010.

Voll, John O. 'Islamic Renewal and the "Failure of the West"'. In *Religious Resurgence: Contemporary Cases in Islam, Christianity, and Judaism*, edited by Richard T. Antoun and Mary Elaine Hegland, 127–144. Syracuse, NY: Syracuse University Press, 1987.

———. 'Renewal and Reform in Islamic History: *Tajdid* and *Islah*'. In *Voices of Resurgent Islam*, edited by John L. Esposito, 32–47. Oxford: Oxford University Press, 1983.

———. *Islam: Continuity and Change in the Modern World.* Boulder, CO: Westview Press, 1994 [1982].

Wagemakers, Joas. 'Between Exclusivism and Inclusivism: The Jordanian Muslim Brotherhood's Divided Responses to the "Arab Spring"'. *Middle East Law and Governance* 12, no. 1 (2020): 35–60.

———. 'De ideologische onderbouwing van de Islamitische Staat'. *ZemZem: Tijdschrift over het Midden-Oosten, Noord-Afrika en islam* 10, no. 2 (2014): 6–13.

———. 'Foreign Policy as Protection: The Jordanian Muslim Brotherhood as a Political Minority During the Cold War'. In *Muted Minorities: Ethnic, Religious and Political Groups in (Trans)Jordan, 1921–2016*, edited by Idir Ouahes and Paolo Maggiolini, 177–200. London: Palgrave, 2021.

———. 'Legitimizing Pragmatism: Hamas' Framing Efforts from Militancy to Moderation and Back?' *Terrorism and Political Violence* 22 (2010): 357–377.

———. 'Making Definitional Sense of Islamism'. *Orient: Deutsche Zeitschrift für Politik, Wirtschaft und Kultur des Orients* 62, no. 2 (2021): 7–13.

———. 'Things Fall Apart: The Disintegration of the Jordanian Muslim Brotherhood'. *Religions* 12, no. 12 (2021): 1–17.

———. *The Muslim Brotherhood in Jordan.* Cambridge: Cambridge University Press, 2020.

Wagner, Mark S. '*Hukm bi-ma anzala 'llah*: The Forgotten Prehistory of an Islamist Slogan'. *Journal of Qur'anic Studies* 18, no. 1, (2015): 117–143.

Wainscott, Ann Marie. *Bureaucratizing Islam: Morocco and the War on Terror.* Cambridge: Cambridge University Press, 2017.

Waltz, Susan. 'Islamist Appeal in Tunisia'. *Middle East Journal* 40, no. 4 (1986): 651–670.

Warburg, Gabriel R. 'Muslim Brotherhood in Sudan'. In *The Oxford Encyclopedia of the Islamic World*, Vol. IV, edited by John L. Esposito, 174–181. Oxford: Oxford University Press, 2009.

Warren, David H. and Christine Gilmore. 'One Nation Under God? Yusuf al-Qaradawi's Changing Fiqh of Citizenship in the Light of the Islamic Legal Tradition'. *Contemporary Islam* 8 (2014): 217–237.

———. 'Rethinking Neo-Salafism Through an Emerging Fiqh of Citizenship: The Changing Status of Minorities in the Discourse of Yusuf al-Qaradawi and the "School of the Middle Way"'. *New Middle Eastern Quick Studies* 2 (2012): 1–7.

Warrick, Joby. *Black Flags: The Rise of ISIS.* New York: Doubleday, 2015.

Wegner, Eva and Miquel Pellicer. 'Islamist Moderation without Democratization: The Coming of Age of the Moroccan Party of Justice and Development?' *Democratization* 16, no. 1 (2009): 157–175.

Wegner, Eva. *Islamist Opposition in Authoritarian Regimes: The Party of Justice and Development in Morocco.* Syracuse, NY: Syracuse University Press, 2011.

Weismann, Itzchak. 'Democratic Fundamentalism? The Practice and Discourse of the Muslim Brothers Movement in Syria'. *The Muslim World* 100 (2010): 1–16.

——. 'Sa'id Hawwa and Islamic Revivalism in Ba'thist Syria'. *Studia Islamica* 85, no. 1 (1997): 131–154.

——. 'Sa'id Hawwa: The Making of a Radical Muslim Thinker in Modern Syria'. *Middle Eastern Studies* 29, no. 4 (1993): 601–623.

——. 'The Politics of Popular Religion: Sufis, Salafis, and Muslim Brothers in 20th-Century Hama'. *International Journal of Middle East Studies* 37, no. 1 (2005): 39–58.

——. *The Naqshbandiyya: Orthodoxy and Activism in a Worldwide Sufi Tradition.* London and New York: Routledge, 2007.

Weiss, Michael and Hassan Hassan. *ISIS: Inside the Army of Terror.* New York: Regan Arts, 2015.

Wereny, Mahmud El-. 'Reichweite und Instrumente islamrechtlicher Normenfindung in der Moderne: Yusuf al-Qaradawis *igtihad*-Konzept'. *Die Welt des Islams* 58 (2018): 65–100.

Wiktorowicz, Quintan. 'Islamists, the State and Cooperation in Jordan'. *Third World Quarterly* 21, no. 4 (1999): 1–16.

——. *Radical Islam Rising: Muslim Extremism in the West.* London: Rowman & Littlefield, 2005.

——. *The Management of Islamic Activism: Salafis, the Muslim Brotherhood, and State Power in Jordan.* New York: State University of New York Press, 2001.

Wilson, Mary C. *King Abdullah, Britain and the Making of Jordan.* Cambridge: Cambridge University Press, 1987.

Winder, R. Bayly. *Saudi Arabia in the Nineteenth Century.* London: MacMillan/St. Martin's Press, 1965.

Wolf, Anne. 'An Islamist "Renaissance"? Religion and Politics in Post-Revolutionary Tunisia'. *Journal of North African Studies* 18, no. 4 (2013): 560–573.

——. 'Secular Forms of Politicised Islam in Tunisia: The Constitutional Democratic Rally and Nida' Tunis'. In *Islamists and the Politics of the Arab Uprisings: Governance, Pluralisation and Contention*, edited by Hendrik Kraetzschmar and Paola Rivetti, 205–220. Edinburgh: Edinburgh University Press, 2018.

——. *Political Islam in Tunisia: The History of Ennahda.* London: Hurst & Co, 2017.

Woltering, Robbert A.F.L. 'Post-Islamism in Distress? A Critical Evaluation of the Theory in Islamist-Dominated Egypt (11 February 2011–3 July 2013)'. *Die Welt des Islams* 54 (2014): 107–118.

Wood, Simon A. *Christian Criticisms, Islamic Proofs: Rashid Rida's Modernist Defense of Islam.* Oxford: OneWorld, 2008.

Woodward, Peter. 'Sudan: Islamic Radicals in Power'. In *Political Islam: Revolution, Radicalism or Reform?*, edited by John L. Esposito, 95–114. Boulder, CO: Lynne Rienner Publishers, 1997.

Zaccara, Luciano, Courtney Freer and Hendrik Kraetzschmar. 'Kuwait's Islamist Proto-Parties and the Arab Uprisings: Between Opposition, Pragmatism and the Pursuit of Cross-Ideological Cooperation'. In *Islamists and the Politics of the Arab Uprisings: Governance, Pluralisation and Contention*, edited by Hendrik Kraetzschmar and Paola Rivetti, 182–204. Edinburgh: Edinburgh University Press, 2018.

Zahid, Mohammed. *The Muslim Brotherhood and Egypt's Succession Crisis: The Politics of Liberalisation and Reform in the Middle East*. London and New York: I.B. Tauris, 2010.

Zalaf, Ahmed Abou El. 'The Special Apparatus (al-Nizam al-Khass): The Rise of Nationalist Militancy in the Ranks of the Egyptian Muslim Brotherhood'. *Religions* 13, no. 1 (2022): 1–18.

Zeghal, Malika. 'Religion and Politics in Egypt: The Ulema of Al-Azhar, Radical Islam, and the State (1952–1994)'. *International Journal of Middle East Studies* 31, no. 3 (1999): 371–399.

———. *Les islamistes Marocaines. Le défi à la monarchie*. Paris: Éditions La Découverte, 2005.

Zelin, Aaron Y. 'The War Between ISIS and al-Qaeda for Supremacy of the Global Jihadist Movement'. Research Notes no. 20. Washington, DC: Washington Institute for Near East Policy, 2014.

Zemni, Sami. 'From Revolution to *Tunisianité*: Who is the Tunisian People? Creating Hegemony Through Compromise'. *Middle East Law and Governance* 8, nos. 2–3 (2016): 131–150.

———. 'Moroccan Post-Islamism: Emerging Trend or Chimera?' In *Post-Islamism: The Changing Face of Political Islam*, edited by Asef Bayat, 134–156. Oxford: Oxford University Press, 2013.

Zollner, Barbara H. E. 'Opening to Reform: Hasan al-Hudaybi's Legacy'. In *The Muslim Brotherhood in Europe*, edited by Roel Meijer and Edwin Bakker, 273–293 (London: Hurst & Co., 2012).

———. *The Muslim Brotherhood: Hasan al-Hudaybi and Ideology*. Abingdon, UK, and New York: 2009.

———. 'Prison Talk: The Muslim Brotherhood's Internal Struggle During Gamal Abdel Nasser's Persecution, 1954–1971'. *International Journal of Middle East Studies* 39, no. 3 (2007): 411–433.

Zuhur, Sherifa. *Egypt. Security, Political, and Islamist Challenges*. Carlisle, PA: Strategic Studies Institute, 2007.

Index

Printed in the United States
by Baker & Taylor Publisher Services